The Sports Strategist

DEVELOPING LEADERS FOR A HIGH-PERFORMANCE INDUSTRY

Irving Rein
Ben Shields
Adam Grossman

NEW YORK | OXFORD
Oxford University Press

Oxford University Press is a department of the University of Oxford.
It furthers the University's objective of excellence in research, scholarship,
and education by publishing worldwide.

Oxford   New York
Auckland   Cape Town   Dar es Salaam   Hong Kong   Karachi
Kuala Lumpur   Madrid   Melbourne   Mexico City   Nairobi
New Delhi   Shanghai   Taipei   Toronto

With offices in
Argentina   Austria   Brazil   Chile   Czech Republic   France   Greece
Guatemala   Hungary   Italy   Japan   Poland   Portugal   Singapore
South Korea   Switzerland   Thailand   Turkey   Ukraine   Vietnam

For titles covered by Section 112 of the US Higher Education
Opportunity Act, please visit www.oup.com/us/he for the
latest information about pricing and alternate formats.

Published in the United States of America by
Oxford University Press
198 Madison Avenue, New York, NY 10016
http://www.oup.com

Library of Congress Cataloging-in-Publication Data
Rein, Irving.
   The sports strategist : developing leaders for a high-performance
industry / Irving Rein, Ben Shields, Adam Grossman.
       pages cm.
   Includes bibliographical references.
   ISBN 978-0-19-934383-6 (hardcover); 978-0-19-026744-5 (paperback)
  1. Sports administration. 2. Sports—Management. 3. Sports—Economic
aspects. I. Title.
   GV713.R45 2015
   796.06′9—dc23

                                        2014000414

Printing number: 9 8 7 6 5 4 3 2 1

Printed in the United States of America
on acid-free paper

To my children, Perry and Lauren—Irving Rein
To my wife, Misha—Ben Shields
To my family, Stewart, Allyson, Seth, and Jordan—Adam Grossman

About the Authors

Irving Rein is Professor of Communication Studies at Northwestern University. He is the author of many books, including *The Elusive Fan, High Visibility, and Marketing Places*. He has consulted for Major League Baseball, the United States Olympic Committee, the National Aeronautics and Space Administration, and numerous corporations.

Ben Shields is Lecturer in Managerial Communication at the MIT Sloan School of Management. He previously served as Director of Social Media and Marketing at ESPN. He is co-author of *The Elusive Fan* and has written many articles and book chapters on sports media and marketing.

Adam Grossman is Founder and President of Block Six Analytics. He has worked with a number of sports organizations—including the Minnesota Timberwolves, Washington Capitals, and SMG @ Solider Field—to enhance their corporate sponsorship and enterprise marketing capabilities.

For more information about *The Sports Strategist*, including exclusive content, go to www.thesportsstrategist.com.

Contents

Preface

What does it take to be a leader in the high-performing sports industry? Fan interest in sports has never been more intense or widespread. The sports industry is now a $750 billion business, with many organizations generating record revenues from ticket sales, broadcast rights agreements, and corporate sponsorships.[1] Innovations in social media and mobile technologies are enabling teams and leagues to increase the frequency and intensity of their interactions with different audiences.

At the same time, unprecedented challenges are making it more difficult for organizations to meet their objectives. Even as the costs of doing business continue to rise, teams and leagues are facing an increasing amount of domestic and foreign competition and new threats to traditional revenue streams. The 24-hour sports news cycle is often dominated by issues of ethics and corruption, which constantly force athletes, teams, and leagues to defend and justify their actions in the face of ongoing crises.

The dynamic environment of the sports industry makes it one of the most challenging and fascinating businesses in the world. The growing complexity also requires every current and aspiring sports professional to constantly evaluate their thinking about the industry.

This includes re-examining the importance of winning on the sports business. When we published *The Elusive Fan: Reinventing Sports in a Crowded Marketplace* in 2006, we started to examine the relationship of how winning on-the-field impacted an organization's off-the-field strategy. However, we only began to explore this issue and what it meant to attract fans.[2]

As we have continued our research on the sports industry since *The Elusive Fan*, one constant theme has emerged. Winning often dominates the conversation about sports business, even though it is not something that can be easily controlled. Moreover, there is a perception that winning spells the difference between the businesses that succeed and those that fail. In *The Sports Strategist*, we examine in more depth the issue of winning and its impact on the sports business. We discovered that the most influential leaders concentrate on the factors that they can control to navigate change, facilitate innovation, and grow their businesses, without relying too much on winning.

We call these leaders sports strategists. The successful sports strategist is the person who has the ability both to narrowly focus on his or her specific role and maintain a cross-disciplinary understanding of how the organization functions as a whole. This integrated approach can help strategists create targeted solutions to critical challenges and provide sports organizations with a sustainable competitive advantage.

Taking a holistic approach has been the catalyst to the success of past leaders in the sports industry. Abe Saperstein was a jack-of-all-trades, master of all.[3] Almost singlehandedly, Saperstein built the Harlem Globetrotters from scratch through a perceptive sense of his audiences' needs and a willingness to adjust his product accordingly. Because of the foundation Saperstein built, the Globetrotters has appeared in over 115 countries, entertaining more than 120 million fans. The brand has extended into merchandise, television series, and movies.[4] And it's all because of the foundation Saperstein skillfully built.

Billie Jean King is one of the few professional athletes who has leveraged her star power to drive change. She not only identified a way to address gender inequality issues, but she also tapped into previously undeveloped business opportunities for women's tennis through her leadership role in creating the Virginia Slim Series and Women's Tennis Association (WTA). King could have rested on her championship laurels. Instead, her legacy may well be shaped by her contributions to the tennis world off the court.

Both Saperstein and King established themselves as sports strategists by having clear goals, taking considered steps to achieve them, and recalibrating their organizations based on changes in the industry. They ultimately achieved their goals in large part because of their integrated strategic thinking on issues including identity, narrative, revenue, place, and ethics.

In the fast-paced sports industry, however, it can be difficult to find the time to learn about new topics or subjects outside your area of expertise. This book is designed to make this process easier for anyone wanting to accomplish this goal. To further enhance the reader's experience with *The Sports Strategist*, we also provide:

- Blog posts that apply topics covered in the book to current events in the sports industry
- Social media outlets that allow us to engage directly with readers, the media, and organizations
- A website, thesportsstrategist.com, that contains lesson plans and additional material for teaching a class using this book

Who can be a sports strategist? Anyone. You might be a senior leader in need of new ways to think about your business's growth opportunities or organizational structure. You might be a manager looking to take the next step in your career. You might be a student who needs to develop an edge to make yourself more appealing to prospective employers. No matter what your level, experience, or position in the industry, you can be a sports strategist and deliver impact. By creating a new strategic game plan, *The Sports Strategist* provides analysis, recommendations, and tactics for you to succeed in today's constantly changing environment.

Acknowledgments

While the book is focused on individual leaders, it could not have been completed without a team effort. We would like to thank Jeffrey Eiden for helping to develop material for the "Crafting a Crisis Blueprint" and "Constructing Enduring Narratives" chapters and John Sisk and Matthew Spector for helping to develop material for the "Reinvigorating Sportscapes" chapter. Greg Swiatek was instrumental in finding material for numerous chapters during the research phase. Emily Olcott, Lynn Miller, Lauren Rein, Andrea Kravitz, Aileen McGraw, Sam Fishell, Alex Fernandez, Eytan Boclin, Robin Hoecker, Amina Asim, Andy Garden, Jordan Grossman, Stewart Grossman, and Josh Barr were critical to helping to research and edit the manuscript.

In addition, we would like to thank all of the students in the Sports Strategy and Leadership classes at Northwestern University who gave feedback on the ideas and structure of the book. The students in the Masters of Science in Communication (MSC) program were particularly helpful in providing input for the book during the crisis communication seminar. Sharron Shepard and Madeline Agaton at Northwestern provided administrative support for work on this project.

We would like to thank Northwestern University, ESPN, and Block Six Analytics for all their support. From ESPN in particular, we appreciate the support of Sean Bratches, Aaron Taylor, Jeff Gonyo, and Chris Brush. We also could not have completed the book without the encouragement of our families. They provided us with the best strategies for how to deal with the stress and the challenges that come with the writing, editing, and publishing of a high-performance book.

We would also like to thank the following colleagues who provided comments on the initial proposal, including:

Stephen Argeris
George Mason University

Jason W. Lee
University of North Florida

Simon Chadwick
Coventry University

Mauro Palmero
East Tennessee State University

Li Chen
Delaware State University

Richard Reider
Marquette University

Joe Cobbs
Northern Kentucky University

Paul Swangard
University of Oregon

Mark Dodds
SUNY Cortland

Brian A. Turner
The Ohio State University

Finally, we would like to thank Oxford University Press for its support during this process. In particular, we want to recognize Patrick Lynch, Maura MacDonald, David Bradley, Christian Purdy, Andrew Varhol, Valerie Ashton, and Ann West for all of their help.

1 | The Winning Business

Andrew Berlin proved that it is better to be good than lucky. On November 11, 2011 at 11:11am, Berlin purchased the South Bend Silver Hawks, a Single-A Minor League Baseball team affiliated with the Arizona Diamondbacks. The team was struggling financially and played in an outdated facility, Coveleski Field, so the first-time owner tried to channel the superstitions of the number 11 to help reverse the organization's fortunes. As it turns out, Berlin needed no such luck; his winning formula started with a synagogue sitting just beyond left field.

Originally opened in 1901, the Sons of Israel Synagogue was the first synagogue ever built in South Bend, Indiana. Located in what was once a bustling downtown neighborhood, membership was healthy for decades, helping spawn five additional synagogues in the area. Over time, new generations of the South Bend Jewish community moved out of the city, and the synagogue's membership began to decline as a result. Since the 1980s, it had gone largely unused.[1]

When Berlin took over the Silver Hawks (renamed the Cubs in 2014), Jewish community leaders proposed that he find a way to renovate and incorporate the building. After some initial hesitation, Berlin decided to turn the synagogue into the team's store. The project would be more costly than building a new store in a more conventional location such as behind home plate. The owner would have to commit a million dollars to build the team's "Ballpark Synagogue."[2] Refurbishing the synagogue's historic chandelier would cost $40,000 alone.[3] However, Berlin quickly realized that restoring the chandelier "is representative of what we're trying to do with the Silver Hawks, the stadium and downtown South Bend."[4]

The Ballpark Synagogue has been a resounding success. Fans now identify it as their favorite part of the stadium[5] and merchandise sales are up 50 percent.[6] The store has been the focus of national attention, with a documentary about the synagogue winning an Emmy in 2013. In that same year, Ballpark Synagogue received national landmark status.[7] Ballpark Digest also named Coveleski Field the 2012 Ballpark Renovation of the Year because of the synagogue. Located within a community that has a small Jewish population, the Ballpark Synagogue is "a focal point of the whole experience [in South Bend]. It's a special piece of history," according to Berlin.[8]

While the synagogue has become the team's crown jewel, Berlin has also been relentless in improving the fan experience at the park. To better understand his customers and what they wanted, Berlin surveyed fans on 36 different touchpoints at the stadium, including the smells, the quality of the customer service, and the experience in the parking lot. Then, as part of his turnaround plan, he and the city invested in upgrading the bleachers to chair-back seats, renovating the upper deck and suites, and adding dedicated areas for families and kids. He even arranged for the team mascot to wear cotton candy-scented cologne. It was all part of Berlin's goal to "create the best-ever ballpark."[9]

Berlin transformed the franchise's fortunes by focusing on improving areas that he could control regardless of the Silver Hawks' win-loss record. In 2012, attendance was up 68 percent.[10] Meanwhile, the team's record was 67–73. In 2013, attendance climbed another 29.5 percent,[11] and the team sold its stadium naming rights to Four Winds Casino.[12] The team finished the year with an 81–58 record and made the Western League championship, but lost to the Quad City River Bandits in a three-game sweep. Berlin said of his intent, "I always want the team to be in first place. But as a business owner, I care more about attendance."[13]

• • •

How can sports organizations and their leaders succeed in the sports business even when they are not winning? Sports leaders today often state publicly that winning is not the only component to creating an organizations' short and long-term strategy. Regardless of a team's record, sports organizations aim for increases in revenue and awareness each year through efforts in ticket sales, marketing, sponsorship, and community relations. In addition, sports decision makers are constantly evaluating how investments in new technologies or events will improve the brand perception of the organization with fans, media, and sponsors.

Yet, deep down, many sports industry professionals still hold a core belief that the money, time, and effort spent on strategic investments to improve the standing of a sports organization only can drive a limited amount of value unless a team is winning consistently. As Former Liverpool FC CEO Rick Parry asserts, "The big issue and the big challenge . . . is to start winning something. That's what fills your stadium and sells your replica shirt."[14] There is, of course, evidence supporting that winning is a catalyst for success in the sports industry. Research has demonstrated that winning can increase attendance, broadcast revenues, and profits in different sports.[15]

So why is focusing too much on winning actually a losing strategy? For starters, winning is a success driver that is difficult for sports business leaders to control. There are many factors that can affect an athletic performance: the opposing team, injuries, weather, and father time, just to name a few. For fans, this unpredictability can be one of the primary attractions of sports – it is unscripted drama at its finest. However, from a business perspective, an over-reliance on winning to sell sports products puts leaders in a more challenging position. When a team or athlete steps onto the field, there are no guarantees of victory, despite which team looks "better on paper." As a result, emphasizing winning as part of an organization's value proposition is a risky approach, especially in today's overly heated competitive marketplace for fans' time and money.

But what if you could have an organization that could win consistently? A closer examination of the concept of winning uncovers something different – that winning is not the magic bullet for all problems facing sports organizations.

The Winning Fallacy

Sports organizations fit into three main categories of winners: perennial winners, perennial losers, and periodic winners.[16] For most sports organizations, there will be seasons when they win championships or make the playoffs and seasons when they will have losing records. Many sports professionals would argue that the best way to maximize success for their organization is to do everything possible to become a perennial winner and avoid being a perennial loser. Regardless of the category to which your organization belongs, however, winning alone will not create a winning business over the long-term.

Perennial Winners

In 2011, The Glasgow Rangers Football Club won its 54th Scottish Football Championship (SFC) and set a world record for the most times a soccer team has won its domestic league championship. In 2012, the reigning kings of Scotland declared bankruptcy and the company owning the team ceased to exist.

The Rangers are the archetype of perennial winners. These sports organizations or athletes can be counted on to compete for their championship on a regular basis. This success enables fans, sponsors, and the media to associate the teams and athletes primarily with winning. The Rangers' championship pedigree, along with its rivalry with the crosstown Glasgow Celtic, defined the team. Controversial former club owner Craig Whyte described the team's mission as to "put as good a team as we can on the pitch and to win trophies."[17]

The Rangers also show the perils of tying an organization's identity to winning. Even as the team racked up titles, its attendance dropped by 14.5% from the 2006–07 season to the 2011–12 season. At the same time, television money made up only a relatively small portion of the team's total revenue and could not cover these losses. As money inflows were decreasing, the team continued to sign increasingly expensive players and coaches to its roster to maintain its winning ways. The only way the team could continue to afford to pay team personnel was by using an illegal scheme that reduced the players' and coaches' income tax burdens. The HM Revenue & Customs (HMRC) assessed the Rangers with tens of millions of pounds of fines for tax avoidance.[18] Combining the team's financial losses with these fines forced the Rangers into bankruptcy. The team eventually relaunched in the SFL's Third Division in the 2012–13 season and moved up to League One for the 2013–14 season. However, the Rangers still struggled financially, as the team lost $23.5 million over a 13-month period ending in July 2013. The situation was so dire that the Rangers asked its players to take a 15% pay cut while its manager accepted a 50% salary reduction.[19]

You might think the Rangers are an extreme example and not every team is going bankrupt trying to win. In fact, the Rangers demonstrate why Union of European Football Associations (UEFA), European soccer's governing body, instituted a financial fair play rule in 2009. UEFA is trying to prevent teams from continually experiencing "repeated, and worsening, financial losses" while trying to pursue a winning strategy. While some clubs can afford these losses because of the wealth of their owners, too many soccer teams were flirting with bankruptcy by spending money they did not have in order to be competitive on the field. This practice was destabilizing soccer leagues throughout Europe and caused UEFA to take action.[20] Teams that fail to balance their books will not be able to compete in UEFA sanctioned events such as the Champions League.

Perennial winners can also be financial losers outside of soccer. If there ever were a basketball team that was as dominant as the Rangers, it would be the University of Connecticut women's basketball team. Since Geno Auriemma has taken over as head coach, the Huskies have won 10 National Collegiate Athletic Association (NCAA) titles. The team has had five undefeated seasons and is consistently ranked as a contender for the national title.

Despite its success on the court, the Huskies have struggled to finish in the black financially. During the team's historic 90-game winning streak from 2009–11, the Huskies lost money every year.[21] This included the team losing over $730,000 even after the Huskies won their second consecutive NCAA championship in 2010.[22] According to the U.S. Department of Education, the Huskies' losses rose to $1.2 million after the 2012–13 season.[23]

The Rangers and the Huskies illustrate that even consistently winning teams can struggle to be profitable. Even with these problems, most people would rather take their chances on being successful with a winning team rather than with a losing team. If perennial winners cannot always make money, then what chance do perennial losers have?

Perennial Losers

The stories and superstitions surrounding the Chicago Cubs inability to win, or often compete for, a Major League Baseball (MLB) World Series title since 1908 have defined the organization's "lovable losers" identity. The Cubs were famously cursed by bar owner William "Billy Goat" Sianis when he and his goat were denied admission to the Fall Classic in October of 1945. Decades later, a black cat's appearance in a 1969 game became the scapegoat for a late season collapse that caused the Cubs to lose the National League (NL) Pennant.

By the 1970s, the Cubs became known as lovable losers because fans, media, and sponsors supported the team even when it was not winning. Whether it was drinking an Old Style beer while eating a Chicago-style hot dog or singing along with broadcaster Harry Caray's seventh inning rendition of "Take Me Out to the Ballgame," people loved the Cubs. Fans kept coming to the "Friendly Confines" of Wrigley Field regardless of the team's performance or high ticket prices. Even when the team lost more games than usual, gate revenues actually increased while television revenues remained constant.[24] For the Cubs, being lovable losers actually had been a winning business proposition.

It is only after the Cubs began to move away from the "lovable loser" identity that the team has begun to see a negative impact. When the Cubs won the NL Central Division title and made the playoffs for the second year in a row after the 2008 season, audience expectations started to change for the organization. As then-manager Lou Piniella stated, "When I came here a couple of years ago, if you told our fans we're going to win two divisions, I think they'd be happy with that. Now if you tell [them] you're going to win a third and not have [playoff] success, they're not going to be happy with that."[25] Since the 2008 season, the Cubs attendance declined for five seasons in a row[26] and television ratings declined by over 64% over the same time period.[27]

We recognize that losing will not be so lovable for every sports organization. In fact, it was not always that lovable for the Cubs. Prior to the 1969 season, the team struggled to attract fans to games. However, there are other teams who have experienced long stretches of losing and have found ways to achieve success. The Toronto Maple Leafs won the last of their 13 National Hockey League (NHL) Stanley Cups in the 1966–67 season. Since the 2002–03 season, the Maple Leafs have only made the NHL Stanley Cup Playoffs one time while often losing in spectacular fashion in both the post season and the regular season. The team lost a 3-goal lead in Game 7 to the Boston Bruins in the 2013 playoffs and suffered a late season eight-game losing streak at the end of its 2013–14 regular season to miss the 2014 playoffs.

Fortunately, the Maple Leafs have a financial cushion to soften the blow of these defeats. The team has a league-leading $1.1 billion dollar organization valuation while also making an estimated $142 million in annual revenue and $48.7 million in annual operating income in 2013.[28] Maple Leaf Sports & Entertainment (MLSE), the company that owns the team, effectively maximizes the organization's advantage of being the sole NHL team in the largest Canadian metropolitan area and also its historic identity as an NHL Original Six team. In addition, it is taking a leading role in building Maple Leaf Square, a modern place marketing venue extension adjacent to the team's arena, the Air Canada Centre. The goal of this project is to create the "epicentre of Toronto's sports and entertainment district."

The hotels, restaurants and shops foster new opportunities for fans, media, and sponsors to engage with the team both before and after games.[29]

A team can achieve financial success while losing, even without the historic pedigree of the Maple Leafs. Prior to making the playoffs in the 2012–13 season, the Golden State Warriors made the postseason only once and had the second worst winning percentage in the National Basketball Association (NBA) over the previous 17 years. Yet, the Warriors sold for a then league-record $450 million for a team that did not own its arena in 2011. One reason for the high purchase price is the Warriors' loyal fan base. Even though many of its fans come from highly affluent areas in San Francisco and Silicon Valley, the Warriors have one of the lowest ticket prices in the NBA which helps the team keep the arena packed with over 18,000 fans per game over the last six seasons. Instead of raising ticket prices, the team renegotiated its local cable television rights deal soon after majority owners Peter Guber and Joe Lacob bought the team that increased annual revenue by $16 million. While attendance and ratings have increased since the Warriors started to perform better on the court after the 2012–13 season, the team has taken advantage of winning seasons largely because of efforts it made off the court during its long stretch of "comic ineptitude."[30]

The Cubs, Maple Leafs, and Warriors demonstrate that being a perennial loser does not mean a sports organization has to be a financial loser. However, many teams and players are neither perennial winners nor perennial losers. They face a different challenge when it comes to winning.

Periodic Winners

The vast majority of organizations fall into this category, where parity rules supreme. Even for the most successful organizations or athletes, winning more than 50% of the time is difficult. The Chicago Bears have the highest overall National Football League (NFL) winning percentage at 57%.[31] Brazil has the best all-time winning percentage of any national soccer team at 63%.[32] Over the past 30 years, 23 of 30 NHL teams have played in the Stanley Cup Finals.[33] Prior to the start of the 2014 season, Roger Federer had won only 29% of the major tournaments he entered even though he has won the most men's Grand Slam titles in tennis history.

This parity means that a number of different teams or athletes are competing for a title in professional sports every year. You may hit it big, but more often than not the probability does not work out in your favor. Even when periodic winners are fortunate enough to win championships, these organizations can still lose money. According to owner Micky Arison, the Miami Heat was unprofitable for the 2011–12 season after winning its second NBA title in only 23 seasons.[34]

Sports professionals can achieve success without focusing solely on winning no matter what category your sports organization falls into as a winner. And just what does winning mean anyway? The definition of winning is constantly in flux with more and more organizations labeled winners every day.

Winning Has Become a Commodity

The concept of winning has been redefined over time. Winning used to be synonymous with championships. Today, the mantra of "everyone gets a trophy" popularized in youth sports is permeating the upper ranks of revenue-generating sports.

The examples of this shift are everywhere. In a bygone era in the NFL, two teams made the playoffs – and the playoffs consisted of one game, the Super Bowl. Today, six teams from each conference advance to the postseason, and there has been discussion of adding more teams to the mix. A similar situation exists in MLB, where it used to be that the league leaders won the pennant and then went to the World Series. Now five teams in each league make the playoffs, with the addition of a sixth team as a possibility on the table. The definition of winning broadens even wider in leagues like the NBA and the NHL, where more than 50% of the teams in the league make the postseason, which for some teams can be construed as "winning." In major college sports, winning is even more pervasive. If a Football Bowl Subdivision (FBS) school wins 6 games, it becomes "bowl eligible," qualifying to potentially play in one of the 35 bowls that are hosted annually. Meanwhile, the NCAA Division I men's college basketball playoff system expanded from 65 to 68 teams in 2010. On the high school level, the institution of the class system in many states, which replaced single state divisions, has expanded the postseason and thus winning opportunities for teams and athletes.

Of course, the meaning of winning is relative to an organization's position and history. A playoff appearance as an 8th seed in the NBA for a perennial loser may feel like the championship, while a championship contender earning that same eighth seed may be met with fan disappointment. But for all intents and purposes, winning now means something different. More teams and athletes can be identified as some sort of winner. And in a world where winning is more accessible than ever before, it's become a commodity for sports organizations. If you can achieve some semblance of winning, what else makes you different? Periodic winners can bank on winning something at some point. The real question is how to differentiate from the legion of other "winners" in the marketplace.

Winning Is Not the Only Success Factor

Winning (however it's defined) can be an important success factor, but it's certainly not the only one. A growing body of academic research is advancing our understanding of the relative influence of winning. We're starting to see that other factors are just as important, if not more so, in explaining why fans consume sports. A study led by Baylor University professor Kirk Wakefield examined MLB attendance from 2000–09 and found that a team's current season winning attendance ranked third behind stadium quality and star players as the most influential factors in predicting attendance.[35] Other work by Temple University professor Daniel Funk and his colleagues measures five key motivational factors in consuming sports: socialization, performance, excitement, esteem, and diversion. Their research showed that fans rated excitement ("I enjoy the excitement associated with the games, I find the games very exciting") much higher than they rated esteem ("I feel like I have won when the team wins, I get a sense of accomplishment when the team wins").[36]

Even if an organization wins, this does not necessarily translate into long-term success. There are many other factors involved. For example, the Florida Marlins have won two World Series championships and fielded a number of competitive teams throughout their 20-year existence. But the franchise has failed to sustain fan interest in the community. Historically, the franchise's owners, most notably H. Wayne Huizenga and then Jeffrey Loria, have presided over dramatic cost-cutting measures after championship seasons, alienating fans in the process. Most recently, Loria gutted a star-studded roster in 2012 after only one underachieving season, which also happened to be the inaugural season of the team's new publicly financed downtown Miami Park, leaving many fans to question the organization's respect (or lack thereof) for its customers.[37] Rather than capitalizing on the momentum of winning two World Series championships, the Marlins have suffered due to a number of factors other than winning – chief among them are distrust of ownership, inconsistency with the team roster, and a poor baseball-watching experience in their previous venue (Sun Life Stadium, which was a converted football stadium). No matter how many games the Marlins win in the coming seasons, the organization will need to find other ways to reengage with the South Florida marketplace over the long-term.

In the end, winning in sports business without winning on the field is no longer a luxury, it's a necessity. For sports business leaders, the opportunity for long-term growth and stability lies in the success factors that can be controlled. We have identified those critical factors and equipped our readers with strategies and real-world best practices to maximize them. Our goal is to help leaders and their organizations capitalize on the times when they do win and withstand the seemingly interminable doldrums of losing. This begins with evaluating the strategic issues that are fundamentally changing the sports industry.

An Inflection Point for Sports Business

Today, the sports industry is at an unprecedented inflection point, where multiple forces are colliding and profoundly altering industry dynamics. Winning alone will not help sports organizations navigate this increasingly complex marketplace. The financial stakes are too high and the competition is too fierce.

Financial Reward and Risk

The prospects for growth in the sports industry have never been better, as many organizations are generating record revenues from ticket sales, media rights agreements, and corporate sponsorships.[38] The figures reported daily in the media for athletes' contracts continue to grow with the size of endorsement deals and franchise valuations. One could argue that the twenty-first century has been the Golden Age for the sports industry, given how large and successful it has become.

But beneath this veneer of prosperity lies a different story. An increasing number of sports managers at the professional, collegiate, high school, and amateur levels are starting to feel financial strain. Because of new technologies, intensifying competition, and issues stemming from the broader domestic and global economy, sports organizations at all levels are facing challenges to their traditional revenue streams. For example, according to league figures, NBA teams collectively lost over $340 million during the 2010–11 season.[39] Player lockouts in the NBA and NHL are indicative of the financial stress that many leagues and teams are facing. The Women's National Basketball Association (WNBA) and Major League Soccer (MLS) often struggle to keep some of the top players in the world because their inability to pay competitive salaries is causing players to defect to Europe and other international leagues.[40]

Of course, the financial pressures are not limited to professional leagues. Universities and colleges are forced to choose between firing faculty, dismissing coaches, and eliminating programs. Because football programs are such significant revenue generators for universities, it is increasingly the case that football coaches are the highest-paid (or among the highest-paid) employees in the state. High school sports are squeezed between drastic funding reductions and declining booster support. From middle school teams to professional organizations, a growing number of sports entities are facing financial predicaments that make it difficult for them to compete on and off the field.

The unpredictability of live sports and its accompanying characters and plot lines are attractive to audiences and advertisers alike. As a result, dollars continue to flow to the industry, with no real signs of slowing. At the same time, the costs for sports organizations to compete are rising precipitously, with athletes, coaches, and facilities being just a few of the escalating expenses. Moreover, the gap between the haves and the have-nots is widening in some sports, leaving the smaller-market or lower-tier entities at a disadvantage.[41] While there is substantial money to be made in sports, it will take a disciplined, strategic approach to growth and management to achieve success.

These financial forces have created new questions about how to develop, distribute, and monetize sports brands of all types, including leagues, teams, athletes, and products. In many cases, the answers will not be readily apparent or easy to achieve. The time when winning was the primary solution has passed. Of course, a winning team or record-breaking athlete will usually drive profits in ways that a losing team or average athlete will not. But by no means does winning alone guarantee prosperity at today's inflection point.

Competitive Intensity

Compounding the financial challenges, sports organizations are now also encountering increasingly intense competition. For example, globalization in sports is in full swing. International soccer leagues such as the English Premier League and La Liga are now making inroads into the United States, often superseding MLS in importance. Other international sports such as cricket and rugby are growing in influence in the United States and other parts of the world. Meanwhile, many leagues from the United States such as the NFL, NBA, and MLB have been building increasingly strong connections with international audiences. Emerging sports such as mixed martial arts, marathon running, and lacrosse are gaining market share at both the professional and amateur levels. Fans have a greater range of sports brands from which to choose than ever before.

Leagues, conferences, and federations are also becoming media companies and distributing their content directly to audiences. The rapid rise of league-owned television channels ranging from the professional NFL Network and NBA Network to the collegiate Big Ten and Pac 12 networks is shifting the landscape of sports media in powerful ways. Meanwhile, digital-only subscription services like

MLB.TV have been met with enthusiasm from millions of fans all over the world. Moreover, with the rise of social networks, athletes can also effectively run their own media companies. Rafael Nadal's more than 12 million Facebook fans[42] and 5 million Twitter followers[43] allow him to reach and influence his fans on a consistent basis and with a controlled message.

There is also the undeniable attraction of other entertainment options outside the sports industry. We are now living in an on-demand world where people can watch what they want, when they want, wherever they want it. Netflix, HBO Go, and the DVR are among the facilitators of this new era of media consumption. Because of the sheer volume of content available, a new viewing behavior called "TV binge watching" has emerged in which viewers watch multiple consecutive TV series in one sitting.[44] Meanwhile, the smartphones and tablets in the hands of hundreds of millions of consumers provide options including gaming, entertainment, and messaging applications. These new forms of entertainment and distribution are further convoluting an already-challenging sports marketplace.

This explosion of technologies is also giving rise to a new class of citizens: the digital natives. They can be found in homes around the world. Parents are documenting their children's innate technological aptitude on YouTube.[45] Babies are increasingly given smartphones and tablets to play with before their first birthday, and some seem to have the facility to use them by the age of two. It may also come as no surprise that seven out of ten children under the age of 12 are considered tablet users.[46] In fact, many parents buy devices like the iPad Mini for their children to use.[47]

This new generation will have a different orientation to life as a consumer and, for the purposes of the sports business, life as a fan. Because of their early and constant use of new technologies such as tablets and smartphones, these digital natives will be unlike any market the sports and entertainment industries have ever seen. Although there is some controversy about how Internet savvy this generation actually is,[48] these fans will simply not know life without technology and will likely be expecting technological experiences everywhere they go, including from sports brands.

As a result of this increasingly competitive environment, sports organizations are now under pressure to constantly improve and adapt their businesses to meet the growing demands from fans, sponsors, the media, and athletes. To justify the price of a full season's subscription, season ticket holders often expect notification about the latest personnel and business decisions as well as constant access to their favorite players through different channels such as social media engagements or in-person appearances. Sponsors count on sports organizations to act as trusted business partners who will help their companies achieve specific revenue goals instead of merely being outlets for venue signage opportunities. Top high school athletes expect state-of-the-art training facilities with the best weight rooms and physical therapy equipment. Today, competing effectively in the sports business requires managing a broader environment that goes beyond what happens on game day and team and athlete performance.

The modern sports organization is complex, and winning is only one piece of the puzzle. In some ways, the modern sports organization bears resemblance to a financial portfolio. Over time, a portfolio with a diverse set of assets has proven to be the most effective approach to surviving the inevitable swings in the market. The same will hold true for the sports organizations that can capitalize on controllable factors beyond athletic performance on the field.

Strategies for Creating a Winning Business

Strategy is one of the most important, but most often misused, terms in business. Leave it to Dwight Schrute, the assistant to the regional manager of Dunder Mifflin on the sitcom *The Office* to accurately represent its nebulous meaning. Schrute once proclaimed, "They say that no man is an island. False. I am an island. And this island is volcanic. And it is about to erupt with the molten hot lava . . . of strategy."[49]

While Schrute's strategic eruption is clearly satirical, actually finding a definition of strategy is no joke. Even experts on strategy do not agree on a single definition. University of Oxford Saïd Business School professor Richard Whittington compares four different perspectives on strategies—the classical, the evolutionary, the processual, and the systemic. McGill University professor Henry Mintzberg articulates the differences between intended strategy (what an organization planned to do) and realized strategy (what an organization actually did). These are only a couple of examples of the approaches that experts have taken to defining strategy.[50]

For this book, we use a definition of strategy that aligns with our primary goals—making individuals better at their jobs and making organizations more successful. This definition comes from Harvard Business School professor Michael Porter, who writes "competitive strategy is about being different. It means deliberately choosing a different set of activities to deliver a unique mix of value."[51] In the context of the sports business, success on the field is something every team and organization is trying to accomplish. The way you deliver true, long-lasting value is by providing something to your customer that is different from what they can get somewhere else. We discuss the factors that will help sports strategists achieve the right mix of differentiation and value for their organizations.

Becoming a successful strategist is about mastering the art and science of making choices. The "kitchen sink" approach can be a convenient crutch when it is difficult to determine viable solutions to difficult problems. In the sports industry in particular, there exist an almost limitless number of options, directions, and tactics to draw upon to respond to the challenges created by today's inflection point. Using this approach, however, is flawed. In fact, Porter asserts, "The essence of strategy is choosing what *not* to do."[52] Moreover, in an environment with limited time, money, and resources, it is simply impossible to try to do everything and see what works. The ability and resolve to make choices is of utmost importance.

To achieve this goal, we have developed the concept of the sports strategist. Sports strategists share a universal set of characteristics that are increasingly important in the dynamic sports industry. There are five critical characteristics that successful sports strategists exhibit in their work:

- Interdisciplinary View – Sports strategists maintain a holistic perspective even as their organizations prioritize increasingly specialized roles. For example, a decision-maker in player personnel should understand how his or her choices impact an organization's identity.
- Problem-Oriented – The most effective sports strategists start with the problem they are trying to solve. Then they identify the methodologies that will help them solve the problem. They never adopt a methodology-first viewpoint on a problem.
- Committed to Differentiation – Sports strategists keep the question of differentiation at the forefront of their minds. They are always answering the question, "How is what I am offering different from others and unique to my customers?"
- Students of Technology – Technology will be central to the sports business for the foreseeable future. Sports strategists recognize that they need to immerse themselves in technologies to take advantage of new opportunities for their organizations.
- Revenue-Focused – No matter where someone sits within an organization, he or she is increasingly expected to help generate revenue. Sports strategists understand how their role contributes to the bottom line and seek new ways to help the organization make money.

The common element among all sports strategists is the ability to analyze the challenges that organizations can best address and determine the best solutions to address these problems. To determine the issues where sports strategists can add the most value, we interviewed industry leaders and completed in-depth analyses on the domestic and international sports markets to determine the approaches that have been successful and those that have not. We then examined the commonalities across all our research and synthesized the core principles into the following eight chapters. These are all factors within a sports strategist's control and can help position an organization for success without an over-reliance on winning.

- Designing an Identity – Sports strategists who design clear, differentiated, and unique identities for their organizations are well positioned for success. Internally, an identity gives focus to an organization's mission and culture and helps influence decisions on a range of issues from athlete personnel acquisitions to marketing campaigns. Externally, fans, sponsors, and the media are more likely to connect with an organization with a strong identity than one that does not stand for something meaningful.
- Constructing Enduring Narratives – The narrative technique is essential to helping organizations better engage targeted audiences. Few communication devices can attract, sustain, and persuade like narratives can. Whether the format is a 140-character tweet or a feature film, the art of storytelling through character, plot, and setting is more important today than ever before.
- Mastering New Technologies – Technological change is coming fast and furiously to the sports industry. Sometimes it seems like there's a new revolutionary platform or innovation introduced every month. To navigate this dynamic new world of technology, sports strategists must become more proactive and less reactive, focusing on adopting new platforms to meet their business objectives.
- Maximizing Revenue with Analytics – All organizations are under pressure to generate more revenue. While there are multiple methods for driving profit, quantitative analytics are proving to be valuable tools in this pursuit. Sports strategists with a fundamental understanding of how to use data to make financial decisions will be better prepared than their peers for the future of the industry.
- Developing Public Support – Sports organizations and the public have a long and intertwined history. Although many teams are private enterprises, they often use the local city or state in their team name. For decades, this arrangement was largely considered to be mutually beneficial. But in recent years, public support for sports has been declining. Since this

support is such a critical source of solvency for the sports world, many sports strategists will be compelled to create new partnerships and business models for the public.

- Crafting a Crisis Blueprint – In the world of 24/7 sports news cycles and social media, seemingly no organization or person is safe from crisis. Often any hint of scandal, whether it comes in the form of gambling, performance-enhancing drugs, or personal attacks, can erode decades of goodwill. The challenge for sports strategists is how to respond to, defuse, and move on from the crisis when it hits.
- Reinvigorating Sportscapes – More sports fans now prefer to watch sports at home than at the venue. On the surface, this presents attendance challenges for the sports industry, particularly for behemoth venues that are built to host enormous crowds. But it also alters the relationship fans have with sports, as the smell of the grass is replaced with the up-close view of a big-screen high-definition TV (HDTV) set. Sports strategists will have to negotiate these new dynamics of the live experience.
- Infusing Ethics into Decision-Making – Ethical considerations are playing an increasing role in how sports organizations evaluate business challenges. Sports organizations increasingly must balance the need for making money with doing right by their various audiences. The use of ethics can help sports strategists improve their organization's decision-making processes.

Before we move on, we want to be clear that this book is solution focused. Every chapter provides a variety of solutions that address how to capitalize on each of the success factors that sports strategists can control. It is also case heavy. Often the best way to develop strategy and innovate is through learning from the successes and failures of others. While some of the cases may be more directly related to your current area of expertise than others, every case is designed to have broader takeaways that are relevant to all readers.

Most importantly, this book is designed to answer the question of how to succeed in sports business without relying solely on winning on the field. It will arm current and aspiring sports strategists with a number of strategies to implement when the situation calls for it.

Sports strategists, it's game time.

2 Designing an Identity

We Brooklyn-ized who we are."[1] Brooklyn Nets CEO Brett Yormark articulated his team's new identity after the New Jersey Nets relocated in 2012. Prior to this move, the team's management faced a number of challenges. It was bringing the first professional sports team to Brooklyn since 1957 when the Dodgers left for Los Angeles. It had taken eight years to build a new arena in Brooklyn's Atlantic Yards after many well-publicized stops and starts. And the team management was in desperate need of rejuvenation, after 35 years of mainly mediocre seasons played in the Meadowlands and Newark. Their response to these challenges was a textbook identity redesign, one that tied the team to the collective identity of Brooklyn, a strategy otherwise known as "Brooklyn-ize."

The story begins with the key players. Chief among them was mogul Jay-Z, who became a part owner of the Nets when developer Bruce Ratner bought the franchise in 2004. Born and raised in Brooklyn's Marcy Projects, Jay-Z instantly imbued the move to Brooklyn with credibility, even though he reportedly owned only 0.16% of the team.[2] The other headliner was Mikhail Prokhorov, who bought the Nets from Ratner in 2010. A Russian billionaire who played professional basketball, his confidence and deep pockets helped elevate the Nets in a market where the Knicks were king. He also quickly became a foil to Knicks owner James Dolan. In 2010, both Jay-Z and Prokhorov graced a billboard overlooking Madison Square Garden (MSG) that proclaimed, "The blueprint for greatness."[3]

With the leadership in place, other elements of the team's "Brooklyn-ized" identity began to take shape. The new logo was particularly influential. With its black and white colors, which reflected Jay-Z's preference for black (he also had a hand in designing the logo), the Nets differentiated themselves from the rest of the NBA, as they were the only team with that color combination. The logo includes a big letter *B* as its centerpiece, which echoes the Brooklyn Dodgers' logo. Also harkening back to the Dodgers heritage, the typography came from the subway signage from that same era.[4] The resulting logo translated well to team merchandise, creating a frenzy of sales when the new hats, jerseys, and t-shirts hit the stores, even attracting New York Knicks fans who could not deny the cool factor of the Brooklyn Nets style.[5]

The Nets' redefined identity was punctuated by its new home, the Barclays Center. The arena is at once a technological marvel and cultural hub, a symbol of the ongoing Brooklyn renaissance. For the smartphone generation, the in-arena Wi-Fi keeps fans connected while at the game, and the Barclays Center app offers a second screen experience with different camera angles of the live game and the ability to watch instant replays.[6] Moreover, the Barclays Center reflects Brooklyn's identity as a supporter of the arts and culture. For example, 55 local vendors supply food and beverages throughout the arena, so if you're looking for a classic Junior's cheesecake or hipster favorite McClure's pickles, the Barclays has you covered.[7] In addition, the basketball court has a "herringbone-patterned" floor that is reminiscent of the parquet floor of the Boston Garden,[8] giving the arena a classic look despite its newness.

The final key element of the Nets Brooklyn-ization was its inaugural marketing campaign. With the two words, "Hello, Brooklyn" as its tagline, the team entered the market with a warm greeting, rather than loudly announcing its arrival. The campaign featured its "Core Four" players: Deron Williams, Joe Johnson, Brook Lopez, and

Gerald Wallace, all of whom had enjoyed success in their NBA careers, but were hardly superstars like Kevin Durant or LeBron James. Each had his own advertisement that educated fans on who they were, as a way to foster a stronger connection between the team and the city. As Nets Chief Marketing Officer and Chief Revenue Officer Frank Mangione put it, "We took a very humble approach because of what the borough means to everyone who lives in it. We took the approach that we're thankful to be a part of this."[9]

The Nets' Brooklyn-ized identity serves as a beacon for the organization, even after Jay-Z sold his ownership stake in the franchise and the team traded for stars Paul Pierce and Kevin Garnett. It provides focus to all aspects of the audience experience. It gives marketing, public relations, and sales representatives a clear, differentiated asset to shape into an overarching communications strategy. It also adds texture to the internal culture, making it feel bigger in purpose, and can help attract and retain top talent on both the player personnel and the business side. Despite decades in the shadows of the New York Knicks, the Brooklyn Nets have now arrived, not just as a formidable competitor in New York City but also as a brand well-positioned for national and international success.

• • •

Identity refers to the characteristics that determine how a person or organization is recognized and remembered. It can be derived from a variety of sources, including behavior, style, heritage, and other differentiators. When sports organizations have a strong sense of who they are, the rewards can be significant and long lasting. A strong sense of identity will result in more disciplined and efficient decision-making. Identity also serves as a guiding law that permeates the culture and directs the overall strategy for every function within an organization, including player personnel, game day operations, marketing, sales, and public relations, to name just a few. Moreover, it can help ensure organization-wide coordination, which tends to be a challenge in the increasingly specialized sports industry. When there is internal clarity on the organization's identity, the product and experience provided to fans, sponsors, and the media are often distinct and much more likely to break through the clutter as a result.

Designing an identity is one of the fundamental tasks for a sports organization. If done successfully, it will inform key decisions across your organization on any number of issues, and help guard against the inevitable peaks and valleys of winning and losing. In this chapter, we discuss two critical elements of identity design:

1. How to build an identity for a sports organization
2. How to implement, maintain, and grow an identity

Identity design is both a strategic and an organizational initiative. It is one thing to develop a unique identity on paper that potentially resonates with fans and sponsors, but if the people within an organization – from the athletes to team executives to stadium vendors – are not living the identity, it will not be authentic or effective. Identity design is a holistic effort that requires leadership at the highest levels and buy-in from all involved. The payoffs can be significant.

Competitive Advantages of Identity Design

In addition to the internal focus it offers organizations, designing an identity has several key benefits that play into the hands of sports strategists. Identity can foster stronger emotional connections with sports fans. Consumer behavior research tells us that people make purchasing decisions based on beliefs about the functional and emotional benefits of products and services.[10] Functional benefits refer to the tangible value a product delivers to consumers. Emotional benefits satisfy a customer's psychological wants and needs. Many companies operate in industries in which the emotional benefits of a product are equally, if not more, important differentiators than the functional benefits.

Coca-Cola beverages are a good example of how the most successful products often have a clear identity that appeals to the emotions of consumers. Coca-Cola's primary functional benefit is quenching thirst with flavored, carbonated water. But there are numerous ways to quench thirst, of course, and despite the lore surrounding Coca-Cola's closely held secret recipe, the basic product is something that can easily be mimicked. In fact, consumers can now buy machines that allow them to produce their own soda at home for a significantly lower cost than buying a Coca-Cola product. Ultimately, the company's emotional connection with its customers is much more valuable than its product's functional benefits. Millions of consumers now associate drinking a Coke with happiness and positivity, bringing to life the company's mantra that "things go better with Coke."[11] As a result, the company will generate billions of dollars of revenue this year not because their consumers want a soda – but because they want a Coca-Cola product.[12]

In sports, emotional benefits often outweigh functional benefits for many fans. It could be argued that most of the important benefits of sports fandom are emotional. That is why identity is such a critical concept. Fans often take on the identity of their favorite athlete or favorite team, and who your favorite athlete or favorite team is says something about you.[13] During the 2013–14 season, the English Premier League had five teams based in London. Even though all are located in the same city, each team has a very different identity. Each team's supporters identify themselves in distinct ways despite the fact that many live within only a few miles of each other.

The other competitive advantage of designing an identity is that it helps sports organizations and athletes achieve differentiation. FC Barcelona stands for world-class soccer. But an equally important component of its identity is the cultural significance it carries both in Spain and internationally. The team embraces its location in Catalonia, which has been seeking independence from Spain for decades, and serves as an important symbol of Catalonia's strength and potential success if it were to become independent.[14] The organization's official slogan "More than a club" helps position FC Barcelona as a cultural emblem. This identity differentiates the team and ultimately helps contribute to its success.[15]

Identity is an important differentiator for athletes as well. If you were a fan of tennis player Andy Roddick throughout his 12-year career, you were not rewarded with many Grand Slam championships (one, to be exact). Despite his considerable talent, Roddick was playing in what was perhaps the Golden Age of men's tennis, competing against all-time greats, including Novak Djokovic, Roger Federer, and Rafael Nadal, which ultimately limited his career winnings and could have rendered him anonymous. But that did not stop him from rising to the upper echelons of his sport based on the strength of his identity. He was a competitive American tennis player (in an era when U.S. men's tennis was comparatively weak), married supermodel Brooklyn Decker, endorsed Lacoste and Reebok, and had an outspoken and engaging personality in press conferences and other public forums. He also bolstered his reputation as a jovial, ready-for-primetime performer by hosting *Saturday Night Live*. Throughout his career, Roddick's identity was the driving force that gave fans many reasons to connect emotionally with him beyond his performance.

Identity design offers a number of advantages for sports strategists. In addition to helping protect against the unpredictability of winning, it can facilitate emotional connections with sports fans and provide valuable differentiation in the marketplace. These advantages take effect only with a clear, distinct, and unique identity.

Building the Identity

If you are defining an identity for your organization, there are a few key areas to consider. None of these is mutually exclusive. In fact, some of the most effective identities combine elements of all three. Developing an identity requires examining the characteristics of the following:

- The Audience – Fans, media, and sponsors
- The Individual – Players, coaches, managers, and administrators
- The Collective – Attributes shared by an entire organization

The Audience

Like most any communication challenge, the audience is often the most logical and effective place to start. Analyzing the target audiences and their unique characteristics can inform identity design and maybe even result in the most authentic identity. Consider specifically the strategies of market image and audience compatibility.

The first strategy is to borrow your identity from the identity of your hometown market (e.g., town, city, state, country). To do so, it is important to understand how the market views itself. What is its image? What are its values? What does it stand for? What are its traditions and history? This market image approach has been successful for a number of organizations. The Brooklyn Nets identity redesign was based entirely on the identity of Brooklyn. The Chicago Bears have for years taken on the tough, gritty, hard-working ethos of the city of broad shoulders. In extreme examples, the identity of an organization can become almost one in the same with its hometown market. In the case of Southeastern Conference (SEC) football teams, the collective psyche of the community rises and falls along with the team throughout each season.[16]

A second audience-driven strategy is to design your identity based on a specific target audience, ensuring that the characteristics of the identity are compatible with the intended audience. Formula One (F1) has capitalized on this strategy through the Red Bull Racing team. Fans of F1 are adrenaline seekers who view open wheel racing as one of the most dangerous forms of the sport. Similarly, Red Bull as a brand takes pride in its edgy identity that is synonymous with danger, excitement, and energy. With two Red Bull sponsored teams, F1 is broadening the scope of its circuit's identity and aligning sponsors with its target audience.[17]

Sometimes an organization's identity can be found simply by looking at the audiences with whom you're trying to connect. If your audience can see themselves and their values in what you do as an organization, the potential for long-lasting emotional connections and loyalty during losing seasons can be much greater than the alternative.

SOUNDERS PUT FANS AT CENTER OF THEIR IDENTITY

Seattle sports fans were reeling. In 2008, they lost their once-venerable NBA SuperSonics franchise to Oklahoma City after months of contentious public debates between the team and the city about a new arena. It was another setback to the collective pride of a passionate, modern, and technologically connected sports city that has a long history of supporting its teams through good and bad times.

Enter the Seattle Sounders Football Club. The team was established in 2007 and introduced as the fifteenth soccer franchise of MLS in 2009. Not only did the team help fill the void created by the loss of the SuperSonics, but it also adopted an innovative and unconventional approach to identity building. The results have been impressive: the highest average attendance in MLS,[18] the highest local TV ratings,[19] and multiple industry awards in sports business.[20]

The reason for its success? The fan is always at the center of the team's identity. As Drew Carey, a famous comedian, game show host, and minority owner of the team declared, the Sounders are "bringing democracy to sports in America."[21] In 2008, the team's ownership opened up the decision regarding the team's name to fans. Although the owners' preference was to distance the new franchise from the other Seattle Sounders of the National American Soccer League (NASL),[22] a majority of fans voted for the Sounders FC name.[23] And that's what it became.

The Sounders have also created the Alliance, a fan association that has input on every aspect of team operations. Most controversially, the Alliance has the opportunity to vote on whether the general manager should keep or lose his or her job every four years. Although some football clubs in Europe have taken a similar tack, this approach is relatively unheard of in

CONTINUED

the United States.[24] But that has not seemed to bother the Sounders' ownership. Majority owner Joe Roth once said, "I've gotten calls from other owners of other teams in other sports who tell me I'm out of my mind. Which tells me it's probably a pretty good idea, actually."[25]

The fans' response to these efforts shows how much they value taking such an important role with the team. The Sounders' festival-like pregame atmosphere brings to mind European soccer traditions in which entire communities march to the downtown stadium in support of their team. The "March to the Match" leaves from Occidental Park, with fans singing, chanting, and walking to make the event their own. Sounders FC scarves have also taken center stage. The symbolic green and blue garments have become a part of the experience, much like those that appear at games in the Premier League in the United Kingdom and the First Division of the Professional Football League (La Liga) in Europe. The "Golden Scarf" is presented at each game to a hometown favorite who exemplifies the "intense passion of Seattle's soccer community."[26]

The team's strategy is fan-centric, intimate, and spontaneous. The franchise has eliminated the distance between the fan and the product. The Sounders' front office understands that the fans define the club's identity and has successfully implemented strategies that give them a feeling of ownership. For many teams and franchises, it takes years to establish culture and traditions. The Sounders accomplished this goal in a matter of months.

The Individual

Sports organizations can select a number of different individuals around whom they can design their identity. Current or former athletes are the first and most obvious choice, as they typically receive the most attention. Coaches, managers, scouts, and advisors are another viable source of identity. In sports with frequent player turnover, these individuals can often be a strong strategic option. There is also the front office staff, including commissioners, owners, presidents, and general managers, who can often be the most permanent fixtures of organizations. For high schools and colleges, notable alumni, students, and faculty are additional possibilities. Even the fan cultures that spring up around teams can embody the desired identity that can extend across the organization.

Many may be familiar with the classic focus group technique in which research-ers assign human personality characteristics to brands. If Best Buy, for example, walks through the door, who would it be? A man or a woman? How old would he or she be? What would he or she be wearing? What would he or she drive? Re-searchers use the answers to these questions to compare consumer perceptions of a brand to what the brand thinks it is. This is a particularly useful, and at times en-tertaining, exercise for brands that sell inanimate objects, as it lends the product a sense of humanity.[27]

Sports organizations do not typically face this problem. The sports industry has the benefit of having an endless and ever-changing supply of compelling charac-ters. If that same focus group were asked to personify Duke basketball, the answer would likely be head coach Mike Krzyzewski. In addition, we often hear the labels "face of the franchise" or "face of the league" attached to star players as a way to define the identity of particular organizations. For example, soccer players Clint Dempsey and Abby Wambach of the U.S. Men's and Women's National Teams have personified their respective organizations. Whether through appearances in the games or through press conferences, free agency signings, endorsements, or crises, it is the people in sports who help drive the industry.

Designing identity through people requires taking a different perspective on building teams and organizations. Historically, the primary focus has often been to put the best possible product on the field, court, or pitch. That often means find-ing the most capable players and coaches and organizing them into a team in the pursuit of success. Personnel decisions are often made based on the primary cri-terion of which players, managers, and administrators give the organization the best chance of winning, but this should not be the only factor considered.

To build a long-lasting and effective identity, sports strategists should consider personnel decisions more broadly. Talent and skill are certainly important fac-tors, but they should be evaluated alongside how an athlete fits with an organi-zation's identity. Of course, it would be a mistake to pass on the opportunity to have a once-in-a-generation player or coach even if he or she does not match a pre-existing identity. Sports strategists can use identity to frame the personnel decision-making process in a more holistic way that merges on-field and off-field factors.

The Stanford Cardinal athletic program demonstrates the value of using this approach. Jim Harbaugh played high school football in Palo Alto, California, and his father was a defensive coordinator for the Stanford Cardinal around that same time. As a hometown native, the younger Harbaugh spent three summers working on field maintenance at Stanford's football stadium. At his first press conference as Stanford's football coach, Harbaugh recalled, "I used to stare down at that field as I was stenciling those numbers. I so very badly wanted to go to Stanford and play for the Cardinal. This was my number-one choice all along."[28] Harbaugh understood the values and history of the Stanford institution and was a natural choice for head coach, even if he was relatively untested at that time in his career. The payoff of that choice was substantial for the Cardinal, with Harbaugh catapulting the team into the national spotlight in his four years as coach. The University of Michigan employed a similar identity-approach at the start of the 2015–2016 season when it hired Harbaugh, a former star quarterback, as its head coach.[29]

The individual can also extend his or her identity across an organization. The Oakland Raiders, under the direction of principal owner Al Davis, were known for their outlaw identity. Davis infused the team's identity with his persona. He dressed in all white and black satin outfits, sued when the NFL blocked his move from Los Angeles to Oakland, and spoke in a rapid, menacing manner.[30] The Raiders purposely signed fast and talented players whom other teams considered difficult to manage and did not want on their rosters. The team was led on the field by idiosyncratic coaches such as John Madden and Art Shell who did not fit the standard profile for this position at the time. This outlaw approach differentiated the team from other NFL organizations. As Davis said about his organization during his Pro Football Hall of Fame Speech, "We were hated, we were feared but we were respected."[31]

While individuals can often serve as the best options for identity design, it is important to point out the risks. A player, coach, owner, or other individual will not stay with the organization forever and may even join a competitor. In addition, if individuals behave poorly and become embroiled in a scandal, there can be a shadow cast over the rest of the organization, especially if its identity is closely connected to the individual. Building around an individual may also tie the organization's fortunes to how the individual performs on the field.

While usually considered perennial winners, the St. Louis Cardinals have often used the organization's stars to build its identity. From fearsome sluggers such as Stan "The Man" Musial and infield magicians such as Ozzie "The Wizard" Smith to masterful managers such as Frankie Frisch and Whitey Herzog, the Cardinals have showcased some of the best personnel talent in baseball. The team at the beginning of the twenty-first century was also fueled by star power. First baseman Albert Pujols and manager Tony La Russa became the faces of the organization's identity from 2001–11. After helping the team win two World Series titles, Pujols and La Russa both left the Cardinals prior to the 2012 season. Losing its stars also meant the team was losing a big part of its identity. As the team's general manager John Mozeliak stated, "When we won the World Series, right away I remember how I was thinking that this is just a fleeting moment in time. . . . The balance of the club was in limbo, directionally, where we may be going."[32]

The Cardinals were facing one of the most complex issues in the sports industry: how to reconstruct an organization's identity after losing its stars. On the one hand, the centerpiece of the sports experience is the players, coaches, administrators, and owners who primarily drive the competitive experience. On the other hand, it is inevitable that these people will graduate, leave, retire, or be fired from the organization.

Rather than signing a famous free agent player or coach after Pujols and La Russa left, the Cardinals have consciously changed its identity management from focusing on star power to building the team's well-rounded image. This repositioning began with promoting their own minor league talent and hiring former Cardinals catcher and novice leader Mike Matheny as manager. The Cardinals were fortunate that players such as pitcher Michael Wacha and first baseman Matt Adams produced on the field quickly to help the team make the playoffs in the 2012 and 2013 seasons. However, this calculated strategy focused on youth and team has successfully altered the Cardinals identity. As owner Bill DeWitt observed, "We had a conscious strategy to build from within. . . . We did a lot of things to build what we have today. I'm pretty pleased with it."[33]

Not every sports organization can alter their identities without star power as the Cardinals have done. The challenge is to continually identify new people and bring them into an organization, develop strategies that maximize any positive associations that stars create with an organization's audiences, and capitalize on people's impact while they are there. Pujols is now part of the new star power identity of the Los Angeles Angels of Anaheim.

The Collective

In the previous sections, we discussed possibilities for deriving identities from audiences and individuals. Another approach is to create a collective identity from characteristics possessed by the organization as a whole. The key to this approach is in selecting characteristics that are differentiated and unique. Three areas to look for these assets are playing style, heritage, and environment.

ANGELS SING A NEW TUNE

When Arturo "Arte" Moreno bought the Angels in 2003 from the Walt Disney Company, the ownership change continued a major redesign of the team's identity based on the emerging Latino market. Founded in 1961 by Western radio and movie "singing cowboy" Gene Autry, the Angels have historically been a relatively junior partner to the dominant Los Angeles Dodgers.[34] For 36 years, Autry was the owner of the team, which was headquartered in the largely Caucasian, wealthy, and conservative Orange County. Over time, the demographics of the area changed dramatically, with Latinos eventually comprising 34% of Orange County and 48% of Los Angeles County.[35] While the Dodgers and San Diego Padres found success earlier in connecting with Latino fans, the Angels needed to refine their game plan. In doing so, they have become one of the most innovative Latino-focused sports teams.

Moreno, a Mexican American businessman, is the linchpin of the Angels' redefinition of their identity. As the first Mexican American to own a professional sports team, Moreno has become an aspirational symbol for Latino fans. He is also an active and accessible owner, frequently appearing at the park, mixing with fans in the concourse, and famously lowering the price of stadium beer.[36] As his actions signify, Moreno's identity is indispensable to the team's image.

Following Moreno's lead, the team demonstrates its understanding of its fan base in other ways. Broadcasts of every game are now available in both English and Spanish. After Pujols signed a record free agent contract with the team, the Angels ran billboards across the market with a simple message: "Albert Pujols: #1 Hombre." In its simplicity and directness, the marketing campaign was a confirmation of the Angels' evolving identity.

The results of their efforts are noteworthy. The Angels have increased Latino attendance from 13% in 2001 to almost 30% by 2013.[37] The club has continuously filled the ballpark with an annual attendance of over 3 million.[38] To help move out from under the shadow of the Los Angeles Dodgers, the Angels embraced the identity of their owner as a guidepost for the decision-making across the organization. It is a distinct identity shift that aligns with one of the fastest-growing fan bases in Southern California and certainly the United States.

Playing Style. A team or athlete can have a signature playing style that can be crystallized into an identity. The Grinnell College men's basketball team put this small Iowa Division III school on the map with its unique system. The team emphasizes three-point shooting and relentless full-court ball pressure, resulting in a frenetic pace and skyrocketing scores. If the team ran a more conventional half-court game, it is highly unlikely it would receive the same attention it does now. Jack Taylor brought the program national attention when he scored a record 138 points in one game. Even NBA forward and unapologetic shooter Carmelo Anthony was amazed at Taylor's feat: "How can you shoot 100 times, though? . . . That's like a video game."[39]

Heritage. An organization's history and traditions are other potential sources of differentiation. Notre Dame's football program is probably the most iconic example of leveraging its heritage to maintain differentiation in the marketplace. This includes its famous rallying cry to "Win One for the Gipper,"[40] the Touchdown Jesus mural that overlooks the stadium, and the "Play Like a Champion Today" sign that players hit as they head onto the field before a game. All of these traditional elements preserve Notre Dame's status as one of the most prominent institutions in sports.

Environment. As the actual home of the organization, the facility environment may be the most experiential extension of the sports team's identity. In 2010, Pennsylvania State University (Penn State) announced that it would support a NCAA Division I hockey program for the first time in the school's history. As part of the transition from a club to varsity sport, Penn State recognized that connecting with the community was critical to achieving a new identity for the hockey program. After receiving a $100 million gift from alumnus Terry Pegula to build a state-of-the-art facility, Pegula Ice Arena became the centerpiece of the inclusive identity it wanted to build for the hockey program. The team used to play at the Greenberg Ice Pavilion, an arena with less than 1,500 seats that resembled a "one-story warehouse."[41] For Pegula Ice Arena, the school was determined to "provide a venue for Division I Intercollegiate competition and serve the recreational needs of the University's students as well as those of the surrounding community."[42] The two NHL-sized ice rinks in one arena exemplify this approach. This unusual configuration enables Penn State to host numerous local and statewide recreational opportunities for the central Pennsylvania community while also providing a 5,000-plus seat venue for its hockey team. Penn State successfully demonstrates how a venue can be designed to embody an organization's identity.

While each characteristic is important, sports strategists should pinpoint where these different elements overlap and synthesize the key themes. Combining all three collective elements will usually lead to the development of a more differentiated identity.

PLAYING FOR IDENTITY

The Carlisle Industrial Institute was an academic institution in Carlisle, Pennsylvania, founded in 1879 to educate Native Americans. Its football team never had Twitter, luxury suites, dynamic ticket pricing, or its own television network, but it was ahead of its time in identity building.

The team's history and legacy are certainly controversial and complex. The general American population viewed Native Americans as uneducated heathens who could not compete with the white man on or off the field. Carlisle founder Richard Henry Pratt aimed to show that Native Americans could be "literate members of local communities" by assimilating them into the country's mainstream culture. Pratt's approach to "civilizing" his students was epitomized by the slogan of "Kill the Indian, Save the Man." According to Pratt, the only way to achieve his goal was to force Native Americans to give up their cultures, religious beliefs, and ways of life to become Americans.[43]

While Pratt's approach clearly has moral and ethical issues, instituting the Carlisle Indians football team did help to change the public perception of the time. Led by stars such as Jim Thorpe, the team barnstormed throughout the United States, putting on a show that infused innovations on the football field with Native American overtones. Coached by the legendary Glenn "Pop" Warner, the team utilized the speed and agility of its undersized players through new formations like the single-wing and quick-strike passes to maximize the team's advantages over its bigger and more powerful opponents. Reenacting the battle for the western frontier (on more friendly terms), the Indians played against schools such as Harvard, Michigan, Minnesota, and Washington. Crowds filled renowned stadiums such as Franklin Field, the Polo Grounds, and Harvard Stadium to watch the Indians play the collegiate powers of the era. The Carlisle Indian Marching Band dressed in full tribal regalia, and a cheering section of Indian Maidens accompanied the team. The team's record of 173 victories makes the Indians the most successful football program in the United States that no longer exists.[44]

The school used its high-profile team to emphasize the importance of education to Native Americans and to combat the negative perception of them that was then prevalent in the United States. Carlisle's public relations department bombarded newspapers with press releases about the team's players and victories while also holding press conferences at every opportunity. The media coverage was extensive and theatrical, as illustrated by a caption to a *Chicago Tribune* cartoon: "The Modern Indian Discards The Tomahawk For The Deadlier Football At The Chicago Coliseum."[45] While the institute eventually shut down in 1917, the leader of the school implemented a new strategy for growing the school's brand through sports. Pratt's decision to tie the image of the school to the athletic program generated excitement and attention in Carlisle through the high visibility of its football team.

The school had a very clear sense of its identity—combining its unique playing style with its Native American heritage—and maximized it at every opportunity. Whether it was on the football field, in the stands, or in the press, the Indians never wavered from who they were and what they represented to different audiences. Carlisle helped lay the groundwork for more recent efforts by institutions, such as Boise State University and Florida Gulf Coast University, to use sports to redefine their image.

Implementing and Maintaining an Identity

Sports strategists can design a unique and differentiated identity for their organizations and clearly articulate it in a plan, but in many ways, how the identity is implemented is as important as designing the identity itself. Implementing an identity across an organization is also not without its challenges. Sports organizations are simply larger and more complex today than ever before. In the early days of the industry, leaders often served in multiple, wide-ranging roles. For example, MLB owner Connie Mack was manager, public relations director, box office administrator, and travel coordinator for his Philadelphia Athletics baseball team over a period of 52 years.[46] In the college ranks, Frank O'Rear Moseley was athletic director, head football coach, and fundraiser for Virginia Tech in the 1950s and 1960s. The Virginia Sports Hall of Fame credits "almost every field and building of the Virginia Tech sports complex [as] a monument to the dedication and unflagging energy and efforts of Moseley."[47] In charge of both the business and sports sides of their teams, these leaders and many others like them navigated enterprise-wide decision-making and execution.

Today, organizations are far more specialized because of the industry growth that early leaders helped stimulate. Many leagues, teams, and athletic organizations have broadened to include seemingly every specialized function of modern businesses, from product development to marketing to sales – and everything in between. Like many industries, specialization has also bred siloes in sports organizations. As a result, achieving strategic alignment and operating efficiently can become more difficult. The TV series *Seinfeld* parodied the specialization of sports organizations when George Costanza was hired as the "assistant to the traveling secretary" for the New York Yankees.[48] In actuality, the Yankees front office has over 40 executives, officers, and senior administrators, all of whom have specific duties and responsibilities.[49] This may be a natural development for sports organizations, but it is a long way from Mack running the entire show.

The reason an identity is so important is that it can connect all facets of an organization in the era of specialization. No matter their specific function, all employees can look to and work toward upholding the identity as a common denominator. The question then becomes how to achieve buy-in to the identity and ensure that it influences decision-making and behavior. To help in this process, we will explore three strategic imperatives: developing institutional rhetoric, fostering collaboration across departments, and maintaining consistency.

Developing Institutional Rhetoric

Institutional rhetoric is the language, signs, and symbols an organization chooses to use in order to communicate its point of view both internally and externally in the marketplace. Constructed through themes, arguments, and special vocabulary, it shapes what the organization thinks of itself and ideally frames how others see it. For the sports strategist, any institutional rhetoric program should stem from the organization's core identity and be based on its philosophy and values.

Dan Gable and the University of Iowa wrestling program exemplify the implementation of institutional rhetoric. While the university was always a hotbed of wrestling, it became a dominant power almost single-handedly through Gable's efforts. He led the squad to 21 consecutive Big Ten championships and a streak of nine NCAA championships between 1978 and 1986.[50] For Gable, however, it was the pain of losing that motivated his success. Before he was a coach, Gable was the Michael Jordan of wrestling. He had a 182–1 record as a collegiate wrestler, with his only loss coming from his last NCAA match before going on to a dominating performance at the 1972 Olympics.

It was that one loss, however, that stuck with him both as a wrestler and a coach and defined the Iowa program. Gable required of his wrestlers total commitment to the sport and to the team. He expected his athletes to train with the devotion of Benedictine monks. He preached perseverance, single-mindedness, and sacrifice to get the most from his squads. The practice room served as the team's sacred temple, where the squad devoted its time and honed its skills to develop the aggressive style he favored. His wrestlers' personal lives, including their families, friends, and diets, were indistinguishable from their team's activities. When describing why his wrestlers went through these efforts, Gable said, "He or she needs inner strength – a strength that has been determined by all of the preparation done to date."[51] Gable's wrestlers had to look no further than their coach to find an example of someone who embodied this institutional rhetoric. His life revolved around the values he espoused to his team and was a critical part of its identity.

Institutional rhetoric can also take many other forms. Traditions such as fight songs, pregame rituals, and signage in stadiums are all viable vehicles to communicate an organization's identity. The key is thinking about the employee and audience experience holistically and ensuring that the language, symbols, and environments all deliver on the core message of the organization.

Fostering Cross-Department Collaboration

In the sports industry, organizations are typically divided into two camps. First is the group of people responsible for team or player operations. This group is in charge of building, coaching, and maintaining a team or athlete. The second group is more traditionally defined as business operations, which consists of marketing, sales, public relations, finance, and other similar functions. The division of responsibilities between the two has traditionally been clear. The team operations are largely charged with putting the product on the field of play, while the business operations are largely charged with generating revenue and building brand equity. Team operations officials do not customarily have serious strategic discussions with those on the business side. In addition, business operations officials would not usually consider asking players, coaches, or managers questions about ticketing, marketing, public relations, or sponsorship strategy.

There are strong reasons for why these divisions exist. The sports industry operates in a performance sector in which certain people have the particular skills to be successful in certain roles. Just as not everyone can have the physical attributes to become a professional athlete, not everyone has the voice to become a famous singer. Because these positions require a specialized skill set, an industry norm of division of responsibilities has developed. Athletes compete, coaches manage, marketing employees communicate, sales associates sell, and rarely do all of them meet to discuss each other's objectives and projects.

As a result of these expectations, many sports organizations' employees have little or no impact on their organization's core product. Only after the team operations staff sign, select, or recruit a player do these business professionals have the opportunity to craft strategies and promotions. Whether a player, coach, or administrator reflects an organization's past identity or matches last season's campaign may not be of strategic importance. If that person can help the organization compete more effectively, then everyone else in the organization will fall in line.

Outside the sports industry, it is not as common for this type of bifurcation to exist. Procter & Gamble (PG), one of the most successful consumer products companies of all time, has built its business model on a framework of interdisciplinary focus. PG does have a group of 1,000 Ph.D.s with unique skill sets in chemistry, biology, or physics who work at developing new products. It also has brand managers whose role is to manage and develop marketing plans. However, brand managers are expected to work with these scientists to develop "strategic choices and vision, product and commercial innovation" for their products.[52] The marketing group, therefore, is deeply embedded within product development, to the point that marketing has become instrumental in developing the product. It is a holistic strategy in which consumer needs are at the forefront and all the various disciplines collaborate to achieve strategic goals.[53]

All parts of an organization have information that is valuable to other departments. Sports organizations should make sharing information between the team and business operations a higher priority. For example, it would be difficult to find people who have spent more time looking into the background, history, and experiences of athletes than coaches, general managers, recruiters, and scouts. Business operations officials could consider soliciting information from team operations officials to gain new insights about marketing or sponsorship campaigns that better meet their audiences' needs.

The Chicago Cubs have utilized this integrated approach as part of the team's efforts to increase sponsorship and advertising revenue. The team works with W Partners, a company partially owned by the same family that owns the Cubs, to sign "legacy partnerships" with large corporate sponsors. As CEO, W Partner's President Wally Hayward asserts, "So when we talk to them about our partnership and where baseball is headed . . . we bring Theo (Epstein, the president of baseball operations) or Jed (Hoyer, the general manager) or Jason (McLeod, the senior vice president of scouting and player development) and the baseball guys in to really sit down and talk to our clients . . . because we think we have the right baseball management and the right vision and plan."[54]

Breaking down silos is essential to ensuring that identity permeates throughout an organization. If team operations officials are going to factor in the organization's brand positioning before making personnel decisions, they should talk to the organization's experts on identity. These are the marketing and public relations officials whose primary job is to be custodians of the brand. This type of communication ensures that the organization is more effective and efficient in implementing a differentiated identity.

A PICTURE IS WORTH A THOUSAND WORDS

Tom Cigarran needed few words to describe how the Nashville Predators team photo highlighted the problems with his organization. While the hockey team had made the playoffs in many seasons since he became an owner in 2007, the Predators were not as successful off the ice, suffering from huge operating losses that would eventually force the owners to contribute $60 million of their personal money to help keep the team afloat.[55] After being appointed chairman and alternate governor in 2010, Cigarran held meetings with members of the team's marketing, corporate partnerships, and ticket operations groups to learn about the team's problems. During the process, he diagnosed one problem that highlighted a major issue within the culture of the organization: the team's official picture did not include most of the organization. In fact, the owners themselves had never been asked to be a part of it. The only participants in the team's photos were players and coaches.

CONTINUED

A PICTURE IS WORTH A THOUSAND WORDS *CONTINUED*

For Cigarran, this showed that the operations team (which included coaches, scouts, assistant general managers, and players) was separate from the other parts of the organization. More importantly, no one on the team on either the operations side or the business side of the organization thought this was particularly unusual. Cigarran disagreed. He felt the picture demonstrated a disconnect; the business people who worked so hard to sell season tickets, luxury boxes, broadcast rights, and sponsorships had no real connection to the players, coaches, and managers. As the co-founder and former CEO of Healthways, Inc. and the former chairman of AmSurg Corp., both multimillion-dollar publicly traded companies on NASDAQ, Cigarran had never seen anything like the corporate culture that existed with the Predators.

Cigarran now requires that all core business departments have regular meetings with the operations team to discuss how best to use players and coaches to maximize revenue. While the relationship continues to develop, the corporate culture has changed dramatically. Cigarran credits the "we're all in this together as one team"[56] mentality as a critical reason that the Predators' revenue increased during the 2011–12 season by 13%.[57] The Predators' business managers now have a front row in the Predators' official picture, along with many other "players" from the business side of the organization.

The story of the Nashville Predators' team picture is representative of the traditional organizational model and how it might be improved. Cigarran recognized that a key to the success of his organization was a strengthened dialogue and interaction among departments. While the steps he took, such as arranging cross-functional meetings and taking a more representative team picture, were simple, they've already paid dividends in the corporate culture.

Maintaining Consistency

The mark of a strong identity is a commitment to consistency. With the competitive pressures of today's marketplace, adhering to a consistent approach may appear increasingly difficult. But sports strategists will often be served well if they can exhibit resilience and not hastily make decisions that veer from an organization's identity.

The Boston Celtics' hiring of former Butler University coach Brad Stevens was a surprising choice to replace championship-winning coach Doc Rivers. Stevens was only in his thirties and had never been an assistant coach in the NBA. The Celtics faced criticism for this selection for two reasons. First, the organization previously had had an unsuccessful experience with Rick Pitino, who came directly from the University of Kentucky. Second, the only former college coach with a winning record in his first NBA job in the past two decades was P. J. Carlesimo.[58]

However, the hire made strategic sense from an identity perspective. The iconic organization's emphasis on tradition as articulated by the team is: "The Boston Celtics are 'the Franchise,' Celtics Green is 'the color,' and the winking leprechaun that serves as the team's logo symbolizes five decades of NBA tradition."[59] While young for the role of coach, Stevens was a throwback to an earlier era. His teams thrived while playing in the legendary Hinkle Fieldhouse, a National Historic Landmark. Stevens loved coaching in Hinkle because the venue is for "somebody who appreciates tradition, somebody who appreciates history. And often times those are people who appreciate team."[60]

At the same time, Stevens had taken a nontraditional approach in leading Butler to two NCAA tournament finals. He used statistical analysis to create the optimal five-person lineups to maximize the point differential during the course of games and hired the first assistant coach of analytics on a college basketball team.[61] The Celtics are moving forward with a coach who not only is at the leading edge of his profession but also embraces the traditions of the sport. The marriage of the Celtics team with an Indiana-bred wunderkind was consistent with who the team is and what Stevens had become.

While taking the long view is always important, maintaining consistency for the sake of consistency is not advisable either. Telltale signs of an identity in need of repair include the usual quantitative success metrics such as sustained declines in attendance, ratings, sponsorship revenue, and merchandise sales. Beyond the numbers, the departure of critical personnel who have previously defined an organization's identity may also spell the need for a new identity, unless their personality has successfully extended across the franchise. Finally, demographic or behavioral shifts in the fan base may also force a redesign. The optimally designed identity, however, can be built upon and strengthened over time.

STEEL CITY CHARACTER

The Pittsburgh Steelers were founded in 1933 and have since cultivated one of the strongest identities in sports. Built around the Rooney family, which has owned the team since its inception, the Steelers are a mom-and-pop family business that happens to run a highly successful NFL franchise. Because of the team's heritage, it also embodies (and perhaps defines) the characteristics and values of Pittsburgh as a community, including work ethic, togetherness, and resiliency. Through both on-field success and adversity, there is no question that the Steelers are Pittsburghers' hometown team.

To maintain their identity, the Steelers organization has attempted to be more strategic about whom they welcome into the Steelers family. One of the most influential acquisitions current owner Dan Rooney has made was the hiring of Kevin Colbert in 2000 as director of football operations. Not only had Colbert helped the perennially struggling Detroit Lions reach the playoffs for six straight seasons in the 1990s, but he was also born and raised in Pittsburgh, attending North Catholic High School and graduating from Robert Morris College with a bachelor's degree. In Colbert, Rooney had both a skilled decision-maker and a hometown boy, leading him to say: "Kevin is a great fit for our organization. We always try to look for good people, and his work ethic and humility are among the many reasons he is one of the NFL's top executives in his field."[62]

In his player personnel decisions, Colbert employs traditional methods of scouting and evaluation. But he also understands the Steelers' identity and the different expectations that the Steelers' leadership and fans have for the team. In addressing season ticket holders in 2013, Colbert explained his philosophy on acquisitions:

> Any player we are looking to add to the team, we always have to try to judge whether he is the type of people we want to add to our team. Really, when it comes down to it, when we add a player, we pretty much say as an organization that we trust this player will be a good person as well. When a player betrays that trust, he no longer can be a part of our organization. We've had to move on from significant players in those regards. I think the part not seen is the number of significant players we choose not to bring in, and I'm talking about first-round-type talent

that can certainly help us win on the field. There have been players
of that nature in the past that we have bypassed because we just didn't
think they would be a good fit as people. We are not perfect. We don't
claim to be perfect. So, we just try to do the best we can to get not only
the best player but the best person as well.[63]

As Colbert acknowledged, the Steelers' efforts at identity management
have not been without challenges. Santonio Holmes is one such example.
In February of 2009, Holmes was named the Most Valuable Player (MVP)
of Super Bowl XLIII. By February of 2010, he was a defendant in a lawsuit
for assaulting a woman with a glass bottle at an Orlando nightclub and
was also facing a four-game suspension for violating the league's substance
abuse policy.[64] The organization responded quickly, making it very clear
that no individual player was more important than the Steelers' identity.
The team traded Holmes for a fifth-round pick to the New York Jets in
April of 2010.[65]

Rooney, Colbert, and the entire Steelers organization faced the greatest
threat to their identity when franchise quarterback, Ben Roethlisberger, a
two-time Super Bowl winner, was accused of sexual assault in Lake Tahoe
and Georgia.[66] His alleged behavior directly conflicted with the Steelers'
identity, yet at the same time, he was indispensable on the field, putting
the organization in a difficult position. The Steelers reportedly called seven
teams about the possibility of trading Roethlisberger for the opportunity
to receive a higher pick in the 2010 draft.[67] The team also cooperated with
the league on a six-game suspension for Roethlisberger for the 2010 season. What they did not do is take a hardline stance by trading or waiving
him. One could argue that not trading the team's star shows the Steelers
lack of commitment to its identity. By NFL standards, however, even con-
sidering trading a quarterback as successful as Roethlisberger was still a
significant signal of its commitment to its identity.

The long tenure of the Rooneys is a big reason why the Steelers have
cultivated this powerful identity built around family. They sign players
and hire coaches and executives who fit this specific culture, even pass-
ing on those who may be more talented on paper. But this has not been
an easy or foolproof strategy, as the difficulty surrounding the decision
CONTINUED

about Roethlisberger can attest. But, like all families, there are ups and downs and degrees of forgiveness. According to Steelers offensive coordinator Todd Haley, who patched up his previously rocky relationship with Roethlisberger, "I don't know about the so-called 'old Ben.' I just know Ben now. He's a great leader and a great quarterback. He's also a good person. That's all I see."[68] For the most part, the organization has stuck to its blueprint of high character and strong work ethic. The Steel City has been and will likely always be a Steelers' city.

Today's heated competitive environment is forcing sports strategists to think differently about how to operate and organize. It is no longer enough to compile a roster of the best players; put them out on the field, court, course, or diamond; and hope that their performance will single-handedly keep fans – and dollars – coming into the business. For an identity to work, team operations personnel must thoroughly understand the strategy behind that identity and use it as a filter for decision-making. Organizations that work more effectively across departments to design and execute a cohesive identity will be best suited to addressing the dynamic challenges in the marketplace and can extend the identity authentically to various audience touchpoints.

Conclusion

Branch Rickey is most famously known as the Brooklyn Dodgers' co-owner who signed Jackie Robinson, the first African-American player in MLB. While signing Robinson was a turning point in baseball history globally, Rickey's decision also had a significant local impact. At the time, the Dodgers were playing in the same city as the New York Yankees and Giants. Signing Robinson differentiated the Dodgers' identity from its New York rivals while also having a profound impact on the team financially both in the short and long-term. The team set a then-MLB attendance record in the season after signing Robinson,[69] at a time when sports organizations had few other ways to make money outside of ticket revenue. The Dodgers still have millions of loyal African-American fans today because of Rickey's decision to sign Robinson in 1947.[70]

However, Rickey's focus on innovation in sports extended far beyond his relationship with Robinson. As a Dodgers executive, Rickey opened the first modern spring training venue, encouraged players to use batting helmets, and hired the first full-time statistician well before Bill James and Billy Beane pioneered the concepts made famous in the book and movie *Moneyball*. [71] As a risk-taking sports strategist with a social conscious, Rickey became the leader in shaping the Dodgers' progressive identity with Robinson as one strong example of his approach.

Rickey demonstrates how thinking strategically about identity should be a foundational consideration of how a sports strategist should operate. Identity is how fans, sponsors, and other audiences will recognize and remember the business amidst a proliferation of other options in a crowded and competitive marketplace. Identity is also the filter through which many sports organizations should evaluate decisions on a wide range of issues, including personnel, growth opportunities, and crisis management. In the remaining chapters, identity will factor into all of the topics we discuss, given how central it is to any sports organization succeeding without relying solely on winning. It is especially relevant in creating, distributing, and managing narratives.

3 | Constructing Enduring Narratives

Ndamukong Suh, Detroit Lions superstar and *Sports Illustrated* 2010 Sportsman of the Year,[1] navigates the familiar streets and landmarks of his hometown, Portland, Oregon. He drives the new Chrysler 300, an upscale, male-targeted luxury car. This TV commercial, entitled "Homecoming," is one of a series by advertising agency Wieden+Kennedy, dramatizing the inspirational story of a young individual who overcame hardship and maintained the discipline necessary to reach stardom. In the commercial, Suh surveys the boarded-up windows of his hometown as he darts across bridges, through tunnels, and past a youth football practice as a pulsing and seductive hip-hop track from the Geto Boys promotes a sense of self-assurance, tenacity, and forward movement.[2] Like Suh, Chrysler positions itself as a dogged fighter who has emerged victorious and returned home from testing times. Both are on a quest to "show where they're going, without forgetting where they're from." The commercial seamlessly ties together disparate narratives of the athlete's biography, urban rejuvenation, and masculine achievement in order to advertise Chrysler's product.

However, this compelling narrative became controversial as Suh developed a reputation as one of the dirtiest players in the NFL. Most notably, on Thanksgiving Day 2011, Suh intentionally stomped on an offensive lineman during a nationally televised divisional game against the Green Bay Packers.[3] Unfortunately for Chrysler, one of Suh's Chrysler commercials was aired immediately after the ugly incident took place.[4] Suh's association with ideals of perseverance and humility were quickly being replaced by associations with maliciousness and rage. Chrysler had tied their showcase car to an emerging star whose storyline had turned for the worse. As a result of the emotional association of Suh with the Chrysler personality, the defensive lineman's growing reputation as an unruly villain became a threat to the integrity of the brand and created a frenzy of media inquiry as to whether Chrysler would cease to sponsor the tarnished Suh.[5]

...

In the Suh commercial, there were three possible beneficiaries of the narrative: Chrysler, Suh, and the Lions. Through the creation and distribution of the narrative, these three players entered into a symbiotic relationship by which each provided value to the other parties while simultaneously receiving something positive in return. For Chrysler, the decision to use a narrative as opposed to more straightforward rhetorical techniques (e.g., presenting factual information about the performance of the car) was carefully made during a time when the company was seeking to dramatically change consumer attitudes toward their brand. Chrysler was plagued not only by negative consumer sentiments about the quality and longevity of its vehicles, but also by a battered brand image in the wake of its bankruptcy.[6] By taking an indirect approach in using a prominent professional athlete's star power, Chrysler did not have to confront its own failures and weaknesses, but instead constructed a new narrative about the rebirth of their car and their brand as symbols of aspiration. Through the emotional heat of Suh's story, Chrysler created associations between the car and the characteristics of determination, loyalty, and style.

Suh was not only paid for his services by Chrysler but was cast in a favorable light through his story. The principle narrative centered upon a star player rooted in his city and neighborhood. The commercial implied that Suh maintained loyalty to his home and family, whereas others in similar positions had compromised their morals when confronted with stardom.

The last potential beneficiary of Chrysler's decision to include the Suh narrative in its commercial was the Detroit Lions organization. Heading into the 2011 season, the club shared the same struggling reputation as Chrysler. The Lions posted an anemic .290 winning percentage over the previous five years, including an infamous 0–16 season in 2008.[7] But games weren't the only thing the team was losing. Between 2000 and 2010, attendance levels plummeted 25% as embittered fans lost interest in their hometown franchise.[8] Like Chrysler, the Lions desperately needed a revamped identity. Suh's tenacious personality served as a catalyst of change for both organizations. To viewers who were aware of the Lions' saga, the commercial suggested the rebirth of the team as a young, aggressive squad that no longer accepted futility.

Chrysler and Wieden+Kennedy recognized the inspirational power in celebrating the resurrection of these once-great institutions. The ad might have been framed as a story about a loyal, hard-working football player who stayed true to his roots. To American viewers who had suffered through the economic meltdown of the late 2000s, however, the message of rebirth resonated strongly: Chrysler, Detroit, and America appeared to be on the rise again.

However, even the most carefully crafted narrative is vulnerable to change, and Suh's head-stomping incident ultimately overshadowed the advertisement's intention. Surely Chrysler knew of Suh's reputation as a hot-tempered, physical player before the incident took place.[9] Chrysler made an emotional connection with the audience via Suh's star power and backstory that wouldn't have been possible with a straightforward, literal message. Simultaneously, however, Chrysler tied its brand to the identity of a star athlete who had a history of misbehaving on the field and the potential for bad publicity.

The Suh commercial demonstrates how powerful the storyline can be. Chrysler could have produced a commercial that featured the car, described the model's innovations, and even compared it to rival vehicles that did not match its quality. Such a commercial, however, would have likely gone unnoticed in a crowded, novelty-seeking advertising landscape.

In the age of intense competition for limited attention spans, the narrative is a key factor in effective communication. There is always another tweet to read, article to scan, or video to watch. As a consequence, consumers can often devote only short bursts of attention to the vast amount of information flooding the marketplace. Therefore, the storyteller must be able to engage the audience in order for the sports organization to compete in the industry.

Mastering the art of constructing a narrative can prove to be an advantageous differentiator for sports strategists, but one that has risks as well. In this chapter, we demonstrate the key points of narrative and its persuasive power. An effective narrative needs a clear set of goals, an understanding of its target audience, and the execution of key principles. All of this must be accomplished through a variety of constantly evolving communication channels. The winners in this communication space will be the organizations willing and able to master the most cutting-edge forms of narrative.

Locking In Memories

Using persuasive stories offers a fundamental means of connecting individuals to one another. Unlike other vehicles for sharing information, stories have the unique ability to create vicarious relationships: they allow followers to temporarily inhabit alternate worlds by virtue of enveloping characters and settings. The transportation-imagery model, proposed by Green and Brock, suggests that members of a narrative's audience often mentally transport themselves to the world of the story. While escaping from their own reality, these recipients, the researchers argue, are more likely to detach from previous attitudes and beliefs than if directly confronted with an argument. Ideally, when recipients return from the narrative world, they bring back with them new perspectives influenced by the underlying message of the story.[10]

Narratives achieve this goal by locking a memory in the audience member's mind for an extended period of time. The sports world is full of plotlines familiar to fans that achieve this goal. New York Yankees' center fielder Joe DiMaggio's 56-game hitting streak is an example of a star athlete's pursuit of a historic record. But organizations rarely have control over these serendipitous storylines. Therefore, most organizations must carefully construct storylines based on a familiar, recognizable product, while differentiating it in a novel way to generate fan interest. Rather than relying on serendipitous events to produce memorable storylines, sports strategists can create anticipation among audiences by using narrative techniques.

Legendary broadcaster Bill Stern first hosted the *Colgate Sports Newsreel* beginning in 1937 and went on to reinvent and massage the concept of the sports narrative for nearly 20 years. His sports broadcast lasted 15 minutes, combining performance art, insightful sports analysis, and masterful sports storytelling. Stern was among the first to recognize that sports has always been a form of theater and entertainment.[11] He brought the show to life with his expressive voice and well-timed pauses, accompanied by a cast of stage actors, a musical quartet and organist, and all the hoopla of early vaudeville. His stories used real facts (the great racehorse Man of War never won the Kentucky Derby), half-true anecdotes (legendary sportswriter Grantland Rice told famous crooner Frank Sinatra he would have better luck as a singer rather than a boxer after seeing him fight), and creative, if untrue, tales (outlaw Jesse James beaned inventor Thomas Edison in a semi-professional baseball game causing Edison to go deaf).[12] His critics and imitators were many, but he understood better than anyone the power of a well-constructed storyline. Whether it's the modern Olympics, the Final Four, or the Rugby World Cup, the narrative can be as important as the game itself.

Stern understood how to weave together the key elements of a classic narrative: dynamic characters, unexpected plotlines, immersive imagery, and vivid settings. More importantly, Stern recognized that a narrative reaches beyond a simple sequence of events. The successful narrative incorporates and emphasizes certain positions and perspectives, shaping events rather than simply reciting facts.

STAR LIGHT, STAR BRIGHT

Jeremy Lin became the ultimate overnight sensation, rising from an obscure benchwarmer to an internationally recognized superstar in less than a month's time. Scoring at least 20 points in nine of ten games in February 2012, Lin led the New York Knicks to an 8–2 record[13] that included his dramatic buzzer-beating three-point shot against the Toronto Raptors.[14] Lin captured global attention not only through his on-court performance, but also through his personal story. An undrafted Asian American player out of Harvard University, earning the league's minimum salary, Lin slept on teammate Landry Fields's couch for his first few weeks on the team.[15]

Lin instantly came to symbolize the ultimate underdog, achieving the improbable and allowing hardcore and casual fans alike to live vicariously through his narrative. The archetype of Lin's character – the underdog – is well known and has always been present in sports, but the speed at which Lin's story reached global audiences differed in this scenario. The American consumer was inundated with Lin updates from both mainstream media and their own personal social networks after each improbable performance. Facebook and Twitter streams were flooded with cheers and jeers of "Linsanity." In February 2012, social media sites mentioned the young star nearly 1,600 times per hour (four times more than any other NBA player during that time period).[16] The sheer amount of "Linsanity" coverage made it nearly impossible for consumers to avoid his story.

However, the media frenzy died down after Lin suffered a season-ending injury.[17] In many ways, the Lin story illustrates the strengths and weaknesses of the new sports narrative realities. His powerful story caught the nation unaware and ignited a flurry of fan admiration, media attention, and sponsorship offers. Once injured, Lin's story no longer captured as much public attention. The Knicks appeared to decide that the Lin storyline would not justify the increased cost of renewing Lin's contract. The price of maintaining the Lin narrative was not something the Knicks were willing to pay, and the Houston Rockets acquired his rights in the 2012 offseason.[18]

The challenge for Lin and the Rockets was to reshape the point guard's narrative after his meteoric rise to fame. With the signing of James Harden and Dwight Howard, the Rockets no longer needed Lin's star power. In addition, Lin's slow start and tough finish to the 2012–13 NBA season left many audiences disappointed after his meteoric rise.[19] At the same time, both Lin and the Rockets recognized the potential for international marketing and sponsorship opportunities as a result of both Lin's popularity in China and the enduring fame of the Rockets' former center, Chinese-born Yao Ming.

Therefore, Lin and the Rockets took proactive steps to modify the storyline. Lin reached out directly to the Chinese market by visiting the country prior to the start of the 2013–14 season and opening up a training camp for prospective basketball players.[20] The Rockets' general manager Daryl Morey engaged traditional and new media outlets to try to manage audience expectations about Lin's on-court performance and to praise his leadership skills.[21] After becoming famous for events largely out of his control, Lin continued to take similar steps to shape his identity after being traded to the Lakers.

The importance of locking in a memory has become even more crucial in a digital age defined by audience choices and short attention spans. Equipped with new technology, consumers can access more information and media than ever before with relative ease. The result is a constant message bombardment that can cause information overload. A study conducted by video metrics solutions provider Visible Measures illustrates the impact of these consumption patterns. When watching short-form online video content, 20% of viewers abandon the video within just 10 seconds of playback, and nearly half stop watching before the one-minute mark.[22]

While this study was limited to online video consumption, it demonstrates the difficulty of keeping an audience tuned in to a message. Consumers can now choose what content to read, watch, and contribute to, and select what content to ignore. Today's social media not only encourage viral sharing of captivating stories but also make it possible for an individual to join and interact with a particular narrative, which adds new voices and dimensions to the story. Powerful narratives have the potential both to capture and retain the attention of large audiences who become engrossed in following a story as it unfolds.

To accomplish these goals, sports strategists should understand the three phases of narrative design. They are:

- Assessing the Audience – Sports organizations should complete an analysis of their fans, media, sponsors, and employees to identify the best ways to connect with their audiences.
- Identifying Storylines – Sports strategists will need to identify the most effective narrative type to reach their target audiences.
- Building the Narrative – Sports organizations should construct storylines by effectively using plot, characterization, and setting.

Assessing the Audience

Every narrative objective must be associated with a specific intended audience. The better an organization understands its relationships with its audiences, the more effectively it will be able to target and persuade those audiences. Therefore, the ability to predict how an audience will receive and interpret a message is crucial to that narrative's success. Elements of every story must be adapted to adequately engage the targeted audience. The growth of digital and social media has resulted in an unprecedented increase in the amount of available consumer information, which means that sports strategists can tailor specific narratives to select audiences.

When identifying specific demographics, value groups, and lifestyles, organizations can narrow their focus to enhance audience connections. One way to target messages to appropriate audiences in the sports industry is to categorize fans into segments defined by levels of engagement. The Audience Engagement Ladder (Figure 3.1) provides a framework for organizations to effectively identify

SUPERFANS

- Can afford to fly to road games and playoff games
- Viewed as high-priority targets by management and receive special treatment for their loyalty
- Super-affluent supporters, recognizable fans or celebrities, such as Spike Lee (NY Knicks) and Jack Nicholson (LA Lakers), who are closely tied to an organization's brand image

AVIDS

- Highly engaged fans whose life is defined by a team or sport
- Attend every home game, sometimes dressing up, and watch every away game
- Members or leaders of fan clubs
- Have strong opinions on every upper-management decision
- Remain engaged throughout offseason, closely following personnel and budget decisions
- Spend significant amount of money on tickets and memorabilia

INTERACTIVES

- Watch all preseason, regular, and playoff games, and frequently attend home games
- Active participants in conversations regarding team across all media channels
- Long-time sports radio listeners and callers
- Heavy Internet users, frequently blog about team and comment on other fan pages
- Play fantasy sports, paying close attention to individual player performances across all teams

WATCHERS

- Watch games on television but rarely attend games for the full experience
- Will catch updates on team through local sports news and readily available media
- Recognize individual players or coaches but don't follow team's offseason developments
- Stay updated on team's performance, but ultimate outcome of season doesn't determine their happiness
- Will only attend games as social events

CASUALS

- Rarely make a point of watching games
- Randomly catch updates through local news
- Occasionally seek out information on team's performance or standing
- Generally aware of playoffs but will only watch if team has legitimate chance of winning

UNENGAGED

- Almost completely unaware of and uninterested in team or league developments
- Never watch games and often actively avoid them
- Only become aware of sports stories when headlines break into mainstream news coverage
- Most-often-ignored group and seemingly least attractive for targeting
- Can be converted up the ladder via friends' excitement, social media, community events, or fantasy sports

FIGURE 3.1 **Audience Engagement Ladder**

target audiences based on a scale of customer involvement, interest, and need.[23] Which rung fans occupy on the ladder is determined by their level of engagement. Different narratives should be written for the specific rungs in order to more effectively engage certain groups.

With a growing sports consumer market, emerging international segments, and an expanding set of media channels, there are more opportunities than ever to reach and move audiences up the ladder. Since 2004, the Washington Capitals have signed numerous Russian hockey stars to its roster in different seasons, including Alex Ovechkin, Dmitry Orlov, Sergei Fedorov, and Alexander Semin. When the Capitals drafted and signed these players, the team became one of the most popular sports organizations in Russia and among Russians living in the United States. As Evgeny Agoshkov, head of the Russian Cultural Centre in Washington, observed, "If you have a Russian delegation here, and the Capitals are playing, it's a must. That's the best place to take them, and they always want to go."[24]

Despite the team's collection of Russian talent, many Russian audiences could not attend games in person, and most could not watch games on television until 2011.[25] In the past, this would have made it difficult for the Capitals to connect with Russian fans, and this demographic would be ranked as "casuals" on the Audience Engagement Ladder. Today, digital technology makes these connections much easier. For example, the Capitals promote a number of team-related blogs on its official site[26] while often providing official credentials to these bloggers. These outlets include *The Russian Machine Never Breaks* (*RMNB*), which is "the relentlessly fun Washington Capitals blog hopelessly devoted to Alex Ovechkin and other Russian Caps."[27] Even with its narrow focus, this blog has more than 10,000 Facebook likes and more than 15,000 Twitter followers.[28] The Capitals' use of star power and technology has helped the team engage Russian fans and move them up the Audience Engagement Ladder.

The Capitals also demonstrate how competition for audience attention has never been greater. In this dynamic environment, sports organizations must learn to design more compelling narratives to break through the clutter. It is critical to identify where different fans fall on the Audience Engagement Ladder and take specific steps to move people up the ladder when possible.

Moreover, not every person is going to be a target to move up the engagement ladder. There are some sports audiences who are not going to support a team, no matter what marketing technique you use. There are also diminishing returns in continually targeting superfans, as they are likely to support an organization no matter how they are approached. An important place to start is identifying which audience members are likely to move up and which audience members are likely to stay put or move down the ladder.

Leading political strategists are now using this approach to win elections. In his book *The Victory Lab: The Secret Science of Winning Campaigns*, Sasha Issenberg demonstrates how successful political campaigns increasingly do not target every voter. For example, there are millions of people who will not vote for a Democratic candidate because they are staunch Republican voters, and vice versa. In addition, there are voters who will always vote for a certain political party or candidate with little or no contact from a campaign. As a result, campaign strategists compile detailed profiles about potential voters and target the people who will be most valuable to their campaign – those people who can be persuaded to vote for a specific candidate and need to be contacted by a campaign with a specific message.[29]

The ability of sports organizations to use the data they have collected about different audiences allows them to determine both which people are more likely to move up the Engagement Ladder and how to use narratives to achieve these goals. Narratives can target specific needs with the hope of converting the less engaged into more active and dedicated customers. The key is finding the audiences and messages most likely to increase engagement and not using marketing resources that will have little or no impact on an audience member unlikely to support an organization. A thorough consideration of audience engagement can reveal which people are most likely to climb the ladder, therein enabling organizations to convert them into more active customers.

Identifying Storylines

An organization must first identify the strategic goals it hopes to achieve through its choice of storylines. Sports organizations and leagues aim to achieve all types of objectives, including improving a team's record, increasing game attendance, gaining market share, fostering community goodwill, boosting merchandise and concession sales, charging higher media rights fees, and building new venues. These goals very often interconnect, and leveraging storylines is often an efficient way to achieve them. Articulating the narrative will be far easier if an organization clearly defines its goals and knows exactly what message it needs to convey.

Narrative Types

For any narrative to grow into an effective branding tool for a sports organization, the storyline should ideally be connected to the positioning and goals of the organization itself and its branding, slogans, and themes. Stories can originate from various sources, each presenting a different set of opportunities and challenges for effective communication. There are five primary ways in which sports narratives are developed.

The Organic Narrative. The organic narrative is a storyline that comes about with little involvement from the sports organization. Oftentimes, these narratives seem to be served on a silver platter for marketers and public relations staff, since they originate unexpectedly from homegrown sources such as individual athletes. Ideally, organic narratives enhance the brand of the sports organization and are widely distributed by the media without the sports organization's involvement. One inspiring example is Jason McElwain, an unlikely hero of Greece Athena High School's basketball team in Rochester, New York.[30] McElwain, an autistic teen, had been the team's student manager for two years until his coach gave him the chance to suit up and play in the fourth quarter of the last game of the season. To the shock of everyone in the stands, including his coach, Jason sank six consecutive three-point shots and finished the game with 20 total points in less than five minutes.

McElwain's speech and language pathologist, Andy McCormack, was present at the game and convinced local news stations to air its highlights on that evening's newscast. With little effort from the school, this underdog story caught the attention of the entire nation in only a few days. Jason quickly became a celebrity, meeting star athletes and then-president George W. Bush, and even winning an ESPY Award for Best Moment in Sports in 2006 (beating out Kobe Bryant's 81-point performance in a game).[31] As a result of this widely distributed story, Greece Athena High School's athletic program received overwhelmingly positive recognition as a value-based, socially conscious program. Jason, his coach, and the school instantly became symbols of acceptance across the nation that will likely endure for years after the event. Even with little or no action taken by the athletic program or school itself to promote the story, Jason's organic narrative became a defining moment in the program's history.

The Directed Narrative. The directed narrative is a storyline that is entirely contrived by the sports organization. In this type of narrative, the organization realizes that creating its own storyline will enhance the value of the brand and acts purposefully to distribute its message. In order to be successful, the directed narrative must be credible and relatable. An example of this narrative type is the

University of Chicago's transformation from an exclusively academic-focused institution to one that promotes and supports a well-rounded education.

If you were to think of the college that was home to the first Heisman Trophy winner and the coach after which the Big Ten Conference would name its championship trophy, the University of Chicago would probably not be your first guess. The Maroons had one of the most powerful college football programs in the country during the early part of the twentieth century, with a record that included national championships in 1905 and 1913.[32] In 1939, however, the University of Chicago, one of the founding members of the Big Ten Conference, ended its football program. Then-president Robert Hutchins banned the sport because he wanted to change the positioning of the school to focus on academics. He declared that "football has no place in the kind of institution Chicago aspires to be."[33] For the next 30 years, Chicago cemented its reputation as a university in which academic study overshadowed all other aspects of college life.

By the mid-1980s, however, Chicago was facing a narrative crisis as potential students chose other universities over "the place where fun comes to die."[34] Something had to change. Chicago decided it needed to change its narrative to be more competitive in attracting students. The school committed more resources to improving student life, including building more dormitories and adding new extracurricular activities. Chicago also placed an increasing importance on athletics. In the words of former Chicago athletic director Tom Weingartner, "We were losing students who wanted a better quality of student life, and part of the solution was athletics, more coaches, better facilities."[35] Using athletics has enabled the former academically focused institution to show different audiences how it has adapted its core mission to focus on "enrich[ing] the lives of our students and contributing to a vibrant, collective, and diverse campus community that inspires excellence."[36]

Chicago's narrative recalibration is working. According to a 2010 article in The Chronicle of Higher Education, "Never has the University of Chicago been more popular. It received a record 19,347 applications for this fall – a 43-percent increase over last year – for a freshman class of about 1,400 students."[37] In 2013, Chicago received a record 30,369 applications and accepted less than 9% of applicants.[38] Chicago could not have achieved this type of success without recognizing that the school needed to change its narrative and broaden its perspective on university life.

The Shaped Narrative. The shaped narrative is created when an organization capitalizes on an existing storyline in order to add branding value. This narrative can be viewed as a hybrid of the organic and directed narratives, as it comes about not by organizational invention but by purposefully shaping and distributing it to the audience via the athletic program. The shaped narrative often occurs when the organization becomes aware of a storyline it deems potentially valuable and decides to tailor it into a narrative that achieves the organization's market objectives. This is the most common narrative form, because organizations take a role in the development of nearly every event describing their team.

One of the most effective executions of the shaped narrative in sports came in the wake of one of the worst natural disasters in U.S. history. After Hurricane Katrina enveloped major portions of the Gulf Coast in 2005, the city of New Orleans was devastated, suffering immeasurable damage and catastrophic loss. The New Orleans Saints were forced to evacuate the city and play all regular season games on the road as thousands of New Orleans citizens took refuge in the damaged Superdome stadium. The Saints became a vagabond team, playing "home" games in San Antonio, Baton Rouge, and even New Jersey. As the Saints ended the year with a dismal 3–13 record, it became increasingly clear that the city's devastation had impacted the team's performance and the team needed an overhaul. The Saints fired Coach Jim Haslett and replaced him with Sean Payton,[39] drafted University of Southern California star running back Reggie Bush in the first round, and signed free-agent star quarterback Drew Brees.[40]

By reconstructing the organization, the Saints helped shape a narrative that became part of New Orleans' urban revitalization and renewal. The marketing team launched campaigns that distributed this narrative of parallel ascendance of the city and the team. The restoration of the Superdome mirrored efforts to rebuild the city. In addition, the Saints organization challenged citizens to embrace the new faces of the team as a representation of the rebirth of New Orleans.[41]

The Saints' narrative became part of the foundation for the team's success. The team sold out all 73,000 seats for every home game for the next five years, starting with the September 25, 2006 homecoming game at the Superdome after repairs were completed.[42] The culmination of the resurgence efforts came in February of 2010, when the Saints defeated the Colts 31–17 in Super Bowl XLIV. The victory represented a symbolic revitalization of the city, spearheaded by its football team. The Saints emerged from the damage of Katrina as a symbol of hope, shaping a powerful narrative that intertwined with the needs of its sponsoring city and fans. The shaped narrative requires combining strong audience analysis with an understanding of how to effectively adapt a message to align with an organization's positioning.

WHEN DOES A TIE MEAN A WIN?

In the entire history of the Harvard-Yale football rivalry, there is one game that endures in public memory. The 1968 matchup between the Harvard Crimson and the Yale Bulldogs was remembered by the *Wall Street Journal* on the game's fortieth anniversary as the "greatest football game you probably never saw."[43] For the first time since 1909, both schools entered the last game of the season undefeated. Yale, considered a national powerhouse, was ranked sixteenth in the country. Harvard, on the other hand, was known for its "Boston Strangler"[44] defense and tenacity but had a weak offense that was clearly inferior to that of the mighty Yale Bulldogs. The game came down to the last 42 seconds, with Yale holding a commanding 29–13 lead. Harvard, led by backup quarterback Frank Champi, improbably scored two touchdowns and converted two two-point conversions to tie the game as time expired. The stunned Yale fans left Harvard stadium deflated by the sudden and unexpected turnaround. The game was forever immortalized by a *Harvard Crimson* headline proclaiming, "Harvard Beats Yale, 29–29."[45]

This game's longevity is surprising, since the two Ivy League schools have since become relative footnotes on the collegiate football sports scene. Except for the loyal fans and the regional media, there was little national interest in this game at the time it was played. So why has this game grown in popularity while simultaneously overshadowing countless other comebacks by schools such as Alabama, USC, Notre Dame, Ohio State, and other football powerhouses? The storyline of the unlikely comeback is engaging, but not nearly enough to warrant continued interest in the game 40 years later.

What enables the game to last in public memory are the complementary off-field narratives that tie into the on-field result. The personal and cultural storylines underlying this historic game were compelling enough to inspire Harvard alumnus Kevin Rafferty to produce a book and documentary focusing on the 1968 contest.[46] The 2008 documentary adds context to the dramatic comeback by weaving together game footage with player interviews and photos of the time period, introducing layers of added meaning and symbolism to the Crimson's unlikely "victory."[47]

CONTINUED

WHEN DOES A TIE MEAN A WIN? *CONTINUED*

The cultural and sociological backdrop to the game is one such storyline. At the time, the Vietnam War was at its peak of intensity, and demonstrations for peace swept the nation, with class and race issues driving these protests. Harvard, a hotbed for protest activity, was swarming with students criticizing the war and the university's complicity with Reserve Officers' Training Corps (ROTC) recruiting on campus. At the same time, Harvard defensive back Pat Conway had recently returned to the team after fighting at the Battle of Khe Sanh, one of the bloodiest conflicts of the war. While football often uses wartime imagery to describe on-field battles, Conway's actual war experience provided a new layer to the narrative of the game.

By comparison, Yale was relatively unaffected by the mass demonstrations. The Bulldogs' biggest contribution to the game's legacy was the star power of many of the participants. Quarterback Brian Dowling, nicknamed "God" around campus, became a nationally recognized figure after being immortalized by fellow classmate Garry Trudeau as "BD" in a widely read comic strip, *Doonesbury*. Also, a prominent star on the team was Calvin Hill. He was such a good running back that that the Dallas Cowboys selected him in the first round of the 1969 NFL draft, and he made the Pro Bowl four times. The Bulldogs' fullback, Bob Levin, was dating then-Vassar student and acting-icon-to-be Meryl Streep at the time of the game. Harvard's squad also featured some high-profile characters such as future-movie star Tommy Lee Jones, who was not only a starting guard on the team but also the roommate of later vice president Al Gore. Streep's and Jones' fame have grown substantially since their involvement with the game, and that has brought more attention to Harvard's historic comeback as time has passed.[48]

With his 2008 documentary, Kevin Rafferty became a master storyteller of the game and its subsequent popularity. He set the scene of the game, with each team representing a different storyline: Harvard was in the unfamiliar position of being cast as the rebellious, scrappy character, while Yale held its more traditional place as the conservative establishment and overwhelming favorite. Harvard's "win" symbolized a comeback for the underdog.[49] There is no question that the wild finish deserved a footnote in college football annals. It was Rafferty, however, who understood and orchestrated the various components of this narrative to reshape perspectives on the weight and cultural significance of this game for a wider audience.

The Improvisational Narrative. The improvisational narrative is an individual's and organization's attempt to recontextualize a preexisting narrative that threatens to hurt a player or team. Star Notre Dame linebacker Manti Te'o was the center of a media whirlwind after the 2013 Bowl Championship Series (BCS) National Championship Game, when it was revealed that his girlfriend, who he claimed had died from leukemia during the 2012 season, never actually existed.[50] Throughout the season, Te'o had cited his girlfriend's health battle as inspiration for his on-field play, but these allegations painted Te'o as a liar who had created a fictional girlfriend to engender sympathy.

With their backs against the wall, Te'o and Notre Dame advanced a counter-narrative, claiming that Te'o was a victim of an elaborate Internet hoax in which a former friend created an online personality with the intention of duping Te'o. Te'o said that he eventually realized that his girlfriend was a hoax but did not make the information public because he was humiliated. He now wants his story to serve as a cautionary tale about the dangers of online identity appropriation.[51] By reframing a negative narrative in a sympathetic light, Te'o deflected criticism and changed his narrative enough for the story to mostly recede from public scrutiny. Later that year, Te'o was drafted by the San Diego Chargers in the second round of the draft.[52] The improvisational narrative forces an organization to immediately and creatively reframe an unplanned story. Narratives can be unexpected and volatile, and the most skilled strategists need to be able to reshape them to avoid catastrophic damage to their player or organization.

Multiple Narratives. Multiple storylines are difficult to control but necessary to manage in a media universe more open to debate through new communication channels. Most often, an organization presents a positive storyline only to be quickly met with contradictory narratives. There have always been at least two sides to every story – and the new media world ensures that multiple sides are presented.

NASCAR learned just how quickly an organization can lose control of a narrative with its promotion of Amber and Angela Cope. These twin racecar drivers were marketed for their sex appeal as blonde bombshells, as illustrated by a provocative *Maxim* cover story designed to promote and publicize NASCAR. The organization used the Cope twins to attract more casual audiences to the sport.[53] The narrative quickly spun out of control, however, and alienated many traditional fans. Amber Cope cut off popular driver Kevin Harvick near the end of a 2012 Nationwide Series race at New Hampshire Motor Speedway, forcing him into a second-place finish. After the incident, the sport's core fan base unleashed a storm of invective through digital media channels, not only calling out NASCAR for straying from its roots, but also refueling an old storyline of NASCAR as a discriminatory organization toward women. One fan expressed his disgust by tweeting, "Sorry, #NASCAR, but the only pole [Amber Cope] will take is in a strip club."[54] The emergence of multiple, dueling storylines complicated NASCAR's original intent in showcasing the Cope sisters. Anticipating and orchestrating how a message unfolds are critical to controlling multiple narratives.

By becoming familiar with the narrative types, a sports organization can become more effective at turning promising storylines into opportunities to build brand equity. Each of the five narrative types requires a different level of development and distribution effort from the organization to maximize the potential for persuasive success. Regardless of whether they are developing an independent or an interrelated narrative, sports strategists must be precise and strategic in their cultivation and communication of the storyline. As previously discussed, the narrative has the potential both to create value for the sports organization and to detract from an audience's perception of a team or player. If the organization determines that a storyline is useful in achieving their internal goals, it is then vital to understand the various pieces that must come together seamlessly in the creation and distribution of a story.

Building the Narrative

In the past century, narratives were easier to control. Through a traditional public relations department or spokesperson, the organization would attempt to manufacture favorable storylines, which were then disseminated to audiences by the media. In fact, there was often a willing agreement between the sports organization and the media to filter the content in a mostly positive manner. The goal for sports promoters and industry leaders was simple: control the media to control the message. For example, author Jane Leavy illustrates the friendly relationship that the media had with sports stars in the 1950s and 1960s in her book *The Last Boy: Mickey Mantle and the End of America's Childhood*.[55]

But in today's digital marketplace, those messages are increasingly edited, reframed, and reconstructed by nontraditional communication agents, often leading to unintended consequences. Organizations that once expected audiences to accept their carefully orchestrated press releases, marketing plans, and player interviews now face an open-ended dialogue among owners, players, fans, and media outlets. In response, they are often forced to recast or reshape their story-lines to address any negative interpretations promoted by their audiences. Care-fully constructing, managing, and distributing storyline content is crucial to that content's effectiveness – and more challenging than ever.

In order to construct an engaging and marketable narrative, sports storytell-ers must understand the building blocks of story development. They should take inventory of their most valuable assets – the players, personalities, records, tradi-tions, community ties, and venues – with the most compelling storyline potential. Three essential elements for any effective sports narrative are plot, characteriza-tion, and setting. Developing each of these ingredients and then combining them into powerful storylines can enable sports organizations to enhance and reframe their messages.

Plot

Plot is the series of events that involve the main characters of a story. Multiple plotlines often intertwine to create one story. Plot is driven by conflict, and ef-fective plotlines confront characters with difficult challenges or obstacles to overcome. Discovering and inventing plotlines that resonate with the audience is the primary objective of the message developer. Plotlines drive character development, redefine relationships, lead characters to overcome seemingly in-surmountable obstacles, or simply affirm the basic values of an organization or player.

In sports, certain plots are more influential and popular than others. While there are countless stock plotlines in all sectors of life, the sports universe features a number of powerful and immediately familiar ones that have withstood the test of time.

The Underdog. In this storyline, a player or team that was undervalued, over-looked, or outmatched overcomes the odds to upset a favored opponent or achieve a stunning feat.

- Florida Gulf Coast University basketball team becomes the first 15-seed to make it to the Sweet Sixteen.
- Quinnipiac University, formerly a Division III hockey program, becomes a Division I Frozen Four runner-up.
- Former bodybuilder Y. E. Yang defeats both Tiger Woods and the field to win the 2009 PGA Championship.

The Comeback Kid. A once-great player or team that has fallen from prominence fights an uphill battle to reclaim long-lost glory.

- Jennifer Capriati, a former highly ranked tennis phenom, overcomes shoplifting and drug arrests to win multiple Grand Slam titles.
- Josh Hamilton recovers from a devastating addiction to drugs and alcohol to win MLB's MVP award.
- Minnesota Viking running back Adrian Peterson returns from a torn ACL injury to rush for over 2,000 yards and win the NFL MVP award.

The Incredible Feat. A team or athlete completes a rare, historic accomplishment that exceeds prior expectations of what is possible.

- Usain Bolt becomes the first sprinter to win back-to-back Olympic gold medals in the 100-meter and 200-meter events.
- University of Mount Union's Division III football team wins 110 consecutive regular season games.
- Novak Djokovic defeats Rafael Nadal in the Australian Open final – a 5-hour, 53-minute match, the longest Grand Slam men's singles final in recorded history.

The Santa Claus. Sports organizations and players act selflessly by giving back to their communities.

- St. Louis Cardinals' nonprofit foundation raises $10 million to help local kids.
- David Beckham visits terminally ill children in Australia.
- NFL wide receiver DeSean Jackson surprises a young boy, who had been previously bullied, by giving him his jersey on national television while playing for the Philadelphia Eagles.

The Rivalry. Two teams or players engage in an ongoing, intense, and often-fierce competition, enhanced by historical, geographical, or circumstantial significance.

- The rivalry between Pat Summitt's University of Tennessee Lady Vols and Geno Auriemma's University of Connecticut Huskies lifts the popularity of women's college basketball to new heights in the 2000s.
- The annual Massillon Washington vs. Canton McKinley rivalry is the only high school football game in the country to get a betting line in Las Vegas.
- The Ultimate Fighting Championship (UFC) markets the rematch between Chris Weidman and Anderson Silva during UFC 168 as "the biggest fight in UFC history."[56]

The Tradition. An established game or ritual carries historical significance that transcends the outcome of the game.

- North Carolina coach Roy Williams starts all Tar Heel seniors during Senior Night.
- Detroit Red Wings fans toss octopi onto the ice during playoff games even though the NHL prohibits fans from throwing anything onto the ice.
- The winning driver of the Indianapolis 500 chugs a bottle of milk in the Winner's Circle and kisses the bricks on the track.

The Love of the Game. A player, franchise, or league makes an expression of dedication to a sport that overshadows personal glory or monetary gain.

- The PGA Tour showcases its players' longstanding passion for the game in its "They Were Born for This" marketing campaign.
- Sixteen years after a high school game between Easton and Phillipsburg ends in a tie, the middle-aged players return to relive the experience and settle the score after months of intense training and preparation.
- After surviving a shark attack and losing her left arm, 13-year-old Bethany Hamilton returns to her professional surfing career only 26 days later. She goes on to compete in countless surfing championships.

The Great Sacrifice. A player or team forfeits titles, games, or financial or personal gains for something else perceived to have greater value.

- Tracey Barnes gives up her spot on the U.S. biathlon team for the Sochi Olympics to her sister Lanny, who became sick during the Olympic trials.
- Pat Tillman foregoes a multimillion-dollar contract with the Arizona Cardinals and loses his life while serving in the U.S. Army in Afghanistan.
- Meghan Vogel, Ohio high school track champion, helps a fallen runner cross the finish line at the expense of her chance to win the 1,600-meter state title.

While these are among the most commonly constructed storylines, there are infinite possibilities for engaging plots, such as "The Overnight Sensation" (Yasiel Puig), "The Famous Sports Family" (Archie, Peyton, and Eli Manning), and "The Fall from Grace" (Mike Tyson). These recognizable plots have proven effective over time, generating a consistent response from audiences across generations, even as the sports industry has continued to grow and evolve.[57]

Characterization

Characterization is the process by which storytellers create and present subjects through a narrative. These subjects represent the principal players in a story and advance the narrative's progress. An effective storyteller will provide the audience with compelling personalities that add depth and complexity to the narrative. Without well-developed characters, a contemporary story loses much of its emotional appeal. Multiple character attributes – such as appearance (NBA power forward Chris "Birdman" Andersen's mohawk and tattoos), motivation (British native Andy Murray's dramatic Wimbledon victory), behavior (Bob Knight's fiery temper), and speaking style (Mohammad Ali's poetic verse) – create an engaging and differentiated storyline. Beyond these attributes, storytellers must carefully consider two factors when selecting characters to feature in their storylines.

Stretch and Reach. Stretch and reach refer to how much flexibility the character has to engage an audience. There are two main questions to consider in determining a character's potential connection with an audience. First, how long will a character's fame last, and how far can it be stretched over time? Is the character likely to be in the spotlight for a day, a month, a year, or a generation? Or will that visibility transcend time? The longer a character remains a part of public memory, the greater recognition he or she carries. Focusing on subjects whose fame and recognition will stretch over time can provide organizations an instantly identifiable common bond with core audiences over generations. Longtime Milwaukee baseball broadcaster Bob Uecker is memorialized with two bronze monuments to remind fans of the fond memories they had listening to the man *Tonight Show* host Johnny Carson called "Mr. Baseball."[58]

A second consideration is how far the fame of a person such as Uecker reaches. Is this person recognized only at a local level? Or does his or her fame reach a regional, national, or international level? Geographic reach can be visualized as a pyramid, with the base consisting of the many locally known characters, gradually thinning out until only a few characters with international recognition stand atop the summit. Selecting a subject with geographic reach enables organizations to engage a wider audience. In 2001, Ichiro Suzuki burst onto the MLB scene with the Seattle Mariners, becoming the first Japanese non-pitching everyday position player in the majors. His record-breaking performance, magnified by his international appeal and fame, allowed the team to attract more international audiences.[59] This combination of time-related and geographic visibility creates a spectrum of stretch and reach that serves as a template for selecting possible characters to drive a narrative.

Depending on the level of competition and size of the audience base, some sports organizations may not be able to choose characters with international reach or who are ingrained in society's collective consciousness across generations. Not every sport has the luxury of a world-famous soccer legend such as Pelé associated with its brand. However, strategically analyzing which members of your organization will be most well-known by an organization's targeted audience over time is critical to selecting characters around which to base a narrative. Connecting with these audiences will produce a higher probability of persuasive success.

Star Power. While stretch and reach determine a character's stature in society, star power can be thought of as the character's ability to connect with and excite the audience. It attracts the publicity that sponsors and teams seek, but they cannot always generate on their own. The star often engages audiences as they identify with and appreciate a star's backstory, values, and relationships, allowing them to forge deeper connections with the sport.

Yet the opportunities for the star to overshadow the sport itself have grown substantially, in large part because of digital communication channels, which provide more transparency and access into stars' personal lives and stories. Organizations no longer possess as much control over their star players' narratives and, by extension, their fans' feelings about them. This can compromise an organization's ability to build a cohesive, positive narrative. Star power has become an increasingly risky proposition, as favorable public sentiment regarding well-known figures can sour quickly, adversely affecting the associated organization.

Given the risks of utilizing star power in narratives, organizations must evaluate the benefits of their heavy use of marquee players to attract fans. Clearly Kevin Durant, Tom Brady, Alex Morgan, and Lionel Messi are identified as stars with outstanding athletic ability and aesthetic appeal. But in an era of free agency in which superstars exercise unprecedented mobility and ever-increasing power, organizations should not exclusively rely on unwieldy and uncontrollable star-based storylines. Instead, they should seek to redefine star power to encompass their own settings, environments, and ancillary characters. This expansion of the traditional definition of star power can be seen as sports franchises and leagues reconfigure the concept to include stadiums, food, entertainment, and familiar franchise figures. In the midst of decades-long futility, the Kansas City Royals inducted their long-time groundskeeper George Toma into the club's Hall of

Fame – only the twenty-fifth inductee to receive that honor. In recognizing Toma's contributions to the franchise, the Royals created their own star narrative in which a groundskeeper took on a new role as fan favorite and reinforced and expanded the concept of the team.[60]

The expanding star power universe includes everything from the famous Milwaukee Brewers' sausage race to diehard fans such as the Vancouver Canucks' Green Men. The Dodger Dog is celebrated by fans as the majors' best foot-long dog – despite being only 10 inches.[61] But size doesn't seem to matter: the Dodgers traditionally sell a league-leading average of 2.2 million dogs per season.[62] The glorification of such a common sports food staple and its close association with the Dodgers' team brand underscores the importance of creating new "characters" for fan consumption. Sports organizations should rely not only on traditional star players, but also conduct a thorough inventory of their assets to dig out new characters and events as key elements to build their narratives.

Setting

Setting is when and where a narrative takes place. Sports have traditionally been defined by the time during which their competitions occur. College football owns New Year's Day, while high school and college basketball teams brand their season-ending tournaments as "March Madness." Similarly, golf enthusiasts' migration to Augusta National each April for the Masters means that spring has arrived. The Indianapolis 500 every Memorial Day marks the beginning of summer. MLB's World Series champions have been determined during the Fall Classic. In each case, these sports have staked out specific ownership of dates and times both on the annual sports calendar and in the sports audience's mind.

The time of games or events plays an important role in creating the live experience. Whether it is the sweltering heat of a high school basketball gymnasium or the crisp, cool autumn air of a college football stadium, sports provide instantly recognizable and memorable settings. The stadiums, arenas, and fields are firmly entrenched as defining links between fans and their teams. Millions continue to visit centuries-old cathedrals such as Wimbledon, Parc des Princes, and St. Andrews. Newer venues, such as the $1.1 billion Yankee Stadium[63] and the University of North Dakota's ornate $110 million hockey arena,[64] attract throngs of fans with their modern-day luxury and amenities.

Settings not only engage the viewer in a collective experience but also have the ability to outshine other competing negative storylines, such as a bad game or athletes' poor off-field behavior. Tour de France organizers have increasingly

HOUSE OF BLUES

When Gene Bleymaier decided to dye the artificial football turf of the Boise State University (BSU) Broncos a vivid blue in 1986, he probably had no idea of the massive impact his decision would have on both the Broncos' identity and the role of the setting in college football culture.[65] Founded in the 1930s as Boise Junior College by the Episcopal Church, Boise State started off as a small, unknown school, not achieving four-year college status until 1969.[66] When Boise State played against the more established University of Idaho in 1973 for the first time and beat the Vandals 42–14, it was clear that Broncos football had arrived (as had a vicious Broncos-Vandals rivalry).[67]

It was Bleymaier's decision to dye the traditional green turf blue, however, that became the catalyst to the school building its narrative around its football team. As BSU's athletic director at the time, Bleymaier saw installing blue turf as an opportunity to match the blue uniforms of the players and stand out from their college football counterparts' seas of green: "I guess that I'm the type of person that when I paint my house I paint it a different color so the neighbors notice you did something."[68]

Ever since Bleymaier's dye job, BSU's blue turf has become a distinctive and unique aspect of Broncos football. This can be seen by Boise State's frequent Thursday night appearances on ESPN. The Thursday night college football slot was a wasteland, and viewers had few other options for a football fix. Once Boise State started playing games during this time of the week, fans and broadcasters alike were transfixed and sometimes puzzled by the spectacle of blue-clad Boise State players on blue turf that contradicted every expectation of a normal football setting. These games also provided a recruiting advantage for Boise State. Because high school athletes across the country could watch the Broncos' wide-open offensive on the blue turf during nationally televised games, they were excited to play on the blue field and Boise State could recruit new players it was unable to target before.[69]

The 2007 Fiesta Bowl was a turning point for Boise State. University president Robert W. Kustra cites the Broncos' historic win as a milestone that resulted in much more than athletic glory: "When we won, I made a conscious decision to take that experience and leverage it with everything we do across the university."[70] Immediately after the Fiesta Bowl, which featured a stunning 43–42 overtime victory and a live marriage proposal from a Boise State player to his cheerleader girlfriend,

CONTINUED

Boise State saw its application rate increase by 40%.[71] The university managed to raise more than $175 million for its new business school after the Fiesta Bowl win. This fundraising, combined with a massive renovation of its academic and athletic facilities, has helped reposition the school as an up-and-coming university.

But none of this would have happened without the blue turf that reinvented the concept of a football setting and differentiated the Broncos from their college football counterparts. Boise blue symbolized the ambition and creativity of this previously unknown institution. The blue turf has become such an iconic part of Boise State's identity that Japan's Hosei University installed its own blue turf to honor the exchange program between the two universities. In doing so, Hosei University became the first institution to license a playing surface as a Boise State trademark.[72]

The blue turf has also symbolized controversy and been criticized by different audiences, as illustrated by ESPN's Chris Berman calling the field "the blue plastic tundra." The blue turf has also led to several NCAA disputes.[73] In 2012, the Mountain West conference banned Boise State from wearing blue uniforms on their blue turf. When the Broncos threatened to leave the conference for the Big East, the Mountain West conceded to their wearing the matching blue uniforms. In March of 2013, the NCAA playing rules oversight panel echoed the Mountain West's concession when it rejected a proposal that would have barred matching uniforms and fields.[74]

Even with, and perhaps because of, the controversy, the payoff for Boise State's blue turf has been substantial. Boise State has used the success of the football team as a catalyst to transform its image from a regional commuter school to a leading academic institution in the northwestern United States. According to Kustra, "If we had to pay for the marketing and the P.R. in The New York Times and the L.A. Times and every newspaper and radio station that mentions Boise State, we couldn't begin to cover it in our budget and it would well exceed the $3.5 million estimated proceeds that we will take home from [the Fiesta Bowl]. We have been given an advantage that very few universities have."[75] Its iconic blue-on-blue trademark will continue to live on and define Boise State's identity. Looking at BSU's meteoric rise as a global academic institution and its national reputation as a leading football powerhouse, it is clear that Bleymaier was right about the blue turf – the neighbors sure did notice.

emphasized setting in recent years to deflect criticism from the ever-widening steroid scandals involving its top cyclists that have threatened the integrity of the event.[76] The rampant drug use of past champions and competitors could have caused irreparable damage to the sport. After all, who wants to watch a parade of chemically enhanced cyclists cheating their way to the winner's circle? Despite these problems, television ratings have increased.[77] One explanation for the Tour de France's immunity to the widespread doping crisis stems from the event's setting – a rolling tourism extravaganza through some of the most beautiful terrain in the world. While still under suspicion of using performance-enhancing drugs (PEDs), the cyclists involved are not just featured as competitors but also as tour guides to an upscale fan base intrigued by the lush French countryside.[78]

Additional innovations in television broadcasts allow for new ways of creating narratives using setting where none existed before. For example, MLB has taken advantage of new camera angles and editing capabilities to effectively inject more drama into the game of baseball on television. Up until the late 1990s, a frequent complaint among television-viewing fans was the slow pace of televised game broadcasts. For years the game had been shot from a static, wide-screen angle with little movement, except for special events such as the World Series. A full nine-inning broadcast often looked more like a series of postcards than an intricate, interactive sporting event.

In order to communicate this setting on television, the league and its broadcast partners made the decision to use multiple cameras and place microphones on managers to give the game a dynamic and emotional rhythm. Innovations such as handheld cameras, "Skycam," and on-screen graphics now frame duels between pitchers and batters as pulse-pounding showdowns featuring close-ups of catchers flashing signals, managers grimacing after called strikes, and pitchers mopping their brows before a deciding pitch. The game has not changed, but the translation of the setting has, and the game has been transformed from an unimaginative viewing experience to a more interactive, dynamic broadcast. The extended pauses that once posed the biggest challenge to retaining viewer attention now present endless opportunities to inject new storylines into broadcasts.

Sports teams and leagues are not the only organizations that understand the power of setting. Broadcasters also utilize unique environments to attract audiences. ESPN has relied significantly on setting in creating one of its most successful and most-watched franchises, *College Gameday*.[79] The show has earned a rabid following among audiences nationwide by taking what was once a standard pregame studio show and morphing it into a traveling pigskin circus, visiting college campuses and highlighting the most anticipated games of the week. While viewers no doubt appreciate the talented and colorful cast of anchors and analysts, there's no mistaking the real star of the show: the scenic college campuses with their fired-up students, cheerleaders, and mascots. Each week features a new setting, producing novelty and excitement that turn a traditional pregame show into a Saturday morning institution that is often more anticipated than the games themselves.

The NHL recognized an opportunity to maximize setting as a narrative device when it launched the NHL Winter Classic in 2008.[80] In an effort to generate fan interest earlier in its regular season, the league decided to play a marquee game on New Year's Day. The NHL now holds the annual game in outdoor venues such as Fenway Park and Ralph Wilson Stadium – a nostalgic twist on a game that is typically played indoors – reintroducing cold weather elements and transforming a midseason game into a distinctive event. Additionally, these New Year's Day matchups usually consist of two teams with a fierce and storied rivalry, such as the Philadelphia Flyers and the Boston Bruins. By competing with college football, differentiating the setting of its product, and supercharging traditional rivalries, the NHL has created an event that has quickly become a marker to kick off the new year. The NHL Winter Classic redefined the league's product in a novel, exciting, and memorable way while helping the organization generate over $30 million in revenue for a single event in 2014.[81] It also has effectively carved out a place in the annual sports calendar and the sports audiences' collective consciousness.[82]

The setting is an important component of a storyline in building a narrative. Once constructed, narratives need to be evaluated for their efficacy in reaching and engaging their target audiences. In addition, narratives are dynamic creations, with changes in characters, plots, and settings potentially impacting storylines. Evaluating the narrative risk is the final phase of effective narrative design.

Narrative Risk

Constructing narratives does not come without risk. The narrative can be more of a gamble than a straightforward argument with traditional support. Stories depend greatly upon not only the medium but also on the audience's ability to interpret them. Their effectiveness relies upon the audience's knowledge, values, and willingness to make inferences about a given narrative.

Aristotle first described the concept of enthymeme, a persuasive technique in which the communicator purposefully omits parts of the argument with the intention that the audience will come to the intended conclusion without complete and explicit prompts. The strategy is designed to encourage the audience to fill in the missing pieces of the message. A well-conceived enthymeme has the benefit of increasing audience belief in the message and communication intensity.[83]

In today's crowded communication environment where 30 seconds can be a long time, the enthymeme is well suited to short media messages. Moreover, the strategy recognizes that the complete, detailed argument is often not a realistic alternative when time and attention spans are short. Former NBA star and current TNT basketball announcer Charles Barkley effectively used this approach after being arrested for drunk driving in 2009. While taking responsibility for what happened, the most effective part of Barkley's apology was thanking famous former NBA players and current executives, referees, and broadcasters that "took the time to check on me."[84] This one sentence encouraged fans and the media to take into account his good standing within the NBA community. He also set the stage for the audience to consider his actions as part of a disease or disorder that needed treatment rather than something that should cause him to be fired from TNT or receiving jail time.

Sometimes, an attempt at an enthymematic message can backfire, as the audience either fails to understand it or feels manipulated by it. For example, when LeBron James staged his now infamous ESPN "The Decision" special, in which he publicly declared his choice to leave Cleveland and "take [his] talents to South Beach," the special was originally intended, in part, to showcase James's generosity.[85] On the program, LeBron strategically surrounded himself with children of the Boys and Girls Club, and he promised to donate his proceeds from the televised special to the charity.[86] The message that the audience was intended to complete was that James was a selfless humanitarian. However, the event stirred up a firestorm of public disgust at James's perceived selfishness and lack of respect for his hometown. The enthymematic message of the Boys and Girls Club's appearance set up an unresolved conflict between his character and his motives.

Stories inherently communicate messages through enthymemes, inviting an audience to consider the greater meaning behind a narrative's plot, characters, and setting. A story's interactive appeal is potentially more persuasive and less likely to be forgotten. Ultimately, if the audience does not pick up on the narrative's intent, its persuasive power is lost or, potentially worse, misunderstood. Much of the associated risk of employing stories to achieve business goals results from the fact that these narratives often change and evolve when conflicting information surfaces. Sports organizations or individuals who use real-life characters and plot points to create narratives must take on uncertainty in not only how the story will unfold in the future, but also how the media and consumers alike will receive and discuss it.

Conclusion

Narrative has the potential to be a more effective persuasive technique than more traditional argument structures of assertion and evidence because of its ability to disarm its audience. At the same time, misuse of the narrative or the introduction of conflicting information can cause confusion, misunderstanding, or even offense. The ability of technology to transmit stories quickly, easily, and to large audiences heightens the risks and rewards of the narrative.

Even with the potential downside of narratives, sports strategists should focus on developing well-constructed and powerful stories. The potential emotional impact tied to a story can be highly persuasive and can encourage audience members to come to an implied conclusion themselves. Because the audience derives the meaning behind the communication rather than having it force-fed to them, the persuasive power of narrative has the ability to be strong and long lasting.

Moreover, sports strategists should consider using narratives as more than simply a way to build brand equity or to deflect negative attention away from a sports organization. A narrative both influences and is influenced by topics covered in the following chapters. How an organization decides to use technology or generate revenue will be shaped by its past narratives and future storylines.

4 Mastering New Technologies

In 2006, Second Life emerged as the new media darling of the year. Millions of people joined this "virtual world" to live in a 3-D alternate reality. They created avatars, dressed them in the latest fashions, built the homes they always wanted, and lived active social lives – even getting married – all from their computers. But just like in the real world, Second Life did not necessarily come cheap. In one month alone, "residents" spent $5 million on goods and services, none of which physically existed.[1]

With more than 7 million residents and plenty of positive press, Second Life became an intriguing proposition for big brands. It was positioned as a fast-growing, immersive environment that could very well be the future of digital communication and monetization. To capitalize on the potential opportunities, Toyota, Coca-Cola, American Apparel, Aloft Hotels, and many others built virtual presences on the platform. Coke, for example, launched the Virtual Thirst Pavilion, where residents competed to create a new vending machine for Second Life that would dispense many different items (with the notable exception of a cold-to-the-touch and physically drinkable can of Coke).[2]

The allure of new technology and a rapidly growing user base also attracted sports brands to Second Life. Adidas and Reebok launched retail stores that sold virtual shoes that gave avatars an "extra bounce" in their step.[3] The NBA took a slightly different approach, building its headquarters where fans could purchase jerseys and apparel as well as watch classic games and other league videos.[4] Perhaps MLB proved to be the most innovative, simulcasting video of the 2006 Home Run Derby from Pittsburgh into a virtual ballpark.[5]

Despite creative thinking and experimentation, none of the sports presences was a game-changer. Brands in other sectors also saw very limited success. In fact, within only a few short years, most of the brands quietly departed Second Life. And Second Life as a platform, although still in operation at the time of publication, has faded out of the mainstream technology conversation and is mostly an afterthought for large brands.

Second Life's shortcomings as a viable branding tool were many, but two stand out. First, while the headlines screamed otherwise, the actual number of users and usage of the platform was much lower than initially estimated. By 2007, the unique users count was closer to 4 million – not 7 million – because people often created multiple avatars. Moreover, only about 25% of those users visited the site at least once a month.[6] There simply was not a large enough audience on the platform to drive meaningful business results. At one point, then–NBA commissioner David Stern said, "I think we've had 1,200 visitors. People tell us that's very, very good. But I can't say we have precise expectations. We just want to be there."[7]

Stern's comment highlights the other key shortcoming of Second Life. Most companies approached the platform without well-developed goals or a strategic plan. At the height of the hype, Sibley Verbeck, the head of the Electric Sheep Company, which helped brands build virtual presences, observed of clients' strategy for virtual worlds, "They don't know. Mostly it's 'We've been reading about virtual worlds – is there anything for us?'"[8] In every case, the ultimate answer was not much.

...

Second Life tells a cautionary tale about the next-big-thing mentality. Human nature often gravitates toward the new and shiny, especially in the technology spheres where change happens regularly. When a new technology platform launches and grows quickly, brands have a tendency to rush to capitalize on the potential opportunities so as not to miss out. In some cases, this first-mover approach results in benefits such as gaining a competitive advantage, defining and shaping the economics of a platform, and being perceived as an innovator. At the same time, it also represents sizable risk, with the resources required to experiment often greater than any potential returns. Moreover, new technology platforms can distract organizations from their core focus and other opportunities that may matter more to the bottom line. One must delicately balance experimentation and restraint, and it is often not an easy balance to strike.

What makes this issue important for sports strategists? You will face decisions on what to do with new technology platforms more so than any other generation before you. Technological change and adoption is simply faster today than it was in the past. For example, the radio was invented in 1897, and it was 31 years before just 25% of the U.S. population adopted it. It took 26 years for the television to reach that same adoption benchmark, 16 years for the personal computer (PC), 13 years for the mobile phone, and 7 years for the Web. With each new media platform, historical trends suggest people's rate of adoption takes less and less time.[9] Moreover, as adoption rates increase, media behavior changes as well. For the first time, in 2013, people in the United States were spending more time using digital devices than watching television.[10]

Today, we see an undeniable acceleration of these trends. In 2013, companies could pick from a number of technology options to reach and engage sports audiences: Facebook, Twitter, YouTube, Foursquare, Tumblr, Instagram, Google+, Pinterest, Wordpress, and Vine (and that is just a sampling of the options in the social media space). There were a host of second-screen TV apps such as Viggle, GetGlue (now known as TVtag), and Zeebox (now known as Beamly) trying to break out, not to mention the ever-expanding universe of mobile and tablet applications and the elder statesmen of the technology class, websites and search engines. While media fragmentation was an issue in the early days of the Web, the clutter is reaching unprecedented levels in the mobile and social era in which we now live as the number of players continues to proliferate.

To complicate matters further, the pace of technological change shows no signs of slowing down. Ray Kurzweil, respected futurist and author of *The Singularity Is Near*, argues that the power of exponential growth is taking hold. He believes modern civilization in the twenty-first century alone will progress not by 100 years but by "more like 20,000 years" based on the current rate of technological change.[11] He even goes so far as to predict that "within several decades information-based technologies will encompass human knowledge and proficiency, ultimately including the pattern-recognition powers, problem-solving skills, and emotional and moral intelligence of the human brain itself."[12] Microsoft Hololens, a wearable computer in the form of a headset that responds to voice commands and hand gestures, is an early step in this direction, as it augments reality with holograms only the wearer sees.

It might not be in your job description, but all sports strategists will be confronted with new technology platforms daily and must have a blueprint for how to respond and allocate your limited resources. We used to live in an era when some companies could afford trial and error because there were fewer technology platforms to try. Now, with new opportunities emerging seemingly daily – from mobile applications to social media to tablets and everything in between – most sports organizations do not have the luxury of experimenting with every technology that hits the marketplace. Today's sports strategist will inevitably need to make choices about which technology platforms to use.

In this chapter, we prepare you for the difficult strategic technology decisions you will face. The technology world changes so quickly that some, if not all, of the innovations we discuss in this chapter may not even be in business by the time you read this book. But that is not the point. Ultimately, this chapter is about the strategic planning process for choosing new technology platforms, the principles of which can be universally applied to the technologies we have not even heard of yet. Faced with a mounting number of options and only limited resources, sports strategists wrestle with a few fundamental questions: Which technology platforms should I adopt? How can I capitalize on technology platforms, integrate them effectively, and develop the appropriate content and experiences to ensure that more sports audiences stay longer and repeatedly come back for more? Finally, how do I monetize new technologies?

To address these questions, we introduce four concepts to help sports strategists adopt, integrate, and maximize new technologies. Each concept is different, yet all of them are designed to work together.

1. Platform Alignment Test – An evaluation process for new technologies to determine strategic fit with a brand
2. Audience Ecosystem – A system of platforms designed to deliver clear, interconnected, and easily navigable fan experiences
3. Immersive Content – A philosophy of developing content for audience ecosystems that provides access, enables control, offers opportunities for fan participation, and rewards fan behavior
4. Monetization – An approach to creating new revenue opportunities through technology or by enhancing existing partnerships

Ultimately, sports strategists should be judicious about which technology platforms to adopt, think holistically about how to capitalize on them, and develop ways to monetize them. By implementing these concepts, you will be in a better position to drive your business forward through new technology platforms.

The Platform Alignment Test

In 2009 and 2010, the key challenge that dominated the media and technology industries harkened back to high school popularity contests. Which brand could amass the most Facebook fans? Some brands were the all-American, well-rounded types who connected with most everyone, so they had no problem making friends on Facebook. Others were like the rich kids who attracted friends because they had the fanciest cars and the latest gadgets (or, in the case of Facebook, gave away the most free stuff). Then there were the brands that did not have a lot of friends, but those they did have were unconditionally loyal. Each approach had its merits, and multiple millions of Facebook users had become fans of (or "liked") brands in only a few years.

After focusing so much effort on growing Facebook fan bases, many brands ultimately found themselves asking, Now what? For starters, just having Facebook fans is only half the battle. Keeping them engaged regularly is critical. Because of Facebook's EdgeRank algorithm, which determines which content users see in their newsfeeds, simply having fans or "likes" does not mean you are reaching them with your message, let alone enticing them to react with a like, comment, or share. The Ehrenberg-Bass Institute in Australia studied fan engagement with the top 200 brands on Facebook and found that only 1.4% of fans engaged with these pages, a curiously low usage number. In the press release for the research, the Institute editorialized, "Facebook is becoming more and more like traditional media. It may be time for advertisers to move on from worrying about how many fans they have to instead explore how many category buyers Facebook can reach, for what cost, and to what effect."[13]

Here is the point: There was a time when brands perceived Facebook pages to be an absolute necessity and most brands created them with whatever resources they could muster. However, some launched without a global view of how this new communication channel connected with their overall business goals and strategy, leaving the organization vulnerable to inefficiency. If you asked a group of social brand managers whether they would do some things differently with their Facebook page presences (e.g., maybe not have as many) if they had a second chance, we hypothesize that the majority answer would be yes.

In the future, brands will undoubtedly confront similar situations. Because of the confluence of mobile devices and social media, new technology platforms with significant user bases will continue to emerge, and sports strategists will be forced to evaluate the potential opportunities they offer.

The Platform Alignment Test is designed to help in this process. The criteria to address in auditing new technologies are:

- Audience Compatibility – Who is the audience?
- Platform Behavior – How does this audience use the platform?
- Business Objectives – How does the platform tie back to your goals?

Audience Compatibility

Like all communication challenges, the first criterion centers on audience. What is the size of the audience on the platform? What is its demographic composition? How active and engaged is the audience? Does the technology align with the overall target audiences? If the platform does not help reach and engage the fans you want, give serious thought as to why you are pursuing this opportunity in the first place. Often audience compatibility – or the lack thereof – is where the next-big-thing mentality does not work.

When GetGlue, Viggle, and Zeebox emerged as second-screen TV-viewing mobile applications, the prospects for increased television ratings were intriguing. Fans could "check in" to live TV programming and earn rewards, view extra content, and connect with other fans via these apps, potentially driving up the amount of time spent viewing and attracting new audiences through incentives. But looking at the size of the audience on each app is when the logic falls short. GetGlue was one of the first movers in this space, accumulating an estimated 4 million users.[14] For the sake of argument, if the goal for a team was to drive more viewership, virtually everyone who downloaded one of these apps would need to be using it and watching the team's game at the same time to measurably impact ratings – hardly a realistic or easy task, especially since these sports audiences might be more likely than others to watch the game anyway (i.e., with or without GetGlue). There is no question that GetGlue/TVtag, and other second-screen apps like it have value, perhaps as a brand loyalty tool. But in any deployment of this technology, weighing the size of the audience base is a key factor moving forward.

In addition to audience size, the number of active users is an important consideration. In the technology space, we often hear of large numbers of users attributed to a particular platform, but that tells only half the story. How many people are actually using a platform is often the more pertinent question. After only five weeks in existence, Google+ had more than 25 million members, becoming the fastest-growing social network ever.[15] Despite the outsized number of users, which hit the 150 million mark[16] after only a year, the real story behind Google+ in its early days was its lack of usage. Some industry commentators called it a "ghost town" and made the joke that the only users were Google employees (and even one in three Google employees was not using the platform).[17] Over time, this perception did change,[18] and Google+ emerged with both audience size and engagement, becoming a credible player in the social media business. But for much of its first year in existence, Google+ forced the question, if a meaningful number of people are not using a platform, is it worth the time and effort to program it? Looking past simple user numbers and focusing on the engagement metrics will often give you the most realistic assessment of a platform's potential.

A final audience compatibility consideration is target alignment. Are you reaching and engaging the audience you want? Pinterest, a social sharing and curation website built on people's interests, launched in 2010 and reached 70 million users by 2013,[19] with the average user spending 15 minutes per visit. This audience is both highly engaged and active. The demographic breakdown, however, historically skews heavily female, at 93% women to 7% men,[20] and the amount of interest in sports on Pinterest pales in comparison to the amount of interest in fashion, home and garden, and travel.[21] Depending on the organizational goals, Pinterest could serve as a viable platform to reach a highly active female audience but potentially may not be the best place to connect with the demographic of male sports fans aged 18 to 34.

The temptation to "fish where the fish are" is always strong. Some technology platforms can claim large numbers of users and high levels of engagement, which will be undeniably attractive. But when evaluating a new technology platform, make sure the fish are aplenty, still swimming, and the ones you actually want to catch.

Platform Behavior

In the evaluation process, sports strategists should also consider how and why people use a technology. Despite having a large and engaged potential fan base, some platforms may not be a perfect match for an organization's identity or narrative. For example, Snapchat is an application that launched in late 2012.

Almost overnight, it became one of the most popular apps, particularly among teens, with more than 5 million users.[22] The app had a simple proposition: users take a picture and send it to another person, but the picture self-destructs in 10 seconds or fewer.

On the surface, the app could be very appealing to sports brands, offering a large user base that skews young and tech-savvy. But because of the way people initially used Snapchat, it did not lend itself as seamlessly to brand integration as other communication platforms. For starters, the potential reach was limited. If a sports organization launched a Snapchat, the team or league could send a "mass Snapchat" to every one of its "friends," but only if it personally requested friendships with individual users, requiring it to build a robust friend list. This would be labor intensive, but it could be done. And some brands did take advantage. For example, Taco Bell and frozen yogurt company 16 Handles were among the early brand adopters of the platform. Acura once made headlines for sending a Snapchat to 100 people.[23] But overall, the number of brands adopting Snapchat, even with 200 million "snaps" sent per day, was low compared to the number of brands adopting other technology platforms. Moreover, for an industry of marketers used to creating indelible content and messages, Snapchat is a different medium – one in which the carefully crafted message disintegrates in a matter of seconds. Another issue was the behavior Snapchat became known for: sexting.[24] Certainly this was not the only use of the platform, but it was a consideration for some brands as they evaluated whether or not Snapchat would align with their strategy.[25]

Snapchat eventually began exploring native advertising, which would enable brands to more effectively target larger numbers of people.[26] The platform also introduced a feature called Stories, through which brands can string together multiple snaps into a narrative that expires after 24 hours. While organizations had been increasingly embracing the Stories feature,[27] many sports brands largely treaded lightly with Snapchat in the early days of the app because of how people behaved on the platform.

Twitter, on the other hand, is a technology platform ideally suited to sports. As Twitter puts it, "Twitter and sports fit together because sports are live, immediate, suspenseful, and fun – and these qualities Twitter mirrors and enhances in real-time."[28] For example, in 2012, two of Twitter's five golden tweets (those that garner significant retweets) were from sports, including T. J. Lang of the Green Bay Packers, who tweeted his frustration after the controversial ending of his team's game against the Seattle Seahawks as a result of replacement referees.[29] More-over, in that same year, the Super Bowl, Summer Olympics, and Euro 2012 joined Superstorm Sandy, the MTV Video Music Awards, and the U.S. presidential elec-tion as the most tweeted-about events.[30] Sports dominates Twitter because its language – scores, stats, breaking news, analysis, opinion – aligns well with the nature of the platform.

People use different technologies for different purposes. Because a technology may align well with your target audience does not necessarily mean it is appro-priate for your identity or organization's content. In many ways, media theorist Marshall McLuhan's prophetic philosophy that "the medium is the message" still holds true today. How a sports organization decides to leverage a technology will inevitably affect the degree to which it achieves its overall goals.[31]

Business Objectives

The final criterion of the Platform Alignment Test is whether the audience and platform behaviors tie back to your business objectives. It may be easy to lose sight of your goals when innovative technologies present many new possibilities, but successful sports strategists should always keep an eye on how platforms can move their business forward. In many ways, it is useful to view technology platforms as a tactic to accomplish broader goals.

Of course, business objectives vary widely. These examples are intended solely to demonstrate how technology platforms can relate tactically to overall goals.

- Increase Consumption of Your Product – The *Sporting News* integrated Face-book social plug-ins into their website to make it easier for audiences to share content with their Facebook friends, thus driving more page views of the site.[32]
- Identity Building (or Rebuilding) – To rehabilitate his identity after his "The Decision" TV special, LeBron James heavily utilized Twitter, Face-book, and Instagram, posting authentic musings and photos that made him more relatable and likeable.
- Direct Revenue Opportunities – The San Francisco Giants partnered with Virgin America on a sponsored #FlytheBeard campaign on Twitter, which rewarded fans who tweeted pictures of the Giants' bearded, yes bearded, plane.[33]

Adopting new technologies is not a zero-cost proposition. In most cases, a technology effort will likely require budget and/or people, all of which can take away from other business functions, depending on the platform. That is why employing the Platform Alignment Test can be useful as a way to determine whether a technology aligns well with the desired audience, platform behavior, and goals of an organization. It should help significantly in the decision-making process.

Finally, if you work through the Platform Alignment Test and determine that a technology platform does not fit your organization, this is an acceptable outcome. Not every platform is going to be ideal, and with so many options available, sometimes patience and waiting for the right technology at the right time is the best course of action. Moreover, depending on your resources, it may be worth experimenting with certain platforms if the answers to the Platform Alignment Test are not clear and convincing. But keep a close eye on audience compatibility, platform behavior, and business objectives throughout the test. In the end, given the rapid technological proliferation, having guidelines on what makes sense and what does not for your organization will help as you navigate these uncertain times.

DO NOT JUST DO IT

By the end of 2011, Twitter reached more than 200 million users. Ashton Kutcher and Lady Gaga had already amassed more than 6 million Twitter followers. Meanwhile, in the sports world, the NBA had been aggressive on the platform for nearly four years, with almost 4 million Twitter followers. The FIFA Women's World Cup Final received more tweets per second (7,196) than the British royal wedding (3,966).[34] Stars like Shaquille O'Neal and Chad Johnson were using Twitter to build their celebrity, even as their athletic performance was declining.

With sports becoming almost synonymous with Twitter, it was curious that Nike, one of the biggest sports brands in the world, did not have a flagship account, @Nike. While it had launched feeds for some of its specialty sports brands – @Nikefootball, for example – conventional brand wisdom suggested that Nike should have a presence on the fast-emerging social media platform.

To Nike's credit, it did not launch its flagship Twitter account just to do it. Rather, the company focused on a strategic opportunity to start its feed. And that moment came at the end of 2011. To coincide with the New Year, Nike finally launched an @Nike Twitter feed (as well as a Nike Instagram feed) on December 31 as part of an overall campaign called #makeitcount. The hashtag also doubled as the campaign tagline, ensuring an easy call to action for the audience. The content plan on the Twitter feed included tweets from Nike athletes sharing their New Year's resolutions to #makeitcount.

Nike could have gone live with its Twitter feed just to have a presence on the platform. But with that approach came potential issues: What if the experience Nike fans received on the Twitter feed was not consistent with the brand? Ultimately, Nike decided to forgo the first-mover advantage in generating a following but ensured that its flagship brand's initial foray into the Twitter space was as integrated as possible. As a result, Nike's Twitter feed grew within a few months to more than several hundred thousand followers, and within less than a year had 600,000 followers. The Instagram account saw similar success, with about 500,000 followers in only one year.[35]

There are a couple of key takeaways from this story. First, the Nike Twitter feed was connected to a larger campaign, not only giving it a unique purpose, but also supporting it with the appropriate marketing campaign to help build its following. Second, Nike tested its approach through other Twitter feeds before launching its flagship presence.[36] It is helpful, if possible, to test and learn with smaller brands for which the risk is much less. Nike had the benefit of getting its feet wet with other feeds, which likely helped inform its efforts for the flagship Twitter feed. At the time of the launch, Perri Shakes-Drayton, 400-meter champion hurdler and Nike UK endorser, was featured in a Nike ad with the quote: "Walk to the stadium, sprint to the finish line."[37] Those words proved to be prescient for Nike on Twitter as well.

There have been many cases in the business world when brands jump into new technologies without having a clear understanding of what they are looking to do, with Second Life as a case in point. The Platform Alignment Test can be a way to avoid these situations. Technology is just a means to an end, not an end unto itself, and should be grounded in an overall philosophy or approach. Knowing when and how to adopt new technology to enhance the fan experience is a key skill for today's sports strategist. The next challenge is getting the most out of the technology you adopt.

The Audience Ecosystem

Convergence has been predicted for decades. Today, it is finally happening, due to the advent of smartphones, tablets, Internet-connected TVs, and the cross-platform applications and software that power them. The term *convergence* has several definitions, but we use the one from Henry Jenkins, a forward thinker on the concept. He defines it as "the flow of content across multiple media platforms, the cooperation between multiple media industries, and the migratory behavior of media audiences who will go almost anywhere in search of the kinds of entertainment experiences they want."[38] This definition is especially apt given the innovations in personal media devices that can be held in consumers' hands, with content providers making their content available on any device in various ways.

Sports is the avatar of media convergence. It is now axiomatic that sports fandom is a multimedia, cross-platform activity. Certainly, audiences may watch a game on television and then read about it in the paper the following morning, but this behavior is increasingly the exception, not the rule. It is far more likely today that fans watch a game on an HD television while also engaging with fellow fans and analysts on Twitter in real time, chatting with friends via text message or Skype, logging on to a website for additional behind-the-scenes content, monitoring fantasy sports teams, or all of the above.

While these new platforms enhance the audience experience, they present new challenges on how to approach developing, distributing, and marketing content on multiple platforms. In response, we believe sports strategists should take a more holistic view of their *audience ecosystem*, which we define as a platform or system of platforms designed to deliver clear, interconnected, and easily navigable fan experiences. The audience ecosystem can be within a single platform or across multiple platforms. The key is how all the platforms work together. Each should be unique, complementary, and interconnected to keep audiences engaged within the ecosystem.

An audience ecosystem is important for two key reasons. First, with so many new platforms, fragmentation is a more pressing problem than ever before. Sports audiences have any number of options for sports content, and it is increasingly difficult to stand out. A carefully constructed audience ecosystem with different touchpoints and entryways can ensure that people spend more time with your brand on more platforms than your competitors. Second, audiences use and consume content on each platform differently. For example, mobile applications are different from Twitter feeds, and YouTube channels are different from TV networks, which means that the way you might program each of these platforms must vary. Audience ecosystems allow platforms to play specific roles in creating and disseminating content and fan experiences. In order to attract and retain fans, coordinating a brand's platforms effectively could very well spell the difference between winners and losers in such a competitive market.

When a fertile ecosystem is created in sports, it can result in audience growth, enhancements in fan experiences, and benefits on the business side. There are few better sports ecosystems than fantasy sports, specifically fantasy football. What started as a backroom, outside-the-mainstream game played by only the most avid of fans has transformed into a dominant form of sports fandom. Throughout the course of its history (the first fantasy football league was created in 1963),[39] technology has been the facilitator of growth and further acceptance of the game, while fantasy football has clearly demonstrated the demand for integrated, converging experiences in the media marketplace.

The advent of the Internet was a transcendent moment for the fantasy sports ecosystem. No longer did league commissioners have to compile scores by hand or send out updates via snail mail. With the help of new websites and the statistical tools that powered them, all these typically time-consuming activities, which also hampered the game's growth prospects, were essentially automated. Once leagues were online, early examples of a growing ecosystem started to emerge. For example, fans could watch the games Sunday afternoon on their television sets while monitoring their fantasy teams online through real-time scoring, which perhaps constitutes one of the first versions of the "second screen." Meanwhile, the smartphone and tablet, along with advancements in fantasy sports applications, have kept fans in control of their fantasy teams no matter where they are, often to the detriment of the friends and family of the most fantasy-obsessed owners. As technology has connected the TV and digital experience more seamlessly, fans have begun to increasingly consume content on multiple media platforms – often simultaneously – within the same ecosystem, encouraging fans to spend more time playing the game.

When the NFL adopted the Xbox One platform, the future of convergence had arrived in many ways. The NFL and Microsoft partnered on an integration for fantasy football that enabled Xbox owners to watch a football game and track their automatically updated fantasy statistics on their television.[40] Now, instead of needing a second screen like a laptop, mobile phone, or tablet, everything would be presented on a single screen through the convergence of TV and digital in the Xbox One environment. From the Internet to this newest form of connected televisions, the integration of new technologies throughout the history of fantasy sports has enhanced and extended the fantasy sports–playing ecosystem.

Adding new technologies into an ecosystem is not without challenges. In these circumstances, it is no surprise that the term "disruptive" is often used to describe how certain technologies upend traditional practices. NBC's coverage of the 2012 Summer Olympics in London is an example of technology's unintended consequences. The event promised to be the most multiplatform experience in the history of sports media. The TV coverage was extensive, with the combined NBC-Comcast television assets like NBC, CNBC, MSNBC, and the newly rebranded NBC Sports Network collectively offering around-the-clock coverage. There was also an extensive digital, mobile, and social game plan in place, giving audiences the ability to watch much of the Olympics live on computers or tablets as part of the TV-everywhere movement. By all accounts, the strategy worked, with a record-breaking 219.4 million Americans watching, making it the most-watched TV event of all time.[41]

With a comprehensive social media plan, NBC's coverage of the 2012 Olympics became a flashpoint in sports media and technology. Many hailed it as the first social media games. The network's push on Facebook, Twitter, and YouTube was significant. Seemingly every graphic included #Olympics, and Ryan Seacrest recorded on-air segments discussing the most talked-about moments on Facebook. In addition, YouTube acted as a primary video hub for great Olympics moments, as did NBCOlympics.com.

Despite these innovative tactics, NBC also encountered challenges in the two-way communication environment of social media. Because the network tape-delayed the most important events for the primetime viewing audience, some people had already heard about who had won earlier in the day, even from NBC itself, on social media. For some active users of the Internet and social media, spoilers were simply too difficult to avoid. That led to complaints in the Twittersphere, trending hashtags like #NBCFail, and a Twitter feed called @NBCDelayed. This feed's sole mission was to highlight the "News and Sports brought to tape delayed [sic] for your viewing pleasure by NBC (Yes, this is a parody account)."[42]

There is a business rationale for holding highly anticipated programming back for primetime in order to charge an advertising premium. The record-setting ratings for the NBC Olympics in London were helped in large part by performances from Missy Franklin and Usain Bolt and a strong showing by the American team as overall leaders in medal count.[43] But as real-time consumption of events across any platform becomes an unwavering expectation of the audience, there will be an increasing demand for all technologies to be complementary, not contradictory, in the audience ecosystem. As Jenkins notes, fans are moving from one media platform to another with rapid speed and are expecting to consume the content they want when they want it.

Sports strategists must balance the benefits of technologies, their accompanying business realities, and fan expectations. NBC's coverage of the Sochi Olympics is a good example of its evolving approach. During the 2014 winter games, NBC promoted its online channels and received a spike in digital viewership while still achieving strong ratings for its tape-delayed events on both its broadcast and cable channels. For example, NBC increased its audience by 3.2 million viewers for 2014 Opening Ceremony as compared to the same event in the 2010 games while also having more than 600,000 people stream the men's halfpipe competition. NBC continues to refine its Olympic audience ecosystem to capitalize on engagement in television and digital channels and maximize revenue.[44]

In the end, with the proliferation of mobile computing, audiences are increasingly engaging with sports across many different channels. Ensuring the effective integration of all these technology platforms is one challenge. How those platforms should be programmed – and with what content and experiences – in this new era of media consumption is another. Both the distribution system and the content must ultimately work together in a coherent ecosystem.

CAR 54, WHERE ARE YOU?

The 1960s sitcom *Car 54, Where Are You?* followed the misadventures of two bumbling police officers in the Bronx who could never quite get it right. Their iconic Plymouth Fury was a cozy hideout that filtered out meddling spouses and irate police chiefs back at headquarters. While these farcical cops could get away with shirking their duties by simply ignoring their walkie-talkies, this modern era of technology demands a new level of transparency. The Hendrick Motorsports racing organization specializes in communicating everything about their cars, drivers, and support team to the public. To facilitate their

CONTINUED

CAR 54, WHERE ARE YOU? *CONTINUED*

audience ecosystem and in cooperation with technology designer Panasonic and social media analyst team Simply Measured, they devised a cutting-edge digital dashboard that manages their social media presence.[45] Housed in an apartment-like complex, the dashboard is a one-stop, all-purpose social media command center, allowing for a myriad of social media to converge and be distributed throughout the Hendrick ecosystem.

The command center is not a new idea in the sports world. Gatorade Mission Control was a first mover, pioneering the real-time social media control room, complete with impressive visualizations of online chatter. The New Jersey Devils are among the other sports organizations that followed suit with their own command center. In the case of Hendrick, the command center provides its teams the ability to hone and control their messages for specific audiences, which is particularly important in a communication environment in which messages are everywhere and often uncontrollable. For example, the popular NASCAR driver Dale Earnhardt, Jr., engaged directly with fans through the command center by participating in a Reddit Ask Me Anything and a Twitter chat session.[46] Moreover, Hendrick has the capacity to produce, edit, and target material from their system designers, engine technicians, and other players in the Hendrick racing-team operations and distribute it directly to fans, sponsors, and competitors alike. The entire team is made available through this command center, peeling away the veneer of team operations and bringing fans into their process through social media.

Integrated social media platforms are the new frontier for developing and targeting specific messages to sports audiences. The ability to control outgoing messages, deliver customized material, and offer sponsors new opportunities is clearly advantageous. The real question for sports organizations is whether this type of execution is appropriate for dealing with the challenges they face. The digital dashboard is innovative but costly and demands a huge investment in time and technology that must be weighed against the other goals of the organization. Moreover, there are many other lower-cost ways to monitor and interact with the social community, using simple tools such as HootSuite and TweetDeck. Regardless of how you engage in this modern technological climate, there is no room for audiences to wonder "Where are you?" when it comes to your sports organization.

Immersive Content

In 2006, *Time* Magazine recognized "you" as the person of the year. It acknowledged the advent of two-way communication technologies that dominated the Internet at the time: YouTube, Wikipedia, and MySpace. Of course, these only represent the beginning of the revolution in consumer content creation. With Facebook, Twitter, Instagram, Vine, and numerous other platforms, sports audiences have become both active consumers of content and content creators of their own. While audiences still demand passive viewing experiences, this new dynamic calls for an even greater emphasis on two-way engagement, particularly as new technologies put consumers at the center of the experience.

The key to a consistently dynamic ecosystem in the future is *immersive content*, which we define as having four key elements: access, control, participation, and rewards. There will always be one-way, lean-back media experiences; sometimes it is just liberating to watch a movie at home with no distractions. But increasingly, the lean-forward phenomenon in which viewers are active participants in defining their sports and entertainment experience is becoming the norm. And as a result, there will be demand for immersive content that can cut through the clutter.

Access

Providing sports audiences with more access to information about the players, the games, and seemingly everything about the sport is not just added value any more, it is expected. In a sign that the industry is headed in this direction fast and furiously, the Masters, not traditionally considered the most open to change, has embraced consumer access. Historically, access to the culture, landscape, and atmosphere of the Masters was limited to exclusive participants and conventional television broadcasts. In partnership with IBM, the Masters introduced a new website and application experience for the 2013 tournament. This took "the Masters to the masses by leveraging digital platforms," as John Kent, program manager and leader of IBM's sports sponsorships, said. He described the company's mission as "all about sharing the history, the tradition, the beauty, the experience here at Augusta National. So our challenge is, on digital platforms, to create an immersive experience that gives the users that sense of place, of *presence*."[47] The Masters' website accomplishes this by offering 360-degree views of each hole, a historical video timeline, and up-to-date leaderboard information. Whether or not fans attend an event, they will crave more access to the players, teams, and facilities. Technology can help facilitate this access more effectively.

Control

Not only are sports audiences demanding access, but they are also looking for control of their entertainment experience, particularly through new technology. With entertainment services such as Netflix and Spotify, they are able to curate their own viewing or listening on their own terms. The sports world is following suit. One example is the new companion television experiences that provide additional, complementary camera angles on sporting events that people can control, such as the NBA/TNT's Overtime digital experience and NBC's Sunday Night Football Extra. In these or other scenarios, it is important that sports audiences have options for how they can personalize and customize their sports content experience, no matter where they are or on what device.

Participation

Sporting events endure as one of the most shared societal experiences, given the thousands of people who gather in stadiums or millions who tune in from home to watch. And because people like to take sides and argue a position, there is an inherent need for fans to participate in some way, shape, or form during an event. The online conversation during a boxing match between Floyd Mayweather, Jr., and Canelo Alvarez in 2013 unfolded as if the Internet had turned into a sports bar. Whether it was blogs, Twitter, Facebook, or websites, fans engaged in pre-match speculation, debate, and judging throughout the contest and reacted to the decision positively or negatively when the fight concluded (with Mayweather winning two of the judge's scorecards and the other judge scoring it a tie). One of the defining characteristics of sports as an entertainment platform is how it elicits opinions and sparks debates among fans. Most any technology experience should find ways to leverage the innate social behaviors of sports fans.

Rewards

Finally, encourage sports audiences to come back to the ecosystem or remain loyal by rewarding them for their behavior. The University of Oregon is one of a number of teams that have begun to pursue a fan rewards strategy.[48] The idea is to incentivize people who engage with the team through social media. The fans who do so earn the most points, which can then be cashed in for prizes. The advantage for fans is that they are rewarded for something they would already be doing – supporting their team – which can help foster even stronger fan loyalty. The university receives free publicity in the form of earned media every time a fan takes an action on one of its social media sites.

Access, control, participation, and rewards are the four key elements of an immersive content strategy that can fuel an ecosystem. These considerations apply to any type of sports content, from news and information to live game broadcasts. A good example of a brand that has constructed a successful ecosystem through immersive content is SB Nation, a collection of sports blogs that cover all major teams and leagues in the U.S. sports leagues and, increasingly, international sports as well. The growth during SB Nation's short time in operation is staggering: it has grown from 5.8 million monthly unique visitors since its debut in 2009[49] to 50 million monthly unique visitors in 2013.[50] Moreover, web visitors spend time on their partner sites, keeping up to date with the latest on their favorite teams and sports.

SB Nation exemplifies why immersive content matters in the new technology marketplace. SB Nation built up and offers content that supports both broad and deep coverage. It covers a wide range of sports but also goes as deeply, if not more so, into each of the sports and teams as a local newspaper might have done 20 years ago. There is coverage of every sport, team, and league. For example, SB Nation's preseason reports for the NFL season include each of its bloggers' complete in-depth breakdowns of camp performances and training camp games, presenting a significant amount of content while also delivering fan access to each of the teams. And all of the platforms are interconnected; when the Dallas Cowboys community mentions the Philadelphia Eagles, that comment is hyperlinked to the Eagles' blog for more information.

The blog network stays fresh because of the people who power it. Unlike a traditional media company that may rely on highly trained and tenured journalists, SB Nation drafts a growing cadre of bloggers – journalists and fans – to produce content on its behalf. This is not to say that the company relaxes quality standards. SB Nation still maintains strong quality control over the accuracy and integrity of its content, but it takes a completely different model for its production. It taps into fans to help them create their content. Co-creation, which is at the core of the SB Nation model, gives consumers the opportunity to create content with a media organization. And it has the added benefit of rewarding fans for all the content they create.

The content is further fueled through participation. It is inherently debatable and conversation-worthy, which encourages readers to participate in the activity on the site as well. In fact, the blogs are not called blogs, but "communities," where fans engage in the "highest-quality conversations and coverage" about sports.[51] There is also the opportunity for readers who build strong enough followings of their own points of view to launch their own communities. It is a constant feed-back loop and reward system that technology has helped facilitate.

SB Nation is a simple but highly effective immersive content environment that balances multiple blogs and content offerings. It is also available across platforms, whether on the Web, through mobile, or in applications. Through the combin-ation of access, control, participation, and rewards, SB Nation has emerged from relative obscurity and become a strong player in the sports marketplace by capi-talizing on new technology.

The advantage of thinking about technology platforms as an audience ecosys-tem is that this perspective ensures that all distribution channels and content work together and complement one another. Effectively orchestrating these plat-forms, while fueling them with the content that will keep fans engaged, is one of the vital technology opportunities for sports strategists.

THE FIVE-TOOL TECHNOLOGY PLAYER

Mike Trudell has made his mark in the sports industry by capitalizing on new media technologies. A journalist by training, Trudell started in sports in 2005, when the industry was still in the nascent stages of navigating the digital revolution. Rather than relying solely on newspapers, radio sta-tions, and television networks to reach audiences with their messaging, he understood that sports organizations had an opportunity to create con-tent and distribute it directly to sports audiences through their own digital communication channels.

Trudell's strategy was to identify underutilized digital media commu-nication channels and create content specifically for them. At his first job with the NFL's Baltimore Ravens, Trudell started as an intern in pub-lic relations. While completing his assigned tasks, Trudell focused his time after hours developing both short- and long-form stories for the team's website to make it a more robust experience beyond the schedule and stats. These efforts helped him to secure a new role producing digital content for NFL Europe's Cologne Centurions and the NFL's Minnesota Vikings.

Building on these experiences, Trudell assembled a multimedia content strat-egy and proposed it to several sports franchises. The plan included reporting on games and practices, writing features and blog entries, and creating pod-casts and online videos. Trudell was quickly hired by the Minnesota Tim-berwolves basketball team, and he became one of the first sports journalists to start broadcasting podcasts on a regular basis in 2006. His podcasts and "WolvesTV" branded video content included interviews with assistant coaches and team experts who provided detailed scouting reports on upcoming op-ponents in each NBA city. Trudell realized that using nontraditional team per-sonnel and sources to foster increased engagement between audiences and the organization provided the Timberwolves with a competitive advantage.[52]

When the NBA's Los Angeles Lakers called in 2008, Trudell brought the cross-platform digital content blueprint he had developed and executed it for the storied franchise, helping lead the team to the top digital presence in the league. As soon as he started in his new role, Trudell used the latest technology to record high-quality video and podcasts that were posted on Lakers.com, Twitter, and Facebook. He worked with the team's manager of new media to use a proprietary tracking tool that allowed them to see where most of the team's click-throughs, unique visitors, and page views were coming from. He also amassed a six-figure Twitter following for his @LakersReporter handle, larger than that of many American sports teams. He now receives thousands of responses, retweets, and questions on a con-sistent basis throughout the season. He has built up so much credibility in the digital space that he has crossed over into traditional media chan-nels. During the 2013–14 season, Trudell was the only person in the NBA reporting for the Lakers' television and radio partners, writing game re-caps and long-form features for the website, and live-tweeting every game. Trudell is covering the team across virtually every media platform.[53]

Trudell is a product of the new media generation. He opportunistically adapted to new technologies and helped sports organizations seize oppor-tunities they may not have known they had. In the process, Trudell has become a model of content creation and distribution. He is an expert in many forms of new media and understands how content should be devel-oped for different platforms and how everything works together. To borrow a baseball term, Trudell – and many other technology-savvy journalists like him – are the new five-tool players on whom the industry will rely for many years to come.

Monetizing Technologies

Longtime MLB commissioner Bud Selig claimed that he had never sent an email in his life, and he bragged that he "never will" in the future.[54] Selig's admission is surprising, because it is rare that a leader of any organization would be able to function without sending out emails. More importantly, his organization operates arguably the most successful technology ecosystem in all of the sports industry.

Major League Baseball Advanced Media (MLBAM) generated almost $700 million dollars in annual revenue for the league in 2013. The MLB At Bat app exceeded 10 million downloads, a 3.4 million year-over-year increase. These offerings enabled MLB fans to access out-of-market games on their computer and mobile devices. MLBAM's ecosystem also extends to other sports and entertainment organizations. MLBAM provided 80,000 hours of live content per year including all live digital video for ESPN and the WWE's 24-hour streaming network.[55]

One of the most important questions facing sports strategists is how to monetize new technologies. In general, there are two ways to think about this question. One is to create new products and experiences through technology. The other is to utilize technology to enhance existing revenue opportunities and partnerships. MLBAM has provided incremental growth for the league in both areas. It has created a new product and experience through the broadcasting of out-of-market games through digital channels and by becoming the digital provider for other sports organizations. It has also provided new ways for audiences to purchase items in traditional revenue categories such as tickets or merchandise. Not every sports organization will be able to achieve comparable success to that enjoyed by MLBAM. But their experience can serve as inspiration for developing your own monetization strategies for new technologies.

Creating New Opportunities

What do the NFL, NASCAR, the Wegmans LPGA Championship, and the American Hockey League have in common? They have all found a new way to monetize their content at a low cost using digital channels. These organizations have partnered with news content distributor SendToNews to develop highlight packages for news outlets to broadcast.[56] The sports organizations provide the footage from their competitions and events while SendToNews packages the content and secures the advertisers to sponsor these segments. News outlets then broadcast these prepackaged segments because they potentially attract large numbers of viewers and already include advertising dollars.

New ticketing platforms can also provide innovative ways to monetize digital assets. Monumental Sports & Entertainment (MSE) introduced a digital ticket system in the 2012 season for the Washington Capitals, Wizards, and Mystics. Instead of paper tickets, each season ticket holder received a personal digital card, similar to a credit or debit card, that contains all their seating information for the year. Season ticket holders swipe these cards to enter the venue on gamedays.[57] The digital ticketing system also enabled season ticket holders to forward tickets to other people via email without going through will call. In addition, it helped them list tickets on Ticketmaster's NHL TicketExchange (hosted by Ticketmaster's TicketsNow) and NBATickets.com Resale Marketplace, the NHL's and NBA's official secondary market, respectively.[58]

The new digital ticket system provides new ways to enhance more traditional revenue streams for MSE. First, the organization knows when and how many times a season ticket holder attends games throughout the year because people have to swipe their cards to get into the Verizon Center, where MSE teams play their games. Ensuring season ticket holders actually attend games is critical to increasing in-game revenue that includes concessions, merchandise, and parking sales. If season ticket holders are not coming to games, then MSE can create new marketing campaigns to help ensure their attendance. Second, the only way for season ticket holders to share tickets is through email using the digital ticket platform. This enabled MSE to generate new, warm sales leads for people who are interested in a team but do not have season tickets. Third, the digital ticket system steers season ticket holders to the secondary ticket market platform owned and operated by the NHL and NBA. MSE captures revenue from secondary ticket sales that more frequently occurred in other marketplaces, such as StubHub, that are now operated by these leagues.[59]

What the MLBAM, SendToNews, and MSE share is their ability to create new digital service offerings with clear ways to derive revenue. For MLBAM, revenue largely comes from the subscription services charged for out-of-market games and new ticket sales. For SendToNews, it comes from packaging content in a way that makes money for news outlets. For MSE, it uses a digital ticket platform to maximize season ticket holder attendance, generate new sales leads, and capture secondary ticket market revenue. These organizations achieve success because they identified tangible ways to monetize digital assets in a manner that makes sense for their target customers.

Strengthening Existing Partnerships Through Technology

In 2013, Verizon announced a four-year, $1 billion extension of its partnership with the NFL. This agreement will allow the company to stream every NFL regular season and playoff game via mobile phones. The agreement also demonstrates the NFL's power to command a premium price for league-wide media rights partnerships. The average $250 million per year that the league will gain is more than leagues such as the NHL make annually from their entire media rights deals – let alone just the mobile component.[60]

More importantly, this agreement shows the increasing emphasis sponsors place on using technology to monetize their corporate partnership agreements.[61] Having the ability to stream all NFL games to mobile phones is a significant differentiator between Verizon and its competitors such as AT&T, Sprint, and T-Mobile. DIRECTV, which started in 1994, has used a similar model with the NFL Sunday Ticket to attract customers to its satellite television platform. Verizon now has unique content that can directly attract new customers who are looking to make a purchasing decision about a new mobile carrier. Want to be able to take your kid to the park on a nice Sunday afternoon and still watch your local over-the-air NFL game? No problem, as long as you get your cell phone service from Verizon. The agreement provides a tangible benefit to Verizon in a way that is easy to explain to the company's key stakeholders – customers, management, employees, and the media.

This is the type of technology deal that sports organizations can pursue with sponsors. It increases revenue for the sports organization while providing a new customer offering that generates direct revenue for the sponsors. Verizon historically had a relationship with the NFL, so extending this rights agreement by capitalizing on new technology was a natural step. Clearly demonstrating to corporate partners how technology can drive new revenue, however, can add significant value to sponsors and sports organizations.

Sports strategists have often considered monetizing technology as the Holy Grail, an aspirational goal that was both expensive and extremely difficult to achieve. The examples highlighted in this section demonstrate the promising possibilities for generating revenue by investing in new technologies and monetizing current digital assets.

Conclusion

Sports audiences now expect multiplatform experiences, and sports strategists must be prepared to deliver them. In this chapter, we laid out a blueprint for how to deal with the issues of technological change and new players entering the marketplace. First, we offered a strategic model for evaluating new technologies as they relate to your business. Then, we looked at the importance of maximizing new technologies by embracing convergence and immersive content. Finally, we discussed emerging tactics to monetize new technologies.

Technology continuously evolves, and it is coming at the sports business quickly. Overall, this is a positive. It presents new ways to create innovative experiences for sports audiences and also represents new revenue opportunities (a topic we'll address at length in the following chapter). It also sets up a challenging situation in which new platforms, companies, and products are launching daily, leaving sports strategists to manage change more frequently than ever before. In many ways, technological change is the new constant and will continue to be a defining challenge and opportunity for the industry.

5 Maximizing Revenue with Analytics

Superfans and nontoxic paint often go hand in hand. No matter where in the world they play, England's national soccer team will guarantee the appearance of seemingly thousands of United Kingdom flags on faces in the crowd. Fans who sit in the Black Hole at Oakland Raiders home games paint their faces silver and black, including various skull designs, to complement their all-black costumes. If it's possible to one-up Raider Nation, Duke University's Cameron Crazies apply a thick coat of blue on their bodies, transforming themselves into a sea of intimidation and possible understudies for the Blue Man Group.

In 2010, Unione Sportiva Triestina, an Italian Serie B league soccer team, took fan paint to the next level. At its 32,000-capacity stadium,[1] Stadio Nereo Rocco, the team closed down a section of 10,000 lower-bowl seats and covered it with a vinyl tarp that had pictures of Triestina fans printed on it.[2] The team now had a stadium full of fans who would always be there to cheer silently and unconditionally.

Why would Triestina make such an out-of-the-box move? For starters, they were continuing to lose money on attendance, with no viable solutions in sight. For the better part of a decade, the team averaged close to 5,000 fans per match.[3] Despite trying all the tricks in the promotional book, their attendance woes persisted, being largely a product of location and demographics. The team plays in an isolated northeastern Italian city with a population of 200,000 people and no immediate suburbs or adjoining cities. Moreover, the city has the oldest age demographic in the country, which doesn't typically bode well for attendance at sporting events. In a stark realization, Triestina's general manager Marco Cernaz lamented, "We'd love to have a full stadium with real supporters. But the reality is that we can't."[4]

Rather than continuing to invest in vain in trying to increase attendance, Triestina saw an opportunity in enhancing other revenue streams. With about 70% of its revenue coming from television, the team reasoned that the stadium would look more exciting and full with the fan tarps, thus potentially increasing the value of its matches for viewers at home. In addition, the tarps represented advertising integration opportunities for brands interested in additional TV exposure. Combined with the savings from closing the stadium sections, which were estimated at about $130,000 per year, the potential new revenue from media rights deals and sponsorships lent credence to Triestina's seemingly bizarre fan tarp experiment.[5]

Covering empty stadium sections with fan-printed tarps is not the answer for many sports organizations. In fact, it was not the answer that could save Triestina. The team declared bankruptcy in 2012, and a new version of the club currently competes in Serie D. However, Triestina's actions were the result of asking the right questions. The team looked holistically at its revenue portfolio to determine which streams were driving the most profit versus costs. It then asked itself how it could accelerate efforts to grow the high potential profit centers. The team's management understood that living and breathing fans should trump the fake variety whenever possible. For Triestina, the best approach to try to breathe life back into its organization was to go against conventional sports business wisdom.

• • •

What approach can sports strategists use to arrive at the best possible revenue management decisions? The strategy of being all things to all people and offering your product at every audience touchpoint will be difficult to sustain, especially as the costs to compete continue to rise for many in the sports industry. Although instinct will always be something leaders trust to varying degrees, there is a benefit in rounding out decision-making processes with additional, quantitative tools, also known in industry parlance as analytics. No matter where you sit in an organization, being familiar with analytics tools and their relationship to revenue will help you gain an advantage, as the sheer volume of consumer data continues to explode as a result of the digital revolution.

This chapter explains how to distill financial and economic information to help leaders at all levels make better strategic decisions. Our goal is to arm you with the critical knowledge of how quantitative analysis can help maximize revenue for your organization. To do so, we will cover three main topics. First, we will ground our discussion in a summary of how most sports organizations make money. Second, we will provide an overview of the key analytics concepts that you need to know. Finally, we will show how these analytics tools can help sports organizations make more money.

The current economic reality in the sports industry demands that all members of an organization help it make money. Every role within a sports organization requires a combination of selling a product or service to external customers (fans, media, sponsors) and selling projects to internal customers (management, players, and other employees). Using quantitative analysis to show how a project, task, or initiative makes money and communicating that economic value to internal and external stakeholders will inevitably lead to more effective decision-making.

How Do Sports Organizations Make Money?

As the sports industry has grown, so too have the number of ways organizations make money. In fact, seemingly limitless revenue opportunities are now on the table. For example, Trabzonspor, a Turkish soccer club, sought to build a hydropower plant to serve as a source of annual revenue for the team.[6] Meanwhile, tennis player Anne Keothavong made one of the first forays into "microtising," or marketing in really small spaces, by painting an advertisement for Sony's 4K Ultra High Definition Television on each of her fingernails.[7] Without question, the industry has come a long way from the days when ticket sales were the universally dominant revenue source, as innovations in business models have expanded the marketplace significantly.

With so many money-making possibilities, it may be difficult at times to maintain strategic focus on what is important in maximizing revenue (and what is not). To help in this process, we have developed the Revenue-Generating Framework, which synthesizes the myriad revenue sources for sports organizations into specific streams. Its intent is to help sports strategists look holistically at their revenue portfolio and make effective decisions based on the performance of each stream.

There are six categories in the Revenue-Generating Framework:

- Game Day – Any revenue from the day of a competition, excluding merchandise. Ticket sales drive the biggest revenue in this category. Concessions and parking often bring in important revenue for most sports organizations as well.

- Media – Every sports organization owns the rights to its games on television, digital, radio, or any other media platform. Sports organizations either become part of a league or conference to sell their media rights collectively to networks or sell their media rights individually.

- Sponsorship – Sports organizations hold the property rights of different inventory items available for sponsorship. In naming rights deals, which are one of the most common forms of corporate partnership, a company signs with a sports organization to have its name, logo, and brand appear in a team's venue. However, sports organizations constantly look for new ways to activate sponsorships that can deliver value to their corporate partners.

- Merchandise – Licensing a sports organization's image, logo, or likeness to sell jerseys, shoes, and equipment is an increasingly important revenue stream.

- Events – Sports organizations host either events that focus on their own teams or competitions for other sports. They also use their facilities to host events not associated with competitions. Organization-focused events include season ticket holder parties, athlete appearances, and fan conventions. Non-organization-focused events include concerts, corporate conventions, and venue tours.

- Subsidies – Subsidies include any revenue not generated by a specific sports organization's individual operating activities. This includes revenue sharing that occurs when a league or conference splits money among all of its teams. It also incorporates public subsidies provided by national, state, or local governments that organizations use for everything from helping to build new professional stadiums to funding the day-to-day operations of a school athletics department. Finally, collegiate and high school teams rely on gifts by alumni, current students, and larger benefactors to help subsidize the cost of their athletic programs.

FIGURE 5.1 **Revenue-Generating Framework**

The Revenue-Generating Framework (Figure 5.1) can be useful to sports strategists in at least three ways. First, it organizes and tracks financial performance in a single model, providing a holistic view of the enterprise's revenue. Second, it enables easy analysis of which revenue streams are performing well versus those that are not and helps to clarify the potential opportunities and strategies for further growth. Finally, it can inform decision-making on organization-wide issues, of which financial implications are only one piece of the puzzle.

The Washington Redskins are a good example of how the Revenue-Generating Framework can be put into practice to aid in decision-making. Heading into the 2013 NFL offseason, the biggest question facing the Washington Redskins appeared to be the health of star quarterback Robert Griffin III's knee. That situation changed when *The Washington Post* columnist Mike Wise asked NFL commissioner Roger Goodell if it was time for the Redskins to change their name, a question that has been hovering over the team for the better part of two decades. Wise's inquiry set off a flurry of activity in both the national and local media, including *Pro Football Talk*, whose editor, Mike Florio, encouraged Griffin to publicly call for an end to the use of the name.[8]

The controversy about the term *redskins* comes from the word's derivation. Critics of the term say that *redskin* "is the most derogatory word you can use to describe a Native American."[9] According to Smithsonian Institution Indian language scholar Ives Goodard, however, the original use of *redskins* has a less controversial origin. It was a term used by the French about Native Americans living in Illinois and later used by President James Madison in a friendly discussion with tribal chiefs about ending alliances with Great Britain. Later in the 1800s, the term *redskin* started to acquire a more derogatory connation as Native Americans and white settlers increasingly battled over land ownership. By 1896, the Webster's Collegiate Dictionary stated that *redskin* was often used in a "contemptuous" manner to describe Native Americans. The term is largely considered offensive to Native Americans today.[10]

Despite the controversy, the Redskins have historically held firm on their position to not change the name, and this time around was no different.[11] The organization's stance is that the team's name is the critical part of its identity. As team owner Daniel Snyder asserts, "The team name 'Redskins' continues to hold the memories and meaning of where we came from, who we are, and who we want to be in the years to come."[12]

But what if the organization did decide to change it? One of the factors in the decision would be the financial impact. We can use the Revenue-Generating Framework to determine the answer to this question from an economic standpoint. It is difficult to envision the Redskins organization losing money in any of its revenue streams based on a name change. For starters, the team is the only provider of a product (the NFL) that is in high demand in a large market (the Washington, D.C. metropolitan area). In this environment, the team will continue to own one of the largest stadiums in professional football, which should keep its game day revenue relatively healthy, assuming large numbers of fans do not permanently boycott the team for the decision. Meanwhile, it would still receive at least an estimated $200 million in media revenues through the NFL's national television deals regardless of its name starting in the 2014 season.[13]

The Redskins could generate more revenue as a result of a name change in two channels. First, the team could sell merchandise with the new name to enhance this increasingly important revenue stream. Second, there are at least some companies that do not want to be associated with a team whose name offends the

Native American community.[14] Many media outlets will no longer use the term *Redskins* in any of their work about the team.[15] Changing the name could enable the team to target those companies that have been reluctant or unwilling to associate with the Redskins and in this way bolster sponsorship revenue. Emory University business school professors Mike Lewis and Manish Tripathi's mascot value analysis found that the team is losing $1.6 million per year because of its association with the Redskins.[16]

Does this analysis mean the Redskins should change their team name? Decisions to drive the most revenue possible should always be considered in the context of the organization's overall goals, audience expectations, and culture. However, the Revenue-Generating Framework establishes that there is seemingly little financial justification for keeping the Redskins name. The analysis shows that the team could actually make more money by changing its name.

As this example demonstrates, the Revenue-Generating Framework tracks a number of key streams through which sports organizations make money: game day, media, sponsorship, events, merchandise, and subsidies. Having this holistic understanding of the revenue portfolio can inevitably help sports strategists make better, more effective decisions. The use of analytics will also be instrumental in driving success (and revenue) for organizations going forward.

What Are Analytics?

In 2003, Michael Lewis's book *Moneyball* spent more than 20 weeks on the *New York Times*' best seller list.[17] His portrayal of Billy Beane's transformation from a can't-miss major league prospect to the numbers-driven general manager of the Oakland Athletics became a classic tome for aspiring general managers and fantasy owners alike. The book gained widespread acclaim because of Beane's innovative use of quantitative analysis to make player personnel decisions, which in many cases upended long-held scouting strategies. In perhaps the ultimate sign of success, the book was adapted into a film starring Brad Pitt in 2011.

Moneyball inspired a legion of disciples in baseball and many other sports. Drawing on analytical frameworks like sabermetrics, pioneered by Bill James in *Baseball America* as early as 1977,[18] general managers, coaches, scouts, and even fans now analyze data on everything from whether paying more for players increases the likelihood of winning a championship to whether quarterback passer ratings are accurate metrics of performance. There have also been numerous books such as *The Wages of Wins* and *Scorecasting* written by economists that challenge the conventional wisdom on predicting player and team perform-ance.[19] Currently, it is harder to think of a hotter term in the sports industry than analytics.

Despite the widespread popularity of the *Moneyball* approach, the use of quan-titative analysis has not spread as rapidly within the business operations functions of sports organizations. This is largely because analytics still suffers from an image problem. In their paper for *Analytics Magazine*, professors Benjamin Alamar and Vijay Mehrotra define sports analytics as "the management of structured historical data, the application of predictive analytic models that utilize that data, and the use of information systems to inform decision makers and enable them to help their or-ganizations in gaining a competitive advantage."[20] While this definition is technic-ally accurate, it is challenging to sift through the jargon of big data to focus on the big results. Analytics often seem reserved for data programmers and statisticians running models that spit out numbers in a language that most people do not under-stand. It's no wonder that the MIT Sloan Sports Analytics Conference, the country's most famous analytics conference, is nicknamed by some as "Dorkapolooza."[21]

While predictive and statistical models can be very complicated, the funda-mental concepts that underlie analytics are not always as complex as they appear. In the simplest of terms, analytics are tools to find, interpret, and use data to make better decisions. There are many factors involved in the decision-making process: previous experience, qualitative evidence, and industry best practices, to name just a few. Analytics is not intended to be a substitute for any of these factors; rather, it is supposed to be complementary to them. In many ways, because of its emphasis on numbers, it often adds valuable objectivity to the decision-making process.

We have identified five fundamental concepts that should help clarify how to find, interpret, and use data. Regardless of your area of expertise, basic knowledge of each of these concepts will make you a well-rounded strategist.

Concept #1: Defining Revenue

Virtually any analysis on maximizing revenue starts with this simple equation:

Revenue = Volume × Price

Every business makes money in one of two ways: either by increasing the volume of goods sold or by increasing the price of each good sold. Using the Revenue = Volume × Price model, organizations can evaluate how decisions will impact future revenue growth and which specific lever to pull (volume or price) to make more money.

Concept #2: Determining Willingness-to-Pay

Willingness-to-pay is the maximum amount of money a customer will spend for a product or service offering. It is an important concept because it helps organizations determine the appropriate pricing strategy for various revenue streams and customers, such as fans, media, and sponsors. In many cases, it is possible to raise prices as long as customers perceive they are still receiving value for a product or service offering. Figure 5.2 illustrates how this model works.

Identifying the consumers' initial willingness-to-pay for a service offering is a challenge facing most sports organizations. Many organizations use historical data or compare their prices to those of other teams and leagues. However, sports organizations should be flexible in adjusting pricing over time. This gives teams and leagues the ability to determine when to increase ticket prices. In 2014, the Chicago Bears could have found themselves in a precarious position when they raised ticket prices on at least some season ticket holders for the twelfth time in 13 years. The team now has the fifth-highest average ticket price in the NFL.[22] This increase also occurred after the team did not reach the playoffs for the sixth time in seven years.

While the announcement was met with the expected fan and media unrest, the Bears had a good reason to increase ticket prices. The reason was willingness-to-pay. Not only does the team play in the largest single NFL market that only has one team, but they also have one of the smallest stadiums in the league. Therefore, the demand for these seats has not decreased even when there have been a number of price increases. In this case, customers feel they are receiving more value than the tickets cost and thus are continually willing to pay higher prices.

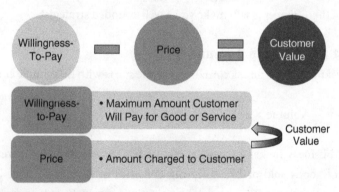

FIGURE 5.2 **Value-Generating Framework**

Concept #3: Mining Data

Because of the sheer amount of data in today's digital marketplace, data mining has become an indispensable analytics tool. Data mining is the process of examining large quantities of data to find patterns or commonalities. It helps find ever-smaller needles in increasingly larger haystacks. Data mining achieves this goal by demonstrating which attributes (or independent variables) drive certain results (or dependent variables). As a hypothetical example, data mining can be used to evaluate how game start times can have an impact on attendance. Evaluating each game over a five-year period can show that fans with children are more likely to purchase tickets to weekend games rather than games on school nights with earlier bedtimes. Based on this information, organizations could target families with weekend ticket packages as a tactic to increase ticket revenue. In this example, the independent variable (family weekend leisure time) drives the dependent variable (purchase of weekend ticket packages).

Companies are increasingly adopting the practice of data mining and using it to maximize revenue. Orbitz, an online travel agency, attracted attention for how it targeted Mac users versus PC users using data mining. Orbitz found that customers who use Mac computers spend up to 30% more per night on lodging because they are more likely to book four- and five-star hotels. In response, Orbitz prioritized more expensive results for Mac users than for PC users during their initial search.[23] While Orbitz's targeting approach was met with some criticism,[24] it was still a clear and powerful example of how data mining can be used to generate more revenue while giving customers a better user experience.

The implications of data mining in sports are wide-ranging. Through customer relationship management (CRM) software, organizations can capture detailed demographic and purchasing habits information on how fans buy products during specific promotions, time periods, or opponent visits. There are also web analytics systems that track how many unique visitors come to a site, where people are accessing a site, and how long they stay on Web pages. And through innovations in mobile technology, organizations can use location-based services to better understand fan behavior in stadiums, such as spending on concessions and merchandise. Because of the affordable cost and growing pervasiveness of digital technology, sports strategists at all levels will be able to capture significantly more data about fans, media, and sponsors. Data mining will be increasingly instrumental in analyzing this data to inform sound decision-making.

Concept #4: Analyzing Regressions

While data mining uncovers the attributes that can drive certain results, regression analysis helps quantify the potential value of these attributes. The reason regression analysis is important is that it can help sports organizations identify the amount that prices can be increased, based on willingness-to-pay.

To show how a regression analysis works, let's return to our family weekend ticket example. In this case, the data mining analysis showed that targeting fans with children with weekend ticket packages would increase revenue. But will the money we spend on marketing to this target audience increase paid attendance and deliver an efficient return? In this case, the independent variable is the amount spent on marketing to this demographic. The dependent variable is the paid attendance. We want to see how much family weekend marketing impacts paid attendance. The regression model would potentially look like this:

Paid Attendance = Impact of Family Weekend Marketing × Amount of Weekend Marketing Dollars Spent + Paid Attendance Levels If No Marketing Occurred

A sophisticated software system is not necessary to run the type of regression analysis illustrated in this example. Applications such as Microsoft Excel can work with the right dataset. If we input the above attributes into Excel and run the regression, we will see results like:

Paid Attendance = 1.5%X + 50

This means that for every dollar spent on marketing to a person with a family for weekend games, there is a 1.5% increase in the likelihood that a person with a family will attend a game. Also, 50 people will attend a game at the current prices even if zero marketing dollars are spent on this demographic.

This example demonstrates the benefit of regression analysis in helping shape the decision-making process. Quantifying the future impact of strategic initiatives can help determine how much an organization can invest in a project and what the potential return on investment will be.

Concept #5: Monetizing Audiences

All potential customers are not created equal. Some will have more impact on revenue than others. To determine this impact quantitatively, organizations can turn to our Audience Monetization Model to determine the relative value of each audience member. The goal of the Audience Monetization Model is to define different people's contributions to specific revenue streams.

Here is how the Audience Monetization Model works (see Table 5.1). An organization looks at the number of in-game attendees for a season at its venue. It then divides the total number of attendees by the amount of money it made from ticket sales, concessions, and parking (which we call Stadium Revenue). In this example, 100,000 fans attended games throughout the course of the year, generating $3 million for the organization. This means that each fan on average delivered $30 in stadium revenue. In the chart, you can see a similar analysis for the Media, Merchandise, and Sponsorship revenue streams.

Table 5.1 **Audience Monetization Model**

Revenue Analysis

Channel	Annual Revenue	Number of People	Percentage of Total Annual Revenue	Average Revenue per Audience Member	Revenue Source
Game Day Attendance	$ 30,000,000	1,000,000	30%	$30.00	Stadium
Average Annual Media Audience	$ 50,000,000	6,000,000	50%	$ 8.33	Media
Number of People Purchasing Merchandise	$ 5,000,000	50,000	5%	$10.00	Merchandise
Number of People Viewing Sponsorship Items	$ 15,000,000	5,000,000	15%	$ 3.00	Sponsorship
TOTAL	$100,000,000	12,050,000	100%	$51.33	

Audience Value

Audience Type	Stadium	Media	Merchandise	Sponsorship	Total Audience Member Value	Relative Audience Member Value
Audience Member One	Yes	No	Yes	Yes	$43.00	1.58
Audience Member Two	No	Yes	No	Yes	$11.33	0.42
Average Audience Value					$ 27.17	1.00

We then examine which audience members contribute to which revenue streams in the Audience Value section. If we find that an audience member does contribute to a revenue stream, then we put a "Yes" response in the column. Each "Yes" response is worth the value in the Average Revenue per Audience Member field. For example, a "Yes" response in the Media column is worth $8.33. We add up all of the "Yes" responses to see how much an audience member is worth in the Total Fan Value column. We find that Audience Member One is worth $43.00. However, we do not just want to see how much an audience member is worth. We also want to compare his or her relative value to that of other audience members. In this example, the average audience value is $27.17, whereas Audience Member One's value is $43.00. Therefore, Audience Member One is worth 58% more to this organization than the average audience member while Audience Member Two is worth 42% less than the average audience member with a value of $11.33.

Combining the results of the Audience Monetization Model with the Audience Engagement Ladder discussed in the "Constructing Enduring Narratives" chapter can help organizations prioritize which customers to target. In this case, an organization should focus its marketing efforts on people with similar profiles to Audience Member One if it will help ensure that they will continue or increase the money they spend with an organization. However, an organization should focus on people with Audience Member Two profiles if marketing spending has little or no impact on Audience Member One. Audience Member Two has the potential to spend more money with a sports organization if they are likely to move up the Audience Engagement Ladder. In a world of limited marketing dollars, this approach can ensure that sports organizations stay focused on the audiences that will deliver the most return on investment.

These 5 concepts – defining revenue, determining willingness-to-pay, mining data, analyzing regressions, and monetizing audiences – provide the baseline knowledge necessary for quantitative analysis in sports organizations. Now let's put these concepts into action.

How Can Sports Strategists Use Analytics to Maximize Revenue Streams?

To illustrate how sports strategists can apply analytics to maximizing revenue, we look at two specific revenue streams – game day and sponsorship. Here, we focus on highlighting key areas of opportunity.

Game Day Revenue

For sports organizations at all levels, game day revenue is primarily composed of ticket sales, luxury suite sales, concessions, and parking. Using the revenue = volume × price concept, there are two main challenges with increasing game day revenue. First, there is a finite amount of product. Regardless of the sport, each organization competes in a fixed number of games every season, which caps the number of tickets and parking spaces that can be sold. Second, the amount to charge for tickets is often difficult to determine. Even with limited amounts of product to sell, many sports organizations still do not reach maximum ticket revenue in their venues. The difficulty of selling tickets throughout the year at prices that truly reflect demand is one of the primary reasons that sports organizations do not maximize their revenue.

Traditional solutions such as hiring more ticket sales representatives, cold-calling different audiences, and offering product promotions have not had as strong of an impact today as they have had in the past, especially in light of the most recent global economic downturn.[25] There is a need for alternative solutions to maximize game day revenue. Analytics can help enhance the volume of products or services sold as well as determine the appropriate pricing strategies.

Decision Tree Modeling. One of the most common analytical frameworks used in data mining is decision tree modeling. Sports strategists may find this tool particularly useful for both completing and graphically depicting data mining analyses.

Here is a sample decision tree (Figure 5.3) that we created for a college's home games. As you can see, the tree is broken down into nodes and branches. The first node is called Home Games, as that is the attribute we are examining for this analysis. The Home Games node then divides into branches called Alumni and

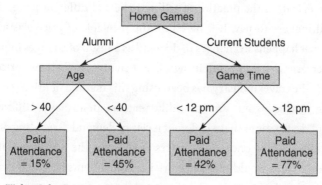

FIGURE 5.3 **Ticket Sales Decision Tree Model**

Current Students. In this example, these are the two groups that are most likely to drive paid attendance. At the Age node for alumni, we identify two age groups that drive paid attendance. Based on our hypothetical data set 15% of alumni over age 40 attend home games, while 45% of alumni under age 40 attend home games. Among current students, 77% attend home games when they occur after 12 P.M.

This decision tree uncovers key insights about value and price. First, alumni under 40 are much more likely to attend (or value) games than older alumni. Second, starting games after 12 P.M. will increase the number of students who will attend games. What is the key takeaway? This college team has a better chance of selling more tickets if it targets alumni under 40 and has games starting after 12 P.M. Making these changes maximizes the ability for an organization to sell tickets and enhances customers' willingness-to-pay for these tickets. Because the games start at times when customers are more likely to attend, the perceived value of the games increases. Completing this decision tree analysis identifies what steps the sports organization could take to increase the volume and price of tickets sold for its home games.

In this example, we looked at only two key attributes: age and game time. Certainly these are not the only attributes that could increase paid attendance. The opponent, win-loss record, weather, and marketing promotions are just a few additional possibilities. This is where data mining can deliver true value by examining thousands of data points in a short amount of time to determine the best attributes for driving revenue.

Dynamic Pricing. Data mining is not the only answer to maximizing ticket revenue. While growing the number of paid attendees (i.e., volume) is critical, the next step in driving revenue is increasing prices. In general, price increases should not be based on fixed increments over predetermined time intervals, but rather on fans' willingness-to-pay.

Dynamic Pricing is the practice of selling tickets at different prices depending on fans' willingness-to-pay. It is based on the principle of price elasticity, which examines what happens to changes in demand as a result of changes in prices. That is, when increases in prices result in significant changes in demand, prices are said to be elastic. The travel industry has been using this method of pricing for years.

In sports, seats at a game are not unlike seats on an airplane. Different games, like different destinations, have different levels of demand depending on a variety of factors. Historically, once ticket prices were set at the beginning of the year, sports organizations would make few pricing adjustments based on demand and were consequently leaving money at the turnstiles.

Now sports organizations are turning to a more agile, real-time way of selling tickets. Companies such as Qcue provide the San Francisco Giants, the San Jose Earthquakes, and other teams the ability to alter the prices of tickets for games before they are sold. The WNBA is using dynamic pricing to increase ticket sales when its biggest stars, such as Brittney Griner and Skylar Diggins, play in different cities.[26] Dynamic pricing enables organizations to price tickets in ways that more closely match demand.

GOING DUTCH FOR PURPLE PRICING

For the many advantages of dynamic pricing, there is one major drawback. Customers can pay different prices for the same seat, which brings up questions of fairness. Moreover, they do not really know all the factors that go into these pricing models. As a result, some customers inevitably delay their purchases, rolling the dice that ticket prices will decrease significantly in the days or hours before a game. We see a similar behavior in the airline industry, when customers wait until the last minute to book a flight to possibly get a cheaper rate.

Although the Northwestern University's men's basketball team had not yet made the NCAA tournament, the athletic department may have developed a new way for the team to win a ticket sales title in dynamic pricing.[27] Northwestern economics professors Jeff Ely and Sandeep Baliga worked with the school's athletic department to create Purple Pricing, named after the school's signature color.[28] Ely and Baliga collaborated with the team to create a "uniform price multi-unit Dutch Auction" for selling tickets.[29] The team sets a price for tickets that continues to decrease until tickets sell out or the auction hits a pricing level that guarantees the maximum revenue for the team. If you are a ticket-buying fan, no matter how much you agree to spend, your tickets will cost you only what everyone else is paying for the same seat.

To bring this concept to life, consider Northwestern's 2011–12 season, when it averaged fewer than 6,000 fans per game.[30] If the average ticket price were $15, Northwestern would make $90,000 per game. However, this pricing strategy might not result in the most revenue. If the team could sell 5,000 tickets at $20 per seat, then it would make $100,000. From a purely economic point of view, it would be better to sell the tickets at

CONTINUED

GOING DUTCH FOR PURPLE PRICING *CONTINUED*

$20 per seat and have fewer fans at the game, as the team would bring in $10,000 more in revenue.

In the type of auction used by Ely and Baliga, ticket prices decrease until the maximum amount of revenue can be obtained. Ticket prices start out high and decrease over time as the game gets closer. Customers buy at the level they think the ticket is worth and are refunded the difference if the price drops. For example, if Northwestern starts off selling tickets at a maximum $40 price point and sells 1,000 tickets, then the team generates $40,000. The team could then move to a $30 price point and sell 1,500 more tickets. This means the team could sell 2,500 tickets at $30 because the people who thought the tickets were worth $40 would happily pay $30 instead. The team would then generate $75,000. The team could then move to a $20 price point and sell 2,500 more tickets. This means that the team could sell 5,000 total tickets and generate $100,000. The team could finally move to a $15 price point, sell all 6,000 tickets, and generate $90,000.

In this scenario, the tickets would be sold at $20, as $100,000 is the maximum amount of money the team can make. People who were willing to pay $40 and $30 per ticket would be refunded $20 and $10, respectively, while people who only wanted to pay $15 would not be able to purchase tickets. Therefore, customers can bid on the tickets at the exact price they think the tickets are worth, and the auction guarantees that they will still receive the lowest possible price they were willing to pay.

Purple Pricing was only used for a certain block of tickets for particular games, underscoring the importance of testing and learning with dynamic pricing strategies.[31] According to deputy director of athletics Mike Polisky, Northwestern increased its revenues by hundreds of thousands of dollars in the games for which it used Purple Pricing.[32] Not only does the uniform price multi-unit Dutch auction elegantly address the most critical problems that are usually associated with dynamic ticket pricing, but it also can still achieve similar results at a lower cost than other dynamic ticket-pricing models and technologies can. While it is too early to call Northwestern's basketball team champions, it is safe to say that Ely and Baliga have put the team in the NCAA tournament of dynamic ticket pricing.

Outsourcing Ticket Sales. The practices of data mining and dynamic pricing will be instrumental for organizations looking to increase game day revenue going forward. Like many other new business services, sports strategists will have to decide whether to build this analytics-based capability in-house or look for outsourcing options. Increasingly, sports organizations at all levels are moving toward the latter and working with firms that specialize in maximizing attendance and revenue. On the collegiate level, schools such as the University of Tennessee, Duke University, Georgetown University, Georgia Tech University, the University of Texas–San Antonio, and Western Michigan University have outsourced their ticket sales operations to companies such as the Aspire Group, IMG Ticketing Group, and Monumental Sports & Entertainment.[33]

Ticketing companies are founded on the importance of quantitative analytics. For example, they use the ideas behind the Audience Monetization Model to target customers who are most likely to purchase tickets to games but have not been contacted before by sports organizations (or, in other cases, have not been contacted effectively). Ticket firms can accomplish this goal because of the vast amount of proprietary data they have collected. In addition, they use professional sales representatives whose primary job is to contact these customers. The combination of data and manpower provides sports organizations with the opportunity to maximize ticket sales revenue in ways they could not accomplish on their own.

One of the other benefits of outsourcing ticket sales is that it can help decrease sports organizations' reliance on season tickets. For years, the prevailing wisdom has been to convert as many fans into season ticket holders as possible. Season tickets guarantee revenue at the beginning of the year regardless of the team's performance. Teams and leagues focus on converting as many fans as possible into season ticket holders, but this may no longer be the best approach to generating more revenue. With the demand for tickets varying game by game, season tickets lock organizations into a fixed amount of revenue, with no ability to adjust prices and account for changes in demand. Having more tickets available for individual purchase provides sports organizations with the flexibility to use the dynamic ticket-pricing models.

By outsourcing ticket sales to the new professional firms, sports organizations can mitigate much of the risk that is associated with having individual game tickets. Because these companies have full-time ticket representatives, they are more likely to be able to respond to changes in ticket demand on a real-time basis. Therefore, these firms can more quickly take advantage of opportunities to sell tickets when games are in high demand. As Aspire general manager Bill Fagan says, "[Schools] don't have the core competency or the expertise to build [in-house operations], and many schools can't pay commissions to their sales consultants because of university rules. They don't have the flexibility and the nimbleness to hire and fire quite like we can in the private sector."[34] In addition, these companies can more efficiently target fans who are likely to buy tickets when demand for certain games is lower.

While the benefits of outsourcing are numerous, there can be reasons not to use this approach. Having ticket sales groups in-house can give your organization more control and accountability over the day-to-day selling strategy. For example, Florida State University (FSU) has recently experienced success in ticket sales and renewals without outsourcing its operations.[35] The school uses this approach because of the cultural advantages of keeping ticketing in-house. According to FSU Assistant Athletics Director for Ticket Sales and Operations Ben Zierden, "We didn't want a team in a war room not involved with our own operational process. We still have that element of control. [The sales staffers] are right there in the office. They're part of our daily meetings."[36] As a sports strategist who may be faced with an outsourcing decision, your best option is to factor in the organization's culture when examining the trade-offs of each approach.

Decision tree modeling and dynamic pricing demonstrate how sports organizations can use new analytical methods to maximize game day revenue. Implementing new quantitatively based frameworks can also help sports strategists enhance other revenue streams. Sponsorship revenue is one area that can significantly benefit by utilizing this approach.

Sponsorship Revenue

The Emirates Group became one of the first companies to integrate performance-based clauses into its sponsorship agreement with the English Premier League team Arsenal. Emirates and Arsenal agreed to a five-year contract that pays the Premier League team £30 million ($48.7 million) in annual fees for a corporate partnership that includes the placement of its name and logo on the club's uniform. While Arsenal has qualified for the Union of European Football Associations (UEFA) Champions League every season for the previous 8 years, it has not won a Premier League, FA Cup, and UEFA Champions League title during this period. If the team fails to qualify for the Champions League or does not perform well in the Premier League, Emirates senior vice president Boutros Boutros said, "there are certain clauses, from 2015, that we pay them a percentage less if they don't perform. It's fair to us and fair to them."[37]

This does seem fair. Sports organizations should be held accountable for their performance with regards to sponsorship agreements. The question is: What is the definition of performance? More specifically, does competitive performance always translate to a successful sponsorship? The fairness component of the Emirates-Arsenal deal appears to focus more on the quantity of impressions. If Arsenal does not qualify for the Champions League then the team will not be able to broadcast its jersey sponsorship to the hundreds of millions of fans who watch the tournament each year. This will decrease the overall number of impressions.

However, this type of analysis does not examine the quality of the impressions. We define quality as the degree to which an organization can help its corporate sponsorships increase partner revenue or meet other corporate partnership goals that do not have a monetary component (e.g., increasing community engagement). Most of the impressions from a jersey or apparel sponsorship go toward increasing brand awareness. Audiences that see a company's logo or brand are more likely to purchase a product or service offering in the future. While these impressions are important, they are not as valuable as sponsorship activation elements that will directly help corporate partners to acquire new customers or retain current customers. Sponsors are increasingly recognizing that all types of impressions are not created equal. They want to see how sponsorships can help generate profitable revenue growth or help further their organization's business goals. Solely generating a large number of impressions should no longer be the standard used to evaluate partnership value.

Today, corporate partnerships must deliver tangible return on investment (ROI), and it is the responsibility of sports organizations to successfully communicate this value to their audiences. Sponsorship can be used to help corporate partners increase revenue while enhancing audiences' overall experience. Sports strategists can achieve these sponsorship goals with an analytics-based approach.

Expanding Sponsorship Inventory. On the surface, it may seem like everything in sports that can possibly be sponsored is already sponsored. Corporate logos are on the field of play in many sports, while jerseys increasingly include sponsor names or logos. Even the backs of some boxers are temporarily tattooed with company logos during fights.[38]

Even though sports teams and companies have identified many different sponsorship opportunities, new corporate partnership activation possibilities still exist, but not always in the most obvious places. One of the most lucrative opportunities that sports organizations can offer is providing access to and facilitating communication between corporate partners. Sports organizations have often built relationships with senior managers who make significant purchasing decisions for their companies. However, most organizations have not utilized this network as a way to help their partners generate money, even though numerous partners have said this is a primary reason that they sponsor teams. According to consulting firm IEG, 51% of companies use their sponsorship spending to enhance their business-to-business communication.[39]

Developing partnership networks for corporate sponsors accomplishes critical goals for sports organizations. First, it creates business-to-business revenue-generating opportunities that exist only because the corporate partner has a relationship with the sports organization. For example, an Information Technology (IT) partner could directly contact the purchasing decision maker for a Quick Service Restaurant (QSR) partner about acquiring a new point-of sale system because of their shared relationship with a team. Second, the value-added service offering provides an ROI that corporate sponsors can easily communicate to the company's management, shareholders, and employees.

Another opportunity that expands sponsorship inventory is the development of engagement marketing campaigns. These campaigns create an environment for customers and clients that influences the creation of positive brand associations and increases the likelihood of purchasing products or services.[40] For example, Under Armour signed an apparel agreement with Tough Mudder, a series of competitions using British Special Forces–designed 10- to 12-mile obstacle courses, in large part because many runners already used Under Armour products during the competitions.[41] The races themselves became one of the most effective ways for Under Armour's customers to engage with the brand. Putting the product into play is a unique way that sponsors can directly target fans and open up new revenue-generating opportunities for the sports organization and corporate partners alike.

These examples show new ways that sports organizations can expand and enhance the sponsorship inventory available for corporate partners. However, corporate partners are frequently unwilling to pay for sponsorship opportunities without clearly understanding the value they are receiving.

Quantifying ROI of Corporate Partnerships. Creating an effective approach to quantifying the value of these partnerships has been difficult. Despite the fact that sports teams and leagues generate millions of dollars annually from sponsorship revenue, few organizations have a reliable estimate on the ROI they generate for corporate partners.

It is not for a lack of effort. Nielsen, Repucom, Quantcast, and other measurement firms provide ratings information to sports organizations that shows how many people consume a team or league's content in both traditional and digital media channels. Meanwhile, companies such as IEG and Joyce Julius have developed their own proprietary methodologies for sponsorship valuations. All of these options have served as important tools for helping sports organizations attempt to determine ROI for their corporate partners.

Despite this progress, challenges still remain in valuing and reporting on sponsorship ROI. Chief among them is the industry's use of a traditional cost per thousand impressions (CPM) model, which has been the dominant yardstick in the media and entertainment industries for decades. Media and entertainment companies have devised different rates that advertisers pay for different channels, programs, and time periods. For years, television programming has generally commanded the highest CPM rates, because it has been the medium that can aggregate the largest audiences, and particularly those demographics most appealing to advertisers. While digital channels can often surpass television programs in the number of people who engage with a brand (based on the number of unique visitors), television programs still command higher CPM rates because customer conversion rates are higher for television than for digital channels.[42]

In general, CPM methodology is not optimal for sports organizations. Outside of major professional sports teams and events such as the Super Bowl, many sports organizations cannot generate the number of impressions that are appealing to corporate partners. At the same time, sports organizations often have direct access to lucrative customers[43] that cannot be easily targeted in other non-sports channels. For example, many sports fans tend to be 18- to 34-year-old men – a notoriously hard demographic for companies to target using traditional advertising.[44] For what sports products may lack in audience scale at times, they can more than make up for in their audiences' demographic profiles.

To this end, there is an opportunity for sports organizations, particularly at the high school and college levels, to demonstrate that the quality of impressions can be more important than the quantity (Figure 5.4). By showing how targeted

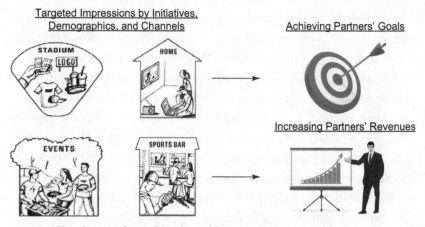

FIGURE 5.4 **How Sponsorship Delivers Tangible ROI to Corporate Partners**
Figure credits: Left: Olga Rogachevskaya; Right, top: Sashkin/Shutterstock; Right, bottom: Nuttapong/Shutterstock.

impressions reach the demographics that sponsors covet, sports strategists add critical texture to what companies are receiving from their investment – direct access to the audience they desire to reach.

HARTFORD VALUES SPONSORSHIPS

Like many schools, the University of Hartford faces off with a big competitor in its backyard. Hartford, a private institution with about 7,500 students, relies primarily on its men's and women's basketball programs to generate in-stadium revenue for the athletic department, which fields 14 sports in the America East Conference. The school's basketball program competes in Hartford, the same city with the highly ranked University of Connecticut men's and women's basketball teams. The Hartford Hawks basketball teams play on campus at the 4,000-seat Chase Arena at the Reich Family Pavilion.[45] In contrast, the University of Connecticut teams play much of their home schedules in the sleek 16,294-seat XL Center in downtown Hartford.[46]

At first glance, it seems unlikely that Hartford could compete head to head with a school like Connecticut, which has one of the most successful combinations of men's and women's basketball programs in the country. In response to this challenge, Hartford has found ways to use Connecticut's "dominance" to its advantage in its pricing, promotion, and sponsorship strategies. According to Brian Gerrity, the school's former assistant athletic director for external relations, Hartford realized it was able to attract smaller corporate sponsors that would be unlikely to partner with the University of Connecticut. To do this, the university developed ongoing relationships with companies, rather than just viewing them as a means to reach new revenue targets. Hartford incorporates its sponsors directly into the decision-making process for event planning and product promotions, encouraging companies to develop deeper ties with the university. In addition, smaller schools like Hartford are often more flexible with the written terms of their sponsorship agreements, allowing them to meet corporate partners' needs throughout the course of the academic year.[47]

To communicate the value delivered to sponsors, Hartford followed the approach outlined in this chapter. The school created a website that

showcased different inventory items and clearly articulated the value corporate partners would receive from sponsorships with the school's athletic department. In addition, Hartford created a portal where sponsors
could see how impressions for specific activation elements created new revenue opportunities and achieved companies' marketing goals on a daily,
weekly, monthly, and annual basis. Hartford discovered that it was helping
partners in the financial services, quick-serve restaurant, and medical services industries achieve an ROI of at least 25% on their sponsorship. This
approach and focus enabled Hartford to grow sponsorship revenue even
while Connecticut is competing in the same space.[48]

Many sports organizations are facing situations similar to that of the University of Hartford. The Hawks were successful because of their ability to customize sponsorship packages and substantially differentiate themselves from the
University of Connecticut. These branded offerings provide potential sponsors
with clear alternatives when making decisions about spending their sponsorship
dollars. Moreover, the use of analytics to communicate the value of sponsorships
to corporate sponsors can be an influential tool in generating new revenue in a
competitive market.

Conclusion

Founding director of the University of South Florida's sport and entertainment
business management MBA program Bill Sutton identified "analytics-savvy,"
"intellectually curious," and "great communicators" as important common characteristics for "under-40 managerial talent" in the sports industry.[49] Regardless
of your specialization, understanding and using quantitative tools to inform
decision-making is increasingly becoming an important part of what it takes to
be a successful sports strategist. Moreover, communicating the ideas that result
from analytical insights is arguably as important as discovering what factors can
grow revenue for an organization.

In this chapter, we reviewed the Revenue-Generating Framework, which includes the six key revenue streams through which sports organizations generate
most of their income: game day, media, sponsorship, event, merchandise, and
subsidies. We also examined the five key analytic concepts on which most analytics

in sports business are based: defining revenue, determining willingness-to-pay, mining data, analyzing regressions, and monetizing audiences. Finally, we applied these concepts to two key revenue streams – game day and sponsorship – to demonstrate how analytics can maximize revenue.

Analytics and quantitative approaches will not solve every problem that sports organizations have in generating more revenue. More traditional methods, such as focus group analysis and audience surveys, can add significant value to the decision-making process. In addition, prioritizing revenue is not always in the best interest of a sports organization. Financial considerations have to be evaluated alongside other strategic priorities.

There is no question, however, that analytics will play an important role on the business side of the sports industry in the foreseeable future. Sports strategists at the high school, collegiate, and professional levels will benefit from knowing how analytics work and how to include quantitative frameworks as part of their decision-making process. Using this approach will help sports strategists not only generate more money for their organizations but also make better decisions.

6 | Developing Public Support

In May of 2012, FIFA announced that the official slogan of the 2014 World Cup in Brazil would be "All in one rhythm."[1] The slogan seemed like an inspired choice for the South American soccer power. Brazilian soccer is famous for a style of play in which dribbles, passes, and shots seem in sync with the sounds of the drumbeats that permeate its hallowed stadiums. Off the field, the slogan encapsulated the "five pillars representing Brazil: cohesive society, power of innovation, striking nature, living football and land of happiness."[2]

The pillars holding up the "All in one rhythm" slogan began to collapse during the 2013 Confederations Cup. This global soccer tournament is considered a test run for a country hosting the World Cup the following year. The initial outcry stemmed from a nine-cent price increase in São Paulo bus fares to help pay for the costs of hosting major sport events. More than $13 billion of public money was being spent to finance construction of 12 new stadiums for the World Cup and the 2016 Olympics.[3] Nine cents may seem like a small amount of money, but the Brazilian minimum wage is only $1.60 per hour. The price increase cost many workers as much as 20% of their weekly income.[4]

The land of happiness exploded in anger, with more than 1 million people filling the streets of Rio de Janeiro, Brasilia, and São Paulo.[5] Throughout the tournament, protestors clashed with police while demanding that public funds go to "hospitals and schools in FIFA standards [sic]."[6] The situation became so volatile that investigative reporter Andrew Jennings advised, "You won't want to wear a FIFA blazer in Brazil. You'll get knocked down."[7] The Brazilian public largely appeared to agree with the demonstrators. President Dilma Rousseff's approval rating dropped from 57% to 30% during the final weekend of the Confederations Cup.[8] Rousseff was transformed from one of the "most popular democratically elected leaders in the world" to a politician who was struggling for reelection in large part because of the protests.[9] Even some of Brazil's most famous current and former soccer players, such as Hulk, David Luiz, and Ronaldo, expressed support for the protestors, even though the demonstrators were rallying against the government's spending on events for their national team.[10]

Despite the protests, FIFA president Sepp Blatter called the Confederations Cup a success and said that he was happy that the "social unrest is now resting."[11] Blatter was in a difficult position. FIFA could not even hint at the possibility of moving the World Cup from Brazil because of the protests without setting off a major crisis for his organization. FIFA could also take comfort in the fact that similar protests in China and Russia prior to the Olympics did not significantly interrupt those events. However, the structural issues facing Brazil could not recede prior to the World Cup.[12] Brazilians may love their futebol team, but they do not love how much money their government is spending to foot the bill for the World Cup and the Olympics.

. . .

Both the World Cup and the Olympics were intended to signal the arrival of Brazil as a global powerhouse on the world stage, much like China capitalized on the 2008 Beijing Olympics. After decades of political corruption and economic malaise, Brazil experienced an economic boom in the 2000s that helped the country achieve record low unemployment rates and high foreign capital investment.[13] To the country's leaders, the World Cup and the Olympics might seem like the perfect stage to showcase the new Brazil. While these global spectacles may still serve as the country's coming-out party, the Confederations Cup protests demonstrated that public support, even in a country as passionate about soccer as Brazil, has its limits.

The situation in Brazil is not an isolated incident. Citizens all over the world are increasingly expressing frustration with the public funding of private sports organizations.[14] In 2013, Zurich voters rejected a referendum on the building of a new $237 million football stadium for the second time since 2008. It was the second sports referendum to be rejected by voters in the same year.[15] Over the past decade, many academics, reporters, and politicians have compiled evidence showing that the perceived benefits of sports organizations do not usually make up for the costs.[16] After completing an evaluation of all academic research on the impact of public financing of new venues on local communities, University of Maryland, Baltimore County economics professor Dennis Coates found that there is "little evidence of large increases in income or employment associated with the introduction of professional sports or the construction of new stadiums."[17] Smith College economist Andrew Zimbalist has asserted that there is overwhelming evidence that sports organizations are at least partially culpable for the financial problems facing their country, state, city, or town.[18]

While communities are growing weary of their governments' sports investments, sports organizations have come to depend heavily on the monetary, legal, and social support of public institutions. Many either cannot afford or are unwilling to finance major expenditures such as building new venues on their own. For example, Dolphins owner Stephen Ross donated $200 million to the University of Michigan at the same time that his team was asking for $350 million in public financing to improve Sun Life Stadium, its home venue.[19] Without subsidies from governments, charitable organizations, and nongovernmental organizations (NGOs), many sports organizations would be forced to lower their expectations for future growth or shut their doors completely.

In this increasingly confrontational environment, sports strategists have an opportunity to propose mutually beneficial solutions for communities and sports organizations alike. We begin by looking at the relationships between sports organizations and the towns, cities, counties, states, and countries that they call home. We will then analyze the issues that have led to the current decline in public support, including the economic and political impact of failed venues and government budget deficits resulting from sports spending. We will also focus on the ways that sports strategists can form better partnerships with public institutions, allowing the public to more easily share in the upside of sports investments while also reducing the risk of future losses of public money. In the final portion of the chapter, we will explore specific steps that can help sports strategists proactively take control of the public support issue and reduce the need for public funding in innovative ways.

State-Sponsored Sports

The relationship between sports organizations and the towns, cities, states, and countries where they compete has historically been so strong that the identity of these areas is largely intertwined with that of their local sports teams or athletes. It is common for a driver to be welcomed to a town or city with signs that display the population and the last time a local sports team won a championship. As the author and critic Scott Raab observes, "Fans see their teams as quasi-public utilities and the players as hometown heroes. . . . Cleveland fans love the city [but] cherish the teams more deeply."[20]

The relationship that these places have with sports has generally been a boon to sports organizations. Most sports organizations at all levels have used public funds to help offset the costs of operating a sports organization, especially when these organizations lose money. Good examples of publicly subsidized sports organizations are Division I college athletic departments. According to the NCAA, the median Football Bowl Subdivision (FBS) school's athletic program lost $12.3 million, the median Football Championship Subdivision (FCS) school lost $10.2 million, and the median Division I school without football lost $9.8 million in 2012.[21] The majority of these athletic programs would struggle if they did not receive public subsidies.

Public support of sports organizations goes beyond financial backing of government or university institutions. Numerous sports organizations have also lobbied for and received legal exemptions that have spawned anticompetitive policies that do not exist in other industries. These exemptions have enabled leagues to create salary caps, restrict player movement, prevent competition, and set licensing standards. Since 1922, MLB has operated with the benefit of an antitrust exemption that enables the league to take steps to determine the expansion, relocation, and contraction of franchises. In addition, the league instituted a draft that forces players to sign with certain teams for a certain period of time while preventing player free agency until 1972. This level of autonomy is not afforded most other large corporations of the same size and impact.

However, the once-seemingly limitless amount of public support for sports organizations appears to be dwindling. Many politicians, community groups, and media members have questioned why governments should commit public resources to sports organizations. Public support has transformed into a public conflict over the role of sports organizations in communities.

The End of the Affair

In 2012, the Kansas City Royals were accused of taking from the poor to give to the rich. A local sports radio host summed up his criticism of the team's use of public financing when he lamented, "The Royals have received at least $12.7 million from taxpayers. . . . By using the money for payroll taxes, the team literally collected taxpayer money to pay their own taxes."[22] According to a report by 810 WHB radio in Kansas City, the Royals originally started receiving public funds in 2006 under the premise of improving Kauffman Stadium, particularly in preparation for the 2012 All-Star Game. By 2012, the team had only used 9% of the funds it had received on the intended stadium improvements; the rest of the money had gone to pay for salaries, telephones, and, yes, taxes.

The Royals did nothing illegal in this situation. The team's agreement with Jackson County requires "reasonable written approval"[23] by the Sports Complex Authority, which the team had secured before distributing its funds. But this did little to soften the public's outcry over the team's reversal and subsequent use of the public's money.

The Royals' alleged usage of funds is an example of the type of action that ignites controversy over public financing of sports venues. Sports organizations and government officials often promise that these investments will stimulate economic growth. Not only does this direct economic growth occur infrequently, but sports organizations are often accused of going out of their way to maximize their own self-interest.

Overpromising and Underdelivering

Most sports teams and leagues simply do not have direct access to the amount of money necessary to finance large construction projects. When businesses make these types of capital expenditures, they generally have two options: equity or debt financing. In equity financing, investors (either people or organizations) exchange money for some form of ownership stake in a company. Many companies raise equity financing by issuing new shares of stock. Debt financing, on the other hand, occurs when a company receives money and has to pay back the principal with interest to a loan originator. This most commonly occurs when a bank loans money to a person or organization.

Many sports organizations prefer debt financing because it can be less expensive (or has a lower cost of capital) than equity financing. Organizations can reap the benefits of the new capital through investments in infrastructure, people, and technology without providing new ownership stakes or generating returns for individuals or entities. In addition, the organization's owners keep any excess returns or profits above and beyond the interest required to pay the debt and do not have to share them with new stockholders.

Because these large-scale projects are so expensive, however, most lenders consider them to be very risky investments. To compensate for this risk, lenders will charge sports organizations high interest rates. As a result, both debt and equity financing can become expensive for sports organizations, to the point where they cannot afford to make renovations or build new venues through these means alone.

Given these financing challenges, it is not surprising that the option of public financing of venues has become so popular for sports organizations. Instead of sports organizations taking on debt, the governments of towns, cities, states, or countries issue new debt. Governments are seen as far less risky to lenders and potential bondholders than are sports organizations because they have more assets on their balance sheets, greater access to revenues through taxes, more collateral to offer lenders, and a longer track record of making debt payments. Therefore, they can issue or accumulate debt at much lower interest rates than sports organizations. In addition, municipal debt is often provided as a tax-free investment opportunity for bondholders. Local governments can also increase taxes, generally through a tax on entertainment and leisure activities, and use this money for the new construction or renovation of sports facilities.

Public entities that finance these large-scale infrastructure projects expect significant short-term and long-term economic benefits. While the venue is being built, local residents see an infusion of new high-paying jobs, particularly in the construction industry. In the long-term, commercial and residential development in the form of new businesses, shopping centers, and/or condominiums around or near the new venue can create new jobs while also increasing tax revenues for governments.

These economic multipliers (in which one dollar of loans can generate numerous dollars in new revenue) drove the explosion of new venue construction over the last 25 years. From 1990 to 2010, at least 260 venues were opened in the United States that used public/private partnership as a primary source of financing.[24] Two-thirds of the teams in the NFL, NBA, MLB, NHL, and MLS played in venues built or significantly renovated during this period. According to the Center for

Public Policy and Administration at the University of Utah, the two main reasons that local governments were willing to spend millions of dollars on these venues were because they were afraid to lose these economic benefits and "owners [could] credibly threaten moving to another city, presumably one willing to publicly finance a stadium."[25]

Some of these projects did achieve the anticipated success for both the sports organization and the local community. For example, the city of San Diego provided $143.8 million of the estimated $294.1 million cost necessary to build Petco Park for the San Diego Padres, in addition to $60 million of infrastructure development for land near the stadium in the Gaslamp Quarter. The building of Petco Park spurred a flurry of new private construction activity that included $593.3 million in hotel, residential, retail, and parking structures near the venue. Property values also increased by over 400% in the area around the stadium.[26] Petco Park did achieve the dual goal of creating a modern venue for the Padres and opening up new economic opportunities in a neglected part of San Diego.

Petco Park is an example of the exception, rather the rule, for publicly financed sports spending. Many studies have shown that facility spending does not spur the expected economic benefits.[27] In fact, stadium-financing agreements tend to have the opposite effect by actually leaving cities in a worse economic situation than before they built these venues or hosted sporting events. The 1976 Montreal Olympics were supposed to cost the city an estimated $300 million.[28] Instead, to finance the games, Montreal incurred $1.5 billion in debt that was not paid off until 2006 – 30 years after the Olympics occurred.[29] Montreal is not the only city that was paying down its debt long after receiving any benefits from a venue. King County in Washington, for example, owed $80 million in payments for the Kingdome in 2010, even though the Seattle Seahawks and Mariners stopped using the facility in 2000.[30] King County was not expected to make its final payments on the venue until 2015.

To complicate matters further, the commercial and residential development that is supposed to occur around venues has often not materialized as planned. In Hamilton County, Ohio, the local government financed an estimated $540 million in debt for the construction of new stadiums for the Cincinnati Bengals and Reds. These stadiums were supposed to serve as anchors for commercial business and real estate growth by spurring new construction for the city's rundown riverfront.[31] Instead, building these stadiums ended up requiring millions of more tax dollars and county resources while returning few economic benefits. Debt payments for the stadiums account for 16.4% of the entire budget for Hamilton

County. Additionally, the deal has largely been blamed for cuts to both education and school services. According to Stanford University economics professor Roger Noll, "The Cincinnati deal combined taking on a gargantuan responsibility with setting new records for optimistic forecasting. It takes both to put you in a deep hole, and that's a pretty deep hole."[32]

Because of the failure of venue construction to consistently spur economic development, the threat of a team moving to a new location is no longer as persuasive as it once was. While Petco Park largely delivered the expected value to the city, the San Diego Chargers are struggling to secure public financing for a new stadium. Even though team president and CEO Dean Spanos has stated that the team will remain in San Diego,[33] it has been widely reported that the Chargers will move to Los Angeles if the local government does not help pay for a new venue.[34] In the past, the threat of a team leaving a city or state would usually be sufficient to induce government officials to scramble to provide public financing. The responses of San Diego officials to the Chargers' threats have clarified the new reality of the current economic environment: publicly financing sports venues has become a lower priority for governments facing massive budget deficits.

Battling Budget Deficits

Many local governments in the United States faced large budget deficits after the global economic downturn of 2008. Unlike the federal government, many local governments are required by law to balance their budgets. As a result, these governments are often forced to make severe cuts that could include reducing the number and salaries of teachers, firefighters, and police officers. When reductions in these essential services occur, nonessential funding takes a significant cut as well.[35]

Athletic programs are one of the first items that state and local governments scale back or eliminate. Alabama community colleges shuttered nearly all their athletic departments after a $3.3 million reduction in state funding.[36] The Duval County School Board in Florida eliminated several high school sports in an effort to reduce a $97 million shortfall for the 2011–12 academic year.[37] Prior to its decision to join the Big Ten Conference, the University of Maryland cut seven programs, including the men's and women's swimming and diving teams.[38] Athletic departments at all levels are facing the real prospect of being downsized or even elimination as governments struggle to keep their communities financially afloat.

Some schools can rely on outside sources to close the financial gap for their athletic departments. Colleges and universities now often charge increasingly high fees to subsidize athletics. Students were assessed over $795 million in fees to support Division I athletic programs at public schools during the 2008–09 academic year.[39] Rutgers University and the University of Washington charge every student $1,000 to support their athletic departments.[40] Pay-to-play fees have become much more common at the high school level as well. In Connecticut, 44 out of 116 school districts charge their students up to $1,450 to participate in each sport.[41]

In response to these escalating costs, NFL linebacker and Saginaw High School alumnus LaMarr Woodley decided to donate $60,000 to cover all high school participation fees at his old school in Michigan. Woodley said he did not want "kids to lose out on an opportunity to maybe earn a scholarship or learn about playing team ball. . . . To miss out on that because your family can't afford $75 was going to be tough."[42] But not every athletic department has an NFL star to cover its operating costs, and schools now need new ways to support their athletic departments.

Uncovering Cost Centers

In 2013, 41 of the 50 highest-paid state employees in the United States were college coaches: 27 football coaches, 13 basketball coaches, and one hockey coach.[43] Coaches' salaries far surpass those of other government employees. For example, University of Iowa head football coach Kirk Ferentz made 28 times more than Iowa's governor.[44] When identifying a scapegoat for the rising cost of college athletics programs, one could easily point a finger at college coaches. Coaches' compensation, however, is only partially responsible for the rising costs of NCAA Division I schools. While total expenses for these programs increased by an average of 13.13% from 2010 to 2012, coaches' compensation as a percentage of operating expenses actually decreased by an average of 0.43% during the same time period.

Rather than being the sole cause of the increase, coaches' compensation is another example of the monetary increase in many standard areas of running Division I programs. The 2013 *NCAA Revenues/Expenses Division I Report* shows that "coaches' compensation," "administrative compensation," "facilities maintenance and administrative support," and "participation and game expenses" have largely remained constant or increased slightly as a percentage of operating expenses. Yet, total costs for college athletic programs have increased by a significant margin. This means that schools are spending more money on each of these areas on an annual basis, not just on coaches' salaries.[45]

We highlight Division I schools in this section because these programs face many of the challenges that have given rise to the public support conflict. Many sports strategists work for organizations for which revenues cannot keep up with rising costs. Short of discovering a game-changing revenue stream, the only way to deal with these deficits is to receive some form of public subsidy. For colleges and high schools, this primarily means that government entities need to provide at least some funding. At the same time that schools have become increasingly reliant on subsidies, governments are reducing the funding they provide for sports programs. Given these types of challenges, sports strategists will need to develop solutions that demonstrate why the public should continue to support sports organizations.

Supporting the Public

There are two key ways in which sports strategists can maximize public support for their organization. The first is to identify and create opportunities for mutually beneficial partnerships between the public and sports organizations. The second is to take proactive steps to engage with government officials, community leaders, foundations, and charities in ways that ensure that public resources flow to sports organizations.

Creating opportunities for communities to directly benefit from sports investments is critical. Governments have largely been dependent on more volatile income sources, such as increases in tourism, real estate development, and taxes, to recoup investments in sports organizations. Rather than promising traditional forms of economic impact that have a history of underperforming, sports strategists have the opportunity to demonstrate how their organizations can provide more tangible returns on investments. This strategy includes:

- Sharing Means Caring – Sports organizations can create new opportunities for individuals in the community to reap the benefits of public investments.
- Doing Well by Doing Good – Sports organizations can provide unique sponsorship and marketing opportunities that help governments and NGOs bring increased awareness to public policy issues.
- Identity Marketing – Sports organizations can help build the identity of the countries, cities, and towns in which they operate.

We start by examining ways to demonstrate the tangible benefits provided to communities that maintain or increase public support.

Sharing Means Caring

One of the fundamental challenges of taxpayer support of sports organizations is that the public does not receive most of the benefits of these investments. Sports organizations are often the ones who profit the most, by selling more tickets, increasing the number of luxury boxes available, and generating more parking revenue. As a tactic to increase public support and give the public more access to the upside to their investments, sports strategists can explore new investment opportunities in both equities and bonds. Not only can these investments foster a stronger audience connection with the team, but they can also help supply the financial backing that many organizations so sorely need.

First, we will examine how issuing equity can achieve this goal by looking at Manchester United's initial public offering (IPO). After exploring the possibility of listing its stock in Singapore, the English soccer club Manchester United offered 10% of its equity to public shareholders on the New York Stock Exchange (NYSE).[46] Why did Manchester United take this approach? As mentioned earlier in this chapter, issuing equity is typically a more expensive form of raising money than taking on new debt.

Taking a closer look at Manchester United's IPO, however, demonstrates that sports teams do not always operate like traditional companies. Sports teams can raise money through stock sales with terms that are very advantageous to the organization. There is demand for sports teams from at least some investors, regardless of the terms of buying the stock. For example, Manchester United's $100 million IPO[47] was structured so that the incumbent owners, the Glazer family, "will personally keep one-half of the capital raised, will retain complete control of the team and won't be beholden to shareholders."[48]

Even given the favorable terms for the Glazers, Manchester United's stock sale did open the door for a wider range of people to become owners in the club. When a company increases its profits, then shareholders' stock will often increase in value. The shareholder can also receive a dividend in return. When the team does well financially, all equity holders – not just management or employees – benefit. If the team does not do well, equity holders can trade the stock just like they would for any other company on the NYSE. Manchester United's IPO provides its fans with the opportunity to take real advantage of the economic upside of the team's performance on and off the pitch.

The rewards for sports audiences owning equity can be intangible. The NFL's Green Bay Packers have taken an even more organization-friendly approach with their stock than have Manchester United. Since 1923, the Packers have issued more than 5 million shares of stock in their club.[49] Shareholders do receive some tangible benefits by buying stock. For example, the money raised in 2012 was used to build more seats and renovate the stadium, which reduced the 96,000-person waitlist for tickets.

However, having the opportunity to buy tickets to the game is not usually the return that investors are looking for in a stock. Packers shareholders receive no dividends and cannot resell the stock "except back to the team for a fraction of the original price."[50] Even with the current terms of the most recent equity offering, "Green Bay Packers stock is still selling like hotcakes."[51] What the Packers shareholders do receive is the ability to solidify their emotional connection with the team. All Packers shareholders can take credit every time that the team they own does well on or off the field. Developing this emotional, rather than functional, connection further builds the relationship between the fans and the Packers while helping to enhance the identity of the organization.

To be clear, it is usually more advantageous for sports organizations to have governments issue debt on a team's or league's behalf. However, both Manchester United and the Green Bay Packers demonstrate that sports organizations can gain access to equity capital with terms almost as favorable as those of government debt. That is largely because equity holders of sports teams are different from equity holders of other companies. Sports equity holders are usually less interested in monetary returns from owning a sports stock than are investors in other industries.[52] Other sports teams have begun to issue stock as well. Twenty-two European soccer teams already have stocks traded on public exchanges.[53]

Raising equity capital has not always worked for sports organizations. The Midwest Sliders of Minor League Baseball's Frontier League planned an equity offering in 2009 to finance the construction of a $9.5 million 3,900-seat stadium.[54] However, the Sliders were not successful in raising money using this approach, and the team was sold to a new ownership group.[55] The Cleveland Indians were the last major American sports team to have a public offering, and the investor response was "tepid at best."[56] The Boston Celtics and Florida Panthers also had similar experiences when they tried to go public.[57] Given the advantages that equity offerings provide, however, sports strategists should consider issuing stock as a potential way both to raise money for and to create stronger fan relationships with their organizations.

Outside of equity, where can sports organizations turn to raise money that better guarantees a significant return on public investment? Another opportunity for the public to share in the upside of investment in sports teams is through social impact bonds (SIBs) or pay for success bonds (PSBs). A major problem with traditional arrangements between governments and sports teams is that governments need to make interest and principal payments on debt payments. In addition, the Tax Reform Act (TRA) of 1986 limits the ability of governments to issue tax-free municipal bonds "if more than 10 percent of the debt for a facility built mainly for nongovernment use was to be repaid with revenue from a private business."[58] As a result, governments are legally required to take on the significant risk in issuing debt, because sports organizations cannot contribute more than 10% to help pay for municipal bonds.

Because of these issues, governments have been increasingly wary of using municipal bonds to fund sports venue construction. Instead, sports organizations and governments can explore using different types of bonds that better tie a sports organization's financial performance to debt payments. Originally launched in 2010 to ensure better outcomes for paroled prisoners, SIBs return money to investors only when certain objectives are met by bond issuers. An example of an organization that has successfully used SIBs is a British charity called St. Mungo's. The charitable organization received approximately $4 million to help ensure that a specific number of London's homeless population have a place to sleep and eat. Investors received cash when benchmarks are reached such as the number of nights stayed at St. Mungo's or the number of hospital visits.[59]

While SIBs have already gained traction in Europe and the United States, they have not yet found a foothold in the sports world. The SIB framework would make it easier to finance sports projects through debt, because it creates an accountability structure for all parties. Sports organizations would be required to meet specific benchmarks, such as selling a certain number of season tickets, instead of promising uncertain tax increases. Government entities would be required to pay back bonds only when organizations met those benchmarks. Debt holders would be committed to a sports organization's success, as they would receive payment only when a team or league met its goals.

SIBs are an example of how governments can reduce their risk with publicly backed sports funding. While equities and SIBs can help the public participate in the upside of sports investments, sports organizations can also demonstrate their value to communities by launching public awareness campaigns for initiatives that are important to governments and that reach target demographics.

Doing Well by Doing Good

In 2006, the Boston Red Sox helped promote the state government's new law that required residents to purchase or secure health insurance as soon as possible. This campaign helped Massachusetts achieve more than 98% health care coverage for residents in the state by 2010.[60] The Red Sox are an example of an organization that became a marketing channel for government initiatives. More specifically, sports organizations can heighten awareness of issues important to local communities. At the same time, organizations can increase revenue and bring attention to their team or league by partnering with the government. Both the government and the sports organization can benefit from working together to achieve public policy goals.

Sports organizations can provide sponsorship opportunities either to supporters or opponents of a law, campaign, or issue. When used appropriately, working with sports organizations can be a very appealing approach for government organizations, political groups, and politicians. These individuals and organizations often lament the difficulty and cost of conveying to the public what they believe is important information on issues ranging from health insurance to e-filing opportunities for tax returns. This form of public support is beneficial for sports organizations looking to increase their marketing and sponsorship revenue.

The Alabama Development Office's (ADO) partnership with the University of Alabama and Auburn University was an example of a nonpolitical campaign that supports a government initiative. The ADO used the national championship football teams from the University of Alabama and Auburn University to promote local businesses. The slogan for the campaign was: "Alabama, consistently producing champions both on the field and in the work force."[61] Alabama and Auburn's football successes created a unique opportunity for the state to build awareness of its initiative and connect with a national business audience.

While not every college or university has a national championship–caliber football team, many schools can develop these types of campaigns. Athletic departments often command national, regional, or statewide attention and can provide a spotlight on issues important to local governments. Building awareness about governmental issues can be a competitive advantage for sports organizations. This is another avenue through which sports organizations can clearly demonstrate the value of support provided via public funds.

THUNDER POWER

It seems unlikely that anyone in Kentucky would need to travel to another city to learn about basketball. But in defiance of conventional wisdom, Louisville Mayor Greg Fischer led a contingent of officials to Oklahoma City in October of 2012 to learn what Louisville could take away from Oklahoma City's experience with the Thunder, its NBA team that helped revitalize the downtown area.[62]

If you had asked people what they knew about Oklahoma City prior to the arrival of the Thunder, most would have talked about the bombing of April 1995 or the failure of many oil businesses. So how did Oklahoma City become a "Big League City"?[63] Starting in the 1990s, the city government passed laws that created a business-friendly environment and spent millions of dollars redeveloping the downtown area. The city, led by officials and businessmen such as Clay Bennett, also made a large bet on sports teams as a critical component of its revitalization plan. The city spent $357.7 million creating a new arena, minor league ballpark, and convention center in the 1990s and 2000s.[64] Even with this investment, Oklahoma City was not guaranteed a major professional sports team, although its efforts to accommodate one were numerous. The Ford Center (now the Chesapeake Energy Arena) was even built to conform to NHL requirements in the hope of landing a hockey team.[65] Oklahoma City saw the impact that an NBA team could have on building its national profile when the New Orleans Hornets temporarily relocated there after Hurricane Katrina.

When the Thunder arrived in 2008, then–mayoral chief of staff David Holt called it the "most significant positive development in the city's history since the Land Run of 1889."[66] City officials used the Thunder to help the city gain national attention in a way that only a sports team could accomplish.[67] Not only was the name of the city now in the sports news virtually every day, but the Thunder was integral to the city's many marketing campaigns as well. For example, the Greater Oklahoma City Chamber of Commerce produced a promotional video that featured the Thunder's imminent arrival as the centerpiece of the city's redevelopment efforts in 2007.[68] When the team reached the NBA finals in 2012, "banners

CONTINUED

THUNDER POWER *CONTINUED*

[hung] from skyscrapers and in office windows, and downtown you [were] more likely to see Thunder t-shirts than coats and ties. Thunder fever [had] taken over this city."[69]

These investments are paying dividends for Oklahoma City. Its population has increased by 15%, and its property values have risen 472% since 2000, according to the Oklahoma City Chamber of Commerce.[70] The Thunder has been a critical driver of these successes. As Mayor Mick Cornett observes, "[The Thunder are] helping to engage people with the arts, parks and character of our city and helping us retain our young people while drawing in other young professionals."[71]

When Louisville officials came to visit Oklahoma City, they already understood the allure of basketball to a community. What they learned in Oklahoma City is how a sports team can set an urban renaissance into motion and position a middle-market city on the national scene.

Professional sports are not the only vehicle that can help cities or towns create a differentiated identity. Branding itself the "amateur sports capital of the world," Indianapolis has welcomed Olympic teams to practice and compete in world-class facilities for decades.[72] The idea was born under the administration of Indianapolis mayor William Hudnut, who with community leaders, crafted a plan to revitalize the city's core identity. Starting small and then growing its stable of organizations, Indianapolis has been successful in drawing amateur sports, like U.S. gymnastics, and governing bodies, such as the NCAA, to base their operations in the city. The focus enables the city to differentiate itself from its competitors and has drawn a great number of visitors and athletes alike. This campaign to attract amateur sports events and organizations has generated more than $1 billion for the Indianapolis economy and attracted more than 4.5 million spectators from outside the city.[73]

High school sports teams can also be used by cities and towns to build an identity. Head football coach Ed Thomas was a driving force in helping the Aplington-Parkersburg High School football team define the small town of Parkersburg, Iowa. The lessons that he preached to the football team about hard work, dedication, and commitment were embraced by the town during his sermons as an Elder

at the First Congregational Church. When Parkersburg suffered a devastating tor-
nado in 2008, the football team became a beacon of the town's rebuilding efforts.
Thomas's commitment to completely reconstruct the high school's field only a few
months after the storm received national attention because of its incredible feat
plotline. His off-the-field success was matched on-the-field as well. Even though
the high school's typical enrollment is 200 students, Thomas coached 4 future
NFL players. When Thomas was murdered in 2009, the town and the nation
grieved his loss. His death inspired a book called *The Sacred Acre* that reached
number 29 on *The New York Times* Bestseller's list. The town's ability to recover
from this tragedy was Thomas and the team's lasting legacy for Parkersburg.[74]

Reducing a Risky Business

Building public awareness, sharing the upside of sports investments, and creating winning campaigns are opportunities to demonstrate return on public investment. Sports strategists also have to minimize the perceived risk associated with
sports organizations securing public funds. Because of the problems we identified earlier in the chapter, many public entities are wary about investing more
resources into sports organizations. Therefore, sports strategists need to initiate
efforts that enable their organizations to directly engage with public audiences in
specific and targeted ways. Potential tactics include:

- Launching Grassroots Campaigns – Sports organizations directly tap into
  communities to conduct fundraising activities and build goodwill.
- Government-Focused Positions – Sports organizations can create or increase the size of their government affairs groups to target specific legislation and help ensure that the organization has an open dialogue with
  community leaders.
- Straight Talk on Lobbying – Sports organizations can consider how lobbying at a state or federal level can help inform and engage lawmakers.

Launching Grassroots Campaigns

Targeting local communities has traditionally been a difficult proposition for
sports organizations. In particular, fundraising is a major challenge at the high
school and collegiate levels. Traditional tactics have included employees or volun-
teers making hundreds of calls to people who are often not interested in making
donations.

Grassroots campaigns directly address this issue because they are designed to engage specifically with audiences who want to contribute their money, time, and abilities to helping a sports organization succeed. In the past, grassroots campaigns were difficult to execute on a larger scale because of the significant amount of resources required to make them effective. New mobile and Web-based technologies have eliminated many of the traditional challenges associated with grassroots campaigns.

WORKING THE CROWD

Veronica Mars was a television show that was broadcast on UPN and the CW television network from 2004 to 2007. It launched the career of Kristen Bell and developed a dedicated cult following. In 2013, series creator Rob Thomas had the idea to independently fund a movie based on the TV show using Kickstarter, an online funding service that allows people all over the world to give monetary contributions of any size to sponsored projects. If a project completely meets its funding goal, then Kickstarter applies a 5% fee and the project receives the rest of the cash. If it is not completely funded, then everyone who made a donation receives his or her money back. Thomas knew that 3 million people had watched each episode and determined that he only needed $2 million in funding to launch the project. The *Veronica Mars* Movie Project generated more than $5.7 million in pledges in only 30 days.[75]

Crowdsourced funding platforms are a promising fundraising channel for sports organizations. They can be used to finance both large and small projects that likely will not receive money from traditional fundraising methods. For example, Buena High School in Ventura, California, raised $1,608 from 40 backers over a 21-day period to support the painting of an "Aquatic Sports Mural" on its campus in collaboration with its students.[76] It is unlikely that an athletic department or government funding would have supported this project.

There are already hundreds of projects on Kickstarter that have the "sports" label. Kickstarter, however, is not the only crowdfunding option available for sports organizations. The New Zealand sailing team raised $42,445 to compete in the Youth America's Cup Regatta through ThrillPledge.[77]

RallyMe is the official crowdsourcing platform for many of the U.S. Winter Olympics sports federations. The U.S. women's ski jumping team raised $32,950 through a "rally" that supported the team's debut in the 2014 Sochi Olympics.[78] Other crowdsourcing platforms through which sports organizations can raise money include Indiegogo and Team Bus. At a time when many sports organizations are looking to generate money through new channels, crowdfunding platforms provide a new opportunity to facilitate grassroots campaigns that directly target engaged audience members.

Sports organizations can use other grassroots tactics to help increase funding, particularly when they can no longer rely on government support. For example, the University of Minnesota successfully completed a campaign to build a new baseball stadium. However, the school could not rely on traditional subsidies, because the state had already contributed nearly half of the financing for a new football stadium in 2009.[79] In addition, the government had already committed hundreds of millions of dollars to the construction of venues for the Minnesota Timberwolves, Wild, Twins, and Vikings.[80] Any request for a new baseball stadium built with state funds would have come at a time when the government was already financially overcommitted to Minnesota's professional sports.

Instead of relying on state funding, the University of Minnesota launched a grassroots campaign to raise money from public nongovernmental sources. The Golden Gopher Fund received a $2 million gift from the Pohlad Family Foundation in addition to securing numerous six-figure contributions. These larger contributions enabled the school to focus on smaller donations that helped increase the number of people and organizations supporting the team. These efforts helped raise a total of $7.5 million, enough to construct a new stadium that opened in 2013.[81]

An important element of the University of Minnesota campaign was its use of star power. Baseball Hall-of-Famer and former Gopher Paul Molitor has been a critical component of this grassroots effort's success.[82] Not only was Molitor an honorary campaign chair, but he also participated in fundraising events and was featured prominently in marketing materials.[83] Molitor is not solely using his own financial resources to help the program like Woodley did with Saginaw High School. Instead, Molitor's commitment brought positive awareness and attention to the baseball team at a time when it needed the publicity to generate momentum for the campaign.

Not every sports organization has a popular former star on whom it can rely to help raise funds for the school or organization. Oftentimes the best person to help create and lead a grassroots campaign is a player, coach, or administrator who may not be famous nationally but is well known within a local community.

FROM COACH TO CHIEF MARKETING OFFICER

When describing the University of California, Berkeley's baseball program in 2010, the *Wall Street Journal* reported that the team "was a money-sucking sponge that drew few fans and even fewer sponsors to its no-frills campus ballyard."[84] The team's public financing well had run dry after 118 years, and it was no longer receiving enough subsidies to continue the baseball program.[85]

Cal's longtime coach David Esquer faced one of the toughest predicaments of his career. He could either watch his team play its final games in the spring of 2011 or organize a campaign to save the squad. The latter option required the coach to become the architect of a campaign to revive Bears baseball. He personally led his team's campaign efforts, cold calling alumni, designing a "Save Cal Baseball" website, and hosting a three-day tournament at the San Francisco Giants' AT&T Park. Esquer even went so far as to ask the fans and players at the team's rival Stanford for contributions to save the program.[86] These efforts helped Cal baseball raise $10 million – enough money to support the program for the next 10 years.

While high schools and smaller colleges may not be able to raise millions for their programs, many sports organizations have succeeded in raising money on a smaller scale. North Merion High School football coach Doug Bilodeau combined social media and humor to help raise $7,000 for his program in Oregon by posting a picture saying, "Will Work For Helmets" on his team's Facebook page.[87] Massachusetts' Hull High School athletic director Jim Quatromoni's grassroots efforts included raising $6,000 in sponsorships by competing in a triathlon and mobilizing parents, athletes, and boosters to raise money through raffles and parking cars to save his school's sports programs.[88]

An increasing number of athletic programs need to close budget gaps and can no longer rely on state funding or activity fees to ensure their teams' survival. One way to stem the tide of financial hardship is to capit-alize on the strong relationships coaches and athletic directors have with their communities. The job description for athletic leaders can now in-clude "chief marketing officer" (CMO).

Grassroots campaigns can be effective in gaining the support of local commu-nities on specific issues. However, sports organizations will also need to directly engage with community officials, politicians, and leaders to maximize public support. Working with government affairs groups or government staffers is an important step toward building these relationships.

Government-Focused Positions

Despite the close relationship that exists between sports organizations and gov-ernments, few athletic departments, leagues, or teams have personnel whose job it is to focus on developing public support. The lack of government affairs experts is especially surprising at the high school and collegiate levels because of how re-liant these sports organizations are on government subsidies. For example, the University of California–Riverside receives 85.5% of its funding from subsidies that include "student fees, direct and indirect institutional support and state money."[89] Despite Riverside's dependence on state support, none of the athletic di-rectors on staff (executive, associate, or assistant) has the job focused on working directly with government organizations.[90]

It is true that many collegiate athletic departments rely on lobbyists, public af-fairs officials, or government relations departments employed within their insti-tutions to monitor and coordinate their activities with state or local governments. For example, Oberlin College's Office of Community and Government Relations "builds and maintains relationships with local, state, and federal governments, as well as with local community members and organizations"[91] for the entire school. As of 2013, the athletic department had no one focused on this type of community leadership role, despite having three assistant athletic directors.[92] The potential problem with this approach is that each school's departments will have different priorities and relationships with governmental organizations. A larger govern-ment affairs department at a college or university is less likely to advocate for the best interests of its athletic department.

Creating government affairs positions can help build public support for sports organizations. For example, the University of Texas at Tyler's athletic department has a vice president of student affairs and government relations whose job includes working with state and local governments as well as with community leaders.[93] This person is an athletics-focused advocate working within the school's administration. This approach enables the athletic department to form its own relationships with state officials while ensuring that any steps taken align with the university's overall priorities.

Straight Talk on Lobbying

After point guard Chris Paul was traded to the Los Angeles Clippers, the team acquired the nickname "Lob City." Paul's perfectly weighted and timed alley-oop passes to his teammates led to highlight reel dunks that left fans and commentators speechless. However, the Clippers team is not the only entity that has earned the Lob City label by leaving people speechless. Washington, D.C. is the nation's political "Lob City," as government lobbying is the lifeblood of the town. Because members of Congress and their staffs cannot be experts on every piece of legislation that comes to a vote, they often rely on outside sources to provide them with information and advocate for their positions. Since the country's inception, companies, unions, and trade associations have used lobbyists to influence decision-makers in all branches of government. In 2013, $3.21 billion dollars was spent on 12,281 lobbyists for Congress and federal agencies.[94]

The main reason that these organizations are willing to spend such large amounts of money on lobbying is that it works. According to the *Economist*, the top 50 companies that spent the most money on lobbying as a percentage of their total assets received an 11% higher return on investment than the S&P 500 from 2002 to 2011.[95] Lockheed Martin, the largest federal contractor in the nation, received $39.8 billion in federal contracts while paying only $15.8 million in lobbying fees in 2003–4 – a ratio of $2,517 earned for every $1 spent.[96]

Even though some sports leagues and teams do have a history of working with lobbyists, they have not invested as heavily in the practice as companies in other industries. Sports organizations spent between $2.9 to $5.1 million dollars annually on congressional lobbying from 2003 to 2013, including $4.4 million in 2013.[97] Even though this may seem like a significant amount of money, overall spending by leagues and teams on lobbying is comparatively low, especially since the size of the domestic sports industry was estimated to be $470 billion dollars in 2013.[98] By comparison, individual companies such as Google, General Electric, and AT&T each spent more than $15 million on congressional lobbying in 2012.[99]

While Washington may be the ultimate Lob City, sports strategists should not pursue only federal lobbying to achieve their public support goals. Lobbying state, county, and city governments can generate comparable returns on investment for sports organizations as well.

THE UFC FOUGHT THE LAW . . . AND THE UFC WON

In the past, many states had laws that made it illegal for any organization to stage mixed martial arts competitions. For the UFC, the world's largest mixed martial arts organization, this was a huge strategic problem. The organization's inability to operate in states such as Illinois and Pennsylvania meant that the UFC was potentially losing millions of dollars because it could not hold live events in large markets. More importantly, these laws characterized UFC's brand in ways that the organization has tried to avoid. Violence is an integral aspect of competition for many other sports, but state governments do not ban them. These laws against mixed martial arts organizations perpetuated a misconception that its competitions are no better than barroom brawls.

In attempting to overturn these laws, the UFC faced significant challenges. Each state had different legislation that prevented mixed martial arts fighting. Additionally, the dispute put politicians in a difficult quandary, as sponsoring legislation that supports (or at least allows) violence is usually not a smart political move. The visceral action exhibited in UFC fights that thrills the organization's fans could easily be used in a negative political ad or as a rival politician's talking point during reelection season. For legislators, overturning laws preventing mixed martial arts fights was not a high priority.

The UFC needed to take control of the situation and persuade state legislators to adopt their point of view and introduce legislation that would overturn these mixed martial arts bans. The foundation of this strategy was lobbying state government officials. The UFC's first step was to address the perception issues regarding its sport while also highlighting the economic benefits of staging matches. The organization and its lobbyists spent time demonstrating to legislators how their fighters are well-conditioned athletes who constantly hone their abilities. The UFC also committed to

CONTINUED

THE UFC FOUGHT THE LAW . . . AND THE UFC WON *CONTINUED*

helping politicians who supported overturning bans on mixed martial arts by making campaign contributions to their reelection funds and working with them to respond to any attacks from opponents or rival campaigns. By educating politicians on mixed martial arts' athletic and financial benefits and helping fight off would-be detractors, the UFC was able to effectively team with governments to pass legislation beneficial to its organization.[100]

The UFC's lobbying efforts have not always been successful. The New York state legislature had failed to pass a law that would allow mixed martial arts fights, even though the UFC has earned the support of the governor.[101] However, states that had previously banned mixed martial arts fighting such as Illinois, Pennsylvania, Indiana, Massachusetts, Wisconsin, and Alabama now allow the sport within their borders. According to the *Sports Business Journal*, this change occurred because of a "shift in attitude toward the sport by many legislators."[102] The UFC's success in changing existing legislation can largely be attributed to its efforts in lobbying state legislators to counter misconceptions about its sport.

The UFC is an example of an organization that utilized lobbying to pass legislation that enabled competition in different markets. However, other organizations have different needs beyond fighting for the right to operate in new locations. There are a number of instances in which sports organizations could have capitalized on specific pieces of legislation to help them better address strategic challenges.

An example is the American Recovery and Reinvestment Act of 2009 (ARRA), which included $164 billion in funding for education, infrastructure, energy/environment, and transportation spending.[103] Many sports-related entities or partners did not take advantage of the opportunity to secure ARRA government funding. Those that did received relatively small amounts, given the size of the legislation. The San Diego Hall of Champions Sports Museum received $123,754 to make "energy efficient upgrades" to its facilities.[104] The city of Norwalk, California, was awarded $332,700 for the installation of an energy-saving roof on its Arts and Sports Complex.[105] These examples demonstrate the funding opportunities that can exist for sports organizations in just a single piece of legislation.

There have been other pieces of legislation that lobbyists and government affairs officials could have examined to achieve the goals of sports leagues, teams, and athletic departments. For example, government funding can be used to help enhance security at sporting events. In 2009, the Department of Homeland Security (DHS) and the FBI issued a security warning about "terrorist interest" in attacking a sports stadium or arena.[106] In 2011, the DHS ranked an attack on a venue as one of the "most devastating possible acts of terrorism."[107] Even though sports organizations have spent $2 billion per year worldwide on security for their venues, only one-third of U.S. sports arenas have the appropriate security measures in place to help prevent a future terrorist attack, according to the National Center for Spectator Sports.[108]

Sports strategists can work with the DHS as well as with congressional and state appropriations committees to increase subsidies that sports organizations receive from the government. For example, the SAFETY Act allows sports organizations to receive indemnification from "important legal liabilities" through the DHS by meeting certain safety and antiterrorism standards.[109] Sports strategists should work with lobbyists and government affairs officials to ensure that sports organizations can benefit from this type of federal and state legislation.

Arizona State University (ASU) showed how knowledge of the local legislative process can provide unique opportunities to finance sports spending. In 2010, the Arizona State Legislature passed a bill that enabled state-supported schools to create a "special revenue district." In these areas, schools could charge in-lieu assessments instead of property taxes on any new private development. ASU can then use these in-lieu assessments to pay for the building or development of new athletic venues and facilities. In 2013, ASU decided to lease 300 acres of a special revenue district for private development and use the assessments as the way to pay for the debt of financing renovations of its Sun Devil Stadium. The estimated $100 to $500 million cost to upgrade the football stadium will now not be paid by local taxpayers. Instead the businesses in the revenue district will help pay down any new debt at no additional costs because the business would have to pay property taxes if they were not paying these assessments.[110]

ASU would never have had this opportunity if it had not understood how legislation could achieve its strategic goal and worked with the state legislature to pass a new law that created a novel method to finance new stadium construction. Understanding the benefits that come from this type of legislation show how lobbyists and government affairs staffers can provide sports organizations with significant competitive advantages. Investing in these resources can help ensure that sports organizations do not miss out on opportunities to receive public subsidies or to benefit from new legislation.

Conclusion

Public support for sports organizations is at a crossroads. In the 1980s and 1990s, governments would seemingly do just about anything to attract a big-name event or keep local teams from moving. Today, many governments are hesitant to issue bonds to finance new sports venues, reduce taxes, build transportation infrastructure, or bid on large events such as the Olympics. For every team, such as the Atlanta Braves, that is able to secure a public-private partnership with little fanfare, there are teams, such as the Minnesota Vikings or D.C. United, who have very public struggles in building publicly financed venues. Local governments are also slashing athletic department funding as part of the effort to comply with legislation that requires balanced budgets. At the same time, sports organizations have largely become more dependent on public funding to run their operations.

Sports strategists should consider taking specific actions to demonstrate how their organizations can deliver value to their communities. It is critical that sports organizations take control of their efforts to secure key sources of funding. Grassroots campaigns, relationships with government affairs figures, and lobbying are all possibilities that often work best in tandem. The relationship between sports organizations and the public is strained in many ways, but these tactics are designed not only to help repair the relationship but to provide mutually beneficial results.

7   Crafting a Crisis Blueprint

The Great Gatsby, Field of Dreams, and *Boardwalk Empire* share a common plot point. They all feature the 1919 Black Sox gambling fix as one of their storylines. Although it has been almost a century since this scandal occurred, why have the Black Sox remained such a pervasive part of the artistic consciousness? The scandal has been etched in people's memory because it was one of the first times that sports so clearly violated the public's trust.

The crisis started with a stunning upset. The formidable 1919 Chicago White Sox lost to the underdog Cincinnati Reds five games to three in the World Series. Even after initial whispers about the fix began to spread, much of the media continued to back the players, team owners, and the league as a whole. Around the time the scandal broke, sports editor Joe Vila wrote, "Personally, I don't believe for a moment that anything was wrong in the [1919] World Series."[1] In fact, something *was* wrong – very wrong. Eight White Sox players had conspired with notorious gamblers, including Arnold Rothstein, to intentionally lose the championship and receive a big payday.

The scandal uncovered many significant problems with America's national pastime. MLB was run by a three-person committee that was fractious and ineffective in dealing with the league's problems. Players habitually complained about being underpaid, and the leaders of baseball leagues spent more time politically maneuvering for power instead of addressing the league's issues. For example, notoriously frugal White Sox owner Charles Comiskey refused to pay to launder his players' clothing.[2]

Baseball executives' initial response to the gambling charges was inadequate and hesitant. Even though the players were tried in court and ultimately found innocent of any crime, the Black Sox scandal pushed baseball into full-blown crisis mode as it questioned the game's principal and most important asset: credibility. Ultimately, Judge Kenesaw Landis was appointed as the first-ever commissioner of baseball in 1921 and thus became the supreme arbiter of all baseball matters. One day after their acquittal in a criminal court trial in 1921, Commissioner Landis banned the eight players involved in the scandal from ever playing professional baseball again. The league also launched a public relations initiative in an attempt to repair its image and to provide information to the media. It also began paying much more attention to betting and unusual or suspicious play on the field.[3] Soon after the league took these steps, ballpark attendance and audience interest in the game stabilized. By 1924, MLB set a new record for attendance with 9.6 million fans attending games.[4]

It was Eliot Asinof in the book *Eight Men Out*, however, who articulated why the Black Sox have remained the iconic sports crisis. He asserted that "if baseball was corrupt then anything might be – and probably was. If you could not trust the honesty of a big league world series, what could you trust?"[5] Up until that point, baseball had a reputation among most fans and sportswriters for being a wholesome, patriotic, and upstanding American game. The scandal was the first time audiences questioned why they placed so much value in their sports heroes. It would not be the last.

• • •

The Black Sox scandal was only one of the many crises that baseball would face. Betting among players, PED scandals, owner misbehavior, and feuds over financial obligations with city and community partners are among the many issues that baseball has confronted. Like most highly visible sports organizations, the league is an ongoing crisis target and is constantly seeking effective solutions to the issues it faces.

In the sports world, nothing threatens a franchise or league's future more than scandal. Whether it comes in the form of betting, drugs, sex, fraud, or personal attacks, any hint of scandal in sports can erode decades of goodwill and success. When reflecting on the state of college sports, *USA Today* columnist Christine Brennan asked, "Has there ever been an academic (and we use that term loosely) year with more lying, cheating, poor leadership, and all-around misbehaving in football and men's basketball than the 2010–11 school year?"[6] Brennan's lament applies not only to collegiate sports but also seemingly to the sports industry in general. The litany of threats to and problems with sports at the youth, high school, collegiate, and professional levels over the last few years includes the following:

- The coaches of the Tustin Pee Wee Red Cobras in California were suspended from Pop Warner football after being charged with creating a bounty scheme in which they paid children to injure players on opposing teams.[7]
- Two Steubenville High School football players were found guilty of raping a 16-year-old girl, while other students attracted international media attention for posting "lurid text messages, cell phone pictures and videos, and social media posts surrounding the sexual abuse of the girl."[8]
- The NCAA has censured prestigious Division I NCAA football programs at Penn State University, the University of Miami, Ohio State University, the University of Oregon, Boise State University, the University of North Carolina, and the University of Connecticut for improper conduct.
- The New England Patriots released Aaron Hernandez only months after signing him to a multimillion-dollar long-term contract extension after he was arrested for first-degree murder and gun-related charges.

To guarantee that fans, the media, sponsors, community leaders, and politicians continue to support leagues, teams, and players, sports strategists must reassure these key audiences that their commitment to maintaining credibility, transparency, and trust is unwavering. Nothing reveals more about a sports organization's character than when it is caught off-guard and forced to publicly respond to a crisis. In this increasingly contentious marketplace, all actions and discourse are under a microscope and need to be carefully planned, executed, and grounded in effective communication practices.

This chapter is broken into two parts. The first analyzes the common characteristics of a crisis and its causes. The second highlights solutions to avoid crises and manage them once they occur. By the end of the chapter, sports strategists should be able to more effectively identify, manage, and navigate crises, a situation that can occur regardless of on-the-field athletic performances.

What Is a Crisis?

A crisis is an unexpected event that threatens the integrity of an organization and its ability to conduct its everyday affairs.

Crises usually share many components:

- Allegations Against the Person or Organization – These accusations range from the exaggerated and deceitful to the specific and factual about acts, including challenges to procedures, unethical or illegal behavior, and performance failures.
- Uncertainty about the Details of What Happened – Not only may the charges sometimes be vague, but the details of the story will often remain elusive as the crisis unfolds. The challenge is trying to respond rationally under circumstances of imperfect information.
- Lack of Control over the Diffusion of the Story – In the Internet age, leaks move around the globe with astonishing ease and often disappear as quickly as they arise. They are prized because they catch sports organizations in their most unguarded moments that may show their true intent rather than the sculpted media release.
- A Person or Organization Is Immediately Put on the Defensive – The crisis event forces the organization to answer charges to defend its honor and integrity.
- A Person or Organization Lacks the Ability to Choose the Circumstances of the Response – The place, time, and type of the person's or organization's response is not usually chosen by the accused, but by the media.
- The Public Often Assumes that You Are Guilty – Historically, the media has used crisis to assume the mantle of the righteous. Whether the claims are valid or not, being placed in the spotlight often causes people to think the person or organization has done something wrong.

As originally articulated by crisis management expert Steven Fink, these components can appear over the course of four stages.[9] We have adapted his work to apply to sports organizations. This four-stage model emphasizes the importance of anticipating and recognizing the stages and addressing them continuously throughout the process of crisis resolution.

The *provocation stage* is the time during and just after the crisis-igniting event takes place. Often there are warning signs that indicate a crisis is likely to occur. At this stage, there is increased communication activity about the organization and the crisis as audiences begin to take notice.

The *action stage* occurs when the crisis has fully reached the public and becomes controversial. Characterized by attacks, counter-charges, and escalating media involvement, the interplay between the social media sphere and the mainstream media creates a spiraling effect that amplifies the crisis. The action stage is also marked by the emergence of communication teams, press conferences, media appearances, and other forms of public debate.

The *management stage* is marked by ongoing attempts at recovery and repositioning of issues. The communication team reduces its public presence while decision-makers continue to confront the crisis through smaller meetings, internal restructuring, and other efforts to recuperate from the situation.

The *post-crisis stage* is when the controversy has dissipated and a new normalcy emerges, but the crisis' consequences continue to leave a clear mark on the organization. In the post-crisis stage, decision-makers often reflect on the future of the organization and how it can best avoid and manage crises that emerge later.

Sports strategists can use these stages to frame a crisis once it occurs. It is also critical to understand what conditions cause a crisis situation to emerge before determining the appropriate frame or response.

The Causes of Today's "Crisis of Crises"

The most striking recent development in crisis management is the audience's new centrality to the communication experience. The old days of the audience as a passive participant in the sports world are rapidly fading. In his book *An Accidental Sportswriter*, Robert Lipsyte observes that most sportswriters and media disregarded major problems in the industry in the 1960s. He contrasts the disinterest of sportswriters in reporting the "family squabbles or drunkenness or screwing around" of star players at the time with the watchdog mentality of contemporary sports journalism.[10] Lipsyte illustrates how the volume and quality of information demanded by the marketplace has increased dramatically. The audience now insists on knowing both the Herculean feats as well as the human imperfections of their team's star players.

The rise of the Internet initiated a monumental shift in power and control from large sports organizations to individual audiences. Social media is an obvious example: Facebook, Twitter, and other platforms provide audiences with outlets to share opinions about and directly interact with sports organizations and players. In fact, about one-fourth of tweets sent by athletes are direct responses to fans.[11] Players who share their views add another dimension to fans' experiences, enhancing how their audiences consume the sport. Social media enables athletes and fans to connect in ways that better enhance the fan experience, but they also spawn a variety of opportunities for athletes to build their identities off the court or field.

When right fielder Nick Swisher played for the Yankees, he became a social media phenomenon whose online stardom overshadowed his on-field performance. He was baseball's version of Justin Bieber: hip, Web-savvy, and celebrity-connected. An early adopter of Twitter, with a following of over 1.6 million, Swisher emerged as an asset for not only the Yankees, but also for advertisers such as Mercedes-Benz, which chose him over better-performing baseball stars for marketing campaigns. Swisher illustrated the power of his social media fan base in 2010 when he launched a four-day Twitter campaign that earned him 9.8 million fan votes and the last spot on the American League All-Star team.[12] Swisher demonstrated how social media provides athletes a new avenue both to build fan relationships and grow their endorsement portfolios.

It has been decades since audiences have had similar casual and direct contact with top-tier athletes. In 1941, legendary Boston Red Sox outfielder Ted Williams became the last MLB player to hit over .400 in a season. After the final game of that year, Williams left the ballpark and stopped for a chocolate milkshake at a local diner on his stroll to his hotel. This was not unusual even for the often abrasive Williams, as he frequently stopped in malt shops with an entourage that included his "best friends" – policemen, theater managers, and the Red Sox clubhouse attendant.[13] It was customary for athletes of this time to take public transportation, eat in mainstream restaurants, and work in the offseason for supplemental income. Later in the twentieth century, sports organizations and agents took steps to increasingly isolate athletes from fans. Casual interactions were replaced with chartered planes and special parking lots. This approach became true even at nonprofessional levels, as universities more frequently established housing and special dining facilities for varsity football and basketball student athletes that separated them from other students.

While social media is not the same as grabbing a malt with Williams, it reconnects the athlete and the audience. These feelings of intimacy are the foundations of loyalty and have fundamentally changed how both sports organizations and their star athletes engage with their fan bases. If audiences feel that they belong to a community in sports, they are more likely to form a deep emotional connection with a team and its players. This explains why sports organizations are using digital communication channels to increase a fan's sense of connection to the game and its stars.[14]

This new interplay also enhances the risk and danger of a crisis. Fans are empowered by their desire to live vicariously through the team's athletes or management. Avid fans fantasize about scoring the winning touchdown in the Super Bowl or having the power to decide which college superstar their favorite NBA team will select in the first round of the draft. The fans' desire to be closer and have more access to the sport and its athletes fuels their vicarious consumption of the game. Digital technologies, most notably fantasy sports, provide the fan with new avenues to role-play as leaders of sports organizations.

As the deep emotional connection between audiences and the team or player grows, the potential for disappointment reaches new heights. As a result, if team behavior or actions do not comport with audience expectations, they are likely to ignite a backlash. When these deep bonds splinter, the emotional response to an issue can be extreme.

An example of the changing expectations of fans occurred in New Zealand when Adidas initiated a geographic price-differentiation strategy for jerseys of the All Blacks, the country's iconic rugby team. The Rugby World Cup edition of the All Blacks' jersey was selling for more than twice as much in New Zealand retail stores as it was in the United States and Britain. While this may have gone unnoticed in the pre-Internet era, today's consumers have the ability to compare prices online and share information in the blink of an eye. Fans took to blogs and the company's Facebook page to accuse Adidas of price-gouging loyal All Blacks fans. Adidas steadfastly refused to lower its price. The company's response threatened to tarnish its brand, and company representatives' claim that their support of rugby sports in New Zealand justified the pricing further fueled the outrage. One dismayed retailer reported, "We've had a number of customers come into the stores, throw Adidas products onto the floor, and say, 'Look, you might as well burn this.'"[15] During the action stage of the crisis, the company was forced to cancel a major corporate event and even took its name off company cars to lower its profile in New Zealand. Adidas did not take into account the national pride associated with New Zealand's All Blacks and the advent of technology that gave fans access to global information

The All Blacks jersey crisis demonstrates that fans are both willing and empowered to take action if they feel mistreated. Fans today are armed with a plethora of new content and communication channels to gather information and speak their minds. The combination of these ingredients can ignite a crisis. Not long ago, Adidas's multiple pricing strategy was common practice and would have gone unnoticed. In today's communication landscape, however, a review of crisis possibilities should routinely include an analysis of global interconnectedness and consumer empowerment. For sports organizations, there is a new recipe for accountability, and many of the old assumptions about fan interaction and business practices need to be reexamined.

Social media channels are not used just by sports fans to vent frustration when a bond with a sports organization has been broken. Sports strategists have to be prepared for the potential damage that can be done to their organizations' identities when athletes are able to instantly speak their minds on sensitive and sometimes inappropriate issues. Social media coverage is a double-edged sword: teams' successes are celebrated and their failures are magnified. Sports organizations spend the majority of their social capital on building their reputations, and it takes only a minor slip-up to erase their hard-earned equity.

UH-OH, TWEET!

Twitter makes it easy to broadcast what's on your mind – maybe too easy. When star players or coaches publish offensive tweets that can be read by millions of followers, it can reflect poorly on the players, their team, and the sport in general. In some cases, turbulence-causing tweets are forgotten or swept under the rug. Unfortunately, others resonate and strike directly at an organization's credibility. The following are some of the most controversial messages sports figures have tweeted since Twitter became a staple in athletes' communication toolbox:

Marvin Morgan, Striker for Aldershot F.C.
Tweet: "Like to thank fans who booed me off the pitch. Where's that going to get you! I hope you all die."[16]
Reaction: Aldershot called the tweet "totally misguided and inappropriate" and stated that Morgan "accepts that his actions were incorrect and ill disciplined." The club fined Morgan two weeks' wages and placed

him on the transfer list.[17] For generations, players have lashed out at critical fans, often resulting in suspensions or other disciplinary procedures, but these were (for the most part) contained incidents. With Twitter, Morgan was able to go beyond screaming at jeering fans. He publicly broadcasted his spiteful message to the Twitterverse.

Johnny Manziel, Quarterback for Texas A&M University

Tweet: "Bullshit like tonight is a reason why I can't wait to leave college station . . . whenever it may be."[18]

Reaction: Manziel quickly hedged by saying he loved College Station and the university. This tweet, however, became part of a larger narrative of how the quarterback considered himself to be more important than the program since winning the Heisman Trophy. The university's response fed into the storyline because it did not distance itself from his comments or take any action against the quarterback.

Paul Bissonnette, Left Wing for Phoenix Coyotes

Tweet: "[Ilya] kovalchuck's gana have to give lap dances for 20 years instead of getting them now that he got rejected. sorry communist. back to the soviet."[19]

Reaction: Bissonnette apologized for his crude comment about the former Russian-born New Jersey Devils left winger's contract problems and deactivated his Twitter account temporarily. However, after fans started a "Free BizNasty" campaign to get him tweeting again, Bissonnette started a new account under a different handle shortly after.[20] While he later reestablished his identity as a funny and blunt commentator on hockey life, Bissonnette demonstrated the danger of misrepresenting the team's values with off-the-cuff comments.

These examples show that uncensored comments from prominent athletes can pose a major risk to their affiliated organizations. In all three examples, the athletes did not appear to consider how audiences might perceive their messages. Twitter is a powerful platform that offers real value to sports organizations. To mitigate potentially negative consequences, however, organizations must educate their players and coaches on appropriate social media participation in order to prevent crises and hold these

CONTINUED

UH-OH, TWEET! *CONTINUED*

individuals accountable for their online remarks. Once firm rules for online conduct have been established, organizations should routinely ensure
that players and coaches understand them through periodic mentoring
and training sessions. Additionally, the organization might choose to create a transparent system of incentives for social media behavior. These systems remind all involved not only to consider the potential repercussions
of their comments but also to realize Twitter's potential benefits.

Sports organizations face a unique challenge compared to companies in other
industries. Unlike many other businesses, sports organizations emphasize the
narratives that surround their players, coaches, and administrators. The components of their identities are vital to the emotional appeal of sports. By attaching a
team to an individual's appeal, sports organizations knowingly place themselves
in a vulnerable position.

Gilbert Arenas's skills on the basketball court and antics off it made him the
superstar of the Washington Wizards in the late 2000s. The negative elements of
Arenas's erratic behavior came to light in December of 2009 when he and another
teammate drew pistols on each other in the locker room over a gambling debt.
The Wizards suffered from months of bad publicity, suspensions, and personnel
changes.[21] In contrast to the sports industry, Walmart does not need to promote
its logistical stars that create and operate the company's world-class distribution
chain to its core customers. While Walmart often highlights associates in its marketing campaigns, customers primarily come to the company's stores for the low
prices rather than to engage or follow its employees.

In addition, the relationship between athletes and the organization has
changed. In the past, athletes typically viewed themselves as employees of sports
organizations, and they were reluctant to discuss disagreements with management in public. Today, a public battle can quickly ensue between organizations
and players, because both are highly visible entities, with some athletes bigger
than the team itself. This conflict reveals one of the major fault lines in the new
media environment.

Consumers are often more interested in hearing from those intimately involved
in the action, such as players and fellow fans, than in listening to the seemingly
faceless administrators who run the sports organizations. The athlete's newfound

voice, and ability to express his or her opinion to whomever will listen, can create scenarios in which the interests and opinions of individual players do not coincide with the communications developed by their parent organizations or sponsors.

But it is not just the athletes who can set off crises for sports organizations. Coaches, general managers, owners, and other executives within organizations can also create difficult communication challenges. Frank McCourt is an example of an owner who caused his team to threaten its bond with his audience. In 2010, the embattled McCourt became involved in a bitter divorce lawsuit with his ex-wife in part to determine ownership of the Los Angeles Dodgers. With the team already facing financial difficulties, McCourt was forced to accept a $150 million bankruptcy loan from MLB. Fans responded emotionally to the seemingly irresponsible and erratic behavior of the front office. Popular Dodgers blog *Mike Scioscia's Tragic Illness* published a post entitled "The Collected Sins of the Frank and Jamie McCourt Era" that offered a laundry list of the owners' shortcomings and went viral throughout the Dodger online community.[22]

The Dodgers, one of the most iconic teams in baseball and in all of professional sports, are ingrained in the very fabric of Los Angeles. The bond between the team and its fans spans entire lifetimes. L.A. parents purchase Dodger-themed bib and creeper sets for their babies, celebrate birthdays in the stands, reschedule weddings around key games, and even elect to eternally rest in a Dodger blue casket. The close relationship that the Dodgers organization had worked to build with its fans later amplified those same individuals' anger with the team's poor management. As the level of intimacy that a fan feels toward a sports organization is heightened, so too are the possible repercussions resulting from the club's management problems. The subsequent sale of McCourt's ownership stake to a Guggenheim Partners-led consortium was a timely bailout of what was escalating into a full-scale revolt. In this case, according to the *Los Angeles Times*, "Dodgers fans deserve great credit. They played no small part in McCourt's undoing. Their outrage was heard in every letter to the editor, in every comment left on the Web, and mostly, in every seat that went unused."[23]

The "crisis of crises" facing sports is the result of audiences' increasing engagement expectations, organizations' desire to foster more intimate relationships with their consumers, and the rapid multiplying of new media channels. Moreover, an organization's credibility is increasingly more vulnerable, because communication controversies can come from anywhere, occur quickly, and threaten the organization's carefully constructed identity.

When reputational stakes are high and increasingly attacked, understanding effective strategies to manage a crisis is essential. We have identified steps that enable a sports strategist to effectively evaluate and respond to crises. However, one of the best forms of crisis management is to avoid these types of situations in the first place.

Preventing a Crisis

While seemingly obvious, it is critical to ensure that all members of a sports organization are alert to activities that put the team or league at risk. Management needs to define and control organizational messages by working with the three key groups that have increasingly frequent audience interactions: administrators, coaches, and players. All three groups must understand the goals and identity of the organization and how to best communicate them to the general public. The most effective strategies not only educate their outreach targets but also make them aware of the consequences of their actions. Setting a clear expectation of ethical and appropriate behavior in contractual agreements, personnel meetings, and in-house communications is an important preventative step toward avoiding potential crises.

Many organizations recognize that they need up-front training to educate these groups and avoid oncoming crises. However, it is becoming increasingly difficult for organizations to regulate the ongoing communications of their players and employees. Audiences have grown accustomed to hearing from athletes on an informal and frequent basis. Much of this communication occurs through digital and social media channels, emphasizing the need for sports organizations to promote appropriate online behavior.

Numerous sports organizations have taken aggressive action by instituting monitoring practices to control online behavior that is potentially dangerous to the organization. For example, the University of Mississippi and the University of Texas have partnered with UDiligence, an online service that monitors their student athletes' social network pages for any comments referring to drugs, sex, racial slurs, and profanity.[24] Through similar initiatives, sports organizations are taking steps toward preventing crises.

It is unclear, however, how effective these policies will be or if they will be sustainable for long periods of time. Unresolved privacy and free speech legal issues surrounding players' autonomy make matters even more complicated. States, such as Wisconsin, have already introduced legislation that would protect the social media privacy of athletes.[25]

TENNESSEE VOLUNTEERS INFORMATION

Pat Summitt, the University of Tennessee's legendary women's basketball coach, had won eight national championships when she was diagnosed with early-onset Alzheimer's at the age of 59 in 2011.[26] Summitt decided (and was cleared by her doctors) to continue to coach. She acknowledged, however, that she was vulnerable to limitations and an undefined timetable regarding her mental decline.

Tennessee's handling of the looming medical issue is an example of how an organization can effectively deter a potential crisis. The university recognized the potential problem at the outset, moved quickly to ask the right questions, gathered the important information, and established its priorities to guide its responses. If mismanaged or addressed only in response to outside inquiries, Summit's health issue could have been detrimental to her legacy and could have impacted the credibility of the entire Tennessee athletic community. At the time, the athletic program was already dealing with self-imposed sanctions after infractions committed by its football and men's basketball program.

The university, however, took control of the situation immediately. Summitt informed her assistants and her team about her condition before any information was released to the public. They were understandably stunned but determined to help her overcome her limitations.

The university subsequently released the story to the media. The women's interim athletic director, Joan Cronan, told the *New York Times* that she had three concerns guiding her response to the situation: Summitt's coaching future, potential recruiting fallouts, and distracting from the team's efforts.[27] In its statement, the university left no doubt that it fully supported Summitt. The university also established an action plan, explaining that Summitt's long-time assistants would begin taking on more coaching duties over time. The action plan preempted any unexpected questions from the media. Furthermore, Tennessee framed the storyline to emphasize that it was fully aware of the attention this decision would bring to the university.

The media response was favorable, and Cronan was forthright in discussing the delicate nature of the situation and how the university was approaching it.[28] The public's response to Summitt's determination to manage this debilitating disease at the highest level of sporting competition portrayed her as a hero in a college sports environment besieged by

CONTINUED

questionable behavior.[29] Summitt resigned after the 2011–12 season and became head coach emeritus of the program.

There are lessons to be learned from Tennessee's ability to anticipate and prevent a media crisis. The university could have released Summitt from her duties under the guise of medical concerns or let the situation play out without publicly responding, hoping that it would resolve itself. Tennessee could have justified either approach in order to protect Summitt in a difficult personal situation. Tennessee's response to Summitt helped rebuild the credibility of the athletic program while softening the blow of its football and basketball sanctions.

Proactive crisis management can also help sports organizations maximize revenue and mitigate reliance on star athletes. The combination of Tiger Woods's injuries and personal life problems that began in 2009 could have ended the PGA Tour's run of success both on and off the course. Woods's 12-year run of historic performances had made him the PGA Tour's number one draw. With Woods at his competitive nadir in 2010, year-on-year final round viewership declined by approximately 34% and stayed below 2.5 million viewers in 2011.[30]

Woods' decline could have generated a crisis for the PGA Tour. Instead, the organization signed record television broadcasting rights deals with NBC and CBS. The new agreement will bring in $800 million annually to the organization beginning in 2011, a 33% increase in the amount of money that the tour made from its previous agreements.

How could the PGA Tour have signed a record contract in the midst of a potential crisis? The key to the organization's new broadcast rights agreement is that the organization understood its television partners' revenue models. The PGA Tour's critical insight was to ensure that its broadcast partners could sell their advertising inventory during broadcasts regardless of ratings fluctuations. The PGA Tour proactively gained commitments from sponsors to buy approximately 75% of the advertisements during tournament broadcasts. As Sean McManus, the chairman of CBS Sports, said about a new agreement, "It's as close to a guarantee as you're going to see in big-time sports today."[31]

The PGA Tour is an example of how sports organizations can prevent crisis and become less dependent on star performers. By understanding how broadcast networks make money, the PGA Tour created a risk-reducing approach that enabled the organization to command a price premium even as the organization confronted a crisis with its star performer.

No matter how proactive a sports organization is in monitoring for potential problems, there will be certain situations in which a crisis is impossible to prevent or avoid. Before responding to a crisis, sports strategists need to determine how different issues will impact their organizations.

Evaluating the Crisis

When a crisis strikes, it is critical to acquire as much information about the crisis-inducing event as quickly as possible. Unlike a normal, orderly audit of practices, an organization in crisis will be pressed to respond or comment in a very short time frame. The most essential questions that organizations should answer are: What are the charges? Who are the key players and stakeholders? What information is missing, and how quickly can we get it? And, most pressingly, should we respond?

Conventional wisdom among crisis advisers and spokespersons is that a quick response is necessary to frame the encounter. Framing the encounter enables organizations to maintain control in the fast-moving communications environment. But there is a problem with assuming that the fast response is always the best approach. It seems counterintuitive to refrain from responding to a crisis, but in some situations silence may be the wisest choice.

BARTMAN TAKES AN INTENTIONAL WALK

The Chicago Cubs were only four outs from playing in their first World Series in almost 60 years when Florida Marlins second baseman Luis Castillo hit a seemingly harmless fly ball off a fastball from Cubs ace Mark Prior. As the ball rose skyward down the third base line, Cubs outfielder Moisés Alou ran over to the left field stands and raised his glove to make the catch. Suddenly, a look of disgust came over his face as the ball ricocheted off a fan's outstretched hand and into foul territory. Alou then riled up the Wrigley Field crowd by slamming his glove against his leg and then visibly reacting with shock and disgust toward the person who prevented him from making the catch. Even though

CONTINUED

BARTMAN TAKES AN INTENTIONAL WALK *CONTINUED*

many fans did not see the initial incident, they did see the outfielder's actions and assumed that someone had prevented Alou from making a sure out.

That someone was Steve Bartman. A longtime season ticket holder and fan, Bartman quickly became the Cubs' enemy number one. Anger swept through the "Friendly Confines" as people screamed, threatened, and threw beer at a fellow fan. Bartman, who sat stoically while wearing headphones over a blue Cubs cap in his front row seat, was finally escorted from the field by security guards. Outside of the ballpark, some Cubs fans turned into an angry mob, chanting "Ass – !" at Bartman.[32] At the same time, the Marlins unleashed a flurry of hits and scored eight runs in the eighth inning. Cubs fans were shocked by the sudden turn of events as their team suffered a humiliating defeat. The series ultimately ended with the team's elimination in the seventh game of the National League Championship Series.

Bartman has become an iconic symbol of how sports-induced emotions can induce irrational behavior. The Bartman reaction has been referred to as "the darkest moment in Wrigley Field history."[33] Immediately following the incident, reporters surrounded his home and relentlessly hounded him for a statement. A prominent restaurateur bought the ball from a seatmate of Bartman for over $100,000 and proceeded to blow it up in front of a national television audience in an attempt to erase the memories of the painful incident.[34] The crowning insult came from then-governor Rod Blagojevich of Illinois. The man who later would be convicted of seventeen criminal counts bragged that Bartman "will never get a pardon from this governor!"[35]

Despite the media attention and unbridled rage from disgruntled fans, Bartman chose to release only a short apologetic comment through his brother a few days after the incident. He has remained silent despite insistent demands (that continue to this day) for an explanation of what happened. Bartman could have cashed in on his instant notoriety. He could have written a book or appeared on TV talk shows, turning his unfortunate incident into a profitable endeavor. Instead, he chose not to respond to requests for comment and maintained his privacy as a citizen. This approach enabled Bartman to earn sympathy from many of the same fans who cursed at him years earlier and the media has begun to rethink and regret its vitriolic attacks. By not responding to his critics, Bartman endured a rare personal sports catastrophe and handled it with remarkable aplomb.

Some questions that potential respondents must ask when deciding whether to respond are: How credible is the source of the charge? Who is the person or organization that is making it? What reputation does he or she have for accuracy in the public sphere? Is there a public and prevalent demand for a response? How will our position change if we wait to respond versus responding now?

Answering these questions will not always lead an organization to respond slowly or refrain from responding at all. In fact, this analysis can expedite an organization's response to a crisis – particularly when the charge is so personally painful or harmful that denial or avoidance could immediately become the default course of action. While it is usually in the best interests of a sports organization to anticipate and ward off a media backlash by promptly confronting the issue, the threat of harsh punishments from admitting fault head-on can cloud the judgment of the accused. This was illustrated in Penn State's response to child sexual abuse allegations.

In November 2011, former Penn State assistant football coach Jerry Sandusky was charged with 48 felony counts of child sexual abuse over a period of 15 years.[36] Rather than immediately distancing themselves from Sandusky when the abuse first came to light, key figures in the Penn State organization, including legendary coach Joe Paterno, failed to take any more than the minimum action required by law. When news of the charges and allegations surfaced, the media and general public were outraged by what seemed to be a university cover-up. Penn State's failure to promptly and transparently respond to the Sandusky allegations[37] resulted in Paterno's firing as well as the eventual removal of the university's president, vice president, and athletic director. In addition, the school initially received some of the harshest sanctions in NCAA history, including a "four-year bowl ban, $60 million fine, vacating 112 wins and four years of reduced scholarships."[38]

While the NCAA later reduced many of the sanctions, Penn State leadership's inability to recognize the most important stage of crisis management caused long-term damage to the school. Any initial evaluation of a situation depends on an organization's willingness to confront potential consequences. Penn State's leaders failed to take the appropriate measures that could have prevented serious consequences. That decision led to the perception that the university had prioritized protecting its image over reporting abuse. This was not only an example of poor judgment, but also an error in evaluating the potential consequences of the situation.

Responding to a Crisis

Once an organization decides to respond, it must evaluate potential choices and identify the possible reactions they might receive. A crucial skill in crisis management is the ability to prepare for how the public and the media will react to an organization's actions or statements. The sports strategists that anticipate these groups' initial reactions are more likely to maintain control of the dialogue and navigate the discussion on their own terms. In many ways, the crisis encounter has elements of a chess match: it is an ever-changing environment that requires anticipation and adaptation prior, during, and after every move. For every question answered, statement released, or tweet sent, there will be a public reaction that could potentially change the dynamic of the situation. In this sense, strategizing how to address a crisis parallels game theory, which outlines models for making decisions based on predictions of how other parties will react and respond. Any organization in crisis must recognize that a response cannot be one-dimensional. It must be analyzed through a prism of possibilities, each with multiple consequences.

Response Choices

In formulating a response to a crisis situation, an organization typically relies on its core identity and values. Most organizations depend on the institutional rhetoric they have developed to maintain their identity. As discussed in Chapter 2, institutional rhetoric is a set of communication concepts that an organization utilizes internally or externally to express its point-of-view.

The initial response may be exclusively in the form of a prepared media statement. An organization typically sets out talking points that usually start with the relevant facts, continues with the framing of an argument, and ideally concludes with an action statement that embodies the essential ideas that the organization wants the media to circulate. This prepared statement is often the single place where an organization has complete control over the argument by producing, shaping, and performing a defense without interruption. Opening statements are typically delivered at a press conference. After the statement is delivered, the organization is open to questions, and it becomes more difficult to control the message.

The decision of whether to deliver the response verbally or in a written statement necessitates strategic planning. The oral statement allows for more interaction, questions, and answers. It also enables the respondent to express emotions. If presenting an oral media statement, the spokesperson must plan the delivery, style, and tone of the message. Today, many successful spokespersons employ a conversational style throughout their presentations. An informal style reflects the changing communication environment of the digital era that emphasizes intimacy, accessibility, and sincerity. A conversational style uses a mix of short and longer sentences, avoids jargon and complicated phrasing, makes eye contact with the audience, and emphasizes vocal inflection with pauses to punctuate and clarify main ideas. The speed of delivery should be at a pace that is slow enough to understand but rapid enough to demonstrate confidence and deter the media from interrupting.

However, the oral statement also exposes the spokesperson to difficult questions that he or she may not be expecting. The written response has the advantages of more control and precision but lacks an opportunity for interaction with fans, media, and sponsors. An effective written statement needs to be grounded in audience analysis to anticipate the point of view of people who could question the organization's credibility. As a result, the most effective written statements concisely state the facts and are designed to be understood by different audiences. Only issuing a written response, however, may portray a person or organization as unwilling to face the accusers. Therefore, it is important to deliver the written message strategically through the various digital channels to maximize its impact.

Too often, the response team rejects the press conference and opts for the written statement because the message can be controlled and involves less uncertainty. Sports strategists must weigh the advantages and disadvantages of the oral and written statements by assessing their comfort level, appetite for risk, and information availability.

BOYS WILL BE BOYS

Michael Phelps enhanced his reputation after winning eight gold medals at the 2008 Summer Olympics and breaking Mark Spitz's record for most gold medals won in a single Olympics.[39] His performance was visually and emotionally compelling, as the television cameras cut between Phelps's dominance in the pool and his mother's passionate cheering. It was sports at its most photogenic: dedication, world-class achievement, family support, and childhood dreams all wrapped into one package. The August 2008 issue of *Sports Illustrated* featured the "All-Time Olympian" Phelps on its cover, bedecked with his eight medals.[40] Sponsors fiercely competed

CONTINUED

for the privilege to tie the emotional connection of his achievements to their products. Speedo, Visa, Omega, Hilton, and Kellogg all struck partnerships with Phelps.

Phelps's image as America's golden boy was threatened, however, just a short time after the 2008 Olympics. The now-shuttered British tabloid *News of the World* purchased a photo of him smoking marijuana out of a bong at a party.[41] The widespread image of Phelps as America's poster boy was in danger of being replaced by one that portrayed him as yet another entitled star failing to understand his responsibility and influence. To make matters worse, Phelps had been arrested in 2004 for driving under the influence, an incident that gained new life as the media attempted to illustrate a trend in Phelps's misbehavior.[42] Phelps's image as a symbol of discipline and achievement conflicted with his out-of-the-pool behavior.

On the same day that the bong exposé was published, Phelps released a statement saying, "I engaged in behavior which was regrettable and demonstrated bad judgment. . . . I acted in a youthful and inappropriate way, not in a manner that people have come to expect from me. For this, I am sorry. I promise my fans and the public – it will not happen again."[43] While Phelps's apology was immediate and concise, it was also stilted and caused many critics to doubt his sincerity or whether he learned from his misstep.[44]

Two days later, Phelps gave an interview to his hometown newspaper, the *Baltimore Sun*. He said, "Seeing my mom reminded me of how it was the day after I got my DUI, and I swore to myself I'd never do that again. This is just a stupid thing of mine that I did, and I have to live with it."[45] With this statement, Phelps directly addressed his behavior and expressed regret for his actions in a forthright manner. Phelps's response also subdued the controversy and shifted public opinion away from viewing him as a villain or proponent of corruption. Only one sponsor, Kellogg, decided to jettison the swimmer.

In the end, his sponsors, the Olympic Committee, and the media essentially excused Phelps's behavior and cast it as a learning experience for the swimmer.[46] This episode parallels the closure achieved after the DUI incident. Both in 2004 and 2008, Phelps's more candid responses pleading for forgiveness for his youthful indiscretions helped ensure no real harm occurred. These outcomes illustrate the importance of recognizing the cultural context of a crisis and the ways in which the accused fits into it. Phelps's Herculean, All-American brand could better withstand these charges with a simple, contrite response from the swimmer rather than a prepared statement. Although much of this chapter addresses strategies that can be used by agents, lawyers, and public relations teams, it's important to recognize when their intervention may actually impede resolution or worsen the crisis by obfuscating the athlete's authenticity. Phelps's marijuana mishap and DUI arrest demonstrate it can be best to let Michael be Michael. At least until he reaches middle age.

Once deciding on the channel for a crisis response, sports strategists can focus on the message. William Benoit, professor of communication at the University of Missouri, has written extensively about repairing an individual or an organization's image after facing an external attack or crisis. Benoit identifies five types of responses – denial, mortification, evasion of responsibility, reducing offensiveness of the event, and corrective action – from which an accused party can choose, each with its own advantages and drawbacks.[47] Using Benoit's five categories as a foundation, we will discuss how these response strategies have been used both successfully and unsuccessfully in the past and how sports strategists can apply them in the future. It is also important to recognize that these categories are often combined and adapted to the specific situation.

Denial. In this response, the accused party claims that he or she did not perform the action in question. This strategy's strength is its brevity, decisiveness, and simplicity. If credible, then the denial can ultimately vindicate the accused, regardless of previous attacks. In 2006, three members of Duke University's men's lacrosse team were indicted for rape. Despite the overwhelming initial response from students, professors, and the media condemning the players over the alleged activities, the accused never wavered in their denials. When the charges were ultimately dropped, the players demonstrated how denial can be a successful crisis management strategy even when faced with a torrent of criticism. As Duke University president Richard H. Brodhead later admitted, "They have carried themselves with dignity through an ordeal of deep unfairness."[48]

If the denial is based on false information or deliberate deceit, however, it amplifies the crisis and ultimately causes more severe consequences. External audiences are usually more upset with a false or questionable denial and more vindictive in their response towards a sports organization because their trust has been violated. In this regard, denial is thus the ultimate high-risk, high-reward image restoration strategy.

BEGGING FOR THE DEATH PENALTY

Franklin High School in Stockton, California received the most drastic punishment ever handed down to a high school football program in 2007: the dreaded death penalty. High schools and universities often commit recruiting violations and are punished accordingly, but the death penalty – which cancels all games and practices and effectively eliminates the future of the program – is seldom considered because of its long-term destructive impact. Franklin's violation and ensuing crisis management missteps demonstrate how misreading the crisis environment can result in far more serious consequences.

The initial charge filed by the California Interscholastic Foundation (CIF) accused Franklin of illegally recruiting ten American Samoans to play for the school's football team. A six-month investigation by the CIF's Sac-Joaquin section, led by Commissioner Pete Saco, found Franklin High School guilty of 54 infractions committed over a three-year period.[49] The charges included paying for travel and lodging expenses for players and their families and providing false information so that the American Samoans could gain eligibility.[50] The original sanctions imposed against Franklin were substantial and included imposing a five-year ban on competing in the football playoffs, making three current American Samoan players ineligible, and forfeiting 19 victories accrued over the prior three seasons.[51]

The CIF's ruling stunned the Stockton Unified School District (SUSD), which had adamantly denied the allegations against Franklin and had stood by the high school since the launch of the investigation. The district released a public statement to the media the same day the original punishments were handed down, claiming that the CIF's findings were invalid and without authority. The statement also made personal attacks that questioned the integrity and impartiality of Commissioner Saco: "Nothing in the CIF rules supports Commissioner Saco's insistence on turning these matters into a media circus, which also demonstrates that his actions and intentions are not in good faith."[52] An impassioned backlash against the CIF amplified the school district's heated words, which included a counterattack from Franklin's head football coach and media interviews with disgruntled Franklin players and students. Furthermore, Franklin defied the CIF's edict by playing the three ineligible American Samoan players.

In response to Franklin's defiance, the CIF increased its punishment. Franklin's football program received the death penalty for the next three seasons.[53] All of Franklin's winter and spring sports teams were suspended from the 2007–8 season's playoffs.[54]

The SUSD and Franklin's handling of the crisis escalated the animosity between the two sides and therefore worsened the school's punishment. It was Franklin's initial response to the CIF's decision that added three rings to the "media circus." Instead of initially seeking a collaborative solution in a less public setting, Franklin and the SUSD used public channels in an attempt to pressure the CIF to back down. Franklin and the SUSD could have better managed this crisis, but they failed to recognize the perils of their responses. The CIF not only held the higher ethical ground, but ultimately made the rules and had the united support of other schools in the district.

An important step to responding to a crisis is analyzing the situation, audience, power relationships, and available communication channels. The school district could have set a precedent of cooperating with the CIF in its initial response to the crisis instead of reacting with aggression and hostility. Minimally, Franklin and the SUSD should have ensured that all stakeholders in the situation understood the school board's position and how it would affect them. This might have impacted not only their eventual punishment but also the ways in which the coach, players, and students chose to respond to the situation. By not setting a cooperative framework in their response, Franklin and the school district quickly lost control of the situation.

Furthermore, Franklin and the SUSD failed to recognize how their argument's quality, delivery style, and message tone played critical roles in the effective management of the crisis. It was inevitable that the public personal attacks on the commissioner would escalate the intensity of the

CONTINUED

BEGGING FOR THE DEATH PENALTY *CONTINUED*

crisis – questioning his "good faith" was an invitation for a stern rebuke. The responses from the SUSD and the Franklin community were neither strategically calculated nor controlled, which detracted from their ability to resolve the issue efficiently.

After internal reflection and suffering, Franklin and the SUSD publicly apologized and distanced themselves from their previous statements. The CIF accepted that Franklin had recognized its failings, and in acknowledging the collateral damage associated with penalizing future student athletes, reduced its sentence.[55] Call it time off for lesson learned and good behavior.

Mortification. In this strategy, the accused party displays regret and offers an apology for the incident. Mortification, similar to denial, directly confronts the issue. With this strategy, however, the accused party admits guilt, takes full responsibility, and asks for forgiveness. If done to the audience's satisfaction, mortification demonstrates honest accountability for the mistakes as well as a sense of vulnerability with which the audience may empathize. Mortification and apologies, however, have become so popular as a response strategy that they are now suspicious paths to redemption. Critics and pundits pick apart apologies piece by piece and analyze them for authenticity and sincerity. In order to be effective, mortification must be perceived as direct and genuine.

Consider NFL quarterback Michael Vick's public apology after his conviction for illegal dogfighting: "I'm sorry. . . . What I did was horrendous. Awful. Inhumane. And I've no excuses for my actions."[56] Gail Collins of the *New York Times* commented that "Vick took responsibility for his behavior and expressed his shame for what he had done so effectively that I wondered if he had hired an apology coach. And he's making anti-dog-fight speeches for the Humane Society of the United States."[57] Mike Tierney of the *Atlanta Sports Examiner* wrote in admiration of Michael Vick's apology, "There are half-assed, roundabout, phony apologies by athletes for their transgressions. And there is a Michael Vick apology. . . . His remarks provide a template for athletes in trouble."[58] By leaving no doubt that he was at fault for his actions, Vick successfully executed a mortification response.

Too often, half-measured apologies end up with unintended negative consequences. Former NBA guard Tim Hardaway claimed, "I hate gay people" in a 2007 interview when he was asked if he could accept an openly gay active NBA player. When talking about his comments in an interview three days later, Hardaway stated, "I don't hate gay people. I'm a goodhearted person. I interact with people all the time. . . . I respect people. For me to say 'hate' was a bad word, and I didn't mean to use it." Hardaway never actually apologized for the content of his statement, instead suggesting he merely should have used different language. His backhanded apology cost him an endorsement deal and caused him to be banned from making appearances at NBA-sanctioned events during the 2007 All-Star weekend.[59] While Hardaway did later fully apologize for his statement and even became the first person to sign a gay marriage petition in Florida in 2013, Hardaway's initial comments and lack of apology have largely shaped his post-NBA career identity.[60]

Evasion of Responsibility. Removing the blame of alleged misbehavior from the organization or person. According to Benoit, examples of evasion of responsibility include proposing that the behavior was in retaliation to someone else's offensive act, citing a scarcity of important information, suggesting the behavior in question was an accident, and advocating that the action was done with good intentions.[61] Evasion of responsibility shifts the focus of the charge onto someone or something else, framing the organization or player as a victim.

PLAYING THE BLAME GAME

When Alex Rodriguez dropped his lawsuits against MLB and the Major League Baseball Players Association (MLBPA) in 2014, many people felt that "baseball's long nightmare is over."[62] For months, Rodriguez battled allegations both from the media and from MLB that he had taken any PEDs received from Anthony Bosch of Biogensis of America, a now-defunct Florida anti-aging clinic. One of the reasons that Rodriguez's evasion of responsibility was so controversial is because he had previously used a mortification response strategy when accused of taking PEDs in 2009. Rodriguez admitted to reporter Peter Gammons that he had used PEDs from 2001–3 only days after *Sports Illustrated* reporters Selena Roberts and David Epstein alleged that he took the drugs during that time.[63]

Rodriguez used an evasion of responsibility response strategy when the MLB accused him of, and later suspended for, violating the league's

CONTINUED

PLAYING THE BLAME GAME *CONTINUED*

substance-abuse policy in 2013. Even after an arbitrator reduced his suspension from 211 to 162 games, Rodriguez sued MLB and claimed the league was perpetuating "this injustice [as the] first step toward abolishing guaranteed contracts in the 2016 bargaining round, instituting lifetime bans for single violations of drug policy, and further insulating its corrupt investigative program from any variety [of] defense by accused players, or any variety of objective review."[64] Rodriguez also sued the MLBPA and accused "the players union of breaching its duty to represent Rodriguez fairly."[65]

Rodriguez was widely criticized for not accepting responsibility for his actions. In response to Rodriguez's very confrontational claims, *Boston Globe* columnist Dan Shaughnessy stated that Rodriguez is "the most hated man in sports, one of the most hated people in all of America. He is a living, breathing, ballplaying piñata – the Prince of Loathe."[66] Rather than being redeemed for his actions, Rodriguez's crisis-response strategy was expensive both in terms of the dollars spent on his legal defense and on the credibility he lost with fans, media, and sponsors.

In contrast, the New York Yankees have emerged relatively unscathed from Rodriguez's crisis. The organization will not have to pay most of the $25 million of Rodriguez's 2014 salary, and it has deflected much of the criticism of the star's PED use. Instead, the Yankees have put most of the blame for the situation on Rodriguez. As one Yankees' official stated to the *New York Daily News*, "This is typical Alex. Instead of taking responsibility for his actions, he blames everybody else. It wasn't the Yankees who introduced Rodriguez to Anthony Bosch."[67] By largely placing culpability on the star rather than the organization, the Yankees have successfully navigated the crisis.

The Yankees' crisis avoidance approach will not always work. In an era where athletes' actions are increasingly placing themselves and their organizations at risk for a crisis, sports strategists should consider if or when to distance their organizations from a crisis generator. In this situation, Rodriguez alienated the public at large and was never able to establish a credible defense, which limited the potential effects on the Yankees organization.

Reducing Offensiveness of the Event. In this strategy, the accused reframes the incident to minimize public outrage. An organization or person can emphasize its redeeming qualities in an attempt to downplay the negative impact of the misbehavior. The benefit of attempting to reduce the offensiveness of the event is similar to that of evading responsibility: the audience's attention and anger is redirected away from the accused organization. Trying to reduce offensiveness, however, may be perceived as manipulative. This is essentially the "who's on first" response that shifts the focus from the issue at hand to a more favorable storyline.

After years of facing accusations that he used PEDs, Lance Armstrong admitted to doping throughout his cycling career in an interview with Oprah Winfrey. Armstrong primarily used a three-pronged approach to redirect the negative attention. Rather than saying he misled the public on several different occasions, Armstrong contended that "I view this situation as one big lie that I repeated a lot of times." In addition, Armstrong argued that he was only doing what other riders were doing, and it would not have been "humanly possible" for a cyclist to win the Tour de France seven times without PEDs.[68] Armstrong also claimed that he would take steps to help Livestrong, the cancer foundation he founded in 1997, restore its reputation and relationship with cancer patients.[69] While largely criticized for his approach to his apology, Armstrong attempted to reduce the offensiveness of his misdeeds by taking tangible steps to minimize the fallout from his PED admission.

Corrective Action. In this strategy, the accused party offers a plan to fix the problem at hand or to prevent it from happening in the future. Corrective action is often a strategy best used in conjunction with mortification. Employing corrective action has several advantages: it is clearly action-oriented and resolution-based and often makes the public feel that the situation is being taken seriously and properly handled. The drawback is that the corrective action itself could be seen as manipulative, ineffective, or too little too late. When Ohio State University (OSU) was first accused of violating NCAA rules regarding inappropriate player compensation in 2011, then-president E. Gordon Gee was asked if he would fire the school's head football coach. Even though coach Jim Tressel had allegedly withheld knowledge of these rules violations from the school and the NCAA, Gee flippantly responded, "I hope he doesn't fire me."[70]

With his comments, Gee appeared to subjugate his major public university's presidency to its football program. After fans and media widely criticized his initial comments, Gee took steps to regain his credibility with different audiences.

He wrote in a media statement, "The current problems in our football program are correctable and will be addressed."[71] Tressel resigned and the players involved received a five-game suspension for the following season. Later that fall, three OSU players were quickly reported and punished by the university for an incident involving unauthorized benefits, demonstrating the new enforcement policy. In this case, utilizing corrective action helped put an end to this downward-spiraling crisis.

However, Gee later became an example of one of the pitfalls of corrective action when discussing conference realignment in college sports. For years, the Big Ten had strongly considered adding the University of Notre Dame to be part of its conference. In response to Notre Dame joining the Atlantic Coast Conference (ACC) for all sports other than football, Gee stated, "The fathers are holy on Sunday, and they're holy hell on the rest of the week. . . . You just can't trust those damn Catholics on a Thursday or a Friday."[72] While making this inappropriate joke at a private event months earlier, Gee announced his resignation only days after his comments became public. While Gee did eventually apologize to Notre Dame officials, there was no corrective action that could be taken both because of his past behavior and the obvious offensiveness of these remarks.

It is critical that organizations understand how these response options are best employed in combination to create a comprehensive identity-restoration strategy. In addition, it is difficult to claim that any one response strategy is always better than another. Each crisis situation differs, and a response must be chosen for and tailored to the unique situation. Sports strategists must carefully analyze the charges, key figures, and all available and relevant information while also anticipating the crisis's trajectory before selecting a strategic response.

Preparing Crisis Respondents

A crisis respondent is traditionally a spokesperson who represents an organization on a number of levels. In sports organizations, the media increasingly wants to talk to owners, executives, and players and bypass the formal avenues of information dissemination. Because there is such a demand for knowledgeable respondents in a sports organization, preparation for communication with the media is necessary on an organization-wide level.

Staging crisis simulations can help organizations become better prepared to establish open and clear communication channels during periods of calm and turmoil alike. These simulations, not unlike theatrical rehearsals, mimic a crisis environment and allow key stakeholders to rehearse and workshop crisis responses. Running practice sessions encourages crisis respondents to share information with each other in a timely manner and ensures that all the players can respond to different issues in an effective manner.

Simulations also expose potential problems with an organization's crisis response. For example, one of the common problems that prevents effective crisis response is personal antipathy. Departments, groups, or people might have previous disagreements with each other that can impair communication during a crisis. Identifying and potentially solving these problems during a simulation can prepare an organization to better respond to an actual crisis.

An unavoidable and much-feared reality in crisis response is a lack of control over questions. Some organizations try to neutralize this threat by limiting time for questioning, establishing ground rules, or choosing not to comment. In some cases, organizations intentionally use respondents who cannot answer certain questions because they lack expertise in particular areas. However, these tricks of the trade are risky. The media may feel that the organization is attempting to spin the story, which inevitably will affect the public's perception of the organization's sincerity.

When answering each question, a spokesperson should follow a consistent and effective response structure based on the tenets of public speaking: introduction, body, and conclusion. This means that a respondent should reframe the question with an introduction, provide specific support in the body, and summarize the message in the conclusion. Ideally, this will all be done in a compressed period of time. This three-part sequence gives organizations control over the message and deters interruptions, preventing the media from distorting the story.

In general, there are three categories of questions: the obvious, the probable, and the off-the-wall. Most organizations are well prepared for obvious and probable questions but fail to prepare for what they perceive as unlikely topics or questions. The off-the-wall question "that comes out of nowhere" can upset even the most carefully planned responses. In preparing a respondent for a crisis, most simulation exercises should designate their time accordingly, with around 50% going to obvious questions, 35% to probable questions, and 15% to off-the-wall questions. This distribution is a good baseline, but organizations should analyze and decide what allocations are most effective for their specific needs.

Some questions simply ask for explanations or clarifications, while others may be more aggressive in tone and content. The respondent must understand not only the question itself, but also its context. The most obvious type of question asks for an explanation for an act or behavior: What did you do? Why did you do it? When did you do it? What are you going to do about it? The respondent should be prepared to answer all four questions directly and briefly, and should demonstrate comprehensive knowledge of the situation. These are the most fundamental of inquiries, but generally the most muffed as well. There are myriad reasons for why a spokesperson may be unable to respond effectively: lack of information, misunderstanding of the question, legal restraints, or refusal to accept the terms of the charge.

Some questions are based on misinformation or ignorance of the subject. In training simulations, these types of questions are typically overlooked because organizations assume the media or public possess general knowledge and awareness of the issue(s). What makes this type of question volatile is that the response can reveal character flaws in the respondent as a result of the unsettling nature of the question. Examples are: "Why can't you just find the best high school players and sign them today?" or "Since you have so many empty seats in your ballpark, why can't you just give the tickets away?" These can become tough questions to answer that require long explanations and run the risk of alienating fans and sponsors alike.

One type of aggressive question is the *ad-hominem*, a personal attack on the respondent. An example of an ad-hominem is: "Why have you deliberately neglected the health of your players by avoiding the truth about steroids?" These questions can be jarring, as they are designed to challenge the respondent's character and professionalism. It is important to distinguish between a legitimate question that is relevant to the crisis and an ad-hominem attack. Instead of responding to the personal attack, reframing the question to return focus to the key themes is an effective strategy to deal with the ad-hominem. The ad-hominem attack is intended to put the spokesperson on the defensive. As a general rule, being defensive detracts from your credibility and convolutes your overall message.

Spokespersons must also prepare for other trap questions. When encountering these types of trap questions, it is important not to let the questioner dictate or frame your answer. It is essential to move the question back to the key talking points that were outlined in the thematic statement. Common examples include:

- Pick Your Poison – The questioner poses two unacceptable choices from which the spokesperson is asked to choose. An example either/or question is, "Since you lost Saturday, are you going to fire your defensive coordinator or hand in your own resignation?" In this case, a sample response could be, "It is a long season, and we do not make decisions on a single game. We constantly evaluate ways to make the team better." The respondent is not accepting the questioner's premise but the respondent is reframing the question and providing an answer that is consistent with an organization's values and positions.

- Secret Agent – The questioner references information from an unknown or unverified place: "I have it on good authority that you are planning on moving your team to Dubai. When will the final decision be made?" A crisis respondent can expect this type of question in a variety of circumstances because it enables the questioner to ask about topics without taking responsibility for the content. There is never a good reason to verify an unsubstantiated question, and that should be the policy of the organization.

- Jeopardy – A series of questions are asked rapid-fire: "When did you know that the upcoming season would be cancelled? Who made that decision and why? Can we expect a statement from you on the costs of the decision and when the players' parents will be notified of the decision to resume play?" The respondent must control and define what questions he or she will answer. A straightforward statement might be something like the following: "I can only answer, at this point, that we are in the process of working out the details of what the cancellation will mean for all of the participants. The details will be released as soon as we have consulted with everyone who is affected."

- Try a Little Tenderness – The questioner is so impassioned by the issue that he or she uses an emotional appeal to cast your organization in a negative light: "When are you going to stop selling unhealthy vendor food? Everything is loaded with nitrates and gluten and you're endangering my child's life." There is no one good answer to such passion. An expression of understanding of the questioner's plight and reassurance that all necessary measures will be taken is a good start. And if there are actual processes that are being employed, mention them.

Planning for question-and-answer sessions requires the ability to respond to both rehearsed and unexpected inquiries with assurance and swift adaptation of material. It is also the interaction that carries the most risk, as it threatens to expose the organization's weaknesses and can be easily edited and distorted by the media. Crisis situations demand not only knowledge of the issue at hand, but also anticipation, practice, and communicative agility.

Conclusion

Crisis has clearly become a critical management issue in the contemporary sports world. It's not that behavior and ethics in sports were pristine over the past century, as illustrated by the 1919 Black Sox Scandal; chicanery has been as much a part of sports as has been celebrated victories. While some skeptics questioned the legitimacy of these practices, for the most part the media in years past was acquiescent, flattering, and often cooperative in repressing scandalous stories. Today, money, competition, and cultural and technological changes have intensified the relationship among the sports organization and its fans, the media, and sponsors. Increased competition paired with multiplying communication channels threatens the past covenant between the media and sports organizations that once shielded organizations from crisis. The communication universe now teems with information that circulates faster than ever among a highly engaged audience equipped with the tools to interact with players and sports organizations. Crisis can now strike from the most unlikely of places – and can blow up in a matter of minutes.

To combat these raised stakes, a sports organization must think strategically about how to properly anticipate and manage a crisis in the new sports environment. Determining the type of response, style of delivery, and desired channels of communication dictates the extent of the damage. In today's digital world, these decisions must be made in shorter periods of time. Successful sports strategists recognize the persistence of the recent changes in the sports environment and approach these changes proactively. As the great Yankees catcher Yogi Berra once said, "The future ain't what it used to be."[73]

8 Reinvigorating Sportscapes

The NFL has long owned Sunday afternoons in autumn. From the festive parking lots holding morning tailgates to the hard-hitting afternoon action on the gridiron, devoted fans have filled stadiums across the country with regularity. For years franchises could count on these loyal customers to show up, even as ticket, parking, and concession prices all escalated.

After peaking at more than 17.3 million people in 2007, action at the turnstiles has slowed.[1] Between 2007 and 2012, average game attendance dropped 4%.[2] Even though attendance increased slightly in the 2013 season, the NFL is well aware that the in-stadium experience has difficulty competing with fans' access to games, scores, and highlights through dozens of digital channels. In 1998, over half of fans said in an ESPN poll that they would rather attend an NFL game than watch it at home. In contrast, a 2011 poll showed that only 29% of fans preferred to be at the game, the sharpest drop of any major sport measured over that span.[3]

The NFL is not the only major football league worried about getting people to its games. The Southeastern Conference (SEC) has led all NCAA college football conferences in attendance over the last 15 years by averaging over 75,000 people at each game.[4]

However, overall conference attendance at SEC stadiums declined from 2010 to 2012, with nine schools experiencing decreases from 2011 to 2012. Even national football powerhouses such as the University of Alabama and University of Georgia had over 30% of their student tickets unused from 2009 to 2012. The primary catalyst for these attendance issues is that the experiences audiences have at home can exceed the ones they have at stadiums. College students are watching the games in their dorm rooms or Greek houses because their access to high-definition televisions, high speed wireless Internet, and faster mobile networks provides a better sports experience than they can find at the stadium.[5]

To combat declining attendance, the NFL and SEC have made a number of efforts to replicate the high quality and convenience of the home-viewing experience. For example, the NFL ordered all of its teams to display real-time fantasy football stats throughout their stadiums in 2011.[6] Up until then, the decision to show player stats from competing games rather than focusing on their own contests had been left to each of the league's 32 franchises. The SEC hired a market research firm in 2013 to examine the game day experience and make recommendations on how the conference can address the problem.[7]

Even as both organizations experienced attendance increases during their 2013 seasons, the NFL and SEC recognized they still faced a difficult challenge. As NFL executive vice president Eric Grubman asserted, "The at-home experience has gotten better and cheaper, while the in-stadium experience feels like it hasn't. That's a trend that we've got to do something about."[8] Mississippi State University athletic director Scott Stricklin cautions, "We can't afford to lose a generation [of ticket buyers]."[9] Without making significant changes to the in-venue product, even these dominant leagues could suffer significant attendance decreases in the future.

• • •

From the racetrack at Churchill Downs to the "Theatre of Dreams" pitch at Old Trafford Stadium to the manicured baseball diamond at AT&T Park, venues have long held a special place in the sports world. These structures serve as more than just places where spectators gather to watch their teams compete. These sites continuously build community spirit and forge common bonds among local residents rallying around their home teams. Visit virtually any high school stadium on a Friday night in the fall in the United States, and you will quickly realize that the families in the stands are as much a part of the experience as the football players on the field. In the sports industry, "place" serves multiple purposes: reinforcing community ties, generating civic pride, and driving local business development. The physical sports venue is a de facto community center – a place where people from all different backgrounds gather.

Over the past 20 years, the concept of place has gradually expanded. This new paradigm has been sparked by a series of technological changes that have not only enhanced the live, in-person experience but also enabled audiences to consume events through emerging digital and mobile channels. The proliferation of communication and social networking platforms has made audience participation and interaction outside the traditional venue experience easier than ever. Sports organizations now struggle to find a balance between keeping the in-venue experience unique and adding new components to it, including streaming video and fantasy sports.

Against the backdrop of the constantly improving experience in people's homes, at official team bars and restaurants, and on mobile devices, sports strategists must consider how to continue drawing people to their venues. Developing and reinvigorating sportscapes becomes the central approach to meeting new attendance challenges. Originally developed by Baylor University professor Kirk Wakefield and University of Mississippi professor Hugh Sloan, the concept of the "sportscape" explores how audiences interact with five stadium factors and team loyalty. They identify the five stadium factors that comprise the sportscape as parking, cleanliness, crowding, fan control, and food service. While team loyalty plays an important role, the authors conclude that "stadium design and stadium services also directly influence spectators' desire to stay, and hence, attend games at the stadium."[10]

Today's sports strategists are expanding the concept of sportscapes to drive attendance, incorporating both traditional in-stadium attractions and activities outside the stadium's walls. This strategy includes incorporating technology, public transportation systems, neighborhood attractions, and local establishments into an organization's sportscape. The concept is not unlike the approach that environmental marketers have taken with theme parks, shopping malls, casinos, and even supermarkets to deliver holistic consumer experiences with no details overlooked. When executed successfully, the best sportscapes give people a compelling reason to leave their lairs – having an experience they cannot get elsewhere. While these issues have existed since the beginning of the modern sports industry, never before have they been so front and center as the living room competes with the stadium experience.

An Overview of Sports Venues

The venue is the foundation on which sports is built. From ancient Greece's stone amphitheaters to today's technologically charged arenas, sports venues have always been more than just a site for matches or games. They are unique environments that are home to spectacles and memories that go beyond wins and losses. As soccer legend Pelé once said of London's original Wembley Stadium, "Wembley is the cathedral of football. It is the capital of football and it is the heart of football."[11]

The modern history of sports venues begins at the turn of the twentieth century with the boom in construction of large football stadiums and city-based ballparks. Across the U.S., the resulting wave of iconic structures can still be seen from Philadelphia's Franklin Field (1895) to the University of Texas' Memorial Stadium (1924). Yale University's stadium became the archetype for many venues. The school decided to build its football program a 70,000-seat building – the largest stadium built since the Roman Coliseum. Named the Yale Bowl in 1914 after its configuration, it became the model for the Rose Bowl, the L.A. Coliseum, and Michigan Stadium (also known as the "Big House"). Even then, Yale acknowledged that it needed to step up from its quaint Yale Field to reinvent the college football experience for its fans.[12]

Indoor venues built during this time were often used to house multiple events. In Minneapolis in the first half of the twentieth century, there was really only one place to experience indoor sports – the Minneapolis Auditorium. During the week, one could watch boxing, wrestling, roller derby, the world champion Minneapolis Lakers, and, for two weeks, the musical ice skating show Ice Follies. The audience was largely made up of men lighting up cigars and creating a cloud of smoke that lingered over the athletes. In the concourse, there was an ever-present aroma of Harris Tweed overcoats, Colgate aftershave, and hot dogs. The typical person bought a ticket, picked up a program, purchased some refreshments, and paid for parking. This represented the extent of the night's revenue for the sports organization. The Minneapolis Auditorium was typical of the all-purpose venues built during this era. They were characterized by the era's state-of-the-art design and civil engineering, which comprised soaring external edifices, dimly lit and narrow corridors, and concrete or wooden seating.

A half century later, a wave of mammoth cookie-cutter stadiums gave the sports world a series of domes: Astro, Metro, King, and Super. While they were criticized for their lack of warmth and intimacy, these all-purpose arenas introduced many innovations still used today, including climate-controlled environments, mall-like food and shopping options, and jumbo-sized electronic scoreboards and advertising signage. While these enhancements initially attracted people to these venues, the sterile environment, poor playing surfaces, over-amplification of sound, and growing expenses ultimately hampered their appeal.[13]

Many sports teams recently chose to build new facilities to remedy these weaknesses. Sports organizations often tried to invent a new audience experience by positioning stadiums as the centerpieces of larger retail, entertainment, and leisure complexes. In some cases, these sports structures have effectively redefined the traditional sports place and reinvented fans' sports experiences. Organizations have increasingly built stadiums in already-established urban areas or constructed new venues in suburban areas that attract fans to entertainment complexes designed around their teams.

One of the most obvious beneficiaries of the sports facility boom is MLB. In the last 20 years, almost every team in the league has built a new ballpark. The parks often combine cutting-edge technology with a thematically unified design that captures the spirit of the city. The first venue of this era was Camden Yards in Baltimore, which is a modern version of a 1920s ballpark that uses historical neighborhood icons as a major design strategy. What made this stadium a meaningful change in marketing sports places was its integration of the surrounding area into the park; the B&O Warehouse building, the longest building on the East Coast, is the stadium's defining visual and serves as the backdrop behind the right field wall.[14] Instead of building the sports facility as an isolated place, the designers embraced the city landscape and embellished it.

Colleges and universities have also been rapidly renovating and expanding their sports facilities. From 1997 to 2014, more than $5 billion was estimated to have been spent on facilities.[15] The University of Michigan's $226 million makeover of Michigan Stadium included new luxury boxes and club seats, wider aisles, better seat comfort, new turf, overall upgrading of technology, wood paneling, and decorative aesthetic upgrades.[16] The University of Maine also spent close to $5 million on its hockey and basketball facility, Alfond Arena. It received new seatbacks, clear glass for viewing, improved air quality, and concourse improvements throughout the arena.[17] These renovations demonstrate the ongoing race to meet audience expectations at all levels of college sports.

Even high school sports programs feel pressure to construct new, lavish sports facilities. Schools justify these improvements as efforts to energize school spirit and civic pride while boosting alumni donations and recruiting top local talent. The city of Allen, Texas, has built a $60 million, 18,000-seat high school football stadium by passing a $119 million bond to fund construction.[18] It is the most expensive high school stadium ever built and incorporates many of the architectural and infrastructural enhancements that define top-notch college and professional facilities.

Eagle Stadium in Allen is only one of many examples of high schools building elaborate facilities to meet market expectations. For example, Episcopal High School in Virginia completed a total athletic facility renovation, which included a multimillion-dollar, 60,000-square foot athletic center and numerous renovations to the gymnasium, field house, and weight room. The major facility renovation is prominently displayed on the private school's website as evidence of its competitive advantage over its rivals.[19] Christian Herr, an architect who worked on the Allen project, claims other districts will try to build bigger stadiums. "There's a competition – not only on the field, but off the field – where they're going to want larger stadiums as well."[20]

DUCK SWAG

Historically, most facilities money goes into the playing venue. That makes sense because the other facilities, such as coaches' offices or training rooms, are not seen as a marketing asset. In addition, the paying customers usually receive most of the benefits of place-building, which include fan-oriented amenities, technological upgrades, and luxury suites and skyboxes for corporate sponsors and business executives. When the Oregon Ducks opened their new Football Performance Center, a gift from Nike co-founder and Oregon alumnus Phil Knight estimated to have cost as much as $138 million, alarm bells rang throughout the sports world.[21]

Constructing a state-of-the-art training facility for the exclusive use of college athletes and staff is not new. The University of Alabama recently spent $9 million to upgrade its already-well-equipped Mal M. Moore

Athletic Facility and Kansas State spent $18 million on its basketball train-
ing facility.[22] With the construction of the Ducks' cutting-edge complex,
however, it was clear that a new standard for recruiting and retaining players had emerged. That standard has everything to do with innovations in
sportscapes that enable these types of facilities to generate new forms of
star power for sports organizations.

What makes the Ducks' brand-new Hatfield-Dowlin Complex so impressive and threatening is its intention to change the competitive environment of college sports through the power of place. The 145,000-square
foot complex consists of three black, interconnected, rectangle-shaped
building units made of granite, steel, and glass. The sleek interior of the
complex is outfitted with Ferrari leather-upholstered furniture, luxury
Brazilian wood floors, countless flat screens, and Nike regalia. Features
include two film-viewing auditoriums, a 25,000-square foot weight room,
a barbershop, multiple players' lounges, an exclusive-access war room for
coaches and their staff, an on-site cafeteria, and art installations showcasing the Ducks' history.[23] The polished black façade of the Hatfield-Dowlin
Complex symbolizes innovation, power, and exclusivity. In the words of
one of the project's lead designers Eugene Sandoval, "It's about not being
afraid to make history."[24]

Oregon head coach Mark Helfrich said of his new facility, "If a building was a superhero, that's it."[25] One of the major problems in developing
star power has been how easily it can evaporate. In high school or college sports, stars get injured, fail to meet academic standards, or graduate.
At the professional level, players get traded or retire in addition to also
sustaining injuries. All of these hazards translate to a risky cost-benefit
decision on how much to bank on them. The Oregon solution is to build
a place that will not get injured, fail a class, or graduate. The building is a
star that can endure over generations and attract, instruct, and showcase
the athletic program's more fleeting star power.

The sports strategist is now faced with new opportunities to develop star
power based on architecture and place innovation. Not everyone is going
to have a generous benefactor bankrolling massive construction projects,
but looking at the sports complex for building permanent star power is a
promising development.

These stadium enhancements are not limited to team sports. In recent years, the United States Tennis Association (USTA) transformed the Billie Jean King National Tennis Center in Queens, New York, from a sea of blue hard courts into an entertainment center, including exhibits and interactive displays. The site lures spectators not only to the Grand Slam competition but also to its attractions, including the Heineken Red Star Café, a new champagne terrace, and the International Tennis Hall of Fame within the Chase Center.[26] No longer just a tennis tournament, the U.S. Open now feels like an upscale state fair. The incorporation of these new buildings off the courts underscores the importance of offering fans entertainment outside the traditional court of play. The USTA is among many organizations seeking to expand their physical presence beyond their venues.

We are witnessing on all levels the most aggressive investment ever in sports facilities. It has become a facilities arms race, as organizations jockey to have the latest and greatest venue. At the same time that the industry continues to build better facilities, it also increasingly faces challenges to attendance largely because of technological advancements.

Tension Between In-Venue and Virtual Experiences

Do new technologies threaten attendance? This is a question that has been debated for as long as the modern sports industry has been in existence. Leagues and teams have historically hesitated to embrace new technologies – and for logical reasons. Enjoying a game in the comfort of a living room presents a convenient alternative to the in-person experience game day organizers work so hard to market. As far back as the 1920s, MLB viewed radio, the transformative medium of the era, as a threat to its attendance numbers. In fact, most team owners banned the broadcasting of games from their ballparks. The Chicago Cubs were an exception and began broadcasting their games in 1924.[27] By 1932, however, the league had started recognizing the benefits that comprehensive radio exposure could provide by tapping into a broader audience base and monetizing radio sponsorship. Six years later, the largest market in the United States, New York City, finally received daily game coverage when the owners of the Yankees, Dodgers, and Giants agreed to allow radio broadcasters into their parks – but only after General Mills forged a sponsorship agreement with the teams.[28]

Professional and collegiate sports had a similarly strained relationship with television networks in the early days. The NFL blacked out television broadcasts in the 1950s in home cities where games were played.[29] The NCAA restricted the number of college games on television, fearing that television coverage might slow their business at the turnstiles.[30] In the 1980s, college football conferences and some individual schools were conflicted on whether to sign broadcasting contracts with ESPN to cover their games.[31] More than three decades later, conferences and teams now create their own cable networks to televise and market their games to regional and national audiences.

While leagues and franchises faced similar challenges from new media in the past, today's threats seem especially pervasive and daunting. When expanding access to their competitions through new media and digital channels, sports strategists must be careful to avoid making the in-venue experience into a lower-quality alternative for audiences. The proliferation of affordable high-definition (HD) televisions has made home viewing much more attractive to customers and more often their preferred option. Broadcasts and mobile applications are providing a viewing experience that is increasingly superior to that offered by the live venue environment. In some cases, fans in the stands have become less connected to the game than fans at home. They struggle to achieve the same sophisticated viewing experience, often relying on mobile technologies to gather game information – if they can get wireless service. They may even phone a friend at home for final verdicts on close strikes or first downs. What started with slow-motion instant replay in the 1960s has evolved into yellow first down lines, strike zone boxes, and behind-the-scenes locker room access, all of which have not been available for most in-venue attendees.[32] The leagues' broadcast partners have further enhanced home viewing, even enabling viewers to control in-game camera angles with multiple field perspectives. Meanwhile, the leagues themselves have made it easier for their audiences to catch every moment from their living room La-Z-Boys or their favorite sports bar. For example, the NFL's Red Zone channel enables viewers to watch every scoring drive in real time on a premium cable sports package.

Of course, television is only one of many platforms on which audiences can now access games, highlights, scores, and news. Online outlets and mobile applications grant consumers even more control over how and where they consume sports content. Moreover, technological advancements in broadband and mobile download speeds and satellite coverage enable more live, real-time streaming than ever before. This technology further threatens the value of the in-person experience.

Fans used to go to the game. Television brought the game to them. And now, they can take the game wherever they want. The ability to "attend" a game has more options than ever before. How should sports strategists respond to both maintain and grow attendance at the venue itself, while also continuing to derive more revenue from digital and mobile platforms?

With the right combination of in-venue appeal and interactive digital experiences, sportscape strategy does not have to be an either/or proposition. The sportscape is the foundation of reinvigorating the attendance experience. To build or enhance a sportscape, sports strategists should examine three components of the environment: inside the venue, outside the venue, and within a conceptual venue.

Inside the Venue

Many companies outside of the sports industry face a similar challenge as sports organizations. Online retailers have threatened to drive physical stores out of business. In response, these brick-and-mortar businesses have been forced to focus on the customer experience to showcase the value of their service: Apple stores contain sleek Genius Bars, Ikea provides Swedish meatballs, and REI locations emulate a mountain resort. Whether it is an iPad, a futon, a new pair of rock-climbing shoes, or a ballpark hot dog, the product is now only part of the equation in a world where these goods can be delivered directly to your living room.

In an ideal scenario, sports strategists could design sportscapes from scratch. In many circumstances, that is not the case. Most organizations are working with an existing venue and engaging audiences within the constraints of the current facility. This venue may be 80 years old and not coming down anytime soon. Moreover, budget constraints may allow only for small changes to the sportscape.

Regardless of the situation, there are both small and large ways to enhance sportscapes. We will examine three main factors that can facilitate this change: the in-game experience, technology integration, and eventizing.

In-Game Experience

What does a differentiated in-game experience look like in a successful sportscape? Typically, audiences are engaged in the experience whether their team is winning or not. Of course, this does not mean that the surrounding entertainment should detract from the game action. Nor should it veer too far from the organization's identity to keep audience attention just for the sake of doing so. But at the same time, in-game experiences can play a vital role in complementing the main event.

Minor league baseball stadiums are leaders in this area. There have been 49 new AAA minor league ballparks built in the United States to replace older facilities in the last 20 years. A study by Summit Economics shows that all but one of these new parks led to attendance increases.[33] It is not just the new venues that have at-tracted audiences. It is what these teams have done inside the venue that has been key to their success.

DRAGONS FLY IN DAYTON

The Dayton Dragons are a single-A Midwestern League minor league base-ball team in Ohio that has set a new record for consecutive ticket sellouts at 1,000 games and counting, breaking the long-held Portland Trailblazers' streak.[34] The Mandalay Group, which owned the franchise until 2014, ac-complished the feat in a Rust Belt city that has lost 40% of its population in the last 50 years.[35] Since the new ballpark was built and the team was founded in 2000, the Dragons have remarkably never played in front of an empty seat at home.[36] More importantly, the ballpark is the centerpiece of a promising urban renewal development in downtown Dayton.

The popularity of the Dayton Dragons isn't tied to team performance – in fact, the Dragons often find themselves at the bottom of their division. The two-story, 8,200-capacity ballpark is designed to fit seamlessly into the surrounding environment; there is no "grand entrance," but two friendly, unpretentious entryways that mirror the design of the neighborhood.[37] The ballpark possesses a vintage design, quality sightlines, and a right field section dedicated to lawn chairs and family seating. The atmosphere created by the ballpark is a central element of Mandalay's entertainment-based strategy.

In addition to the ballpark's structure, the Dragons experience combines in-game events and giveaways, meticulous customer service, and com-munity involvement to create a wholesome, family-friendly atmosphere. Executive Vice President Eric Deutsch said he wanted to create an envi-ronment that was "almost Disneyesque"[38] in its devotion to entertainment. Colorful mascots named Heater and Gem roam the park to the delight of kids and parents alike, while the green-caped superhero "Roofman" throws Softee-ball souvenirs down into the crowd.[39] The Dragons also strengthen their ties to the city of Dayton by hosting nonprofit concession stands dur-ing games and raising money for church groups and youth enrichment programs.[40] The staff is friendly and well-trained, the product of a 10-point

CONTINUED

DRAGONS FLY IN DAYTON *CONTINUED*

written pledge to customer service developed by the team's management. As a walking manifestation of this pledge, Bob Murphy, the team's president, and Deutsch are there after every game, win or lose, to wish patrons a good night as they walk home. "I've been around to a ton of different ballparks," says season ticket holder Jonathan Maurer, "but you never get tired of going to a Dragons game."[41]

The Dayton experience illustrates how organizations can energize their customer base by reimagining the live event. The Dragons' ballpark is a stage that exceeds expectations by housing an entertainment experience for all ages. The team is an anchor for a struggling city, providing a site for community building and neighborhood revitalization. Mandalay understood that a sports franchise can be greater than the sum of its wins and managed this sportscape accordingly.

The Dragons' approach to in-game entertainment is an example of how the venue experience can be different from the at-home experience. After all, it is unlikely that Roofman will hurl Softee-balls at you while you watch the game at home. Many sports organizations, however, cannot rely solely on a differentiated live-game experience. Sports organizations must also be able to replicate at their venues critical elements that many people associate with the at-home experience. Improvements in technological capabilities make this an easier proposition for sports strategists.

Technology Integration

At a sporting event today, it is not unusual to see fans around the stadium looking down at their phones while the game is going on. The always-on culture in which we now live tethers audiences to their mobile devices whenever and wherever they are. Rather than view this as a threat to the audience experience, sports strategists should seek to capitalize on mobile and other technological experiences to transform sportscapes into even more engaging environments.

When incorporating these new technologies into the fabric of the stadium, it is important not to diminish or distract from the live event for those who want a more traditional experience. As Dallas Mavericks owner Mark Cuban cautions, "The last thing I want is someone thinking that it's a good idea to disconnect from the unique elements of a game to look at replays or update their fantasy standings or concentrate on trying to predict what will happen next in the game."[42] By striking the right balance between the live and digital experiences, organizations can attract audiences that demand technology without alienating audiences that want to focus solely on watching the game with no distractions.

Personalizing the technologies available to fans inside the venue effectively addresses this dilemma. The new MetLife Stadium in New Jersey offers wireless access, along with a stadium app that enables fans to access up-to-the-minute team information, parking alerts, and information on which concession lines are the shortest.[43] Patriots owner Robert Kraft also equipped Gillette Stadium with wireless access to kick off the 2012 season. The Patriots joined an increasing number of Wi-Fi-ready NFL venues, including Lucas Oil Stadium, the Georgia Dome, and the Mercedes-Benz Superdome. NFL commissioner Roger Goodell observed, "We believe it's important to bring technology into the stadiums. We've made the point repeatedly that the experience at home is outstanding, and we have to compete with that in some fashion, making sure we create the same type of environment in our stadiums."[44]

As early as 2009, the Pittsburgh Penguins NHL team offered live-action video replays to season ticket holders on their mobile phones. Dubbed the "Yinzcam," the application enables fans to view and create their own instant replays from different camera angles, such as the bench cam and goalie cam.[45] Some European sports clubs have also upgraded their technology to meet their fans' expectations. Hamburg Sports Club, one of Germany's most popular soccer organizations, implemented a wireless local area network (LAN) system to provide fans faster and more widespread Internet access in the stadium.[46]

Some stadiums are designed to compete with the at-home experience while also providing organizations with new information about their customers. Kansas City's Sporting Park in MLS and the San Francisco 49ers' Levi's Stadium in the NFL are making technology an integral, but not intrusive, element of the audience experience. Kansas City's Sporting Park boasts a $6 million high-density wireless network that powers Uphoria, the team's in-stadium wireless application. In addition to showing video replays and unique camera angles, Uphoria provides an easy way to collect data about in-game audience preferences. "When you walk into the stadium, I'll know everything about you," CEO Robb Heineman says. "If I know that every time you come to a game you're getting three beers and two hot dogs, maybe the next game I'll offer you an all-inclusive package for an extra seven bucks."[47]

At Levi's Stadium, the San Francisco 49ers have partnered with Sony to fully integrate audiences' own mobile devices into the live action. Tablets and smartphones provide access to exclusive high-resolution camera angles, real-time stats, and background information about star players. "It's not about putting in physical cameras and screens," says Sony President and CEO Kazuo Hirai. "It's about the experience."[48] These teams are combining personalization and data mining to customize the experience for a diverse audience base and are setting the standard for technological sportscapes.

Implementing new technologies underscores organizations' increasing recognition that people not only multitask at games but also demand information, entertainment, and comfort during breaks in the action. Infusing technology into venues is a significant financial investment, but one that most sports executives view as crucial to maintaining relevance in an ever more crowded sports marketplace.

Eventizing

In recent years, leagues and franchises have increasingly repurposed locations traditionally associated with other sports or teams to create a memorable live event. These organizations attempt to capture attention by eventizing certain games, or holding them in nontraditional stadiums and arenas often meant for other sports. By turning a location into an event, organizations hope to supercharge the stakes of the game and enhance its narrative impact.

Eventizing is not a new concept. Historically, it has been associated with competitions such as the Olympics, All-Star games, and golf tournaments. Perhaps the best example of this approach is championship boxing matches, which were often held in ballparks and stadiums dating back to the early twentieth century. The most notable was the "long count" heavyweight championship fight between Jack Dempsey and Gene Tunney that attracted 105,000 fans to Soldier Field in 1927.[49] The bout could have been held in Madison Square Garden in New York, but it would have restricted the number of fans and altered the open-air special event feature of the match.

What was true then remains true today: places can meaningfully transform an experience when repurposed for special sporting events. College football programs also recognize the value of moving games into nontraditional spaces to eventize regular season contests and create excitement among audiences. For example, the Pinstripe Bowl is an annual college football bowl game played in the new Yankee Stadium. Founded in 2010, the Pinstripe Bowl was the first college bowl game to be played in New York City in nearly 50 years.[50] Playing a game in Yankee Stadium generated interest by placing football in a baseball environment. In most cases, eventizing creates a novel sportscape that, while temporary, fosters memorable audience experiences, cuts through the clutter, and creates the potential for unique storylines.

SHOOTING BASKETS ON LAND AND SEA

The Carrier Classic demonstrates the power of the sportscape. On Veteran's Day in 2011, the NCAA transformed a typical college basketball game into a place-based event, staging the matchup on the surface of the USS *Carl Vinson*, a 95,000-ton, fully functional aircraft carrier.[51] Before a crowd of over 8,000 – mostly comprised of military personnel – number-one-ranked North Carolina faced off against Big Ten powerhouse Michigan State on the carrier's flight deck. Paying tribute to the men and women of the U.S. armed forces, the two teams suited up in patriotic uniforms, weaving each team's color scheme with the camouflage pattern of military outfits.

The place-based event carried symbolic weight. The NCAA, barraged with charges of unseemly money-grubbing and general malaise in fixing its problems, utilized the patriotism of the armed forces to gain goodwill with sports audiences. President Barack Obama, wearing a brown leather bomber jacket, addressed the crowd as their commander-in-chief, expressing his excitement for the event along with his gratitude for the sacrifices made by the nation's armed forces personnel. He also reinforced the importance of the USS *Carl Vinson* itself, which had aided in Haitian relief efforts after a 2010 earthquake and, perhaps most notably, released Osama bin Laden's body out to sea after his death.[52] In this way, the location took on an emotional life that dramatized an otherwise routine sporting event. Coupled with the game's coincidence with Veteran's Day, the Carrier Classic was a particularly effective example of sportscapes imbuing the game with a set of values that differentiated it from other special events.

The Carrier Classic was a ratings hit, becoming ESPN's most viewed November college basketball game in history.[53] The NCAA originally planned to stage more games on aircraft carriers in the 2012 season. Because of some logistical challenges of staging outdoor events such as wind and rain, games staged on aircraft carriers proved difficult.

Rather than lose the appeal of a military setting, the NCAA moved these games indoors. In 2012, Michigan State and Connecticut squared off at the Ramstein Air Base in Germany in the first Armed Forces Classic. The game itself was a thriller, with the unranked Huskies defeating the Spartans 66–62. Players signed autographs for military personnel and visited wounded soldiers in nearby hospitals, proving that sometimes, the

CONTINUED

SHOOTING BASKETS ON LAND AND SEA *CONTINUED*

location is even bigger than the sport itself.[54] Starting in 2013, the NCAA scheduled five more Armed Forces Classics with games taking place inside of military bases. While the location for these games has changed from carriers to bases, the takeaway for sports strategists is that place can carry a symbolic value that can magnify a game's importance.

Outside the Venue

The outside environment of athletic complexes has become increasingly integral to the audience experience. Everything from the parking lot to the surrounding neighborhood comprises the sportscape that seeks to create a memorable audience experience. Sports strategists should view the audience experience at their venues holistically, taking into consideration all aspects of the exchange, from the moment customers purchase their tickets to the moment they return home from attending a game. To make the overall experience more engaging, there are a number of possibilities to employ, including tailgating rituals, engagement with surrounding neighborhoods, venue extensions, and sport-themed destinations.

The Ritual of Tailgating

Tailgating has become a $20 billion a year industry with an estimated 50 million Americans participating each year.[55] Although the exact origin of tailgating is disputed, many claim that the practice dates all the way back to the first college football game between Rutgers and Princeton in 1869.[56] Over the subsequent decades, the growth of automobile sales, the expansion of leisure time, and the mass consumption of sports products made tailgating a staple of football.

While rivalries, chants, retired numbers, jerseys, and mascots all powerfully mark the ritualization of sport, tailgating has now become in itself a ritual escape for fans. Before University of Mississippi football games, fans flock to the Grove, the designated tailgate park for the Rebels and "the mother and mistress of outdoor ritual mayhem."[57] For Rebels fans, the Grove is a place for a mixture of socialization, politicking, and partying. The festivities begin the night before the game, well before the team's players walk through the venerated park to enter the stadium. Whether the team wins or loses, the Grove is a fan magnet and guarantees good times. In the words of one Mississippi tailgater, "We may not win every game. But we've never lost a party."[58]

Rather than being incidental to the experience, Mississippi shows how sports institutions are beginning to recognize that tailgating is essential to sports events. To some people, tailgating may mean even more than the game – it provides a chance to interact with fellow tailgaters in a fun, social, and festive environment. As such, teams rely on tailgaters for television spots during pregame coverage, and local news programs frequently flash images of parking lots full of decked-out fans. As evidence of the growing popularity of tailgating, the Big Ten Network (BTN) aired a show entitled *Tailgate 48* that took place at different Big Ten schools, capturing the color of the weekend and culminating with the tailgates. Every week, the BTN devoted an entire episode to these tailgates and the surrounding sportscape.[59]

More recently, teams have begun to systematically capitalize on the deep emotional value of tailgating and have devoted resources to make them a part of the extended experience of the football weekend. Marketing researchers Jenna Drenten, Cara Peters, Thomas Leigh, and Candice Hollenbeck observed that tailgating creates a group experience in which audiences can see each other and interact, enjoy the game, and build a community in the process.[60] For example, with a stadium situated in an urban area without a large parking space, the Minnesota Vikings took advantage of train-traveling fan experiences by turning tailgating into "railgating." Dozens of food trucks sat next to the Hiawatha light-rail line, providing fans with an incentive to commute downtown on game day rather than staying at home. According to Minneapolis mayor R.T. Rybak, the food trucks "add more sizzle" to the game day experience while providing vibrancy to a neighborhood awaiting a new stadium in 2016.[61]

Colleges are increasingly monetizing pregame tailgate events. The University of Oregon aligned with TailgatePal to provide 22 premium tailgate sites that are available at the stadium's recently completed and adjacent soccer and lacrosse field. These sites' differentiating features include a convenient location, no requirement for a parking space, and a full complement of large-screen TVs with a complete slate of NCAA football games.[62] The sites are intended to provide all the amenities necessary for people to have a turnkey experience and are one more step toward industrializing tailgating.

While teams that support these tailgate activities stand to benefit from the level of audience engagement, teams risk alienating audiences when they distance themselves from cherished pregame rituals. Some tailgaters are not ticket holders and are there for only that part of the game day experience.[63] For some teams, this is viewed as a real loss in potential game day revenue. San Diego Chargers administrators came under fire for a new stadium proposal that eliminated 19,000 parking spaces, essentially destroying the team's tailgate culture.[64]

The excitement of the tailgating atmosphere is one of the most compelling reasons to leave the house, travel to a venue, and engage in the sportscape experience. As sports strategists design their own sportscapes, considerations such as the configuration of parking lots, who will be let in, and where people will be allowed to park are important in deciding how to make the most of the game day experience. Ultimately, strategically integrating tailgating into the sportscape will not only give people more of a reason to come to the venue, but will also deepen their experience while they are there.

Engagement with Surrounding Neighborhoods

When Pittsburgh Pirates owner Barney Dreyfuss decided to build Forbes Field in 1909, location was critical. Reasoning that downtown Pittsburgh was not yet a viable commercial location, Dreyfuss built one of the first concrete athletic facilities in America on nine acres of land in the city's Oakland neighborhood. Over time, it became the first home of the Steelers as well as a venue for concerts, circuses, and a wide range of entertainment events. The walk from the trolley to the park felt like it was an extended experience of the playing field. There were numerous restaurants, bars, and hot dog palaces, as well as Gus Miller, a legendary corner newspaper vendor.[65]

Dreyfuss was shrewd in recognizing that location, location, location was critical to the success of his ballpark. He did not expect the Pirates to be the sole drivers of economic growth in this neighborhood. Rather, he valued the resources already available and constructed a venue that engaged with previous development. For example, Forbes Field was constructed near the intersection of 15 trolley lines and the University of Pittsburgh.[66] People could easily get to the ballpark from the surrounding areas at a time before the widespread use of automobiles. Dreyfuss was one the first owners to recognize that accessibility would be a critical element of the sportscape. By building the venue at the Oakland location, Dreyfuss helped the team grow with the neighborhood.

Dreyfuss's approach represents one of the most important place-marketing initiatives in today's sports industry: the rise of the sports-based neighborhood. The key element of these neighborhoods is that sports organizations take advantage of the existing infrastructure to facilitate future growth. For example, the construction of the MCI Center (now the Verizon Center) in Washington, D.C., during the mid-1990s is largely credited with revitalizing the Chinatown neighborhood in Washington, D.C. However, the neighborhood already provided former Washington Wizards and Capitals owner Abe Pollin with significant advantages. The location of the new venue would enable easy Metrorail subway access, as the city's red, yellow, and green lines all stopped at the Gallery Place-Chinatown station adjacent to the venue.[67] This enabled people from both the city and surrounding suburbs to more easily attend Capitals and Wizards games.

While Chinatown was largely underdeveloped at the time, the neighborhood was also close to where many Washingtonians already lived and worked. Chinatown is adjacent to Capitol Hill, the neighborhood where many federal government buildings are located. In addition, Chinatown is near the Dupont Circle and Adams Morgan neighborhoods, where many of the city's younger demographics lived. Once the venue was completed, it became the catalyst to the neighborhood's future development, with many new bars, restaurants, and businesses built near the venue. However, Chinatown's rise as a sports neighborhood occurred in large part because of already existing advantages that could easily contribute to the area's development.[68]

Not all sports-engaged neighborhoods require a new venue or permanent location. The Boston Red Sox conceived the idea of a pop-up neighborhood that emerges just before a home game and disappears just as quickly after the last out. Fenway Park's Yawkey Way is an adjoining street transformed into a Boston Red Sox sportscape. The franchise recognized the value of the street and in 2003 cut a deal with the city to close it to the public and install the team's own vendors there.[69] The Red Sox monetized the street by controlling the comings and goings of people and creating a festival-like atmosphere that offers people a reason to come early to games at the park. Prior to each game, Yawkey Way fills with throngs of Red Sox fans eager to pick up the newest jerseys and caps from the team store. Others play fast-pitch challenges and chat with program purveyors. Still others indulge in pregame food and drinks. The team's creation and management of these spaces have helped sustain audience interactions and enhance the social connection people have with the team. It is a valuable model for sports programs that cannot build self-sustaining neighborhoods but have the resources to create these temporary community environments.

Venue Extensions

By extending beyond the parking lots and surrounding neighborhoods, sports strategists can facilitate sportscape attendance and experiences even miles away from the venue. For example, Chicago Blackhawks owner Rocky Wirtz has extended his team's sportscape to include the entire state, enlisting bar owners across Illinois in an expansive off-site place-marketing strategy. The team's Official Blackhawk Bar program now includes more than 130 official team-sponsored affiliate bars. This replicates the communal experience of watching games with like-minded Blackhawk fans outside of the United Center.[70] Of course, bars have long reaped the benefits of showing games on TV, often becoming known for their unofficial team allegiances. Wirtz's program formalized this marketing opportunity by providing memorabilia, jerseys, and other marketing materials to every bar while selecting three bars for special events on game nights. Wirtz, who is also the president of the Wirtz Beverage Group, offered "discount prices on popular drinks . . . in exchange for a hockey-based name on the drink specials and a guarantee of a certain number of TVs featuring the Blackhawks games."[71] The Blackhawks' home ice at the United Center seats more than 22,000 people, but Wirtz is multiplying his unofficial attendance figures by enabling fans to "go to" games off-site.

The Blackhawks demonstrate how the concept of a sportscape has expanded. Organizations do not have to be limited by their venues, the areas around the venues, or the neighborhoods where they compete. Sports strategists can examine towns, cities, states, and countries as extensions of their venues and capitalize on media and technology to create opportunities that bring people together in a common shared experience.

A VIRTUAL PLACE WHERE EVERYONE KNOWS YOUR NAME

While digital technologies have the power to connect audiences both to the game in the stadium and with friends outside, they also redefine sports whose settings are less confined to a single field of play. With the aid of technology, an undefined sports site like a running course can become a clearly recognizable place with meaning. Distance running used to be inherently isolated as an individual sport, but the explosion of interactive technology for avid runners has transformed running into a collective experience.

Bolstered by robust Internet communities, the running and marathon worlds have seen significant growth in recent years. In 2013, a record 541,000 runners completed marathons compared to 353,000 in 2000,[72] while the same year saw a record 1.96 million runners participating in half-marathons, as compared to 482,000 in 2000 in the United States.[73] The sport has successfully increased engagement in the online and mobile channels, as running has leapt from being an intensely personal activity to a social one. It is easier than ever to access information about where and when marathons are taking place, to register for these marathons, and to track runners' progress. The Columbus Marathon was the first to place electronic tags on the runners' numbers that were activated by sensors along the path. Friends and family could learn about runners' times via their Twitter and Facebook accounts. The program, called Tweet my Time, resulted in more than 7,000 real-time tweets, making the Columbus Marathon a trending topic.[74] These advances have transformed running into an interactive community experience in which the concept of place expands past a marathon's physical boundaries and into the world of social media.

This concept is not limited to marathon running. Across the spectrum from the serious to the casual runner, other innovations have changed what it means to be a participant in the sport. Released in 2006, the "Nike+iPod" program (Nike Plus), which paired the iPod MP3 player with a specially designed shoe or phone-based GPS sensor, enables runners to bring their personal running experiences to a growing, interconnected online community. With Nike Plus, runners can track times, distance, pace, and calories burned, as well as log onto the online community, find friends, compare times, and join "challenges." The challenges, in which runners pledge to run a certain amount of miles in a month or a year, are the quintessential community experience, creating a global cohort of like-minded runners and engaging participants in competitions that merge the offline and online.[75]

While other sports scramble to create online experiences that promise perks other than what's on the field, the connections made online between runners help facilitate a virtual world of competitions, challenges, and performance that have taken the sport to the next level. For runners, the running sportscape exists online, and new technology such as Nike Plus is their ticket to the venue. Sports that used to be largely individual – cross-country skiing, triathlons, and swimming, to name just a few – can use this kind of technology to help participants share challenges, applaud achievements, and unite in building a virtual place from the digital ground up.

In the increasingly fierce competition for audiences' money and time, outside-the-stadium interactions can prove to be as important as what goes on inside the stadium. By enhancing activities beyond the venue and the neighborhood, sports organizations can boost audience engagement, increase loyalty, and encourage repeat visits. The more sports strategists engineer their venue experiences in this holistic manner, the better the chances of maintaining a vibrant, well-attended experience at your venue.

Resolving In-Venue and Virtual Tension

At the beginning of this chapter, we referenced the historical tension between in-venue and virtual experiences. Even in this new digital age, if sports strategists develop engaging sportscapes, media can be complementary and synergistic, rather than antagonistic.

One sport that has done particularly well in retaining its audience for live games while also leveraging digital media is MLB. In 1962, average per game attendance was 13,150.[76] In 2013, the average game attendance had grown to 30,504, with total annual attendance reaching just over 74 million.[77] Baseball has been successful in part by building a record number of new ballparks that improve the live experience. Similarly, Minor League Baseball, which was considered a disappearing game in the 1950s and 1960s because of MLB's rapidly expanding television broadcasts, experienced 24 consecutive years of growth from 1985 to 2008, with attendance peaking in 2008 at 51.5 million.[78]

But another critical driver of this growth is MLBAM, one of the most successful digital operations in all of the sports industry. In the Mastering New Technologies chapter, we showed how MLB has monetized digital assets by providing out-of-market games to audiences through its MLB.tv digital channel and At Bat mobile application.[79] Conventional wisdom may suggest that enabling audiences to both watch out-of-market games and more easily stream live games would depress rather than increase attendance.

MLB, however, has realized that enhancing its digital capabilities can actually drive more people to games in two ways. First, MLBAM makes it easier for people to purchase tickets. Over 35 million tickets for games were sold in 2012 through MLBAM.[80] Second, enhancing audience engagement in the mobile and Internet channels increases the likelihood that more people will buy tickets to live sporting events, according to PricewaterhouseCoopers (PwC).[81]

MLB is not the only sports organization to realize that media experiences can drive people to live events. In November of 2011, Fox broadcast the first UFC bouts ever to appear on network television.[82] This event was the culmination of a successful media strategy. The UFC had used television and social media to generate brand awareness and increase in-arena attendance for its events. In 2005, UFC president Dana White and UFC owner Lorenzo Fertitta persuaded Spike Television to broadcast a series called *The Ultimate Fighter* in which contestants competed for a UFC contract. The UFC agreed to pay the production costs for the show in its last attempt to avoid bankruptcy.[83]

The success of *The Ultimate Fighter* was critical to the UFC. Many broadcast and cable channels had feared scheduling mixed martial arts programming because of the brutal nature of the sport. Demonstrating that the show quickly gained a devoted following with its target demographic of 18- to 34-year-old men provided credibility for the UFC with media partners. Moreover, the UFC recognized that it could use its success on television to increase attendance for its live events. For example, the organization promoted ticket sales for its marquee events to an engaged audience during its television broadcasts. This approach has been one of the primary drivers of the organization's ability to charge an average of $245 per ticket while often selling out arenas.[84] MLB and the UFC demonstrate that audiences consuming an organization's content through different technology channels can increase in-person attendance and revenue for sports organizations' live events.

In-venue and virtual experiences have formed a symbiotic relationship. Attending games can deepen audience connections with a team or athlete, which encourages audiences to become more deeply connected with the team (and consume more content through media) when they are away from the venue. At the same time, media experiences across all platforms (TV, digital, mobile, social) can also drive more audience engagement and encourage people to buy tickets to see the team or athlete live. It is a virtuous cycle. The key to this cycle working, however, is that the venue experience must be different from, and in some ways better than, the digital experience.

Conclusion

Sports audiences find many reasons for not attending live events. Their reasons include traffic to games is unbelievable, the parking is too expensive, the weather is too rainy or cold, the Wi-Fi at the venue does not work well, the stadium food is too fattening, and the stairs to the seats are too steep. While some of these objections should not prevent people from attending games played by their favorite teams, the reality is that customers have more choices and are more discriminatory than ever before. In this environment, sports strategists need to give people reasons to attend events at venues rather than to stay at home.

Sportscapes provide both tangible and intangible approaches for sports organizations to address these challenges. They enable sports strategists to explore how concepts of team legacy, institutional history, and cultural significance intersect with the new needs and desires of its core audiences. This includes developing an understanding of how live events and technology can and should work together as catalysts for a better in-venue sports experience.

The successful sportscape also goes beyond the immediate physical structure. Creating a unique in-venue experience is critical to achieving this goal, but it is only one component of a successful strategy. Extending the concept of a sportscape beyond the venue itself and into surrounding environments is vital to enhancing live events. In addition, the venues that integrate and use their surrounding neighborhoods often strike emotional chords that motivate audiences to attend live events. Ultimately, sportscapes provide audiences with a sense of belonging that is greater than the game itself, representing their sport's past, present, and future.

9 Infusing Ethics into Decision-Making

In February 2013, Florida Atlantic University (FAU) announced the largest donation in the athletic department's history. The $6 million gift came from George Zoley, an FAU alumnus as well as the former Board of Trustees chairman and founder of GEO Group. The gift would help offset costs for various athletic expenditures, including the new $70 million football stadium the university had opened just two years prior. In return, the Owls would play their football home games at what would be called GEO Group Stadium.[1]

There was one problem with this agreement. GEO Group is in the business of owning and operating federal and state prisons and illegal immigration centers. It has also been the subject of numerous accusations of human rights violations in its facilities.[2] Through the goodwill gift to the university, the GEO Group hoped that the sponsorship would improve its public image and help combat the negative attention it has received from numerous lawsuits and community protests about the company's operating practices.

Only after announcing the GEO Group's donation did FAU discover a potential line had been crossed. Scathing comments from the media, industry, academia, and fans quickly became the dominant narrative about the new naming rights deal. Critics of the donation almost immediately called the stadium "Owlcatraz,"[3] and the school was mocked on television shows such as The Colbert Report days after the announcement.[4] Ohio University sports administration professor David Ridpath said of the potential partnership, "It does appear we're prostituting ourselves to the highest bidder regardless of what they represent. . . . The sanctity of higher education matters little when the dollars are needed."[5]

Due to the backlash, the GEO Group withdrew its $6 million donation, and the school kept the name FAU Stadium while it searched for another sponsor.[6] Only a few weeks after the GEO Group withdrew its donation, FAU president Mary Jane Saunders resigned from her position, citing the stadium controversy as one of the key factors in her decision. She said, "There is no doubt the recent controversies have been significant and distracting to all members of the University community. The issues and the fiercely negative media coverage have forced me to reassess my position as the President of FAU."[7]

The case of FAU and the GEO Group generated so much controversy because it raised many fundamental ethical questions of right and wrong. To what lengths should a university go to fundraise for athletics as opposed to academics? What message did the prison sponsorship send to the student athletes and the student body in general about the university's values? Have college athletics become too professionalized? Will there ever be an end to the escalating arms race for new revenues and facilities?

In contrast, the New Jersey state-owned New Meadowlands Company, LLC, took a different approach to a controversial sponsor for the venue that hosts the New York Giants and Jets. In 2008, New Meadowlands entered into negotiations with the German insurance company Allianz for a naming rights sponsorship. Allianz has been criticized for its strong ties to the Nazi government, including charges that "the German company insured Adolf Hitler's engineers at the Auschwitz death camp, had a chief executive in his cabinet and allegedly refused to pay off life insurance policies to Jews during the Holocaust."[8]

Even though Allianz had publicly apologized for its role in working with Hitler and the Third Reich, New Meadowlands realized that signing a naming rights deal would bring up painful memories of the Holocaust.[9] Instead of accepting the most money, the company signed a naming rights agreement with MetLife for $400 million over 25 years – less than the proposed Allianz deal.[10] The New Meadowlands venue, now called MetLife Stadium, may have earned less money but avoided a crisis and potential damage to its identity.

· · ·

Both FAU Stadium and MetLife Stadium show how ethical issues in the sports industry are more challenging today than ever before. Throughout sports history, questions of ethics have revolved largely around the competitions themselves and concerned issues such as sportsmanship and fair play. Whether they deal with cheating through PEDs or evaluating player safety in contact sports, these competitive ethics issues are increasingly complex and many times dominate the sports conversation.

At the same time, sports organizations now face a host of new business challenges driven by ethical considerations. Increasingly, sports strategists must balance the need to generate as much money as possible and the need to do right by their various audiences. The issues they confront can range from the degree to which advertising is integrated into the field of play to the size of player compensation in college football and college basketball.

Ethical questions rarely have easy answers. A critical difference between the FAU and MetLife Stadium situations was how the organizations made their choices. FAU did not appear to fully factor ethics into its strategic thinking before agreeing to the naming rights gift. Not only did the decision damage the credibility of the university and its former president, but the school did not receive the naming rights gift. Infusing ethics into its decision-making process ultimately enabled New Meadowlands to make a more effective strategic choice.

To navigate the proliferation of these types of challenges in sports, this chapter offers strategic guidelines for incorporating ethical considerations and thinking into the decision-making process. Our model is comprised of three main principles: transparency, integrity, and inclusivity. Each principle will be addressed throughout the chapter, with examples and cases of how sports organizations have implemented each. By adhering closely to these principles when facing ethical challenges, sports strategists can enhance their organization's decision-making processes. This approach provides organizations with a better chance of obtaining support, goodwill, and credibility from their key constituents while also being in a position to generate more revenue.

Consequences of Crossing the Ethical Line

Some sports professionals may not be sure why they should factor ethics into the decision-making process. After all, sports is a business. One compelling answer for factoring ethics into the decision making process is that the consequences of crossing the ethical line can be severe. The history of boxing is a cautionary tale about the power of ethics. There was a time when boxing stood next to baseball and horse racing as the powerful triumvirate of professional sports in the United States. While all of these sports have experienced ethical challenges, it is boxing that has been infamously undone by corruption.

The Set Up, a 1949 film, illustrated what happened to boxing. Bill "Stoker" Thompson, played by former Dartmouth University boxer Robert Ryan, was a beaten-down, aging boxer whose pride kept him fighting, despite his wife's pleading that he leave the sport. In his next (and ultimately last) bout, Stoker was scheduled to fight an overpowering opponent that most likely would result in another loss. Confident of Stoker's defeat, his manager bet against Stoker with local mob boss Little Boy. Yet Stoker entered the ring knowing nothing of the wager. In a performance of a lifetime, Stoker shocked his opponent, defeating him by a knockout and preventing his manager's payday. The consequence for Stoker was not a bottle of champagne and another shot at a title but a clubbing to the head and the end of his career.[11]

The Set Up is a work of fiction, but it highlights what became the biggest problem with boxing: corruption. Boxing was controlled by promoters, arena managers, and, in some cases, mob bosses who held sway in local communities. The sport thrived on organized gambling, which was illegal in most areas and resulted in many fixed matches.

While taking steps to address illegal gambling, boxing continues to face issues today because of its history of prioritizing money over all other considerations. For example, four major organizations sanction official matches and award titles. This enables boxing to have more championship fights that can generate revenue. This also cheapens the product, because it is impossible for fans to know who is the best fighter in any particular weight class when so many different boxers can say they are the champion. More importantly, the number of different official organizations forces judges to use different scoring systems when evaluating a fight. This fuels the perception that boxing cheats the fan by promoting specific fighters through fixing matches or using its opaque scoring system to arrange wins for certain fighters.

Track and field has encountered a similar problem to boxing with its inability to control its core product. Like boxing, there was a time when track and field stars were among the most venerated sports heroes. The four-gold-medal success of Jesse Owens in the 1936 Olympics is an iconic moment in American history. When Roger Bannister broke the four-minute mile mark in 1954, the event was both globally televised and received front-page headlines all over the world.[12] Sprinter Wilma Rudolph in the 1960s and decathlete Bruce Jenner in the 1970s were as familiar as Serena Williams and Aaron Rodgers are now.

Today, the sport is highly visible only in an Olympic year, with television ratings barely registering for other premier events. The 2013 World Track and Field Championships attracted a peak of only 1.73 million viewers in the United States even with stars such as Usain Bolt participating in the competion.[13] By comparison, the 2012 U.S. Figure Skating Championship averaged 2.75 million viewers,[14] and the average final round of a 2013 PGA tournament attracted 4.1 million viewers.[15]

A major blow to the integrity of the sport was a succession of stars who faced drug charges and disqualifications after using performance-enhancing substances. Three days after winning the 1988 100-meter Olympic final in Seoul, Ben Johnson was disqualified for testing positive for a banned steroid.[16] This high-profile embarrassment to the sport also fueled suspicions that many athletes were taking banned substances to increase performance. These suspicions were confirmed when a number of stars, including Marion Jones, Asafa Powell, and Justin Gatlin later tested positive for performance-enhancing drugs.

Track and field's image problem is not a question of its ability to take corrective action. Athletes now take a number of tests both inside and outside of competitions. Track and field organizations have instituted year-round random drug testing to uncover athletes using performance-enhancing drugs. The issue is that these efforts to clean up the sport came too late and were ineffective in saving the sport from the damage already caused by many of its highest-profile participants. Many fans and media members now are suspicious of successful track and field athletes, given the number of stars who have failed drug tests. In fact, the race and competitions are not over until the drug tests are completed days later. As former USA Track and Field (USATF) CEO Doug Logan lamented, "We cannot yet assure our fans that we are running a clean sport and therein lies the tragedy."[17] Track and field and boxing demonstrate that ethical challenges can be long term in nature. If not addressed fully and systematically, they can endure and ultimately result in erosion and decline for a sport.

Boxing and track and field may also seem like extreme examples of the impact of ethics in sports. Despite the growing awareness of the prevalence of concussions in football, the NFL has signed record media rights deals, achieved high television ratings, and increased the number of international competitions in which it participates outside the United States. The widespread match-fixing crises of international soccer do not seem to be affecting the success of the sport. For example, the Barclays Premier League, La Liga, and the Bundesliga continue to expand into new markets, with some teams having more fans internationally than they do domestically. Manchester United's hundreds of millions–strong Asian fan base exceeds the number of fans it has in Europe.[18] Specialization at the youth sports level continues to grow despite the increasing evidence that participating in multiple activities reduces injuries and athlete burnout.[19]

Yet, a single ethical incident can have a direct and immediate impact on a sports organization. NASCAR sanctioned Michael Waltrip Racing (MWR) for taking illegal steps to ensure that Martin Truex, Jr. qualified as a driver for the 2013 Chase for the Sprint Cup, the organization's version of the playoffs. These maneuvers included having one driver spin out intentionally and another making an unnecessary pit stop. These actions prevented another driver from winning the regular season-ending race at Richard International Speedway and enabled Truex to qualify for the Chase.

The repercussions of making an unethical choice to promote winning had severe consequences for NASCAR, MWR, and Truex. NASCAR had to deal with the perception that drivers and teams were more focused on the dollars that came from winning than on the integrity of the sport. NASCAR fined MWR $300,000 and assessed Truex with a 50-point penalty that caused him to fail to quality for the Chase. Truex then lost his title sponsor, NAPA Auto Parts, only days after the completion of the race, costing MWR millions of dollars. Without NAPA as a sponsor, MWR dropped Truex from its team. MWR's failing to fully factor in ethics in the decision-making process had significant consequences on all levels of NASCAR.[20]

Ethical Challenges in Sports

Making ethically-based decisions starts with a deeper understanding of the different types of ethical challenges in sports. We have identified three categories of these challenges. The first is competitive ethics. These are issues that address the competitions, games, and matches. The second is business ethics. These issues focus on the revenue, marketing, brand, and public relations challenges facing the sports industry. The third is composite ethics, which are issues that combine both competitive and business challenges. Sports strategists will likely deal with issues that fall into all three of these categories during their careers.

Competitive Ethics

In the book *Ethics and Sports*, Swansea University Professor of Applied Ethics Mike McNamee asserts that one of the most common fallback positions of coaching is "bend the rules as much as you can but don't break them or if you do, whatever else, don't get caught."[21] McNamee articulates the seemingly incongruous dichotomy of rules and ethics in sports. The idealized premise of any sporting competition is that everyone plays by the same rules, and those rules are made clear to competitors and audiences alike. A level playing field can determine true winners and losers. On the surface, sports and ethics seem like natural partners, as both stress honesty, fair play, and teamwork. In this environment, participants can learn important lessons about perseverance, overcoming obstacles, and leadership.

A major hurdle with ethics and sports is that competitors are often encouraged to bend but not break the rules. The language of baseball is a particularly good example of this ambiguity. Players are encouraged to "steal bases," while managers look for any opportunity to "steal signs." The rules of the game also do not always apply equally to all competitors. Home plate umpires are notorious for having their own strike zones even though MLB clearly defines the criteria for what is considered a ball and what is considered a strike in its rulebook. Hall-of-Fame pitchers such as Gaylord Perry have admitted to and are celebrated for throwing spitballs while they played.[22] Perry went so far as to try to convince batters that he might throw an illegal pitch even when he ultimately decided not to do so during an at-bat.[23]

Baseball is far from the only sport where the rules are expected to be exploited or tested. Soccer players are infamous for "diving" when they are fouled or tackled. This includes rolling around in immense pain only to bounce back the moment after an opponent receives a penalty or a card. In the NBA, players flopping became such a problem that the league had to develop a new system of fines to discourage the behavior.

Athletes and teams are also celebrated for making their opponents break the rules or look foolish. Deception, misdirection, and confusion are just as much a part of sports as following the rules. Fans cheer when quarterbacks draw defensive linemen offside using hard-snap counts. There also exists a code of ethics in many sports according to which players are expected to break the rules to enforce the order of the game. For example, hockey teams often have enforcers on their rosters whose primary task is to retaliate for perceived misconduct by an opposing team.

Thick rulebooks, numerous officials, large league offices, and vigilant fans are supposed to ensure that the rules of the game are followed. These elements create an expectation that sports organizations should have a clear sense of what is right and wrong. At the same time, fans, media, and sponsors expect an organization's coaches and athletes to push the boundaries of the rules as far as possible without going over the line. This ambiguity demonstrates one of the primary reasons why the relationship between ethics and sports is so difficult to successfully navigate.

Business Ethics

For decades, the prevailing wisdom was that companies should focus solely on maximizing shareholder or equity owners' value.[24] To achieve this goal, businesses were expected to maximize profits by generating the most revenue and reducing all possible costs. Little emphasis was placed on ethics, mission, and values if they were thought to negatively impact shareholder value.

Today, leading companies have found that an ethical framework is good for business. Zappos.com operates in a largely commoditized online retail market. Zappos provides a web portal for its customers to purchase products – primarily shoes – and have them delivered to specific locations. Zappos has made exceptional customer service the cornerstone of its brand differentiation from other retailers. Rather than offshoring its call center, Zappos made its inbound representatives a critical element of its organization. Its management-empowered employees do everything possible to fulfill a customer's order, even if it means talking to them for hours or spending extra money on faster shipping. The company has famously paid potential job applicants $2,000 to not work at the company if they did not fit well with the company's commitment to customer service. Zappos' customer service strategy was so successful that the company grew from a small startup to a global brand that generated tens of millions of dollars in revenue in a matter of a few years. Amazon recognized the value of Zappos' approach when it acquired the company in a $1.2 billion stock deal in 2010.[25]

Zappos is an example of a company that employs a double bottom line when evaluating its performance. Rather than solely looking at financial performance, this kind of company also considers the social impact it has on its employees, customers, and shareholders, as well as other external audiences. In their book *The Solution Revolution*, Deloitte consultants and authors William D. Eggers and Paul Macmillan illustrate how business leaders who employ this framework make better problem-solvers, and many companies that use the double bottom line outperform the S&P 500.[26] A study by business school professors at Stanford University and Emory University found that a company with higher "reputational capital" can increase its cash flow because its "various stakeholders trust it to uphold its commitments."[27]

In the sports industry, organizations are examining new ways to incorporate business ethics into their strategic approach. More specifically, many teams and leagues are enhancing their businesses while continually offering more value to their customers. For example, MLB's Cleveland Indians created a "Lunch and Three Innings" promotion to encourage fans to take their lunch hour at Progressive Field. For $15, fans received a ticket and a $10 voucher to spend at select games. This enabled the Indians to attract customers who otherwise may not have come to a game at Progressive Field during the middle of a workday, while providing fans with an opportunity to see an Indians game.[28] Later in the chapter, we explore more examples of how sports organizations are balancing the need to maximize as much revenue as possible and the need to build strong, long-term relationships with different customers.

Composite Ethics

Many ethical challenges in the sports industry touch on both competitive and business issues. Perhaps no example brings this to life better than the question of whether college athletes should receive compensation in addition to their scholarships. If schools continue to professionalize their amateur athletic programs, then who should be getting paid?

The *O'Bannon v. NCAA* lawsuit highlights the complexity of this question. Former University of California, Los Angeles (UCLA), basketball player Ed O'Bannon is leading a class-action lawsuit against the NCAA, contending that players no longer competing for their college or university should be paid when their likeness or image is used. The complaint originally focused on their inability to receive royalties when EA Sports and Collegiate Licensing Company used their likenesses in its college basketball video game.[29] In 2013, EA Sports settled these lawsuits for $40 million.[30] In 2014, the United States District Court ruled in favor of the players and the NCAA appealed decision.

The larger issue of these lawsuits is the question of whether NCAA athletes should be paid for their performance for their schools' teams. One of the primary reasons that the lawsuits against the NCAA are moving forward is due to the organization's stance that student athletes are sufficiently compensated by receiving tuition and fees, room, board, and required course–related books.[31] When agreeing to compete in college athletics, the NCAA requires students to waive their rights to all future revenue derived from their likeness and image. Financially, this benefits the NCAA, as it is not required to compensate current and former athletes beyond the terms of the athletes' national letters of intent. Ethically, this has caused critics to question how someone could be a student athlete in perpetuity when he or she is not a student or athlete for most of his or her life. In addition, the judge in this case has allowed current student athletes to join the O'Bannon suit to contest whether they should also receive money for the use of their likenesses and images.[32]

Concurrently, the NCAA has dealt with other ethical challenges to the organization's position on paying college athletes. The NCAA received criticism for selling apparel with Reggie Bush's likeness after the organization sanctioned the University of Southern California (USC) because Bush received money while in college.[33] In addition, Johnny Manziel was reported to have signed thousands of autographs that dealers sold for profits.[34] The NCAA suspended Manziel for the first half of the first game of the 2013 college football season for his alleged role in these activities, leaving many to question the consistency of its approach to this issue.[35]

The issue of whether student athletes should be paid illustrates some of the problems at the intersection of competitive and business ethics. From a competitive perspective, critics argue that paying players would compromise the integrity of the game. Big schools with big donors would capitalize on this opportunity to recruit the best athletes. As a result, the schools with the most money to pay players would likely achieve the most competitive success.

Southern Utah University professor David Berri counters that argument by demonstrating that athletes' ability to receive money could actually increase the competitive balance in college sports.[36] Berri claims there is currently a significant amount of competitive imbalance in college sports. From 1950 to 2005, 10 schools were ranked in the top eight of the final Associated Press college football rankings.[37] During the same time period, 45% of Final Four teams came from only 10 schools. Berri has found similar results in sports ranging from men's volleyball to women's softball.[38] The essence of Berri's argument is that schools that have achieved success in the past have been more likely to achieve success in the future, because players want to go to schools with the best track records of success. Without schools being able to offer some form of additional compensation to players, talent and victories will likely continue to be concentrated in a few programs.

From a business ethics perspective, paying athletes would likely be both cumbersome and filled with legal complications. Even though many schools have begun providing athletes with additional scholarship funding starting in 2015, collegiate programs will still not compensate players directly.[39] As Big Ten commissioner Jim Delany at one point asserted, "The Big Ten's schools would forgo the revenues in those circumstances and instead take steps to downsize the scope, breadth and activity of their athletic program."[40] Moreover, it is unclear exactly who would get paid, how much they would get paid, and what the Title IX ramifications of such payment would be, particularly in terms of gender equity.

There is a potential way for athletes to be compensated without amateurism being removed from college sports. The International Olympic Committee (IOC) originally prevented its athletes from receiving any money from "endorsements, memorabilia deals and other business opportunities."[41] President Jimmy Carter signed the Olympic and Amateur Sports Act in 1978, which created the United States Olympic Committee as the head governing body for amateur sports in the United States.[42] One of the outcomes of this act was that it became easier for Olympic athletes to receive money for the use of their likeness and image through sponsorship deals.[43] For example, swimmer Ryan Lochte has made millions of dollars through endorsement deals with companies such as Gillette and Gatorade but does not receive nearly as much from swimming in events.

The NCAA could adopt what is known as the Olympic model to allow college athletes to make money without schools having to pay any additional compensation. According to University of New Haven business professor Allen Sack, college athletes could then be allowed to "take control of their own marketing rights: to hire agents, sign endorsement deals and engage in other 'entrepreneurial' activities."[44] Therefore, college athletes would be able to earn money without having to receive this compensation from the NCAA or their schools.

Whether or not the NCAA decides to adopt the Olympic model, composite ethical issues are threatening the organization as a whole. While the student athlete compensation structure has been in place for decades, it is facing stronger attacks than ever before because of rising revenue, increased media attention, and concerns over fairness. For example, Northwestern University's football players considered forming the first ever union for college athletes to collectively advocate for its position on a variety of issues. The NCAA has to factor in these considerations as it moves forward with its relationships with different audiences.

We end the Ethical Challenges in Sports section with a discussion of the *O'Bannon v. NCAA* case, because it touches on each type of ethical challenge in the sports industry. We have shown how understanding the competitive, business, and composite issues could enable the NCAA to address a problem as difficult as the compensation of its current and former athletes. This discussion is an example of how infusing ethical considerations into the decision-making process can lead to new and better strategic choices.

Ethics-Based Decision-Making

Ethics should not be viewed simply as a potential problem confronting the sports strategist. Ethical considerations can also be used to help sports organizations capitalize on new revenue opportunities and better engage with new and existing audiences. To navigate these considerations more effectively in today's marketplace, three key principles can help guide sports strategists' decision-making: transparency, integrity, and inclusivity.

Transparency

A key principle of ethics-based decision-making is transparency. Transparency refers to the degree to which an organization is open and honest with its audiences. Developing products and service offerings that more effectively align with an organization's core audiences can build goodwill and increase revenue.

Helping Customers to Help the Organization. The Zappos philosophy on customer management is a familiar one in the sports industry. In the "Reinvigorating Sportscapes" chapter, we discussed how the Dayton Dragons marketed a fan-friendly concept to their customers. This team's approach is also an example of combining good business practices with ethical decision-making.

Having a 1,000-plus game sellout streak is a significant achievement, but the Dragons also want someone to actually be sitting in a seat for each game. To achieve this goal, the team has gone so far as to suggest that some of their customers not buy 70-game, full-season ticket packages. Instead, the team encourages them to buy only 17- or 30-game season ticket packages to ensure that they can actually attend all games.[45] For the customer, this locks in their seats for games they can actually attend and saves them money. The Dragons' management can then sell season ticket packages for fewer games to a greater number of customers while also selling more individual game tickets, which are usually priced higher than season tickets. The Dragons also likely earn more money from game day sources such as parking, concession, and merchandise sales. Dayton's strategy builds goodwill, fills the stands, and provides the organization the opportunity to maximize its revenue.

Not every sports organization is going to have a waiting list for its season tickets. However, sports organizations can take steps to ensure that fans have transparency when purchasing tickets. One of the major complaints ticket holders have with sports organizations is their inability to easily resell tickets for games they cannot attend. In the past, a customer's only viable option was to sell tickets to individual brokers or ticket-reselling companies that would provide tickets to another customer at any price they could get. Therefore, neither the original nor the new ticket buyer had any way of knowing the ticket's true price on the secondary market. This lack of transparency brought up questions of fairness for the original purchaser and alienated potential ticket buyers. Since 2000, StubHub and other online portals have become the primary ticket brokers in the secondary market. These companies' websites clearly show the buying and selling prices for tickets for different events in real time on the secondary market.

Sports organizations have long realized that there is demand in the secondary ticket market that they are not capturing. What some organizations have more recently discovered is that customers want teams and leagues to control the secondary market. The NBA found that the majority of its fans who had used a secondary website to purchase tickets had actually visited the team's site first and wanted to go to only one location.[46] By providing the portal through which its fans can purchase all ticket types, NBA teams can generate more revenue from secondary ticket transactions while providing a service that its fans want. As a result, the NBA partnered with Ticketmaster "to create the sports world's first website that will list tickets for games sold by both teams and fans."[47] Ticket buyers can see in one location the tickets directly sold by the teams and tickets available from resellers to make the best purchasing decision for their needs. This approach offers more transparency than ever before in the ticket buying process. The Dragons and the NBA illustrate how adding transparency to purchasing tickets can actually maximize revenue while creating a better customer experience.

Open Source Organizations. Companies in the technology industry are known for fiercely guarding their proprietary technology and strategies. For example, the movie *The Social Network* is framed around multiple lawsuits filed against Mark Zuckerberg for allegedly using the ideas of other people and organizations to start Facebook.

Despite this competitive environment, some leading technology companies are using open source software to create and monetize new products. Open source software is defined as something that "can be freely used, changed, and shared (in modified or unmodified form) by anyone."[48] One of the most successful shared endeavors is Google's Android Open Source Project, which is an operating platform used to run mobile devices.[49] Google has provided the Android system for free to companies such as Samsung, LG, and Sony to power these companies' mobile devices. Google can better serve mobile advertisements and searches through these companies' smartphones and tablets than it can with Apple's mobile devices, such as the iPhone or iPad. Using these open source efforts from different people and firms has enabled Google to generate billions of dollars in mobile revenue.[50] During the third quarter of 2013, the Android platform operated on 81% of smartphone devices shipped; and 75% of all app downloads came from the Google Play app store while enabling companies such as Samsung to take profits and market share from Apple.[51]

On the surface, open source technology seems like it should not work. How can technology companies maintain a competitive advantage if they are allowing other developers the opportunity to see and use some of their best code, frameworks, products, and strategies? Yet, Google shows that transparency can lead to new dollars and added market share by accessing the ideas of many people to create better service offerings and new revenue generating opportunities.

Sports organizations operate in a competitive environment that facilitates open source business practices. Despite being the fiercest of foes in competition, teams in the same league or sport rarely are competing against each other from a business perspective. For example, legislation has often provided sports leagues exemptions from anti-competitive practices not seen in other industries. League rules often dictate that only one or two teams can play in a metropolitan area. Therefore, individual organizations in these areas have unique abilities to target sports customers in ways that businesses from other industries cannot. This creates an ideal environment for teams in the same league or different sports to share best practices in an open source manner.

Many professional and collegiate sports leagues already employ revenue-sharing practices that distribute money earned by an individual team(s) or school to all league members. However, revenue sharing occurs only after money is earned.

Open source practices should be employed so that all league members can earn more money. For example, a team or school that employs a promotion that increases ticket sales for their games can share this practice with other league members. Then, these teams and schools can either use or improve on this promotion to increase revenue. Everyone in the league benefits when an individual organization creates a winning strategy.

FRENEMIES

The 2011 Big City Marketing Summit illustrated how leading sports strategists are recognizing the value of exchanging best practices at the non-professional level. Bill McGillis, then executive associate athletic director at the University of South Florida, realized that colleges that operate in large metropolitan markets face different competitive pressures than those that operate in rural or suburban markets. In particular, collegiate football programs in urban markets have to compete directly with NFL teams.

McGillis experienced this problem firsthand while operating in the Tampa Bay metropolitan market. The University of South Florida lacked the money, facilities, and resources to compete directly with the NFL's Tampa Bay Buccaneers. Rather than trying to address this challenge himself, McGillis invited athletic directors from 15 programs, including such schools as Temple University, the University of Houston, and the University of Washington, to the Big City Marketing Summit to discuss best practices for colleges dealing with professional competition. "I wanted to compare notes with someone who is facing similar challenges and the same great opportunities that I have here," McGillis said. "And that's going to be people at institutions that share a market with NFL teams."[52]

The Big City Marketing Summit enabled sports strategists to communicate with people who are working for programs that are trying to create a differentiated positioning in a specific type of market. It also demonstrated a unique competitive advantage that sports organizations enjoy over businesses in other industries. Most teams in the same league or conference rarely operate in the same markets or compete for the same audiences. By increasing transparency and sharing as much information as possible, these organizations can operate more like partners rather than competitors when it comes to creating better businesses.

Integrity

Another key principle of ethics-based decision-making is integrity. Integrity is an important issue because it is most often tested during times of change. Sports business is part of a constantly evolving industry because of the new rules, media, equipment, and safety issues that impact competitions. Managing expectations, proactively identifying problems, and soliciting audience feedback before implementing changes can help organizations grow and meet new strategic goals.

Building Integrity Through Change. The expectations sports strategists set for audiences when it comes to the integrity of the product are of critical importance. At the same time, sports strategists must be effective in their change management processes in order to deal with new competitive challenges. For example, football and hockey have attempted to limit those collisions that are most likely to cause injury, and soccer has implemented new technology that can clearly identify when a ball crosses the goal line.

However, traditionalists are often upset when alterations are made to the sport they love. They accuse an organization of selling out by fundamentally altering the core product. Traditionalists have a point; sports organizations have spent decades marketing the rules of the game and building audience loyalty. The question for sports strategists becomes how to make changes while still maintaining an organization's credibility with various audiences that have differing expectations.

Lacrosse is a sport that faced this dilemma. Lacrosse had been growing quickly but had yet to occupy a major place in American sports. For example, the number of lacrosse players increased from 253,901 in 2001 to 746,859 in 2013, and there are 17 teams across two domestic professional lacrosse leagues.[53] However, lacrosse is still considered a niche sport that is unknown by most causal sports audiences.

One of the principal reasons for its slow rate of audience acceptance is the game's slow pace of play. Despite being marketed as "the fastest game on two feet", lacrosse can actually move pretty slowly at all levels.[54] During the course of the game, players historically had no time limit on when they were required to take a shot on goal. Therefore, some lacrosse offensive possessions did not involve a significant amount of action. Instead, players would often pass the ball around waiting to find an opportunity for their best shot on goal.

This lack of game action became the catalyst for the NCAA to take action regarding a major rule change for 2013–14. The NCAA instituted a modified 30-second shot clock to increase the pace of play. This means that a team is required to make an attempt on goal 30-seconds after receiving a stall warning from the officials.

While many of lacrosse's supporters want to maximize the speed of play to attract new audiences, there were some wary of significant rule changes. As Colgate coach Mike Murphy stated, "We really could be opening Pandora's box. The intentions of the rules changes are good, to speed up the game. We want to continue to be the fastest game on two feet. But the administration of the rules may be more problematic . . . Some of it was so drastic, that sometimes we might be cutting our nose off to spite our face."[55]

As lacrosse dealt with pace of play issues, amateur wrestling faced a very similar challenge. One of the original sports in the ancient Olympics in 708 B.C. wrestling was ousted by the IOC as an Olympic sport for the 2012 and 2016 games.[56] In order to regain wrestling's Olympic status, Fédération Internationale des Luttes Associées (FILA), the international wrestling association based in Sweden, launched a campaign to revive the sport. It spent $3 million to convince the IOC that it was meritorious of being voted back into the Olympics. FILA also made changes to the rules of the sport at the IOC's request. For example, scoring was doubled, with an emphasis on rewarding more aggressive wrestling moves.[57] The organization used the catastrophic defeat of losing its Olympic status as a catalyst to make critical changes to the sport. It listened to the IOC recommendations while factoring in ideas from high-profile endorsers, media experts, and its own athletes. Wrestling has been reinstated for the 2020 Tokyo Olympic Games. The FILA campaign was a textbook example of how to maintain an organization's core identity while adapting to a changing sports environment.

Professional wrestling is another example of a sport that has successfully altered its positioning while largely maintaining the support of traditional fans. This stepchild of amateur wrestling originally presented staged matches as legitimate contests. The specter of Gorgeous George, the platinum-bobbed showman, staggering across the ring after a fake head-butt was sold to fans as an authentic experience. The wrestlers practiced their moves and holds with the dedication of Broadway thespians. Attempting to mislead fans, however, changed from a competitive advantage to a competitive disadvantage. As audiences became increasingly aware the matches were staged, they questioned why the sports leaders continued to insist that the fights were real.

Instead of keeping up the pretense, professional wrestling eventually acknowledged that the contests were part of a scripted drama.[58] World Wrestling Entertainment (WWE) continues to perform well because it incorporates the matches into a narrative involving larger feuds and conflicts between its stars. The contests have become part of a larger story that the WWE uses to market the organization and its marquee events. We recognize the irony of highlighting the WWE as an example of integrity when its core product is staged matches with predetermined outcomes. Abandoning its flawed ethical position, however, has enabled the organization to be more straightforward with its target audiences.

GETTING SLAUGHTERED FOR A PAYCHECK

If there were ever an example of separate but unequal in sports, it could be found in college football paycheck games. NCAA Division I college football is currently divided into two categories – the FBS and FCS. The 126 FBS teams consist of schools in the power conferences such as the SEC, Big Ten, and Pac 12. The 122 FCS teams consist of teams that compete in conferences such as the Big Sky Conference, Ivy League, and Patriot League. One of the FBS schools' biggest problems was finding teams to compete against outside their conference to fill out their schedule and have enough wins to qualify for bowl games. A major problem for FCS schools was making enough money to finance their football programs and athletic departments.

Paycheck games appeared to solve both problems. FBS teams scheduled games they would likely win while FCS teams would collect hundreds of thousands of dollars in revenue. For example, the University of Northern Iowa generated almost $1 million from playing the University of Iowa and the University of Wisconsin in paycheck games. The money from these games accounted for almost one-third of the school's $3.3 million football budget.[59]

During the 2013 college football season, however, one big issue emerged. UNI beat Iowa, and it was not the only FCS school to win a paycheck game. In fact, eight FCS teams beat FBS teams in a single week while making over $2.3 million in the process.[60] These results seemed to demonstrate that FCS teams were becoming increasingly better matchups with FBS teams while providing revenue for smaller programs that could desperately use the money.

The problem with paycheck games, however, is that the exception is not the rule. Even though eight FCS teams won, 22 teams lost during that same week, with many of the losses being routs.[61] Paycheck game results more frequently look like the University of Wisconsin's 45–0 win over the University of Massachusetts. Savannah State lost by a total of 139 points in games versus Oklahoma State University and Florida State University in a single season. FAU was criticized for exchanging "mismatches for millions" after being blown out in games with the University of Georgia and the University of Alabama.[62]

As a result, paycheck games place many college football programs' credibility in jeopardy with its key audiences. Many fans have to pay for season tickets that include games that they often do not want to attend and cannot resell. Students are increasingly reluctant to attend games that are likely to have lopsided scores.[63] Forcing broadcast partners to give legitimacy to these contests through game coverage and analysis can cause them to lose credibility with the viewers, readers, or subscribers. Sponsors can feel slighted because paycheck games compromise the positive brand associations that many are paying for through corporate partnerships with sports teams.

Because of these issues, these types of games will likely become a thing of the past. The Big Ten Conference has announced that its schools will no longer schedule games with non-FBS members. Schools in other conferences have been examining whether they should end paycheck games as well.[64] FCS schools should be the biggest losers in the elimination of paycheck games, because they will lose a significant amount of money.

Yet, FCS football programs are not in as bad shape as one might think. As Big South commissioner Kyle Kallander asserted, "There are some that rely on the [paycheck game] revenue to improve facilities and fund their programs. But it's not like the sky would fall and [those teams] wouldn't be able to play anymore."[65] In fact, ending paycheck games could actually encourage FCS schools to continue to look at enhancing other revenue streams that do not cause the ethical challenges of scheduling mismatches for profit. For example, some FCS schools could make more money from media rights deals. Because there are an increasing number of regional sports networks (RSNs) and national networks that are looking for programming, FCS teams have opportunities to sign new media rights deals. NBC Sports Network recently signed a new agreement with the Ivy League to broadcast football, men's basketball, and lacrosse.[66] The Big Sky Conference agreed to a five-year contract with DirecTV Sports Network that will reach 8.7 million viewers across 18 states.[67] Campusinsiders.com, a company partially owned by Chicago White Sox subsidiary Silver Chalice Ventures, exclusively broadcasts games for the Patriot and West Coast Conferences on its digital platforms and is helping the company generate an estimated $100 million in revenue.[68]

At a time when teams and leagues are looking to maximize revenue, many organizations believe they cannot afford to make the ethical decision when it means they could lose money. While ending paycheck games could mean less money for some schools, there are additional revenue opportunities for FCS institutions that do not call into question the ethics of scheduling mismatches for profit. In this case, the decision to make games truly competitive could be the impetus for a healthier sports environment for both FBS and FCS college football teams.

Maintaining integrity often demands that an organization adopt new products or change past behaviors. Determining how and when a sports organization should evolve requires making alterations while taking into account the concerns of traditional audiences. Listening to internal and external markets can help facilitate an effective change management process.

Inclusivity

Making a commitment to bringing audiences into the decision-making process builds both goodwill and better businesses. More inclusive organizations break down the traditional barriers between the organization and the customer. They also can gain a competitive advantage by incorporating audience feedback into their strategic decision-making process.

Ask and You Shall Receive. The Dallas Mavericks decided to redesign the team's uniforms for the 2015–16 NBA season. While many teams and leagues have gone through a similar process in the past, they traditionally make the decision without consulting external audiences, because the uniforms are one of the most visible symbols of a team's brand. The Mavericks are adopting a different approach. As Mark Cuban stated, "What's the best way to come up with creative ideas? You ask for them. So we are going to crowd source the design and colors of our uniforms."[69]

The move toward crowdsourcing important decisions is a fundamental change that could address a traditional problem for the sports industry. Sports organizations typically employ a top-down approach in which key strategic decisions are often made by senior leaders, implemented by junior employees, and delivered to audiences. Fans, media, and sponsors have to live with the decision of their favorite sports team and league without having significant input on the process.

Engaging audiences in the decision-making process is a problem in other industries as well. It is one of the reasons that authors such as James Surowiecki[70] have examined crowdsourcing as a technique to address strategic challenges. Rather than pushing out information, organizations can pull information from audiences by having them become stakeholders in the process. For example, companies are setting up online collective decision markets in which their employees can vote on specific projects, tactics, or ideas. Employees use a currency, such as fake dollars or points, to buy shares of a certain idea or initiative. This is similar to the way that investors buy stock in companies that they think will increase in value over time through exchanges such as the NYSE. The company then pursues the project that receives the most buy orders. Senior management uses this approach to secure buy-in from lower-level employees, and more people in the organization have a stake in the project.

Crowdsourcing and collective decision-making do not have to focus solely on initiatives typically found on the business operations side of a sports organization. Organizations can solicit feedback or votes from different audiences on certain types of front office, coaching, and player personnel decisions. In particular, crowdsourcing can be used to help make the decisions that come with predictions of future performance, such as which athlete an organization should recruit, draft, or sign.

This may seem like a risky proposition. Why would any team allow people with varying degrees of expertise in sports to have input on these types of decisions? You only have to listen to a local radio sports show or read some tweets or Facebook posts to see how bizarre recommendations from different audiences can be. Organizations also pay general managers, coaches, scouts, and recruiters to identify and evaluate the best talent for their teams, and they should be held responsible for these types of decisions. Crowdsourcing could become a scapegoat when a decision does not work out in the predicted manner.

In Nate Silver's book *The Signal and the Noise: Why So Many Predictions Fail – but Some Don't*, he examined studies about the prediction power of large numbers of people as compared to a smaller number of experts. The research illustrated that using the collective analysis of many people making independent forecasts is often a more accurate predictor of future performance than individual experts making the same predictions in areas ranging from economics to politics. One explanation for the cause of this gap is that experts are overconfident in their predictive abilities. They often create models based on a nonrepresentative dataset and do not account for how new information can impact their predictions.[71]

Another issue that causes experts to make predictive errors is incentives. Rather than making independent predictions, team officials will often follow other administrators' leads, because it is harder to be blamed or lose your job if you are following industry standards. For example, many football coaches will punt or kick a field goal on fourth down even when going for it is the decision that will most likely increase a team's probability of winning.[72] Because going for it on fourth down is an atypical practice, coaches whose teams are unsuccessful often receive much more criticism than those who take a more conservative approach.[73]

Large groups of sports audiences making independent decisions are more likely to make changes because they do not share the same incentives. External audiences are not going to be monetarily compensated for their efforts or are not trying to keep their job based on a sports organization's overall performance. Instead, they are more likely trying to maximize the emotional value they receive from investing their time and energy in helping with a sports organization's decision-making process.[74]

Many sports organizations already use a form of collective decision-making. As discussed in the "Designing an Identity" chapter, Seattle Sounders fans voted both on the team's name and on whether the team's general manager should retain his position. The NFL, NBA, and MLB are among those organizations that already have fans vote on players they want to see participate in each league's all-star games.

Using crowdsourcing as a method to incorporate external audiences into internal decision-making processes will enhance an organization's engagement with its core demographics. Because they are now included in strategic discussions, audiences are more likely to purchase more products and service offerings such as tickets, merchandise, and sponsorship.[75]

Inclusivity Increases Income. The sports industry has had a complicated relationship with race, gender, and sex issues. Sexual orientation has become one of the most visible ethical issues in sports over the past decade. For example, then-IOC president Jacques Rogge offered his continued support of the 2014 Winter Olympics in Sochi even after Russia passed a law that prevented the advocating of "non-traditional sexual relations" around children.[76] In addition, the IOC stated that it can bar or send home any athletes from the Olympics who protest the Russian law in any manner, because the organization's "charter prohibits athletes from making political gestures during the Winter and Summer Games."[77]

While the IOC's official stance is to support the toleration of all athletes regardless of their sexuality, the organization scheduled its signature event in a country that does not share its position.[78] The IOC was stuck between a heavy financial commitment and its values. With billions of dollars on the line, the IOC appeared to have prioritized its short-term financial priorities over longer-term ethical concerns.

The Sochi Olympics illustrated the challenge facing many sports strategists when it comes to practicing inclusivity. Many sports organizations, such as the IOC, have policies supporting diversity and inclusivity. However, sports organizations often face situations in which different audiences do not share or agree with an organization's values. Can sports organizations afford to take any additional steps that encourage inclusivity when these efforts can alienate previously supportive audiences?

The NHL's relationship with the *You Can Play Project* demonstrates a promising approach to handling this issue. Started by Philadelphia Flyers scout Patrick Burke, the *You Can Play Project* has created a partnership that includes a "significant commitment to education and training for teams, players, media and fans plus the production and broadcast of more public service announcements" on issues involving homosexuality in sports.[79] The key difference between this partnership and other initiatives in the past is that the NHL will be connecting with media and fans and not just its own employees. Working with its customers to promote tolerance helps the NHL show that its actions match its ethics. This new and enhanced support of the lesbian, gay, bisexual, and transgender (LGBT) community through the *You Can Play Project* is a direct message about the organization's commitment to being a leader on this issue.

However, this partnership is only an indirect way to target gay audiences as customers. Like most sports organizations, the NHL has not yet directly marketed itself to LGBT fans in the same way it has with other nontraditional audiences, such as women and minorities. Sports organizations that overlook the LGBT demographic are potentially missing out on a larger financial opportunity. Making up 6.7% of the American population, the LGBT community has an annual buying power that has been estimated to be $790 billion.[80]

The LGBT community is also heavily active in sports. Not only are there hundreds of LGBT sports leagues in the United States[81] but also more than 10,000 people from 70 countries competed in the 2010 Gay Games in Cologne, Germany. [82] A Nielsen study found that gay and lesbian individuals "were more likely to attend pro sports events, play sports, go online for sports news and videos, and play fantasy sports" compared to the average adult.[83] As a result, Nielsen's senior vice president of global digital audience measurement Eric Solomon asserts, "Besides having a great deal of spending power, [gay consumers are] highly active online, especially when engaging with sports content."[84] Websites such as Outsports.com and the Compete Network demonstrate large numbers of gay sports fans could be directly targeted by teams and leagues.

This demographic has already been aggressively pursued by car, apparel, hotel, travel, and restaurant companies. For example, Chevrolet unveiled two advertisements during the opening ceremony of the 2014 Winter Olympic games that featured gay couples.[85] Nike also launched its Be True 2012 campaign to highlight "the achievements of the New York City, San Francisco and Portland communities as progressive leaders of LGBT life with city-specific footwear releases and accompanying hat and tee."[86] This campaign was part of the company's effort to promote its Nike LGBT Sports Summit during Gay Pride Month. Nike used this campaign to increase its revenue from its core apparel products, grow its customer base, and build goodwill with LGBT communities in large cities.

Nike also shows how corporate sports sponsors are increasingly exploring opportunities to work with gay athletes. When Jason Collins announced he is gay shortly after playing the 2012–13 season for the Washington Wizards and Boston Celtics,[87] Nike partnered with Collins as part of its Be True campaign. Collins's announcement also demonstrated how having an openly gay athlete could help a team or league generate new revenue. On the day after Collins's decision to become the first active player in the four major professional American sports to openly declare he was gay, all of the custom jerseys purchased from the Wizards' online store were Collins's jersey.[88] The Brooklyn Nets replicated this success when Collins's jersey became biggest seller at the NBAstore.com only two days after the center signed his first 10-day contract with the team in 2014.[89]

Collins was not the first active major professional athlete in the world to declare he was gay. While playing for the Cardiff Blues in 2009, Welsh rugby player Gareth Thomas announced he was gay in an interview with the *Daily Mail*.[90] This led to the Cardiff Blues being profiled in national, European, and international outlets, including *Real Sports with Bryant Gumbel*, and enabled the team to gain exposure it never would have received without Thomas's announcement. After retiring from rugby, Thomas also signed a promotional speaking agreement and co-founded his own marketing and public relations firm.[91]

Since Collins's announcement, other high-profile athletes have made public their sexuality, such as 2013 SEC co-Defensive Player of the Year Michael Sam. While these athletes had been afraid of losing corporate sponsors in the past, this fear has significantly dissipated. In fact, being openly gay can potentially create new opportunities for athletes, organizations, and sponsors. When British diver and London Olympics star Tom Daley announced that he was bisexual, director of sports marketing and sponsorship at the leading sports agency brand Rapport Nigel Currie asserted that Daley may have "actually improve[d] his marketability because of what he has done and the way he handled it."[92]

These developments could lead to more efforts from sports teams and leagues to connect with LGBT customers. Sports strategists can look to the WNBA as an example of an organization that has actively marketed to this fan base, with efforts including advertising in gay lifestyle magazines and holding LGBT pride nights.[93] Rather than simply being the focus of public relations efforts, LGBT audiences can be targeted as customers to maximize an organization's revenue.

This section laid out the key principles that can help sports strategists navigate ethical challenges and successfully use ethics to increase both goodwill and revenue. Transparency, integrity, and inclusivity are the foundations of sound ethical decision-making that will not only strengthen connections with your audiences but will also create opportunities to earn more money in the future.

Conclusion

As the business of sports becomes more complex, so too will the ethical questions surrounding it. Some of the more difficult sports ethics questions are just beginning to emerge. What happens when athletes can use wearable technologies to help improve their performance? Does the sport of baseball need to change its rules to appeal to the next generation of fans who have very short attention spans and will not sit still for three and a half hours? Will there come a point in time when college and high school athletes will be compensated like Olympic athletes for the use of their likeness and image?

It is impossible to determine every ethics-related question that a sports strategist will face. Instead, specific challenges were used throughout this chapter to demonstrate how to navigate these issues. More importantly, we have shown how using ethical frameworks and principles is valuable to sports organizations. Creating an integrated approach that values the use of ethics in the decision-making process can help sports strategists build better businesses.

Epilogue

When we began editing the "Crafting a Crisis Blueprint" chapter, a small crisis of our own developed. Seemingly every day there was a new league, team, or athlete struggling with a crisis. Even crises that appeared to be resolved reappeared in surprising ways. In 2012, former National League MVP and current Milwaukee Brewer Ryan Braun became the first MLB player to win his appeal to overturn his 50-game suspension for using performance-enhancing drugs. In a press conference after his successful appeal, Braun proclaimed, "I would bet my life that this [banned] substance never entered my body at any point."[1] In 2013, Braun lost that bet when he admitted to taking performance-enhancing drugs and received a 65-game suspension. As we finished writing the book, Braun's story was still changing. Not only did he begin the 2014 season with comparable numbers as he had posted earlier in his career, but jeers turned into cheers when he received an ovation from Brewers fans during his first at bat at Miller Park. In a matter of months, Braun had been the unequivocal face of a franchise, a suspected steroid user, an appeal winner, an embarrassed athlete, and finally a comeback kid.

Braun's rise and fall became emblematic of the speed and nature of change in the sports industry. Denials and combative stances during multiple different crises were too often quickly followed by confessions and admissions of guilt. The latest tweet or headline caused us to reexamine our material in the chapter. Changes to a crisis management chapter, however, could be expected, since crises are by their definition dynamic and unexpected events.

It was the constant change in other chapters we were addressing that became the challenge. In the "Constructing Enduring Narratives" chapter, multiple storylines had to be reevaluated as new information came to light. Ndamukong Suh is a good example of this constant narrative evolution. When we began writing the book in 2010, Suh had just been featured in the Chrysler commercial highlighted in the opening of the chapter because of his ability to connect with the car company's core demographics. By 2012, Suh had been voted the NFL's least liked player by fans.[2] By 2013, Suh had changed his personal narrative enough to be voted team captain.[3] Suh's up-and-down storyline contained many different narrative types and plot twists, including signing with the Miami Dolphins as a free agent in 2015, all in a relatively short period of time.

New technologies have also been making a sports strategist's job both much easier and much harder. It has become easier because new technology allows sports organizations to connect with new and traditional audiences more frequently than ever before. Sports organizations now have new opportunities to monetize technological investments by digitally broadcasting games, selling tickets, and creating new sponsorships. It has become more difficult because the proliferation of digital communication channels means there is more competition and information vying for audience attention. Advances in digital, broadcast, and mobile technologies have made it easier for fans to stay at home rather than attend live events.

At the same time, audience expectations about accessibility to sports organizations are changing. Fans, media, and sponsors want to connect with their favorite athletes and teams at any point throughout the year, whether they are at home or on the road. Not only do audiences want to hear from different parts of the sports organization, but they also want to have control over how, where, and when they receive this communication. Local communities also are increasingly vocalizing their criticism of public investments in sports organizations and using social media to rally support for their opposition.

Interacting in new ways with external audiences was not the only change in communication facing sports strategists. Determining which projects to invest in requires an understanding of how much revenue a new initiative, campaign, or technology can generate for an organization. The most sophisticated analytical models can best add value if they are communicated effectively to internal audiences and aligned with the organization's identity.

Change was everywhere and happened rapidly during our four-year journey on this project. If there was ever any doubt about whether organizations must focus on factors other than winning to achieve long-term success, the day-to-day dynamism and complexity of the sports industry alleviated our concerns.

We repeatedly found that the most effective way of dealing with current and future challenges in the sports industry is the holistic approach at the center of being a sports strategist. Rather than running away from complex issues, sports strategists focus on learning and embracing multiple and integrated ways to drive growth. Looking at different factors and incorporating them into the decision-making process can help their organizations achieve success and gain a competitive advantage. This does not mean that sports strategists have to be experts in every field to achieve this goal. Instead, savvy sports strategists will identify the most important priorities to address problems and take advantage of new opportunities.

The sports industry is at the center of some of the most innovative and creative thinking in business today. At the same time, there is an insatiable demand for new business models and ideas. The successful sports strategist will be someone who approaches challenges with an interdisciplinary view and can lead effectively through periods of change and uncertainty. If you can do this on a consistent basis, you will be in a better position to make an impact on the industry. That should be the goal of every sports strategist.

Notes

PREFACE

1. Horrow, Richard B., and Karla Swatek. *Beyond the Box $core: An Insider's Guide to the $750 Billion Business of Sports*. New York: Morgan James Pub., 2010. Print.
2. Rein, Irving, Philip Kotler, and Ben Shields. *The Elusive Fan: Reinventing Sports in a Crowded Marketplace*. New York: McGraw-Hill, 2006. 94–97. Print.
3. "Harlem Globetrotters Play Their First Game." History.com. A&E Television Networks, 7 Jan. 2013. Web. 23 Jan. 2014. <http://www.history.com/this-day-in-history/harlem-globetrotters-play-their-first-game>.
4. Ibid.

CHAPTER 1

1. Dubkin Yearwood, Pauline. "Ballpark Synagogue." *Chicago Jewish News*, n.d. Web. 16 Feb. 2014. <http://chicagojewishnews.com/2014/01/14/ballpark-synagogue/>.
2. Ibid.
3. Fosmoe, Margaret. "Restored Light Fixture Returns to Former South Bend Synagogue." *SouthBendTribune.com*. South Bend Tribune, 3 July 2012. Web. 16 Feb. 2014. <http://articles.southbendtribune.com/2012-07-03/news/32528215_1_sons-of-israel-synagogue-chandelier-building>.
4. Ibid.
5. "South Bend, Indiana Honored with Emmy Award." *South Bend Silver Hawks*. MiLB.com, 7 Nov. 2013. Web. 16 Feb. 2014. <http://www.milb.com/news/article.jsp?ymd=20131107&content_id=63759552&vkey=news_t550&fext=.jsp&sid=t550>.
6. Dubkin Yearwood, "Ballpark Synagogue."
7. "South Bend, Indiana."
8. Fosmoe, "Restored Light Fixture."
9. Buchanan, Leigh. "Andrew Berlin: How I Saved the Silver Hawks." *Inc.* Inc. Magazine, July–Aug. 2013. Web. 16 Feb. 2014. <http://www.inc.com/magazine/201307/leigh-buchanan/south-bend-silver-hawks-andrew-berlin.html>.
10. Fosmoe, Margaret. "Silver Hawks Attendance Soars 68 Percent This Season." *SouthBendTribune.com*. South Bend Tribune, 4 Sept. 2012. Web. 16 Feb. 2014. <http://articles.southbendtribune.com/2012-09-04/news/33589050_1_hawks-president-joe-hart-andrew-berlin-west-michigan-whitecaps>.
11. Fosmoe, Margaret. "South Bend Silver Hawks Attendance: 245, 471 for 2013." *SouthBendTribune.com*. South Bend Tribune, 17 Sept. 2013. Web. 16 Feb. 2014. <http://www.southbendtribune.com/news/local/keynews/localeconomy/article_7b6ef668-1f08-11e3-a57d-0019bb30f31a.html>.
12. McFadden, Maureen. "New Name: "Four Winds Field at Coveleski Stadium"" *WNDU.com*. WNDU, 5 Sept. 2013. Web. 16 Feb. 2014. <http://www.wndu.com/sports/headlines/BREAKING-Coveleski-Stadium-gets-new-name-222512521.html>.
13. Buchanan, "Andrew Berlin: How I."
14. Mickle, Tripp. "U.S. Sports Executives Who Run Arsenal See Slow Gains, Intense Scrutiny." *SportsBusiness Daily*. Street and Smith's, 15 Aug. 2011. Web. 16 Feb. 2014. <http://www.sportsbusinessdaily.com/Journal/Issues/2011/08/15/Franchises/Arsenal-main.aspx>.
15. Rosner, Scott, and Kenneth L. Shropshire. *The Business of Sports*. Sudbury, MA: Jones and Bartlett, 2004. Print.
16. *The Elusive Fan*, 94–97.
17. "Rangers Football Club Enters Administration." *BBC News*. BBC, 14 Feb. 2012. Web. 16 Feb. 2014. <http://www.bbc.co.uk/news/uk-scotland-glasgow-west-17026172>.
18. Pritchett, Jon L. "What Can We Learn From the Financial Meltdown of Glasgow Rangers FC?" *Forbes.com*. Forbes, 8 Oct. 2012. Web. 16 Feb. 2014. <http://www.forbes.com/sites/sportsmoney/2012/10/08/what-can-we-learn-from-the-financial-meltdown-of-glasgow-rangers-fc/>.

19. Lamont, Alasdair. "Rangers players asked to take pay cuts." Sport Football. 16 Jan. 2014. BBC Sport. 24 Apr. 2014. <http://www.bbc.com/sport/0/football/25769725>.

20. "Financial Fair Play." *UEFA.org*. Union of European Football Associations, n.d. Web. 16 Feb. 2014. <http://www.uefa.org/footballfirst/protectingthegame/financialfairplay/>.

21. Smith, Chris. "When It's Okay To Lose Money: The Business Of Women's College Basketball." *Forbes.com*. Forbes, 29 Mar. 2012. Web. 16 Feb. 2014. <http://www.forbes.com/sites/chrissmith/2012/03/29/when-its-okay-to-lose-money-the-business-of-womens-college-basketball/>.

22. Eichelberger, Curtis. "Women Basketball Programs Lose Money as Salaries Break College Budgets." *Bloomberg Politics*. Bloomberg, 1 Apr. 2011. Web. 16 Feb. 2014. <http://www.bloomberg.com/news/2011-04-01/women-s-basketball-teams-operate-in-red-as-salaries-break-college-budgets.html>.

23. "University of Connecticut." *The Equity In Athletics Data Analysis Cutting Tool*. U.S. Department of Education, n.d. Web. 18 Feb. 2014. <http://ope.ed.gov/athletics/InstDetails.aspx?756e697469643d31323930323026796561723d323031322673656172636843726971746572696913d33313364343336663665366653635363337343639363337353373432363732363437343364333232663331333832663332333303331333432303331333113361333433363361333313334323034313346426726 4743d322f31382f3230313420313313a34363a313420414d> or <http://ope.ed.gov/athletics/GetOneInstitutionData.aspx>.

24. Moskowitz, Tobias J., and L. Jon Wertheim. *Scorecasting: The Hidden Influences Behind How Sports Are Played and Games Are Won*. New York: Crown Archetype, 2011. Print.

25. "Cubs Deal with Great Expectations." *Chicago Tribune*. Chicago Tribune, 18 Feb. 2009. Web. 16 Feb. 2014. <http://articles.chicagotribune.com/2009-02-18/news/0902180073_1_cubs-playoff-familiar-theme>.

26. Ecker, Danny. "Cubs Attendance Lowest Since 1998." *ChicagoBusiness.com*. Crain's Chicago Business, 25 Sept. 2013. Web. 16 Feb. 2014. <http://www.chicagobusiness.com/article/20130925/BLOGS04/130929861/cubs-attendance-lowest-since-1998>.

27. Ourand, John. "Smallest MLB Markets Show Ratings Boost." *SportsBusiness Daily*. Street and Smith's, 30 Sept. 2013. Web. 16 Feb. 2014. <http://www.sportsbusinessdaily.com/Journal/Issues/2013/09/30/Media/MLB-ratings.aspx>.

28. Ozanian, Mike. "The NHL's Most Valuable Teams." Forbes. Forbes Magazine, 25 Nov. 2013. Web. 14 Apr. 2014. <http://www.forbes.com/sites/mikeozanian/2013/11/25/the-nhls-most-valuable-teams/>.

29. "Maple Leaf Square." Maple Leaf Square. Maple Leaf Sports and Entertainment. 24 Apr. 2014. <http://www.mapleleafsquare.com/home.html>.

30. Riper, Tom Van. "NBA: Why The Warriors Are The Best Deal In Basketball." Forbes. 25 Jan. 2012. Forbes Magazine. 28 Apr. 2014. <http://www.forbes.com/sites/tomvanriper/2012/01/25/the-show-must-go-on/>.

31. "History: All-time Win/Loss Records by Team." Pro Football Hall of Fame, n.d. Web. 16 Feb. 2014. <http://www.profootballhof.com/history/stats/win-loss_records.aspx>.

32. "Compare National Soccer Teams." *FindTheBest.com*. FindTheBest, 2014. Web. 16 Feb. 2014. <http://national-soccer-teams.findthebest.com/>.

33. Posnanski, Joe. "Fair or Foul? Parity and American Sports." NBC Sports, 3 Feb. 2014. Web. 16 Feb. 2014. <http://m.nbcsports.com/content/fair-or-foul-parity-and-american-sports>.

34. Rovell, Darren. "Miami Heat Owner Says Team Will Likely Lose Money This Year." Sports Biz With Darren Rovell. CNBC, 2 July 2012. Web. 18 Feb. 2014. <http://www.cnbc.com/id/48047319>.

35. Wakefield, Kirk L. "Is Winning Everything?" Migala Report, 09 Nov. 2010. Web. 05 May 2014. < http://www.thebusinessofsports.com/2011/07/13/is-winning-everything/>

36. Funk, Daniel, Kevin Filo, Anthony Allan Beaton, and Mark Pritchard. "Measuring the Motives of Sport Event Attendance: Bridging the Academic-Practitioner Divide to Understanding Behavior." *Sport Marketing Quarterly* 18:3 (2009): 126–38. Print.

37. Zinser, Lynn. "Jeffrey Loria Trades Away the Marlins' Dignity." *NYTimes.com*. New York Times, 14 Nov. 2012. Web. 16 Feb. 2014. <http://www.nytimes.com/2012/11/15/sports/the-marlins-no-1-problem.html?_r=0>.

38. Horrow, Richard B., and Karla Swatek. *Beyond the Box $core: An Insider's Guide to the $750 Billion Business of Sports*. New York: Morgan James Pub., 2010. Print.

39. Silver, Nate. "N.B.A. Disputes Forbes Analysis Suggesting League Is Profitable." *NYTimes.com*. New York Times, 5 July 2011. Web. 23 Jan. 2014. <http://fivethirtyeight.blogs.nytimes

.com/2011/07/05/n-b-a-disputes-forbes-analysis-suggesting-league-is-profitable/?utm_source=twitterfeed>.

40. Altavilla, John. "WNBA Facing Labor Issues as CBA Expires After Season." *The Courant*. Hartford Courant, 28 July 2013. Web. 23 Jan. 2014. <http://articles.courant .com/2013-07-28/sports/hc-wnba-all-stars-0729-20130728_1_wnba-president-laurel-richie-news-conference-nba-tv>.

41. Herndon, Mike. "NCAA's Step Away From Deregulation Keeps Gap Between Haves, Have-Nots from Widening." *Al.com*. Alabama Media Group, 9 May 2013. Web. 10 Sept. 2013. <http://www.al.com/sports/index.ssf/2013/05/ncaas_step_away_from_deregulat.html>.

42. "Rafa Nadal." *Facebook*. N.p., n.d. Web. 10 Sept. 2013. <https://www.facebook.com/Nadal>.

43. Rafael Nadal (@RafaelNadal). "Rafael Nadal." *Twitter*, n.d. Web. 10 Sept. 2013. <https://twitter .com/RafaelNadal>.

44. Wallenstein, Andrew. "Why Everything You Know About Binge-Viewing Is Wrong." *Variety*. N.p., 23 Aug. 2013. Web. 10 Sept. 2013. <http://variety.com/2013/biz/news/netflix-breaking-bad-everything-know-binge-viewing-wrong-1200586747/>.

45. Mike Wilson Tunes. "Baby Works IPad Perfectly. Amazing Must Watch!" YouTube, 24 June 2010. Web. 14 Jan. 2014. <http://www.youtube.com/watch?v=MGMsT4qNA-c>.

46. Sam Laird. "Kids Go Gaga Over Tablets." *Mashable*. Mashable, Inc., 29 Aug. 2012. Web. 23 Jan. 2014. <http://mashable.com/2012/08/29/kids-tablets-infographic/>.

47. Perez, Sarah. "Report: IPad Mini Gains as the Preferred 'Kids' Tablet' after the Holidays." *TechCrunch*, 15 Jan. 2013. Web. 30 Sept. 2013. <http://techcrunch.com/2013/01/15/report-ipad-mini-gains-as-the-preferred-kids-tablet-after-the-holidays/>.

48. O'Neil, Megan. "Confronting the Myth of the 'Digital Native'" The Digital Campus 2014. 21 Apr. 2014. The Chronicle of Higher Education. 24 Apr. 2014 <http://chronicle.com/article/Confronting-the-Myth-of-the/145949/?cid=at&utm_source=at&utm_medium=en>.

49. "St. Patrick's Day." *The Office*. NBC. 11 Mar. 2010. Television.

50. Mazzucato, Marianna. "Different Views of Strategy." *Strategy for Business*. London: Sage Publications, 2002. 7–9. Web. 23 Jan. 2014. <http://www.sagepub.com/upm-data/9497_019389ch1.pdf>.

51. Porter, M. E. "What Is Strategy?" *Harvard Business Review 74.6*, Nov.–Dec. (1996): 65. Print.

52. Ibid, 70.

CHAPTER 2

1. DeSantis, Alicia. "All Black Everything: A Brooklyn Nets Style Guide." *NYTimes.com*. New York Times, 27 Sept. 2012. Web. 13 Feb. 2014. <http://www.nytimes.com/interactive/2012/09/27/style/brooklyn-nets-logo.html>.

2. Helin, Kurt. "Jason Kidd to Buy Half of Jay-Z's Ownership Share of Nets." *ProBasketballTalk*. NBC Sports, 4 Sept. 2013. Web. 16 Feb. 2014. <http://probasketballtalk.nbcsports.com/2013/09/04/jason-kidd-to-buy-half-of-jay-zs-ownership-share-of-nets/>.

3. Beck, Howard. "Nets Throw First Bucket of Paint at the Knicks." *NYTimes.com*. New York Times, 1 July 2010. Web. 13 Feb. 2014. <http://www.nytimes.com/2010/07/01/sports/basketball/01mural.html?gwh=B4B119BEFAB69073DC0759E2F3D6FE48&gwt=pay>.

4. DeSantis, "All Black Everything."

5. Dell, Chris, and Jonathan Moffie. "Branding Brooklyn: The Rise of the Hybrid Fan." *The Local Fort Greene/Clinton*. New York Times, 8 May 2013. Web. 13 Feb. 2014. <http://www .nytimes.com/interactive/2012/09/27/style/brooklyn-nets-logo.html>.

6. Tucker, Daniel. "Tech-Savvy Brooklyn's Barclays Center? Yep, There's An App For That." *NPR.org*. National Public Radio, 1 Jan. 2014. Web. 13 Feb. 2014. <http://www.npr.org/2014/01/01/258889962/tech-savvy-brooklyns-barclays-center-yep-theres-an-app-for-that>.

7. "Dining." *Barclays Center Brooklyn*. Barclays Bank, 2012. Web. 13 Feb. 2014. <http://www .barclayscenter.com/arena/dining>.

8. Torenli, John. "Building From the Ground Up: Nets' New Court Reminiscent of Boston's Famed Parquet Floor." *Brooklyn Daily Eagle*. Everything Brooklyn Media, 13 Sept. 2012. Web. 13 Feb. 2014. <http://www.brooklyneagle.com/articles/building-ground-nets-new-court-reminiscent-bostons-famed-parquet-floor>.

9. Follmer, Max. "How NBA's Nets Said 'Hello, Brooklyn'." *Brief*. Brief, 15 Nov. 2013. Web. 13 Feb. 2014. <http://brief.promaxbda.org/content/brooklyn-nets-rebranding-case-study>.

10. "The Science of Shopping: The Way the Brain Buys." *Economist.com*. The Economist Newspaper Limited, 18 Dec. 2008. Web. 10 Sept. 2013. <http://www.economist.com/node/12792420>.

11. "1966 Things Go Better with Coke U.S. Ad." *The Coca-Cola Company*. N.p., n.d. Web. 14 Sept. 2013. <http://www.coca-colacompany.com/press-center/image-library/1966-things-go-better-with-coke-us-ad>.

12. "Best Global Brands 2012—Coca-Cola." *Interbrand*. Interbrand, n.d. Web. 10 Sept. 2013. <http://www.interbrand.com/en/best-global-brands/2012/Coca-Cola>.

13. Wann, Daniel L., Merril J. Melnick, Gordon W. Russell, and Dale G. Pease. *Sport Fans: The Psychology and Social Impact of Spectators*. New York: Routledge, 2001. 4–10. Print.

14. Williams, Carol J. "A 250-Mile Show of Support for Catalonia Independence." *LATimes.com*. Los Angeles Times, 11 Sept. 2013. Web. 14 Sept. 2013. <http://www.latimes.com/world/worldnow/la-fg-wn-catalonia-independence-demonstration-20130911,0,7827367.story>.

15. "Values." *FCB*. FC Barcelona, n.d. Web. 23 Jan. 2014. <http://www.fcbarcelona.com/club/identity>.

16. St. John, Warren. *Rammer Jammer Yellow Hammer: A Road Trip into the Heart of Fan Mania*. New York: Crown, 2004. Print.

17. Spurgeon, Brad. "Meet the Red Bull Tribe." *NYTimes.com*. New York Times, 24 May 2013. Web. 14 Sept. 2013. <http://www.nytimes.com/2013/05/25/sports/autoracing/25iht-srf1prix25.html?pagewanted=all&_r=0>.

18. Clark, Dave. "Putting Seattle Sounders' Record Attendance in Perspective." *Sounder at Heart*. SB Nation, 23 Oct. 2012. Web. 23 Jan. 2014. <http://www.sounderatheart.com/2012/10/23/3543532/seattle-sounders-record-attendance-mls>.

19. Ibid.

20. "Seattle Sounders FC Recognized as the 2010 Professional Sports Team of the Year." *Sounders FC News*. Seattle Sounders FC, 20 May 2010. Web. 23 Jan. 2014. <http://www.soundersfc.com/news/articles/2010/05-may/sounders-fc-win-sports-business-journals-team-of-the-year.aspx>.

21. "Chairman Drew Carey." *Sounders FC News and Blog*. Seattle Sounders FC, n.d. Web. 23 Jan. 2014. <http://www.soundersfc.com/alliance/chairman.aspx>.

22. Kumming, Benjamin. "DIY or Prefab? Portland, Seattle and Success in American Soccer Culture." *Pitch Invasion*. Pitch Invasion, 9 Aug. 2009. Web. Jan. 23. 2014. <http://pitchinvasion.net/blog/2009/08/09/diy-or-prefab-portland-seattle-and-success-in-american-soccer-culture/>.

23. "Seattle Sounders FC Selected as Team Name." *Seattle Sounders FC*. MLS Network, 7 Apr. 2008. Web. 23 Jan. 2014. <http://www.soundersfc.com/news/articles/2008/04-april/seattle-sounders-fc-selected-as-team-name.aspx>.

24. Mayers, Joshua. "Sounders FC." *Seattle Times*. Seattle Times Company, 4 Oct. 2012. Web. 12 Sept. 2013. <http://seattletimes.com/html/sounders/2019345450_sounders05.html>.

25. Booth, Tim. "Seattle Brings Democracy to MLS with GM Vote." *Soccer Newsday*. North American Soccer News, 31 Oct. 2012. Web. 23 Jan. 2014. <http://www.soccernewsday.com/usa/r/536558/seattle-brings-democracy-to-mls-with-gm-vote->.

26. "The Golden Scarf—Seattle Sounders Football Club." *Sounders FC News and Blog*. Seattle Sounders, n.d. Web. 12 Sept. 2013. <http://www.soundersfc.com/matchday/golden-scarf.aspx>.

27. Aaker, Jennifer L. "Dimensions of Brand Personality." *Journal of Marketing Research* 34.3 (1997): 347–56. Print.

28. Peña, Michael. "Jim Harbaugh, a Former NFL Quarterback, Is Named the New Head Football Coach." *Stanford Report*. Stanford University, 10 Jan. 2007. Web. 23 Jan. 2014. <http://news.stanford.edu/news/2007/january10/harbaughsr-011007.html>.

29. Dodd, Dennis. "Journey Leads Harbaugh Back to Michigan, Where He Learned from Bo." CBSSports.com. CBS, 03 Apr. 2015. Web. 07 May 2015. <http://www.cbssports.com/collegefootball/writer/dennis-dodd/25135139/long-road-leads-harbaugh-back-home-to-bo-and-to-the-wolverines>.

30. "Raiders Owner Al Davis Dead at 82." *ESPN.com*. ESPN, 9 Oct. 2011. Web. 14 Sept. 2013. <http://espn.go.com/nfl/story/_/id/7074380/oakland-raiders-owner-al-davis-dies-82>.

31. "Hall of Famers—Al Davis." *Pro Football Hall of Fame*. Pro Football Hall of Fame, n.d. Web. 11 Sept. 2013. <http://www.profootballhof.com/hof/member.aspx?PlayerId=51>.

32. Miller, Scott. "Two Years Post-Pujols, Full-Steam Ahead for Series-Bound Cardinals." *CBSSports.com*. CBS Interactive, 19 Oct. 2013. Web. 17 Feb. 2014. <http://www.cbssports.com/mlb/writer/scott-miller/24107819/two-years-postpujols-fullsteam-ahead-for-world-seriesbound-cardinals>.

33. Ibid.
34. Gonzalez, Alden. "Are Angels Gaining on Dodgers in LA Rivalry?" *MLB.com*. MLBAM, 2 Feb. 2012. Web. 11 Sept. 2013. <http://mlb.mlb.com/news/article .jsp?ymd=20120228&content_id=26896926&notebook_id=26904758&c_id=ana>.
35. Rishe, Patrick. "LA-area Latino Fans Will Embrace Pujols." *FOXSports.com*. FOX Sports, 8 Dec. 2011. Web. 24 Jan. 2014. <http://msn.foxsports.com/mlb/story/albert-pujols-will-have-special-appeal-to-los-angeles-angels-latino-fanbase-120811>.
36. "Fan-Friendly Moreno Promises Lower Beer Prices." *SI.com*. Sports Illustrated, 23 May 2003. Web. 24 Jan. 2014. <http://sportsillustrated.cnn.com/baseball/news/2003/05/22/ moreno_ap/>.
37. King, Bill. "Angels Seek Messaging that Will Play Across Both the Hispanic and General Markets." *Sports Business Daily*. Street and Smith's, 24 June 2013. Web. 24 Jan. 2014. <http://www .sportsbusinessdaily.com/Journal/Issues/2013/06/24/In-Depth/Los-Angeles-Angels.aspx>.
38. Ibid.
39. Birch, Tommy. "Grinnell College's Jack Taylor Scores NCAA Record 138 Points." *USA Today*. Gannett, 21 Nov. 2012. Web. 14 Sept. 2013. <http://www.usatoday.com/story/sports/ ncaab/2012/11/20/jack-taylor-grinnell-college-ncaa-record-138-points/1718463/>.
40. "Knute Rockne's 'Win One for the Gipper' Speech." *Archives of the University of Notre Dame*. University of Notre Dame, n.d. Web. 14 Sept. 2013. <http://archives.nd.edu/research/texts/ rocknespeech.htm>.
41. Santaniello, Gary. "Penn State Opens Ice Arena Fit for a Division I Team." *NYTimes.com*. New York Times, 12 Oct. 2013. Web. 4 Feb. 2014. <http://www.nytimes.com/2013/10/13/ sports/penn-state-opens-ice-arena-fit-for-a-division-i-team.html?_r=1&>.
42. Zehngut, David. "Ice Arena." Letter to Design Professionals. 2 Sept. 2010. *Office of Physical Plant*. Penn State University, Aug. 2010. Web. 4 Feb. 2014. <http://www.opp.psu.edu/about-opp/divisions/cpd/images/icehockey%20longlist.pdf>.
43. Ydstie, John, and Sallie Jenkins. "Gridiron Guts: The Story of Football's Carlisle Indians." *NPR News*. National Public Radio, 19 May 2007. Web. 24 Jan. 2014. <http://www.npr.org/ templates/transcript/transcript.php?storyId=10217979>.
44. "Carlisle Indian School Yearly Totals." *College Football Data Warehouse*. College Football Data Warehouse, n.d. Web. 24 Jan. 2014. <http://www.cfbdatawarehouse.com/data/ discontinued/c/carlisle/yearly_totals.php>.
45. Wallace Adams, David. "More than a Game: The Carlisle Indians Take to the Gridiron, 1893–1917." *Western Historical Quarterly* 32.1 (2001): 34–35. Print.
46. Macht, Norman L. *Connie Mack and the Early Years of Baseball*. Lincoln: U of Nebraska P, 2007. Print.
47. "Class of 1979: Frank Moseley." *Virginia Sports Hall of Fame & Museum*. Virginia Sports Hall of Fame & Museum, n.d. Web. 12 Sept. 2013. <http://vshfm.com/inductees/inductee_ details.php?inducteeID=173>.
48. Katcher, Paul. "Best 'Seinfeld' Sports Moments." *ESPN.com*. ESPN, 26 Nov. 2004. Web. 24 Jan. 2014. <http://espn.go.com/espn/page3/story?page=katcher/sports_seinfeld>.
49. "Yankees Front Office." *New York Yankees*. MLB.com, n.d. Web. 24 Jan. 2014. <http://newyork .yankees.mlb.com/team/front_office.jsp?c_id=nyy>.
50. "Dan Gable Profile." *Hawkeyesports.com*. CBS Sports, n.d. Web. 24 Jan. 2014. <http://www .hawkeyesports.com/sports/m-wrestl/mtt/gable_danoo.html>.
51. Gable, Dan. "Dan Gable: Only Teamwork Can Bring Wrestling Back." *USA Today*. Gannett, 12 Feb. 2013. Web. 12 Sept. 2013. <http://www.usatoday.com/story/sports/olympics/2013/02/12/ olympic-wrestling-dan-gable-column/1913955/>.
52. "Marketing—Jobs at P&G: Assistant Brand Manager." *PG*. Procter & Gamble, n.d. Web. 15 Sept. 2013. <http://www.experiencepg.com/jobs/marketing.aspx>.
53. Coleman-Lochner, Lauren, and Carol Hymowitz. "At Procter & Gamble, the Innovation Well Runs Dry." *Bloomberg Businessweek*. Bloomberg, 6 Sept. 2012. Web. 15 Sept. 2013. <http://www.businessweek.com/articles/2012-09-06/at-procter-and-gamble-the-innovation-well-runs-dry>.
54. Harris, Melissa. "Cubs Pitch 'presentation Room' in Push for New Sponsors." *Chicago Confidential*. Chicago Tribune, 11 Oct. 2013. Web. 24 Oct. 2013. <http://www.chicagotribune .com/business/ct-biz-1013-confidential-cubs-20131013,0,1300344.column>.
55. Rau, Nate. "Profit Eludes Nashville Predators Despite On-Ice Success, Public Money. *The Tennessean*. Gannett, 29 Apr. 2012. Web. 24 Jan. 2014.

<http://www.tennessean.com/article/20120429/NEWS01/304290057/
Profit-eludes-Nashville-Predators-despite-ice-success-public-money?nclick_check=1>.

56. Tom Cigarran. Telephone interview by Adam Grossman. 26 June 2012.

57. "Tom Cigarran." *SternBusiness* (2012): 11. Web. 24 Jan. 2014. <http://issuu.com/nyustern/
docs/sternbzspring_2012_final?e=1692101/2847029>.

58. Ryan, Bob. "Brad Stevens Has a Tough Road Ahead in NBA." *BostonGlobe.com*. Boston
Globe Media Partners, 4 Aug. 2013. Web. 14 Sept. 2013. <http://www.bostonglobe.com/
sports/2013/08/03/brad-stevens-has-makings-hit-nba/rKVbXZ3NZNOVU9nehfURrN/
story.html>.

59. "Legacy—Celtics History." *NBA.com*. NBA Media Ventures, n.d. Web. 14 Sept. 2013.
<http://www.nba.com/celtics/history/History_index.html>.

60. Collier, Barry. "A Letter from the Athletic Director." *The Campaign for Hinkle Fieldhouse*.
Butler University, N.p., n.d. Web. 14 Sept. 2013. <http://www.butler.edu/hinkle-campaign/
preserve-hinkle/dear-friends/>.

61. Holmes, Baxter. "Brad Stevens's Latest Hire Also Has Connections to Butler." *BostonGlobe
.com*. Boston Globe Media Partners, 28 July 2013. Web. 11 Sept. 2013. <http://www
.bostonglobe.com/sports/2013/07/28/brad-stevens-latest-hire-also-has-connections-
butler/1dIbg932wzfBfRxoCwFX9L/story.html>.

62. King, Rob. "Candid Talk with Kevin Colbert." *Pittsburgh Magazine*. WiesnerMedia,
Aug. 2009. Web. 24 Jan. 2014. <http://www.pittsburghmagazine.com/Pittsburgh-Magazine/
August-2009/Features-Candid-Talk-with-Kevin-Colbert/>.

63. Labriola, Bob. "Fan Forum with Kevin Colbert." *Steelers.com*. Pittsburgh Steelers, 14 May
2013. Web. 24 Jan. 2014. <http://www.steelers.com/news/article-1/Fan-Forum-with-Kevin-
Colbert/2bfc742a-20a2-4f26-a21b-cf12e8edb0f3>.

64. Leahy, Sean. "Pittsburgh Steelers Trade Super Bowl XLIII MVP Santonio Holmes to the New
York Jets." *USA Today*. Gannett, 12 Apr. 2010. Web. 24 Jan. 2014. <http://content.usatoday
.com/communities/thehuddle/post/2010/04/pittsburgh-steelers-trade-super-bowl-xliii-mvp-santonio-
holmes-to-the-new-york-jets/1>.

65. Ibid.

66. "Woman in Georgia Alleges Assault." *ESPN.com*. ESPN, 8 Mar. 2010. Web. 24 Jan. 2014.
<http://sports.espn.go.com/nfl/news/story?id=4970050>.

67. Schefter, Adam (@AdamSchefter). "Here are teams that Steelers have called about
Roethlisberger: Rams, 49ers, Raiders, Bills, Jaguars, Seahawks and Browns." *Twitter*,
April 2010, 11:15 A.M. Tweet.

68. Freeman, Mike. "Michael Vick, Ben Roethlisberger: Changed for the Better, and Perhaps
for Good." *BleacherReport.com*. Bleacher Report, 26 Aug. 2013. Web. 24 Jan. 2014. <http://
bleacherreport.com/articles/1747701-michael-vick-ben-roethlisberger-changed-for-the-
better-and-perhaps-for-good>.

69. Spatz, Lyle. *The Team That Forever Changed Baseball and America: The 1947 Brooklyn
Dodgers*. Lincoln: University of Nebraska, 2012. 12. Print.

70. Spencer, Lyle. "Rickey's Foresight Shapes Game for Generations." *MLB.com*. MLBAM, 14 Apr.
2012. Web. 17 Feb. 2014. <http://mlb.mlb.com/news/article.jsp?ymd=20120412&content_
id=28519610&vkey=news_mlb&c_id=mlb>.

71. Ibid.

CHAPTER 3

1. Chen, Albert. "My Sportsman: Ndamukong Suh." *SI.com*. Sports Illustrated, 15 Nov. 2010.
Web. 4 Feb. 2014. <http://sportsillustrated.cnn.com/2010/magazine/sportsman/11/15/chen.
suh/index.html>.

2. Brettman, Allan. "Wieden+Kennedy Puts Portland's Ndamukong Suh in Driver's Seat of
New Chrysler Ad." *OregonLive*. The Oregonian, 8 May 2011. Web. 4 Feb. 2014. <http://www
.oregonlive.com/business/index.ssf/2011/05/wiedenkennedy_puts_portlands_n.html>.

3. "Ndamukong Suh Ejected, Denies Stomp." *ESPN.com*. ESPN, 25 Nov. 2011. Web. 4 Feb. 2014.
<http://espn.go.com/nfl/story/_/id/7276717/ndamukong-suh-detroit-lions-ejected-denies-
stomped-green-bay-packers-lineman>.

4. Meier, Fred. "Chrysler 300's Ndamukong Suh Stomps on Ad, May Be Suspended." *USA
Today*. Gannett, 25 Nov. 2011. Web. 4 Feb. 2014. <http://content.usatoday.com/communities/
driveon/post/2011/11/chrysler-300s-ndamukong-suh-stomps-on-ad-may-be-suspended/1>.

5. "Chrysler, Other Sponsors Quiet After Ndamukong Suh's Thanksgiving Stomp." *Sports Business Daily*. Street and Smith's, 28 Nov. 2011. Web. 4 Feb. 2014. <http://www.sportsbusinessdaily.com/Daily/Issues/2011/11/28/Marketing-and-Sponsorship/Suh.aspx>.

6. Bennett, Jeff. "New Chrysler Battling Old Defects." *WSJ.com*. Wall Street Journal, 10 May 2012. Web. 4 Feb. 2014. <http://online.wsj.com/article/SB10001424052702303630404577393044257833510.html>.

7. "Detroit Lions Franchise Encyclopedia." *Pro-Football-Reference.com*. Sports Reference, n.d. Web. 4 Feb. 2014. <http://www.pro-football-reference.com/teams/det/>.

8. "24/7 Wall Street: Seven Pro Teams on the Brink of Collapse." *Xfinity by Comcast*. Comcast, n.d. Web. 4 Feb. 2014. <http://xfinity.comcast.net/slideshow/sports-proteamscollapse/3/>.

9. Freeman, Mike. "Suh's Nastiness Changes Lions' Culture, Makes Him a Dirty Player." *CBSSports.com*. CBS Interactive, 28 Aug. 2011. Web. 4 Feb. 2014. <http://www.cbssports.com/nfl/story/15494946/suhs-nastiness-changes-lions-culture-makes-him-a-dirty-player>.

10. Green, Melanie C., Jeffrey J. Strange, and Timothy C. Brock. "In the Mind's Eye: Transportation-Imagery Model of Narrative Persuasion." *Narrative Impact: Social and Cognitive Foundations*. Mahwah, NJ: L. Erlbaum Associates, 2002. 315–41. Print.

11. "Bill Stern Sports Reel." *OTRcat.com*. Old Time Radio Catalog, n.d. Web. 5 Feb. 2014. <http://www.otrcat.com/bill-stern-sports-reel-p-1099.html>.

12. French, Jack. "Even His Initials Were BS." *Radio Recall*. Metropolitan Washington Old Time Radio Club, Dec. 2008. Web. 7 Feb. 2014. <http://www.mwotrc.com/rr2008_12/stern.htm>.

13. "Jeremy Lin Game-by-Game Stats." *ESPN.com*. ESPN, 2012. Web. 5 Feb. 2014. <http://espn.go.com/nba/player/gamelog/_/id/4299/year/2012/jeremy-lin>.

14. "Jeremy Lin Hits Game-Winning Shot to Lead Knicks Over Raptors." *HuffingtonPost.com*. Huffington Post, 14 Feb. 2012. Web. 5 Feb. 2014. <http://www.huffingtonpost.com/2012/02/14/jeremy-lin-knicks-raptors-winner-valentines-video_n_1277863.html>.

15. Augustine, Bernie. "Before Linsanity Erupted, Jeremy Lin Slept on NY Knicks Teammate Landry Fields' Couch." *NYDailyNews.com*. New York Daily News, 13 Feb. 2012. Web. 5 Feb. 2014. <http://www.nydailynews.com/sports/basketball/knicks/linsanity-erupted-jeremy-lin-slept-ny-knicks-teammate-landry-fields-couch-article-1.1021809>.

16. Tuttle, Brad. "Lintinis? Spiced Chicken 'Lings'? The Latest in Marketing Jeremy Lin & 'Linsanity.'" *TIME.com*. Time Inc., 24 Feb. 2012. Web. 5 Feb. 2014. <http://business.time.com/2012/02/24/lintinis-spiced-chicken-lings-the-latest-in-marketing-jeremy-lin-linsanity/>.

17. "Jeremy Lin Has Torn Meniscus." *ESPN.com*. ESPN, 1 Apr. 2012. Web. 5 Feb. 2014. <http://espn.go.com/new-york/nba/story/_/id/7759848/jeremy-lin-new-york-knicks-surgery-torn-meniscus>.

18. "Source: Jeremy Lin to Ink Offer sheet." *ESPN.com*. ESPN, 6 July 2012. Web. 5 Feb. 2014. <http://espn.go.com/new-york/nba/story/_/id/8133715/source-new-york-knicks-jeremy-lin-agrees-sign-offer-sheet-houston-rockets>.

19. Golliver, Ben. "Jeremy Lin Recounts Sleepless, Tearful Struggle to Live Up to 'Linsanity' with Rockets." *The Point Forward*. Sports Illustrated, 21 Aug. 2013. Web. 22 Sept. 2013. <http://nba.si.com/2013/08/21/jeremy-lin-houston-rockets-daryl-morey/>.

20. "Jeremy Lin in China for hoops camp." *ESPN.com*. ESPN, 25 Aug. 2013. Web. 22 Sept. 2013. <http://espn.go.com/nba/story/_/id/9598744/jeremy-lin-houston-rockets-eager-try-pick-roll-dwight-howard>.

21. Golliver, Ben. "Court Vision: Rockets GM Daryl Morey Defends Jeremy Lin in Reddit AMA." *The Point Forward*. Sports Illustrated, 16 Aug. 2013. Web. 22 Sept. 2013. <http://nba.si.com/2013/08/16/daryl-morey-jeremy-lin-reddit-ama-houston-rockets-andrew-bynum-kevin-garnett/>.

22. *Viewer Abandonment Trends in Short-Form Online Video Content*. Visible Measures, 2012. Web. 5 Feb. 2014. <http://corp.visiblemeasures.com/contact-us/abandonment-research/>.

23. The Audience Engagement Ladder is adapted from Rein, Irving, Philip Kotler, Michael Hamlin, and Martin Stoller. *High Visibility*. New York: McGraw-Hill, 2006. 95. Print and *The Elusive Fan*, 82.

24. Svrluga, Barry. "Five Russians Find Home on the Washington Capitals." *WashingtonPost.com*. Washington Post, 15 Apr. 2009. Web. 24 Sept. 2012. <http://www.washingtonpost.com/wp-dyn/content/article/2009/04/14/AR2009041403494.html>.

25. "VGTRK Acquires NHL Television Rights in Russia." *NHL.com*. NHL, 30 Nov. 2011. Web. 24 Sept. 2012. <http://www.nhl.com/ice/news.htm?id=603831>.

26. "Washington Capitals Blog Roll." *Washington Capitals—Blogs*. Washington Capitals, n.d. Web. 20 Sept. 2013. <http://capitals.nhl.com/club/page.htm?id=42399>.

27. Oland, Ian. "What It's Like to Be a Washington Capitals Fan in Russia." *Russian Machine Never Breaks*. N.p., 10 Jan. 2010. Web. 24 Sept. 2012. <http://www.russianmachineneverbreaks .com/2010/01/10/what-its-like-to-be-a-washington-capitals-fan-in-russia/>.

28. "Russian Machine Never Breaks." *Facebook*. Facebook, n.d. Web. 20 Sept. 2013. <http://www .facebook.com/russianmachineneverbreaks>. Russian Machine Never Breaks (@Russian Machine). "Russian Machine Never Breaks." *Twitter*, n.d. Web. 20 Sept. 2013. <http://twitter .com/#!/russianmachine>.

29. Issenberg, Sasha. *The Victory Lab: The Secret Science of Winning Campaigns*. New York: Crown, 2012. Print.

30. "Autistic Teen's Hoop Dreams." *CBSNews*. CBS Interactive, 28 Oct. 2006. Web. 5 Feb. 2014. <http://www.cbsnews.com/video/watch/?id=1342163n>.

31. Granderson, LZ. "Jason McElwain Continues to Do Great Things." *ESPN.com*. ESPN, 21 July 2008. Web. 5 Feb. 2014. <http://sports.espn.go.com/espn/page2/story?page=grander son/080717>.

32. "Feature Story: Chicago Football Eras." *The University of Chicago*. The University of Chicago, 8 Oct. 2012. Web. 7 Feb. 2014. <http://athletics.uchicago.edu/sports/fball/2012-13/ releases/201303102v73qy>.

33. Hutchins, Robert M. "'college Football Is An Infernal Nuisance.'" *SI Vault*. Sports Illustrated, 18 Oct. 1954. Web. 5 Feb. 2014. <http://sportsillustrated.cnn.com/vault/article/ magazine/MAG1128811/>.

34. Bearak, Barry. "Where Football and Higher Education Mix." *NYTimes.com*. New York Times, 16 Sept. 2011. Web. 5 Feb. 2014. <http://www.nytimes.com/2011/09/17/sports/ ncaafootball/at-the-university-of-chicago-football-and-higher-education-mix.html? pagewanted=all&_r=0>.

35. Ibid.

36. "Athletics Mission and Overview." *The University of Chicago*. The University of Chicago, n.d. Web. 7 Feb. 2014. <http://athletics.uchicago.edu/about/overview>.

37. Hoover, Eric. "Application Inflation." *Admissions & Student Aid*. Chronicle of Higher Education, 5 Nov. 2012. Web. 5 Feb. 2014. <http://chronicle.com/article/Application- Inflation/125277/>.

38. Manier, Jeremy. "College Sends Admission Decisions in Milestone Year for Applications." *UChicago News*. University of Chicago, 15 Mar. 2013. Web. 5 Feb. 2014. <http://news.uchicago .edu/article/2013/03/15/college-sends-admission-decisions-milestone-year-applications>.

39. "Sources: Saints Hire Cowboys' Payton as Head Coach." *ESPN.com*. ESPN, 18 Jan. 2006. Web. 5 Feb. 2014. <http://sports.espn.go.com/nfl/news/story?id=2295741>.

40. Jenkins, Lee. "Brees Is Coming Back with New Orleans." *NYTimes.com*. New York Times, 31 Aug. 2006. Web. 5 Feb. 2014. <http://nytimes.com/2006/08/31/sports/football/ 31brees.html>.

41. Duncan, Jeff. "New Orleans Saints' Success, Super Bowl Win, Rode In on Katrina's Wake." *Nola.com*. Times-Picayune, 27 Aug. 2010. Web. 5 Feb. 2014. <http://www.nola.com/saints/ index.ssf/2010/08/new_orleans_saints_success_sup.html>.

42. Varney, James. "New Orleans Saints Sell Out Renovated Superdome for 2011 Season." *Nola .com*. Times-Picayune, 22 May 2011. Web. 5 Feb. 2014. <http://www.nola.com/saints/index .ssf/2011/05/new_orleans_saints_fans_in_tha.html>.

43. Barra, Allen. "Sports: Football's Unforgettable Tie." *WSJ.com*. Wall Street Journal, 18 Nov. 2008. Web. 15 Sept. 2013. <http://online.wsj.com/article/SB122696675321435371.html>.

44. The Boston Strangler was the nickname of an actual murderer in the early 1960s in Boston.

45. "The Saga of a Great Headline." *HarvardMagazine.com*. Harvard Magazine, Nov.–Dec. 2000. Web. 6 Feb. 2014. <http://harvardmagazine.com/2000/11/the-saga-of-a-great-head.html>.

46. Rafferty, Kevin. *Harvard Beats Yale 29–29: The Story of the Most Famous Football Game Ever Played in the Ivy League . . . as Told by the Players*. New York: Overlook, 2009. Print.

47. *Harvard Beats Yale 29–29*. Dir. Kevin Rafferty. Kino International, 2008. DVD.

48. Ibid.

49. Ibid.

50. Burke, Timothy, and Jack Dickey. "Manti Te'o's Dead Girlfriend, the Most Heartbreaking and Inspirational Story of the College Football Season, Is a Hoax." *Deadspin*. Gawker Media, 16 Jan. 2013. Web. 20 Sept. 2013. <http://deadspin.com/manti-teos-dead-girlfriend-the-most-heartbreaking-an-5976517>.

51. "Manti Te'o Says He's the Victim of "Girlfriend" Hoax." *CBSNews*. CBS Interactive, 16 Jan. 2013. Web. 6 Feb. 2014. <http://www.cbsnews.com/8301-400_162-57564381/manti-teo-says-hes-the-victim-of-girlfriend-hoax/>.

52. Marvez, Alex. "Te'o Is No Joke Among Chargers." *FOXSports.com*. FOX Sports, 25 June 2013. Web. 6 Feb. 2014. <http://msn.foxsports.com/nfl/story/manti-teo-no-joke-san-diego-chargers-rookie-linebacker-rookie-symposium-062513>.

53. "Angela and Amber Cope: Twin Turbos." *Maxim.com*. Maxim, n.d. Web. 6 Feb. 2014. <http://www.maxim.com/maximtv/angela-and-amber-cope-twin-turbos>.

54. Gleeson, Scott. "Kevin Harvick Blames, Fans Rip Amber Cope." *USA Today*. Gannett, 15 July 2012. Web. 6 Feb. 2014. <http://content.usatoday.com/communities/gameon/post/2012/07/kevin-harvick-points-blame-fans-rip-amber-cope/1>.

55. Leavy, Jane. *The Last Boy: Mickey Mantle and the End of America's Childhood*. New York: Harper, 2010. Print.

56. McNeil, Franklin. "Weidman-Silva II to Happen Dec. 28." *ESPN.com*. ESPN, 15 July 2013. Web. 20 Sept. 2013. <http://espn.go.com/mma/story/_/id/9475713/ufc-president-dana-white-says-chris-weidman-anderson-silva-ii-happen-dec-28>.

57. For additional storylines, see *The Elusive Fan*, 227–28.

58. "Brewers Broadcaster Uecker Honored with Another Statue." *FoxNews.com*. FOX News Network, 22 Jan. 2014. Web. 17 Feb. 2014. <http://www.foxnews.com/sports/2014/01/22/brewers-broadcaster-uecker-honored-with-another-statue/>.

59. Howe Verhovek, Sam. "Japan's Baseball Idol Wins Fans in Seattle." *NYTimes.com*. New York Times, 24 Apr. 2001. Web. 6 Feb. 2014. <http://www.nytimes.com/2001/04/24/sports/japan-s-baseball-idol-wins-fans-in-seattle.html?pagewanted=all&src=pm>.

60. "Toma Selected to Royals Hall of Fame." *Kansas City Royals*. MLB.com, 29 June 2012. Web. 6 Feb. 2013. <http://kansascity.royals.mlb.com/news/article.jsp?ymd=20120629&content_id=34145878&vkey=pr_kc&c_id=kc>.

61. "Thomas Arthur, 84, Inventor of Dodger Dog, Dies." *NYTimes.com*. Associated Press. New York Times, 28 June 2006. Web. 6 Feb. 2014. <http://www.nytimes.com/2006/06/28/us/28arthur.html>.

62. "California Legends Farmer John and the Los Angeles Dodgers Get Smokin' Hot for Home Opener." *Bloomberg.com*. Bloomberg, n.d. Web. 15 Aug. 2013. <http://www.bloomberg.com/apps/news?pid=newsarchive&sid=aIrwyHsgZoHE>.

63. "The Business of Baseball." *Forbes.com*. Forbes, n.d. Web. 21 Sept. 2013. <http://www.forbes.com/lists/2011/33/baseball-valuations-11_New-York-Yankees_334613.html>.

64. "The Hipp and Ralph Engelstad Arena Provide the Old and New Minnesota Hockey Venues." *NFHS.org*. National Federation of State High School Associations, n.d. Web. 6 Feb. 2014. <http://www.nfhs.org/content.aspx?id=6694>.

65. "Boise's Blue Field Turns 20." *CBS College Sports*. CSTV, 14 Sept. 2006. Web. 6 Feb. 2014. <http://www.cstv.com/sports/m-footbl/stories/091406abt.html>.

66. "Boise State University." *StateUniversity.com*. N.p., 2013. Web. 6 Feb. 2014. <http://boise.stateuniversity.com/>.

67. Scott, Tom. "38 Years—10 Twists & Turns in the Bronco-Vandal Rivalry." *KTVB.com*. King Broadcasting Company, 13 Nov. 2009. Web. 6 Feb. 2014. <http://www.ktvb.com/community/blogs/scott-slant/38-years--10-twists--turns-in-the-Bronco-Vandal-rivalry-69968742.html>.

68. "Boise's Blue Field Turns 20."

69. Miller, James A., Steve Eder, and Richard Sandomir. "College Football's Most Dominant Player? It's ESPN." *NYTimes.com*. New York Times, 24 Aug. 2013. Web. 21 Sept. 2013. <http://www.nytimes.com/2013/08/25/sports/ncaafootball/college-footballs-most-dominant-player-its-espn.html?pagewanted=all>.

70. Cotton, Anthony. "Colorado Universities Want to Drive New Revenue with Athletic Success." *Denverpost.com*. Denver Post, 28 July 2013. Web. 6 Feb. 2014. <http://www.denverpost.com/ci_23746098/colorado-universities-want-drive-new-revenue-athletic-success>.

71. Ibid.

72. "Japanese University Licenses Blue Turf." *KTVB.com*. King Broadcasting Company, 11 June 2012. Web. 6 Feb. 2014. <http://www.ktvb.com/boise-state/Japanese-university-installs-blue-turf-honors-BSU-158455005.html>.

73. Doyle, Paul. "Joining the Big East: At Boise State, They Sing the Blues." *The Courant*. Hartford Courant, 13 Dec. 2011. Web. 6 Feb. 2014. <http://articles.courant.com/2011-12-13/sports/hc-boise-state-blue-turf-1214-20111213_1_blue-turf-boise-state-blue-field>.

74. "NCAA: Teams' Unis Can Match Field." *ESPN.com*. ESPN, 8 Mar. 2013. Web. 6 Feb. 2014. <http://espn.go.com/college-football/story/_/id/9032290/ncaa-keep-boise-state-broncos-wearing-blue-blue-field>.

75. Boise State University. "Communications and Marketing. BSU President Kustra: This Is a Way to Showcase the University as We Never Have Before in Our History." Boise State University, 18 Dec. 2006. Web. 6 Feb. 2014. <http://news.boisestate.edu/newsrelease/archive/2006/122006/1218fiesta_kustra.shtml>.

76. Prudhomme, Christian. "100% Tour de France!" *Tour de France 2013*. N.p., n.d. Web. 3 Oct. 2013. <http://www.letour.fr/le-tour/2013/us/animations-100th.html>.

77. Roxborough, Scott. "Tour de France Hits Six-Year Ratings High for Eurosport." *HollywoodReporter.com*. Hollywood Reporter, 3 July 2013. Web. 6 Feb. 2014. <http://www.hollywoodreporter.com/news/tour-de-france-hits-six-579761>.

78. Vasquez, Diego. "Your Client at the Tour de France." *Media Life Magazine*. N.p., 15 July 2012. Web. 21 Sept. 2013. <http://www.medialifemagazine.com/your-client-at-the-tour-de-france/>.

79. "College GameDay Corner." *ESPN MediaZone*. ESPN, 13 Dec. 2011. Web. 6 Feb. 2014. <http://espnmediazone.com/us/press-releases/2011/12/csudec13/>.

80. "The 2008 NHL Winter Classic." *SI.com*. Sports Illustrated, n.d. Web. 6 Feb. 2014. <http://sportsillustrated.cnn.com/multimedia/photo_gallery/0801/nhl.winter.classic.pens.sabres/content.1.html>.

81. Botta, Christopher. "NHL Winter Classic Nets $20 Million." *SportsBusiness Daily*. Street and Smith's, 13 Jan. 2014. Web. 7 Feb. 2014. <http://www.sportsbusinessdaily.com/Journal/Issues/2014/01/13/Events-and-Attractions/Winter-Classic.aspx>.

82. Burnside, Scott. "Sources: NHL Finalizing 6 Outdoors." *ESPN.com*. ESPN, 16 Apr. 2013. Web. 15 Sept. 2013. <http://espn.go.com/nhl/story/_/id/9180372/nhl-plans-6-outdoor-games-2014-including-los-angeles-new-york-chicago-vancouver-sources-say>.

83. Aristotle. *The Rhetoric and the Poetics of Aristotle*. Translated by W. Rhys Roberts and Ingram Bywater. New York: Modern Library, 1954. 24–30.

84. "Barkley: I Have to Use Better Judgment." NBA.com. NBA, 18 Feb. 2009. Web. 22 Feb. 2014. <http://www.nba.com/2009/news/02/18/barkley.interview/>.

85. Abbott, Henry. "LeBron James' Decision: The Transcript." *ESPN.com*. ESPN, 8 July 2010. Web. 6 Feb. 2014. <http://espn.go.com/blog/truehoop/post/_/id/17853/lebron-james-decision-the-transcript>.

86. Ibid.

CHAPTER 4

1. MacMillan, Douglas. "Big Spenders of Second Life." *Businessweek.com*. Bloomberg L.P., 16 Apr. 2007. Web. 13 Feb. 2014. <http://www.businessweek.com/stories/2007-04-16/big-spenders-of-second-lifebusinessweek-business-news-stock-market-and-financial-advice>.

2. Rose, Frank. "How Madison Avenue Is Wasting Millions on a Deserted Second Life." *Wired.com*. Conde Nast Digital, 24 July 2007. Web. 12 Feb. 2014. <http://www.wired.com/techbiz/media/magazine/15-08/ff_sheep?currentPage=all>.

3. Bannister, Larissa. "Adidas Targets Avatars with Shop in Second Life." *BrandRepublic*. Haymarket Media Group, 14 Sept. 2006. Web. 13 Feb. 2014. <http://www.brandrepublic.com/news/592537/>.

4. "NBA Headquarters Unveiled in Second Life." *NBA.com*. NBA Media Ventures, 1 May 2007. Web. 13 Feb. 2014. <http://www.nba.com/news/second_life_070501.html>.

5. Terdiman, Daniel. "'Second Life' Makes an All-Star Pitch—CNET News." *CNET News*. CBS Interactive, 11 July 2006. Web. 13 Feb. 2014. <http://news.cnet.com/2100-1043_3-6092913.html>.

6. Ibid.

7. Rose, "How Madison Avenue Is Wasting Millions."

8. Ibid.

9. Kurzweil, Ray. "Mass Use of Inventions." *The Singularity Is Near.* N.p., 2005. Web. 13 Feb. 2014. <http://www.singularity.com/charts/page50.html>.

10. Delo, Cotton. "U.S. Adults Now Spending More Time on Digital Devices Than Watching TV." *AdAge.com.* Crain Communications, 1 Aug. 2013. Web. 13 Feb. 2014. <http://adage.com/article/digital/americans-spend-time-digital-devices-tv/243414/>.

11. Kurzweil, Ray. "The Law of Accelerating Returns." *KurzweilAI.net.* Kurzweil Accelerating Intelligence, 7 Mar. 2001. Web. 13 Feb. 2014. <http://www.kurzweilai.net/the-law-of-accelerating-returns>.

12. Kurzweil, Ray. *The Singularity Is Near: When Humans Transcend Biology.* New York: Penguin, 2006. 8. Print.

13. Creamer, Matthew. "Brand Engagement Rate Still 1%, but Facebook Is OK with That." *AdAge.com.* Crain Communications, 15 Nov. 2012. Web. 13 Feb. 2014. <http://adage.com/article/digital/brand-engagement-rate-1-facebook/238317/>.

14. Snider, Mike. "Social TV App GetGlue Gears Up for Grammys." *USA Today.* Gannett, 8 Feb. 2013. Web. 13 Feb. 2014. <http://www.usatoday.com/story/tech/personal/2013/02/07/getglue-grammys-oscars-march-madness/1898611/>.

15. Hoffer, Steven. "Google+ Fastest Growing Social Network Ever, ComScore Study Says." *HuffingtonPost.com.* Huffington Post, 3 Aug. 2011. Web. 13 Feb. 2014. <http://www.huffingtonpost.com/2011/08/03/google-plus-fastest-growing-social_n_917389.html>.

16. Sawers, Paul. "Google+ Is One Year Old Today, Here's a Look at How It's Done So Far." *TheNextWeb.com.* TNW, 28 June 2012. Web. 13 Feb. 2014. <http://thenextweb.com/google/2012/06/28/google-is-one-year-old-today-heres-a-look-at-how-its-done-so-far/?utm_source=Reddit>.

17. Fitzgerald, Britney. "1 In 3 Google Employees Allegedly Inactive on Google." *HuffingtonPost.com.* HuffingtonPost.com, 9 Nov. 2012. Web. 13 Feb. 2014. <http://www.huffingtonpost.com/2012/11/09/google-employees-google-plus_n_2101174.html>.

18. Sawers, "Google+ Is One Year Old Today."

19. Horwitz, Josh. "Semiocast: Pinterest Now Has 70 Million Users and Is Steadily Gaining Momentum Outside the U.S." *TheNextWeb.com.* TNW, 10 July 2013. Web. 13 Feb. 2014. <http://thenextweb.com/socialmedia/2013/07/10/semiocast-pinterest-now-has-70-million-users-and-is-steadily-gaining-momentum-outside-the-us/>.

20. Indvik, Lauren. "The Most Popular Branded Boards on Pinterest." *Mashable.* Mashable, Inc., 8 May 2013. Web. 2 Oct. 2013. <http://mashable.com/2013/05/08/pinterest-most-popular-brand-boards/>.

21. Ibid.

22. Hoover, Ryan. "Hooking Users One Snapchat at a Time." *PandoDaily.* N.p., 30 July 2013. Web. 13 Feb. 2014. <http://pandodaily.com/2013/07/30/hooking-users-one-snapchat-at-a-time/>.

23. Stampler, Laura. "Acura Sent 100 Followers a Snapchat." *Businessinsider.com.* Business Insider, 29 July 2013. Web. 13 Feb. 2014. <http://www.businessinsider.com/acura-sent-100-followers-a-snapchat-2013-7>.

24. McDermott, John. "Brands Experiment with Photo-Messaging Service Snapchat, Facebook Poke." *AdAge.com.* Crain Communications, 4 Jan. 2013. Web. 13 Feb. 2014. <http://adage.com/article/digital/brands-experiment-photo-messaging-service-snapchat-facebook-poke/238979/>.

25. Kemp, Nicola. "What Marketers Should Know About Snapchat." *Marketing Magazine.* Haymarket Media Group, 13 June 2013. Web. 13 Feb. 2014. <http://www.marketingmagazine.co.uk/article/1186152/marketers-know-snapchat>.

26. Isaac, Mike. "Snapchat Closes $60 Million Round Led by IVP, Now at 200 Million Daily Snaps." *AllThingsD.com.* Dow Jones, 24 June 2013. Web. 13 Feb. 2014. <http://allthingsd.com/20130624/snapchat-closes-60-million-round-led-by-ivp-now-at-200-million-daily-snaps/>.

27. "Washington Wizards and Washington Capitals Join Snapchat." Washington Wiards. NBA.com, 21 Jan. 2014. Web. 21 Feb. 2014. <http://www.nba.com/wizards/washington-wizards-and-washington-capitals-join-snapchat>.

28. "Twitter Media." Twitter Developers, n.d. Web. 13 Feb. 2014. <http://cliffstowing.yourtemplate.ca/default_018.html>.

29. "Golden Tweets." *2012 Year on Twitter.* Twitter, n.d. Web. 13 Feb. 2014. <https://2012.twitter.com/en/golden-tweets.html>.

30. "Global Town Square." *2012 Year on Twitter*. Twitter, n.d. Web. 13 Feb. 2014. <https://2012 .twitter.com/en/global-town-square.html>.

31. McLuhan, Marshall, and Quentin Fiore. *The Medium Is the Message*. New York: Random House, 1967. Print.

32. Osofsky, Justin. "Making News and Entertainment More Social in 2011." *Facebook Developers*. Facebook, 28 Dec. 2010. Web. 13 Feb. 2014. <https://developers.facebook.com/blog/post/443/>.

33. Turnbull, Trevor. "Monetizing Social Media in Sports with SF Giants Bryan Srabian (Part 3)." *SportsNetworker.com*. Sports Networker, 2012. Web. 13 Feb. 2014. <http://www.sportsnetworker .com/2012/04/12/monetizing-social-media-in-sports-with-sf-giants-bryan-srabian/>.

34. "Twitter's 2011 Year in Review." Twitter, 2011. Web. 13 Feb. 2014. <http://yearinreview.twitter .com/en/tps.html>.

35. Felix, Samantha. "Meet The 10 Most Followed Companies on Instagram—Ever." *Businessinsider.com*. Business Insider, 18 Oct. 2012. Web. 13 Feb. 2014. <http://www .businessinsider.com/the-10-most-followed-companies-on-instagram-2012-10?op=1>.

36. Wasserman, Todd. "Just Did It: Nike Finally Opens a Twitter Account." *Mashable*. Mashable, Inc., 30 Dec. 2011. Web. 13 Feb. 2014. <http://mashable.com/2011/12/30/nike-twitter-account/>.

37. "Nike 'Make It Count' Campaign in the Spirit of Preparations for the London 2012 Olympic Games." *CreaTimes.tumblr.com*. CreaTimes, 5 Jan. 2012. Web. 13 Feb. 2014. <http://creatimes .tumblr.com/post/15355455185/nike-make-it-count-campaign-uk>.

38. Jenkins, Henry. *Convergence Culture: Where Old and New Media Collide*. New York: New York UP, 2006. 2–3. Print.

39. Harris, Bob, and Emil Kadlec. "A Nod (and a Wink) to the Founders of Fantasy Football." *Fspnet.com*. Fantasy Sports Publications, Inc., n.d. Web. 13 Feb. 2014. <http://fspnet.com/ wink.pdf>.

40. Murphy, Samantha. "Xbox and NFL Will Bring Fantasy Football to Life." *Mashable*. Mashable, Inc., 21 May 2013. Web. 13 Feb. 2014. <http://mashable.com/2013/05/21/xbox-nfl/>.

41. Etkin, Jaimie. "London Olympics 2012 Ratings: Most Watched Event in TV History." *HuffingtonPost.com*. Huffington Post, 13 Aug. 2012. Web. 13 Feb. 2014. <http://www .huffingtonpost.com/2012/08/13/london-olympics-2012-ratings-most-watched-ever_n_1774032.html>.

42. NBC Delayed (@NBCDelayed). "NBC Delayed." *Twitter*, n.d. Web. 10 Sept. 2013. <https:// twitter.com/NBCDelayed>.

43. Etkin, "London Olympics 2012 Ratings."

44. Poggi, Jeanine. "Uneven Start for Sochi Ratings, but NBC Is Feeling Good." *AdAge.com*. Crain Communications, 12 Feb. 2014. Web. 17 Feb. 2014. <http://adage.com/article/media/ nbc-releases-olympic-ad-inventory/291680/>.

45. Ryan, Nate. "Hendrick Social Media Plan Could Be Prototype." *USA Today*. Gannett, 14 Aug. 2013. Web. 13 Feb. 2014. <http://www.usatoday.com/story/sports/nascar/2013/08/14/ hendrick-motorsports-social-media-reddit-dale-earnhardt-jr-twitter/2657983/>.

46. "Earnhardt Chats with Fans via Reddit AMA, @TeamHendrick Takeover." *Hendrick Motorsports*. HendrickMotorsports.com, 6 Aug. 2013. Web. 13 Feb. 2014. <http://www .hendrickmotorsports.com/news/article/2013/08/06/Earnhardt-chats-with-fans-via-Reddit-AMA-TeamHendrick-takeover>.

47. Maxcer, Chris. "How IBM Works with Masters to Deliver an Immersive Digital Experience." *Poweritpro.com*. Penton, 12 Apr. 2013. Web. 13 Feb. 2014. <http://poweritpro.com/news-amp-views/how-ibm-works-masters-deliver-immersive-digital-experience>.

48. "Ducks Announce Fan Rewards Program." *Goducks.com*. University of Oregon, 30 Aug. 2012. Web. 13 Feb. 2014. <http://www.goducks.com/ViewArticle.dbml?ATCLID=205671563>.

49. Overly, Steven. "SB Nation's Sports Blogger Collective Sees Bias as a Plus." *WashingtonPost. com*. Washington Post, 20 Dec. 2010. Web. 13 Feb. 2014. <http://www.washingtonpost.com/ wp-dyn/content/article/2010/12/17/AR2010121706202.html>.

50. Orlando, Dan. "Vox Media Says Design Helps Charge SB Nation." *BizJournals.com*. New York Business Journal, 19 July 2013. Web. 13 Feb. 2014. <http://www.bizjournals.com/ newyork/news/2013/06/17/vox-media-credits-new-interface-with.html?page=all>.

51. "It Starts with the Fan." *SB Nation*. Vox Media, n.d. Web. 3 Oct. 2013. <http://www .voxmedia.com/media-kit/brand/sbnation>.

52. Mike Trudell. Telephone and email interview by Adam Grossman. 29 September 2013.

53. Ibid.

54. Fischer, Eric. "Eric Fischer Twitter Page." *Twitter*, 15 July 2013. Web. 15 Sept. 2013. <https://twitter.com/EricFisherSBJ/statuses/356786738120765440>.

55. Ozanian, Mike. "MLBAM's Home Runs With Sony And WWE At CES Set Stage For IPO." *Forbes*. Forbes Magazine, 12 Jan. 2014. Web. 17 Apr. 2014. <http://www.forbes.com/sites/mikeozanian/2014/01/12/mlbams-home-runs-with-sony-and-wwe-at-ces-set-stage-for-ipo/>.

56. "Media Clippings." SendtoNews, n.d. Web. 15 Sept. 2013. <http://www.sendtonews.com/press>.

57. "Season-Ticket Holder Digital Ticket Guide." *Tickets*. Washington Capitals, n.d. Web. 16 Apr. 2014. <http://capitals.nhl.com/club/page.htm?id=91793>.

58. "Monumental Sports & Entertainment Introduces Digital Ticket System." *News Presented By Lexus*. Monumental Sports & Entertainment, 01 Oct. 2012. Web. 16 Apr. 2014. <http://capitals.nhl.com/club/news.htm?id=642529>.

59. Gregory Chatzinoff and Josh Brickman. Interview by Adam Grossman. 11 Dec. 2013.

60. Hughes, Jed. "Sports Leagues' Record-Breaking Media Contracts Make Huge Impact on Revenue." *BleacherReport.com*. Bleacher Report, 23 May 2012. Web. 17 Sept. 2013. <http://bleacherreport.com/articles/1193160-sports-leagues-media-contracts-and-make-a-huge-impact-on-player-compensation>.

61. Futterman, Matthew, and Spencer Ante. "Verizon Pads NFL Deal." The Wall Street Journal. 04 June 2013. Dow Jones & Company. 28 Apr. 2014. <http://online.wsj.com/news/articles/SB10001424127887324563004578525060861520512>.

CHAPTER 5

1. Marcotti, Gabriele. "Actual Fans: Are They Necessary?" *WSJ.com*. Wall Street Journal, 21 Sept. 2010. Web. 6 Feb. 2014. <http://online.wsj.com/article/SB10001424052748703989304575503821229703834.html>.

2. Ibid.

3. Greene, Jerry. "Virtual Stadium Fans Could Solve Woes." *ESPN.com*. ESPN, 26 Sept. 2010. Web. 6 Feb. 2014. <http://sports.espn.go.com/espn/page2/story?id=5616909>.

4. Ibid.

5. Marcotti, "Actual Fans."

6. O'Byrne, David. "Football Finance: Top Turkish Club Plans Hydropower Plant." *FT.com*. Financial Times, 14 Aug. 2012. Web. 6 Feb. 2014. <http://blogs.ft.com/beyond-brics/2012/08/14/football-finance-cash-strapped-turkish-club-plans-hydropower-plant/?Authorised=false>.

7. Trenholm, Rich. "Wimbledon Star Sports Ads on Her Fingernails for 4K TV." *CNET UK*. N.p., 24 June 2013. Web. 3 Oct. 2013. <http://crave.cnet.co.uk/homecinema/wimbledon-star-sports-ads-on-her-fingernails-for-4k-tv-50011566/>.

8. Florio, Mike. "Momentum Builds for a Redskins Name Change, and One Man Can Make It Happen." *ProFootballTalk*. NBC Sports, 9 Feb. 2013. Web. 6 Feb. 2014. <http://profootballtalk.nbcsports.com/2013/02/09/momentum-builds-for-a-redskins-name-change-and-one-man-can-make-it-happen/>.

9. Gesaman, Krista. "'Skin Tone." *Daily Beast*. Newsweek/Daily Beast, 4 Oct. 2009. Web. 6 Feb. 2014. <http://www.thedailybeast.com/newsweek/2009/10/04/skin-tone.html>.

10. Skinner, David. "The Real History of the Word Redskin. It's Not What You Think." *Slate*. The Slate Group, 18 Dec. 2013. Web. 6 Feb. 2014. <http://www.slate.com/blogs/lexicon_valley/2013/12/18/redskins_the_debate_over_the_washington_football_team_s_name_incorrectly.html>.

11. "'We Are Very Proud to Be Called Redskins.'" *Redskins.com*. Washington Redskins, 11 Feb. 2013. Web. 6 Feb. 2014. <http://www.redskins.com/news-and-events/article-1/We-Are-Very-Proud-To-Be-Called-Redskins/d4d7c05d-be39-4a27-9244-d06cfae46797>.

12. Snyder, Dan. "Letter from Washington Redskins Owner Dan Snyder to Fans." *WashingtonPost.com*. Washington Post, 9 Oct. 2013. Web. 6 Feb. 2014. <http://www.washingtonpost.com/local/letter-from-washington-redskins-owner-dan-snyder-to-fans/2013/10/09/e7670ba0-30fe-11e3-8627-c5d7de0a046b_story.html>.

13. Badenhausen, Kurt. "The NFL Signs TV Deals Worth $27 Billion." *Forbes.com*. Forbes, 14 Dec. 2011. Web. 6 Feb. 2014. <http://www.forbes.com/sites/kurtbadenhausen/2011/12/14/the-nfl-signs-tv-deals-worth-26-billion/>.

14. Bashir, Martin. "Oneida Indian Nation Pressures NFL's Redskins to Change Name." *MSNBC*. NBC Universal, 9 Sept. 2013. Web. 3 Oct. 2013. <http://tv.msnbc.com/2013/09/09/oneida-indian-nation-pressures-nfls-redskins-to-change-name/>.

15. "Slate.com, Others to Ban 'Redskins' Name from Their Pages." *Chicago Tribune*. Chicago Tribune, 9 Aug. 2013. Web. 6 Feb. 2014. <http://articles.chicagotribune.com/2013-08-09/sports/chi-slatecom-others-to-ban-redskins-name-from-their-pages-20130809_1_native-americans-redskins-american-indians>.

16. Lewis, Mike, and Manish Tripathi. *The Financial Impact of Mascots on Sports Brands*. Rep. Emory Sports Marketing Analytics, 19 Dec. 2013. Web. 17 Feb. 2014. <https://blogs.emory.edu/sportsmarketing/2013/12/19/the-financial-impact-of-mascots-on-sports-brands/>.

17. "Best Sellers: November 2, 2003." *NYTimes.com*. New York Times, 2 Nov. 2003. Web. 6 Feb. 2014. <http://www.nytimes.com/2003/11/02/books/best-sellers-november-2-2003.html?scp=9>.

18. Pierce, Gregory F. *How Bill James Changed Our View of Baseball*. Skokie, IL: ACTA Sports, 2007. Print.

19. Berri, David J., Martin B. Schmidt, and Stacey L. Brook. *The Wages of Wins*. CA: Stanford Business, 2006. Print. Moskowitz, Tobias J., and L. Jon Wertheim. *Scorecasting: The Hidden Influences Behind How Sports Are Played and Games Are Won*. New York: Crown Archetype, 2011. Print.

20. Alamar, Benjamin, and Vijay Mehrotra. "Beyond 'Moneyball': The Rapidly Evolving World of Sports Analytics, Part I." *Analytics Magazine* Sept.–Oct. 2011: n. pag. *Analytics Magazine*. Institute for Operations Research and the Management Sciences, 30 Aug. 2011. Web. 6 Feb. 2014. <http://www.analytics-magazine.org/special-articles/391-beyond-moneyball-the-rapidly-evolving-world-of-sports-analytics-part-i>.

21. London, Jay. "The 2012 Sloan Sports Analytics Conference, a.k.a. 'Dorkapalooza'" *Slice of MIT by the Alumni Association RSS*. Slice of MIT, 6 Mar. 2012. Web. 9 Dec. 2014. <http://slice.mit.edu/2012/03/06/the-2012-sloan-sports-analytics-conference-a-k-a-dorkapalooza/>.

22. Wright, Michael C. "Bears Announce 2014 Ticket Prices." *ESPNChicago.com*. ESPN, 5 Feb. 2014. Web. 7 Feb. 2014. <http://espn.go.com/blog/chicago/bears/post/_/id/4690304/bears-announce-2014-ticket-prices>.

23. Mattioli, Dana. "On Orbitz, Mac Users Steered to Pricier Hotels." *WSJ.com*. Wall Street Journal, 23 Aug. 2012. Web. 6 Feb. 2014. <http://online.wsj.com/article/SB10001424052702304458604577488822667325882.html?mod=e2tw>.

24. Smith, Jake. "Smug Alert: Orbitz Shows Mac Users Higher Priced Hotels by Default." *9to5mac.com*. N.p., 25 June 2012. Web. 6 Feb. 2014. <http://9to5mac.com/2012/06/25/smug-alert-orbitz-shows-mac-users-higher-priced-hotels-by-default/>.

25. Fuller, Marcus R. "Gophers Turn to Outsourcing for Football, Men's Basketball Ticket Sales." *TwinCities.com*. St. Paul Pioneer Press, 19 May 2012. Web. 6 Feb. 2014. <http://www.twincities.com/gophersfootball/ci_20655628/gophers-football-mens-basketball-turn-outsourcing-ticket-sales>.

26. Lombardo, John. "For the WNBA, Time for a Clutch 3." *SportsBusiness Daily*. Street and Smith's, 20 May 2013. Web. 6 Feb. 2014. <http://www.sportsbusinessdaily.com/Journal/Issues/2013/05/20/Leagues-and-Governing-Bodies/WNBA.aspx>.

27. Ely, Jeff, and Sandeep Baliga. "Big News." *Cheap Talk*. Cheap Talk, 11 Feb. 2013. Web. 6 Feb. 2014. <http://cheaptalk.org/2013/02/11/big-news/>.

28. Jeff Ely. Email interview by Adam Grossman. 15 June 2013.

29. Ely and Sandeep, "Big News."

30. Wolverton, Brad. "Many Division I Programs See Big Drop in Basketball Attendance." *Players*. Chronicle of Higher Education, 26 Mar. 2012. Web. 6 Feb. 2014. <http://chronicle.com/blogs/players/big-basketball-attendance-swings-among-division-i-programs/29814>.

31. "Purple Pricing for Select Men's Basketball Games Launches." *NUSports.com*. CBS Interactive, 11 Feb. 2013. Web. 6 Feb. 2014. <http://www.nusports.com/sports/m-baskbl/spec-rel/021113aac.html>.

32. Harris, Melissa. "Economists Share Strategy to Make More Money from Ticket Sales." *Business*. Chicago Tribune, 05 Jan. 2014. Web. 20 Feb. 2014. <http://articles.chicagotribune.com/2014-01-05/business/ct-biz-0105-confidential-tickets-20140105_1_grant-achatz-nick-kokonas-ticket-sales>.

33. Berkowitz, Steve. "Marketers Reshape How College Teams Sell Tickets." *USA Today*. Gannett, 5 Aug. 2011. Web. 6 Feb. 2014. <http://usatoday30.usatoday.com/sports/college/2011-08-05-college-outsourcing-sports-ticket-sales_n.htm>.
34. Ibid.
35. Mahoney, Rod. "What It Takes to Be Consistently Successful in College Football." *Tomahawk Nation*. SB Nation, 9 Feb. 2010. Web. 6 Feb. 2014. <http://www.tomahawknation.com/2010/2/9/1302407/what-it-takes-to-be-consistently>.
36. Berkowitz, "Marketers Reshape How College Teams."
37. Warshaw, Andrew. "Win or We'll Cut Sponsorship, Arsenal Warned by Main Backers Emirates." *Mail Online*. Associated Newspapers Ltd, 22 Dec. 2012. Web. 2 Oct. 2013. <http://www.dailymail.co.uk/sport/football/article-2252281/Arsenal-warned-Emirates-win-cut-sponsorship.html>.
38. McCarthy, Michael. "Ad Tattoos Get Under Some People's Skin." *USA Today*. Gannett, 3 Apr. 2002. Web. 6 Feb. 2014. <http://usatoday30.usatoday.com/money/advertising/2002-04-04-tattoo.htm>.
39. "Best Practices: Sponsorship Activation." *IEG Sponsorship Report*. IEG, 28 Jan. 2013. Web. 6 Feb. 2014. <http://www.sponsorship.com/iegsr/2013/01/28/Best-Practices--Sponsorship-Activation.aspx>.
40. Stern, Daniel. "The Digital Rules of Engagement." *AdWeek.com*. Adweek, 5 May 2008. Web. 6 Feb. 2014. <http://www.adweek.com/news/advertising-branding/digital-rules-engagement-95681>.
41. Tough Mudder. *Tough Mudder, Probably The Toughest Event on the Planet, Names Under Armour Their "Official Outfitter" of Performance Footwear, Apparel and Accessories*. *Toughmudder.com*. N.p., 5 Dec. 2011. Web. 6 Feb. 2014. <http://toughmudder.com/wp-content/uploads/2011/02/Tough-Mudder-and-Under-Armour-Press-Release.pdf>.
42. Vranica, Suzanne. "Web Video: Bigger and Less Profitable." *WSJ.com*. Wall Street Journal, 14 Mar. 2013. Web. 3 Oct. 2013. <http://online.wsj.com/article/SB10001424127887324034804578346540295942824.html>.
43. Paul Dupont, Kevin. "Garden Fans on the Money." *Boston.com*. Boston Globe, 5 June 2011. Web. 6 Feb. 2014. <http://www.boston.com/sports/hockey/bruins/articles/2011/06/05/garden_fans_on_the_money/?page=full>.
44. Rose, Frank. "The Lost Boys." *Wired.com*. Conde Nast Digital, Aug. 2004. Web. 6 Feb. 2014. <http://www.wired.com/wired/archive/12.08/lostboys.html>.
45. "Chase Family Arena." *Hartford Hawks*. University of Hartford Athletics, 27 Mar. 2008. Web. 6 Feb. 2014. <http://www.hartfordhawks.com/sports/2008/3/27/272028327.aspx?id=5>.
46. *XLCenter.com*. XL Center, n.d. Web. 6 Feb. 2014. <http://www.xlcenter.com/>.
47. Brian Gerrity. Interview by Adam Grossman. 4 Jun. 2012.
48. Ibid.
49. Sutton, Bill. "Thoughts on Fan Passion, Owner Perception, Sales Persistence." *Sports Business Daily*. Street and Smith's, 3 June 2013. Web. 6 Feb. 2014. <http://www.sportsbusinessdaily.com/Journal/Issues/2013/06/03/Opinion/Sutton-Impact.aspx?hl=analytics>.

CHAPTER 6

1. Fédération Internationale de Football Association. "Brazil 2014 Slogan Presented: All in One Rhythm / Juntos Num Só Ritmo." *Fifa.com*. FIFA World Cup, 30 May 2012. Web. 12 Feb. 2014. <http://www.fifa.com/worldcup/media/newsid=1641290/index.html>.
2. Ibid.
3. Panja, Tariq. "Brazil Caps Confederations Cup Marked by Protests with Title." *Bloomberg.com*. Bloomberg, 30 June 2013. Web. 12 Feb. 2014. <http://www.bloomberg.com/news/2013-07-01/brazil-caps-confederations-cup-marked-by-protests-with-title.html>.
4. Anbinder, Jacob. "Brazil's Protests over Transit Fare Hikes Illustrate the Dangers of Income Inequality." *Tcf.org*. Century Foundation, 21 June 2013. Web. 12 Feb. 2014. <http://www.tcf.org/blog/detail/brazils-protests-over-transit-fare-hikes-illustrate-the-dangers-of-income-i>.
5. Prada, Paulo, and Maria Carolina Marcello. "One Million March Across Brazil in Biggest Protests Yet." *Reuters*. Thomson Reuters, 20 Jan. 2013. Web. 12 Feb. 2014. <http://www.reuters.com/article/2013/06/21/us-brazil-protests-idUSBRE95J15020130621>.
6. "FIFA Says No Plans to Cancel Confederation Cup amid Huge Protests in Brazil." *Fox News*. FOX News Network, 21 June 2013. Web. 12 Sept. 2013. <http://www.foxnews.com/world/2013/06/21/fifa-says-no-plans-to-cancel-confederation-cup-amid-huge-protests-in-brazil/>.

7. Mayer, Andre. "Brazil Protests Show Cost of Hosting Major Sports Events." *CBCnews* .CBC/Radio Canada, 29 June 2013. Web. 12 Sept. 2013. <http://www.cbc.ca/news/world/ story/2013/06/28/f-brazil-protests-sports-events.html>.

8. Downie, Andrew. "Brazil Wins on the Soccer Field, but Can Protesters Win on the Streets?" *Csmonitor.com*. Christian Science Monitor, 1 July 2013. Web. 12 Feb. 2014. <http://www.csmonitor .com/World/Americas/2013/0701/Brazil-wins-on-the-soccer-field-but-can-protesters-win-on-the-streets>.

9. Soto, Alonso. "Brazil Protests Take Toll on Rousseff's Popularity, Economy Key." *Reuters*. Thomson Reuters, 25 July 2013. Web. 12 Feb. 2014. <http://www.reuters.com/ article/2013/07/25/us-brazil-politics-rousseff-idUSBRE96O1CZ20130725>.

10. Azzoni, Tales. "Protests Get Support from Brazilian Soccer Players." *Yahoo! News*. Yahoo!, 19 June 2013. Web. 12 Feb. 2014. <http://news.yahoo.com/protests-support-brazilian-soccer-players-142353765.html>. "Ronaldo Lauds Brazil's Victory in the Confederations Cup, Says He Backs Protesters." *Reuters Sports*. AOL.com, 1 July 2013. Web. 12 Feb. 2014. <http://on.aol .com/video/ronaldo-lauds-brazils-victory-in-the-confederations-cup--says-he-backs-protesters-517840927/>.

11. "FIFA's Blatter Pleased with Brazil as Host Despite Protests." *CBC.ca*. CBC/Radio Canada, 1 July 2013. Web. 12 Feb. 2014. <http://www.cbc.ca/sports/fifaconfederationscup/story/2013/07/01/ sp-soccer-fifa-confederations-cup-brazil-protests-world-cup-2014.html>.

12. Rigby, Claire. "Brazil's Protests Have Subsided—for Now." *New Statesman*. NewStatesman, 12 Sept. 2013. Web. 12 Sept. 2013. <http://www.newstatesman.com/politics/2013/09/ brazils-protests-have-subsided-now>.

13. Winter, Brian, and Silvio Cascione. "Brazil Economic Growth Disappoints Again." *Reuters*. Thomson Reuters, 29 May 2013. Web. 12 Feb. 2014. <http://www.reuters.com/article/2013/ 05/30/us-brazil-economy-idUSBRE94T00T20130530>.

14. Capozzi, Joe. "Protesting Fans Ejected from Marlins Park for 'Creating Disturbance.'" *Palm Beach Post*. Cox Media Group, 8 Apr. 2013. Web. 12 Feb. 2014. <http://blogs.palmbeachpost .com/marlins/2013/04/08/protesting-fans-ejected-from-marlins-park/>. "Istanbul Downplays Protests Ahead of Olympic Vote." *ESPN.com* ESPN, 25 July 2013. Web. 12 Feb. 2014. <http://sports.espn.go.com/espn/wire?section=oly&id=9508675>.

15. "Voters Reject Football Stadium Plan in Zurich." *AP News Archive*. Associated Press, 22 Sept. 2013. Web. 12 Feb. 2014. <http://www.apnewsarchive.com/2013/Voters_reject_ football_stadium_plan_in_Zurich/id-5e4d16636809436089359e036825e5fa>.

16. Shapiro, Ilya. "Public Financing of Vikings Stadium a Bad Deal for Fans, Taxpayers." *Cato.org*. Cato Institute, 23 May 2012. Web. 12 Feb. 2014. <http://www.cato.org/blog/ public-financing-vikings-stadium-bad-deal-fans-taxpayers>.

17. Coates, Dennis. "A Closer Look at Stadium Subsidies." A Closer Look at Stadium Subsidies. 29 Apr. 2008. The American Magazine. 28 Apr. 2014. <http://www.american.com/ archive/2008/april-04-08/a-closer-look-at-stadium-subsidies>.

18. Zimbalist, Andrew. "Brazil World Cup Olympics Finances—Brazilian Infrastructure Olympics and World Cup Impact." *Americas Quarterly*. Americas Society and Council of the Americas, Summer 2011. Web. 15 Sept. 2013. <http://www.americasquarterly.org/ zimbalist>.

19. "Ross' Gift to Michigan Could Affect Miami Stadium." *The Big Story*. Associated Press, 4 Sept. 2013. Web. 22 Sept. 2013. <http://bigstory.ap.org/article/stephen-ross-give-200m-u-michigan-0>.

20. Raab, Scott. *The Whore of Akron: One Man's Search for the Soul of LeBron James*. New York: HarperCollins, 2011. 20–21. Print.

21. Fulks, Daniel L. *Revenues and Expenses of NCAA Division I Intercollegiate Athletics Programs Report: Fiscal Years 2004 through 2012*. Rep. NCAA, 2013. Web. 12 Feb. 2014. <http://www.ncaapublications.com/productdownloads/2012RevExp.pdf>.

22. Kietzman, Kevin. "Tax Payers Fund Questionable Royals Expenses." *Sports Radio 810 WHB*. ESPN, 31 July 2012. Web. 12 Feb. 2014. <http://www.810whb.com/common/more .php?m=49&post_id=1001>.

23. Ibid.

24. Horrow, Richard B., and Karla Swatek. *Beyond the Box Score: An Insider's Guide to the $750 Billion Business of Sports*. New York: Morgan James Pub., 2010. 101. Print.

25. Ibid.

26. Ibid, 105.

27. Belson, Ken. "As Stadiums Vanish, Their Debt Lives On." *NYTimes.com*. New York Times, 7 Sept. 2010. Web. 12 Feb. 2014. <http://www.nytimes.com/2010/09/08/sports/08stadium .html?pagewanted=all>.

28. Waldron, Travis. "How Brazil's Olympic and World Cup Dreams Turned into a Nightmare." *ThinkProgress*. ThinkProgress, 2 July 2013. Web. 27 Sept. 2013. <http://thinkprogress.org/ sports/2013/07/02/2236331/brazil-world-cup-olympics-economic-nightmare/>.

29. Newton, Paula. "Olympics Worth the Price Tag? The Montreal Legacy." *CNN.com*. Cable News Network, 19 July 2012. Web. 13 Feb. 2014. <http://www.cnn.com/2012/07/19/world/ canada-montreal-olympic-legacy/index.html>.

30. Belson, "As Stadiums Vanish."

31. Belson, Ken. "Stadium Boom Deepens Municipal Woes." *NYTimes.com*. New York Times, 24 Dec. 2009. Web. 27 Sept. 2013. <http://www.nytimes.com/2009/12/25/sports/25stadium .html?pagewanted=all>.

32. Albergotti, Reed, and Cameron McWhirter. "A Stadium's Costly Legacy Throws Taxpayers for a Loss." *WSJ.com*. Wall Street Journal, 12 July 2011. Web. 12 Feb. 2014. <http://online.wsj .com/article/SB10001424052748704461304576216330349497852.html>.

33. Florio, Mike. "Spanos Says Chargers Want to Stay in San Diego." *ProFootballTalk*. NBC Sports, 22 May 2013. Web. 12 Feb. 2014. <http://profootballtalk.nbcsports.com/2013/05/22/ spanos-says-chargers-want-to-stay-in-san-diego/>.

34. Florio, Mike. "If L.A. Move Will Happen in 2013, Chargers Are the Most Likely to Go." *ProFootballTalk*. NBC Sports, 30 June 2012. Web. 12 Feb. 2014. <http://profootballtalk.nbcsports .com/2012/06/30/if-l-a-move-will-happen-in-2013-chargers-are-the-most-likely-to-go/>.

35. Fieldman, Evan D. "A Temporary Band-Aid Pay-to-Play Fees and the Extracurricular Crisis in Sports and the Arts." *Entertainment & Sports Lawyer* 29.3 (2011): 1. Print.

36. Wolfson, Hannah. "Alabama Community Colleges Cut Sports Due to Budget Woes." *AL.com*. Alabama Media Group, 10 Apr. 2011. Web. 12 Feb. 2014. <http://blog.al.com/spotnews/2011/04/ alabama_community_colleges_cut.html>.

37. Carlyon, Hays. "No Money Available for Duval High School Sports, Says Board Chairman." *Jacksonville.com*. Florida Times-Union, 12 Mar. 2011. Web. 12 Feb. 2014. <http://jacksonville .com/news/metro/2011-03-12/story/no-money-available-duval-high-school-sports-says- board-chairman>.

38. Carey, Bill. "University of Maryland cuts 7 sports teams, saves men's outdoor track SI Wire." SI Wire. 03 July 2012. Sports Illustrated. 28 Apr. 2014. <http://tracking.si.com/2012/07/03/ university-of-maryland-cuts-sports-teams/>.

39. Berkowitz, Steve, Jodi Upton, Michael McCarthy, and Jack Gillum. "How Student Fees Boost College Sports amid Rising Budgets." *USA Today*. Gannett, 6 Oct. 2010. Web. 22 Sept. 2013. <http://usatoday30.usatoday.com/sports/college/2010-09-21-student-fees-boost-college- sports_N.htm>.

40. Eichelberger, Curtis. "Rutgers Football Fails Profit Test as Students Pay $1,000." *Bloomberg.com*. Bloomberg, 3 May 2012. Web. 22 Sept. 2013. <http://www.bloomberg.com/news/2012-05-03/ rutgers-football-fails-profit-test-as-students-pay-1-000.html>.

41. Thomas, Jacqueline R. "Legislators Take Aim at Controversial 'Pay-to-Play' Sports Fees." *Connecticut Mirror*. CT Mirror, 8 May 2013. Web. 22 Sept. 2013. <http://ctmirror.org/ legislators-take-aim-controversial-pay-play-sports-fees/>.

42. "LaMarr Woodley Handles Athletic Fees." *ESPN.com*. ESPN, 17 Aug. 2012. Web. 12 Feb. 2014. <http://espn.go.com/nfl/story/_/id/8276648/pittsburgh-steelers-lamarr-woodley-60k-donation- covers-schools-athletic-fees>.

43. Rhodes, Margaret. "Infographic: Who's The Highest-Paid Public Employee in Your State?" *Fast Company Design*. Fast Company, Inc., 25 June 2013. Web. 12 Feb. 2014. <http://www .fastcodesign.com/1672861/infographic-whos-your-states-highest-paid-public-employee>.

44. "State Salaries for Iowa." *DesMoinesRegister.com*. Gannett, 1 Nov. 2012. Web. 12 Feb. 2014. <http://data.desmoinesregister.com/dmr/dmr-public-records/state_salaries.php>.

45. Fulks, *Revenues and Expenses: 2004–2012*.

46. "Manchester United Announce Stock Listing in New York." *CNN.com*. Cable News Network, 1 Aug. 2012. Web. 13 Feb. 2014. <http://edition.cnn.com/2012/07/30/sport/football/ manchester-united-stock-football/index.html>.

47. Futterman, Matthew, and Kevin Clark. "Manchester United Shoots for U.S. IPO." *WSJ.com*. Wall Street Journal, 4 July 2012. Web. 12 Feb. 2014. <http://online.wsj.com/article/SB1000142 4052702304211804577505172266999742.html>.

48. Smith, Chris. "Manchester United IPO: History Says Don't Buy." *Forbes.com*. Forbes, 10 Aug. 2012. Web. 12 Feb. 2014. <http://www.forbes.com/sites/chrissmith/2012/08/10/manchester-united-ipo-history-says-dont-buy/>.

49. "Shareholders." *Packers.com*. Green Bay Packers, 2013. Web. 12 Feb. 2014. <http://www.packers.com/community/shareholders.html>.

50. *Shareholder History & Financial History*. Rep. Green Bay Packers, 2012. Web. 12 Feb. 2014. <http://prod.static.packers.clubs.nfl.com/assets/docs/2012shareholder-history.pdf>.

51. Saunders, Laura. "Are the Green Bay Packers the Worst Stock in America?" *WSJ.com*. Wall Street Journal, 13 Jan. 2012. Web. 12 Feb. 2014. <http://blogs.wsj.com/totalreturn/2012/01/13/are-the-green-bay-packers-the-worst-stock-in-america/>.

52. Belson, Ken. "Investing in Packers, Wallet and Soul." *NYTimes.com*. New York Times, 15 Nov. 2011. Web. 12 Feb. 2014. <http://www.nytimes.com/2011/11/16/sports/football/in-green-bay-shares-of-stock-are-more-than-a-financial-investment.html?pagewanted=all&_r=0>.

53. "STOXX® Europe Football." *Stoxx.com*. STOXX.com, n.d. Web. 12 Feb. 2014. <http://www.stoxx.com/indices/index_information.html?symbol=FCTP>.

54. Shea, Bill. "Minor-League Baseball's Sliders Plan Stock Offering." *Crain's Detroit Business*. Crain Communications, 16 June 2009. Web. 12 Feb. 2014. <http://www.crainsdetroit.com/article/20090616/EMAIL01/306169995/minor-league-baseballs-sliders-plan-stock-offering>.

55. "Midwest Sliders." *Baseball-Reference.com*. Sports Reference, 16 Apr. 2013. Web. 12 Feb. 2014. <http://www.baseball-reference.com/bullpen/Midwest_Sliders>.

56. Prial, Dunstan. "Manchester United IPO a Risky Game." *FOXBusiness*. FOX News Network, 9 Aug. 2012. Web. 12 Feb. 2014. <http://www.foxbusiness.com/industries/2012/08/09/manchester-united-ipo-risky-game/>.

57. Ibid.

58. Kuriloff, Aaron, and Darrell Preston. "In Stadium Building Spree, U.S. Taxpayers Lose $4 Billion." *Bloomberg Politics*. Bloomberg, 5 Sept. 2012. Web. 12 Feb. 2014. <http://www.bloomberg.com/news/2012-09-05/in-stadium-building-spree-u-s-taxpayers-lose-4-billion.html>.

59. "Commerce and Conscience." *Economist.com*. The Economist Newspaper Limited, 23 Feb. 2013. Web. 12 Feb. 2014. <http://www.economist.com/news/finance-and-economics/21572231-new-way-financing-public-services-gains-momentum-commerce-and-conscience?fsrc=scn/tw_ec/commerce_and_conscience>.

60. The Official Website of the Governor of Massachusetts. "Patrick-Murray Administration Celebrates 98% Health Care Coverage in Massachusetts." *Mass.gov*. Commonwealth of Massachusetts, 13 Dec. 2010. Web. 12 Feb. 2014. <http://www.mass.gov/governor/pressoffice/pressreleases/2010/98-health-care-coverage-achieved-in-ma.html>.

61. Rovell, Darren (@darrenrovell). "Alabama uses Bama, Auburn players images hoping to bring new companies to state pic.twitter.com/yMmOBjxm." 31 January 2012, 7:34 P.M. Tweet.

62. "Lou. Mayor Visiting Oklahoma City, Examining Downtown Revitalization." *WHAS11.com*. Belo Kentucky, 22 Oct. 2012. Web. 12 Feb. 2014. <http://www.whas11.com/news/local/Mayor-OKC-visit--175255151.html>.

63. Holt, David. *Big League City: Oklahoma City's Rise to the NBA*. Oklahoma City, OK: Full Circle, 2012. Print.

64. Cadle, Aaron, and Jim Carroll. *Revenue of Economic Impact of Selected Professional Sports Venues and Downtown Revitalizations Efforts in Oklahoma City*. Rep. Legislative Reference Bureau, Apr. 2013. Web. 12 Feb. 2014. <http://media.jsonline.com/documents/LRB+143797+-+Ald+Murphy+-+Sports+Venues+Revitalization+of+Downtown+Oklahoma+City+Report.pdf>.

65. Ibid.

66. Tramel, Berry. "Oklahoma City Thunder: New Book to Chronicle OKC's Ascension." *NewsOK*. NewsOK.com, 16 Apr. 2012. Web. 12 Feb. 2014. <http://newsok.com/article/3774306>.

67. Hoover, Brendan. "Big Leagues." *Oklahoma Gazette*. Gazette Media, 25 Apr. 2012. Web. 12 Feb. 2014. <http://www.okgazette.com/oklahoma/article-15077-big-leagues.html>.

68. "Discover Oklahoma City." *YouTube*. YouTube, 7 Dec. 2007. Web. 12 Feb. 2014. <http://www.youtube.com/watch?v=XtspPuAywfo>.

69. "Oklahoma City Thunder Power!" *OKC Newsroom*. Oklahoma City Chamber, n.d. Web. 12 Feb. 2014. <http://www.okcnewsroom.com/packaged-stories/oklahoma-city-thunder-power!.aspx>.

70. Guarini, Drew. "Oklahoma City Thunder Changed Business for Oklahoma City, Seattle." *HuffingtonPost.com*. Huffington Post, 15 June 2012. Web. 12 Feb. 2014. <http://www .huffingtonpost.com/2012/06/15/oklahoma-city-thunder-seattle-supersonics_n_1594729.html>.
71. Ibid.
72. "Q&A: Indianapolis Sports Strategy." *American Outlook*. Sagamore Institute, 2011. Web. 12 Feb. 2014. <http://www.americanoutlook.org/q--a-indianapolis-sports-strategy.html>.
73. Ibid.
74. Glicksman, Ben. "Two years after death, Ed Thomas continues to impact Parkersburg." Inside High School Football. 1 Sept. 2011. Sports Illustrated. 24 Apr. 2014. <http:// sportsillustrated.cnn.com/2011/writers/ben_glicksman/09/01/ed-thomas-legacy/>.
75. Thomas, Rob. "The Veronica Mars Movie Project." *Kickstarter.com*. Kickstarter, 13 Mar. 2013. Web. 12 Feb. 2014. <http://www.kickstarter.com/projects/559914737/the-veronica-mars-movie-project>.
76. Hanrahan, MB. "Buena High Aquatic Sports Mural." *Kickstarter.com*. Kickstarter, 9 Jan. 2013. Web. 12 Feb. 2014.<http://www.kickstarter.com/projects/367132375/buena-high-aquatic-sports-mural>.
77. "Support NZL Sailors for Youth America's Cup." *Crowdfunding for Sports and Entertainment*. ThrillPledge, n.d. Web. 4 Sept. 2013. <http://thrillpledge.com/projects/support-nzl-sailors-for-youth-americas-cup>.
78. "Soar With Us Into History—Annual Benefit." *Women's Ski Jumping USA's Rally*. RallyMe, n.d. Web. 4 Sept. 2013. <https://www.rallyme.com/rallies/94>.
79. Waldron, Travis. "Foul Play: Five Cities that Want Taxpayer Money to Finance Pro Sports Stadium Boondoggles." *ThinkProgress.org*. Center for American Progress Action Fund, 12 June 2012. Web. 12 Feb. 2014. <http://thinkprogress.org/economy/2012/06/12/496136/ foul-play-five-cities-that-want-taxpayer-money-to-finance-stadium-boondoggles/>.
80. Ibid.
81. Vomhof, John, Jr. "Gophers Proceed with Plans for New Baseball Stadium." *Minneapolis St. Paul Business Journal*. Bizjournals.com, 13 Jan. 2012. Web. 12 Feb. 2014. <http://www .bizjournals.com/twincities/blog/sports-business/2012/01/gophers-proceed-baseball-stadium.html>.
82. "Hall of Famers Proud to Be Maroon & Gold." *Golden Gopher Fund*. University of Minnesota, 4 Feb. 2011. Web. 12 Feb. 2014. <https://www.goldengopherfund.com/Online/ default.asp?doWork::WScontent::loadArticle=Load&BOparam::WScontent::loadArticle::art icle_id=40F99B76-AEDF-4AD0-ABE2-538CCE4C2660>.
83. Ibid
84. Karp, Hannah. "The Cal Baseball Resurrection." *WSJ.com*. Wall Street Journal, 22 Apr. 2011. Web. 12 Feb. 2014. <http://online.wsj.com/article/SB10001424052748704071704576277130580 424792.html>.
85. Ibid.
86. Ibid.
87. Daschel, Nick. "Raising Money for High School Athletics Takes Creativity to New Levels." *OregonLive*. The Oregonian, 26 Apr. 2013. Web. 12 Feb. 2014. <http://highschoolsports .oregonlive.com/news/article/-2642827908847221710/raising-money-for-high-school-athletics-takes-creativity-to-new-levels/>.
88. King, Bill. "High School Sports Running on Empty." *Sports Business Daily*. Street and Smith's, 2 Aug. 2010. Web. 12 Feb. 2014. <http://www.sportsbusinessdaily.com/Journal/ Issues/2010/08/20100802/SBJ-In-Depth/High-School-Sports-Running-On-Empty.aspx>.
89. "NCAA College Athletics Department Finances Database." *USA Today*. Gannett, 16 May 2012. Web. 12 Feb. 2014. <http://www.usatoday.com/sports/college/ncaa-finances.htm>.
90. "The Official Athletics Site of University of California—Riverside." *Staff Directory*. University of California-Riverside, n.d. Web. 4 Sept. 2013. <http://www.gohighlanders.com/ staff.aspx?tab=staffdirectory>.
91. "Community and Government Relations." *Oberlin.edu*. Oberlin College & Conservatory, n.d. Web. 12 Feb. 2014. <http://new.oberlin.edu/office/community-and-government-relations/>.
92. "Staff Directory." *Oberlin College Athletics*. Oberlin College, n.d. Web. 12 Feb. 2014. <http://www.goyeo.com/staff.aspx?tab=staffdirectory>.
93. "Howard Patterson." *The University of Texas at Tyler*. UT Tyler Athletics, 2014. Web. 12 Feb. 2014. <http://www.nytimes.com/interactive/sports/baseball/2013alexrodrigueztimeline.html>.

94. "Lobbying Database." *OpenSecrets.org*. Center for Responsive Politics, 29 July 2013. Web. 12 Feb. 2014. <http://www.opensecrets.org/lobby/>.
95. "Money and Politics." *Economist.com*. The Economist Newspaper Limited, 1 Oct. 2011. Web. 12 Feb. 2014. <http://www.economist.com/node/21531014>.
96. Plumer, Brad. "The Outsized Returns from Lobbying." *WashingtonPost.com*. Washington Post, 10 Oct. 2011. Web. 12 Feb. 2014. <http://www.washingtonpost.com/blogs/wonkblog/post/the-outsized-returns-from-lobbying/2011/10/10/gIQADSNEaL_blog.html>.
97. "Professional Sports, Arenas & Related Equip & Svcs." *OpenSecrets.org*. Center for Responsive Politics, 2011. Web. 12 Feb. 2014. <http://www.opensecrets.org/lobby/induscode.php?id=G6400>.
98. "Sports Industry Overview." *Plunkettresearch.com*. Plunkett Research, Ltd., 2013. Web. 12 Feb. 2014. <http://www.plunkettresearch.com/sports-recreation-leisure-market-research/industry-statistics>.
99. "Top Spenders." *OpenSecrets.org*. Center for Responsive Politics, 2012. Web. 12 Feb. 2014. <http://www.opensecrets.org/lobby/top.php?showYear=2012>.
100. Lorenzo Fertitta. Telephone interview by Adam Grossman. 20 July 2012.
101. Elstein, Aaron. "UFC's Deep Pockets May Feed Ban." *Crain's New York Business*. Crain Communications, 23 Apr. 2013. Web. 12 Feb. 2014. <http://www.crainsnewyork.com/article/20130423/BLOGS02/130429967>.
102. King, Bill. "UFC Goes Another Round in Effort for N.Y. Sanction." *Sports Business Daily*. Street and Smith's, 10 Jan. 2011. Web. 12 Feb. 2014. <http://m.sportsbusinessdaily.com/Journal/Issues/2011/01/20110110/Leagues-and-Governing-Bodies/MMA.aspx>.
103. "Funding Breakdown." *Recovery.gov*. The Recovery Board, 2012–2013. Web. 12 Feb. 2014. <http://www.recovery.gov/arra/Transparency/fundingoverview/Pages/fundingbreakdown.aspx>.
104. "Project Summary." *Grants Award Summary—City of San Diego*. Recovery.gov—Track the Money, n.d. Web. 4 Sept. 2013. <http://www.recovery.gov/arra/Transparency/RecipientReportedData/pages/RecipientProjectSummary508.aspx?AwardIdSur=31598>.
105. "Project Summary." *Grants Award Summary—City of Norwalk*. Recovery.gov—Track the Money, n.d. Web. 4 Sept. 2013. <http://www.recovery.gov/arra/Transparency/RecipientReportedData/Pages/RecipientProjectSummary508.aspx?AwardIDSUR=43769>.
106. "Stadiums, Hotels Attract 'Terrorist Interest,' Feds Say." *CNN.com*. Cable News Network, 22 Sept. 2009. Web. 12 Feb. 2014. <http://articles.cnn.com/2009-09-22/us/us.security.bulletins_1_terrorist-stadiums-bulletins?_s=PM:US>.
107. Keating, Peter. "Industry of Fear." *ESPN.com*. ESPN, 11 Sept. 2011. Web. 12 Feb. 2014. <http://espn.go.com/espn/story/_/id/6936819/stadiums-increase-budgets-heighten-security-measures-protect-fans-espn-magazine>.
108. Ibid.
109. "What Is the SAFETY Act?" *SAFETY Act*. Department of Homeland Security, n.d. Web. 12 Feb. 2014. <https://www.safetyact.gov/pages/homepages/Home.do>.
110. Feiden, Douglas. "Devil of a Stadium Plan." *WSJ.com*. Wall Street Journal, 12 Nov. 2013. Web. 12 Feb. 2014. <http://www.nytimes.com/interactive/sports/baseball/2013alexrodrigueztimeline.html>.

CHAPTER 7
1. Cottrell, Robert C. *Blackball, the Black Sox, and the Babe: Baseball's Crucial 1920 Season*. Jefferson, NC: McFarland, 2002. 119. Print.
2. "Black Sox Scandal." *Baseball Reference Bullpen*. USA Today Sports Digital Properties, n.d. Web. 25 Sept. 2013. <http://www.baseball-reference.com/bullpen/Black_Sox_Scandal>.
3. Anderson, William B. "Saving the National Pastime's Image: Crisis Management During the 1919 Black Sox Scandal." *Journalism History* 27 (2005): 105–11. Print.
4. Stein, Fred. *A History of the Baseball Fan*. Jefferson, NC: McFarland &, 2005. Print.
5. Asinof, Eliot. *Eight Men Out*. New York: Ace, 1963. 197. Print.
6. Brennan, Christine. "NCAA Sports in 2010–11: A School Year for Scandal." *USA Today*. Gannett, 30 Mar. 2011. Web. 11 Feb. 2014. <http://usatoday30.usatoday.com/sports/columnist/brennan/2011-03-30-fiesta-bowl-auburn-ncaa_N.htm>.

7. Watt, Kristin. "Coaches Facing Charges and Other Recent Youth Football Scandals." *Yahoo! Sports*. Yahoo!, 2 Nov. 2012. Web. 23 Sept. 2013. <http://sports.yahoo.com/news/coaches-facing-charges-other-recent-youth-football-scandals-053400562--spt.html>.

8. Almasy, Steve. "Two Teens Found Guilty in Steubenville Rape Case." *CNN.com*. Cable News Network, 17 Mar. 2013. Web. 11 Feb. 2014. <http://www.cnn.com/2013/03/17/justice/ohio-steubenville-case>.

9. Fink, Steven. *Crisis Management: Planning for the Inevitable*. New York: American Management Association, 1986. 20–28. Print.

10. Lipsyte, Robert. *An Accidental Sportswriter: A Memoir*. New York: Ecco, 2011. 33–45. Print.

11. Sylvester, Rob. "WSJ Study Finds Athletes' Tweets to Be Unsurprisingly Self-Referential." *Off the Bench*. NBC Sports, 19 June 2011. Web. 11 Feb. 2014. <http://offthebench.nbcsports.com/2011/06/19/wsj-study-finds-athletes-tweets-to-be-unsurprisingly-self-referential/>.

12. Shpigel, Ben. "Swisher Wins Vote by Fans, and With It Last A.L. Spot." *NYTimes.com*. New York Times, 8 July 2010. Web. 11 Feb. 2014. <http://www.nytimes.com/2010/07/09/sports/baseball/09pins.html>.

13. Hoffer, Richard. "Williams Does It! Bosox Slugger Ends Season with .406 Mark." *SI Vault*. Sports Illustrated, 19 July 1993. Web. 23 Sept. 2013. <http://sportsillustrated.cnn.com/vault/article/magazine/MAG1138455/2/index.htm>.

14. Martin, Amy Jo. "Leadership: How NASCAR Uses Access to Build the Most Loyal Brand Fans Anywhere." *Fast Company*. Fast Company, Inc., 15 Oct. 2012. Web. 23 Sept. 2013. <http://www.fastcompany.com/3002134/how-nascar-uses-access-build-most-loyal-brand-fans-anywhere>.

15. Hutchison, Jonathan. "The Price of a Jersey Sets Rugby Fans Against Adidas." *NYTimes.com*. New York Times, 24 Aug. 2011. Web. 11 Feb. 2014. <http://www.nytimes.com/2011/08/25/sports/rugby/adidas-angers-all-blacks-fans-with-price-policy.html?pagewanted=all>.

16. Gibbs, Thom. "Aldershot Discipline Striker Marvin Morgan after 'I Hope You All Die' Twitter Message to Fans." *The Telegraph*. Telegraph Media Group, 5 Jan. 2011. Web. 11 Feb. 2014. <http://www.telegraph.co.uk/sport/football/teams/aldershot-town/8241900/Aldershot-discipline-striker-Marvin-Morgan-after-I-hope-you-all-die-Twitter-message-to-fans.html>.

17. Klopman, Michael. "Soccer Player Marvin Morgan Tweets Death Wish to Fans." *HuffingtonPost.com*. Huffington Post, 5 Jan. 2011. Web. 11 Feb. 2014. <http://www.huffingtonpost.com/2011/01/05/marvin-morgan-twitter-fans_n_804973.html>.

18. Thompson, Wright. "The Trouble with Johnny." *ESPN.com*. ESPN, 30 July 2013. Web. 2 Oct. 2013. <http://espn.go.com/espn/otl/story/_/id/9521439/heisman-winner-johnny-manziel-celebrity-derail-texas-aggies-season-espn-magazine>.

19. Womeldorf, Ryan. "Verified: Paul Bissonnette and the Power of Social Media." *The Farm Club*. N.p., 27 Mar. 2013. Web. 11 Feb. 2014. <http://thefarmclub.net/2013/03/27/verified-paul-bissonnette-and-the-power-of-social-media/>.

20. O'Brien, James. "Paul 'BizNasty' Bissonnette Makes His (Triumphant?) Return to Twitter, Discusses Homeless People and hoarding." *ProHockeyTalk*. NBC Sports, 30 Aug. 2010. Web. 11 Feb. 2014. <http://prohockeytalk.nbcsports.com/2010/08/30/paul-biznasty-bissonnette-makes-his-triumphant-return-to-twitter-discusses-homeless-people-and-hoard/>.

21. Falgoust, J. M. "Arenas: Gun Episode Now Ancient History." USA Today. Gannett, 12 Apr. 2012. Web. 23 Sept. 2013. <http://www.usatoday.com/sports/basketball/nba/story/2012-04-11/Arenas-happy-with-Memphis-blues-over-Agent-Zero/54188368/1>.

22. Petriello, Mike. "The Collected Sins of the Frank & Jamie McCourt Era." *Mike Scioscia's Tragic Illness*. N.p., 30 June 2011. Web. 11 Feb. 2014. <http://www.mikesciosciastragicillness.com/2011/06/30/the-collected-sins-of-the-frank-jamie-mccourt-era/>.

23. Dilbeck, Steve. "Fans' Disgust Helped Push Frank McCourt to Sell Dodgers." *LATimes.com*. Los Angeles Times, 2 Nov. 2011. Web. 11 Feb. 2014. <http://latimesblogs.latimes.com/dodgers/2011/11/fans-disgust-helped-push-frank-mccourt-to-sell-dodgers.html>.

24. Henry, Jim. "Colleges Do UDiligence to Prevent Social Networking Embarrassment." *AOLNews.com*. AOL News, 1 Feb. 2010. Web. 15 Aug. 2013. <http://www.aolnews.com/2010/02/01/colleges-do-udiligence-to-prevent-social-networking-embarrassment/>.

25. Fieldhouse Media (@fieldhousemedia). "NEWS: Wisconsin recently introduced SB 223, a bill that will protect the social media privacy of student-athletes." 10 July 2013, 9:19 A.M. Tweet.

26. Longman, Jeré. "A History of Fearlessness." *NYTimes.com*. New York Times, 24 Aug. 2011. Web. 11 Feb. 2014. <http://www.nytimes.com/2011/08/25/sports/ncaabasketball/pat-summitt-faces-dementia-with-fierce-determination.html?_r=0>.

27. Zinser, Lynn. "Tennessee's Summitt Reveals Dementia Diagnosis." *NYTimes.com*. New York Times, 23 Aug. 2011. Web. 11 Feb. 2014. <http://www.nytimes.com/2011/08/24/sports/ncaabasketball/tennessees-summitt-reveals-dementia-diagnosis.html>.

28. Jenkins, Sally. "Q&A: Tennessee Athletic Director Joan Cronan." *WashingtonPost.com*. Washington Post, 23 Aug. 2011. Web. 11 Feb. 2014. <http://www.washingtonpost.com/sports/colleges/qanda-tennessee-athletic-director-joan-cronan/2011/08/23/gIQAOxcjZJ_story.html>.

29. Longman, Jeré. "The Usual High Expectations Mingle with Uncertainty." *NYTimes.com*. New York Times, 15 Mar. 2012. Web. 11 Feb. 2014. <http://www.nytimes.com/2012/03/16/sports/ncaabasketball/pat-summitts-health-gives-tournament-different-feel-for-lady-vols.html?pagewanted=all>.

30. Futterman, Matthew. "Tiger Woods Is No. 1 Again, but Golf Hardly Missed Him." *WSJ.com*. The Wall Street Journal. 10 Apr. 2013. Web. 26 Jan. 2014. <http://online.wsj.com/article/SB10001424127887323646604578402891124694264.html>.

31. Ibid.

32. Hoekstra, Dave. "Steve Bartman Catches More Hell in ESPN Documentary." *Suntimes.com*. Chicago Sun-Times, 27 Sept. 2011. Web. 11 Feb. 2014. <http://www.suntimes.com/sports/7888784-419/documentary-revisits-bartman-fallout.html>.

33. Ibid.

34. "Bartman Ball to Be Destroyed Thursday." *ESPN.com*. ESPN, 25 Feb. 2004. Web. 11 Feb. 2014. <http://sports.espn.go.com/mlb/news/story?id=1744055>.

35. Hoekstra, "Steve Bartman."

36. "What Are the Charges Against Jerry Sandusky?" *CNN.com*. Cable News Network, 21 June 2012. Web. 11 Feb. 2014. <http://www.cnn.com/2012/06/21/justice/pennsylvania-sandusky-charges>.

37. Sandusky was convicted on 45 of 48 counts in 2012.

38. Brady, Erik. "Penn State Trustees Would Like Sanctions Reduced." *USA Today*. Gannett, 16 July 2013. Web. 11 Feb. 2014. <http://www.usatoday.com/story/sports/ncaaf/2013/07/16/penn-state-ncaa-joe-paterno-jerry-sandusky-freeh-report/2522359/>.

39. Nista, Monica. "8 Gold Medals for Michael Phelps the Swimming Phenom." *ABC News*. ABC News Network, 16 Aug. 2008. Web. 11 Feb. 2014. <http://abcnews.go.com/Sports/China/story?id=5595376>.

40. "Michael Phelps." *SI Vault*. Sports Illustrated, 25 Aug. 2008. Web. 11 Feb. 2014. <http://sportsillustrated.cnn.com/vault/cover/featured/11001/index.htm>.

41. Brosh, Brendan. "Report: Olympic Swimmer Michael Phelps Caught Smoking Bong?" *NYDailyNews.com*. New York Daily News, 31 Jan. 2009. Web. 11 Feb. 2014. <http://www.nydailynews.com/entertainment/gossip/report-olympic-swimmer-michael-phelps-caught-smoking-bong-article-1.362569>.

42. *The Elusive Fan*, 186–87.

43. "Phelps Admits 'Bad Judgment' After Marijuana-Pipe Photo." *CNN.com*. Cable News Network, 2 Feb. 2009. Web. 11 Feb. 2014. <http://www.cnn.com/2009/US/02/01/michael.phelps.marijuana/>.

44. "Visa Backs Michael Phelps As Criticism Continues To Pour In." *SportsBusiness Daily*. Street and Smith's, 4 Feb. 2009. Web. 11 Feb. 2014. <http://www.sportsbusinessdaily.com/Daily/Issues/2009/02/Issue-95/Sponsorships-Advertising-Marketing/Visa-Backs-Michael-Phelps-As-Criticism-Continues-To-Pour-In.aspx>.

45. Van Valkenburg, Kevin. "Intense Scrutiny Has Phelps Weighing Whether He Will Swim in 2012 Games." *Baltimoresun.com*. Baltimore Sun, 5 Feb. 2009. Web. 11 Feb. 2014. <http://www.baltimoresun.com/sports/olympics/bal-te.sp.phelps05feb05,0,3171313.story>.

46. Shipley, Amy. "Phelps Will Not Face Any Sanctions." *WashingtonPost.com*. Washington Post, 2 Feb. 2009. Web. 11 Feb. 2014. <http://articles.washingtonpost.com/2009-02-02/sports/36768580_1_bob-bowman-michael-phelps-debbie-phelps>.

47. Benoit, William L. *Accounts, Excuses, and Apologies: A Theory of Image Restoration Strategies*. Albany: State U of New York P, 1995. 74–80. Print.

48. Wilson, Duff, and David Barstow. "All Charges Dropped in Duke Case." *NYTimes.com*. New York Times, 12 Apr. 2007. Web. 12 Feb. 2014. <http://www.sportsbusinessdaily.com/Daily/

Issues/2009/02/Issue-95/Sponsorships-Advertising-Marketing/Visa-Backs-Michael-Phelps-As-Criticism-Continues-To-Pour-In.aspx>.

49. Mero, Ted. "Section Throws Book at Franklin." *Lodi News-Sentinel*, 17 Oct. 2007: 1+. Print.
50. "CIF Section Issues 5-Year Playoff Ban Against Franklin H.S. Football for Recruiting Violations." *Prnewswire.com*. PR Newswire, n.d. Web. 12 Feb. 2014. <http://www.prnewswire.com/news-releases/cif-section-issues-5-year-playoff-ban-against-franklin-hs-football-for-recruiting-violations-58687137.html>.
51. Burke, Garance. "High School Football Coach Resigns amid Recruiting Scandal." *USA Today*. Gannett, 1 Nov. 2007. Web. 12 Feb. 2014. <http://usatoday30.usatoday.com/sports/football/2007-11-01-3425480781_x.htm?csp=34>.
52. Stockton Unified School District. "CIF-SAC-Joaquin Section & Stockton Unified School District Announce Breakthrough Resolution in Football Dispute." *Recordnet.com*. N.p., 14 Nov. 2007. Web. 12 Feb. 2014. <http://online.recordnet.com/projects/franklinsanctions/CIF_Settlement.pdf>.
53. Burke, "High School Football Coach Resigns."
54. Ibid.
55. "Franklin's 'Death Penalty' Reduced." *Lodi News-Sentinel*, 15 Nov. 2007: 13–14. Print.
56. "Michael Vick Blogs Apology for Dog Fighting." *Just Jared*. Celebuzz, 17 Aug. 2009. Web. 12 Feb. 2014. <http://www.justjared.com/2009/08/17/michael-vick-blogs-apology-for-dog-fighting/>.
57. Collins, Gail, and Ross Douthat. "Michael Vick's Apology." *NYTimes.com*. New York Times, 19 Aug. 2009. Web. 12 Feb. 2014. <http://opinionator.blogs.nytimes.com/2009/08/19/michael-vicks-apology/?_r=0&gwh=7D714169C754150B99E7FCA32F643DBA>.
58. Tierney, Mike. "It's a Completion: Vick Issues Complete Apology on '60 Minutes.'" *Examiner.com*. Clarity Digital Group, 16 Aug. 2009. Web. 12 Feb. 2014. <http://www.examiner.com/sports-in-atlanta/it-s-a-completion-vick-issues-complete-apology-on-60-minutes>.
59. "Hardaway Apologizes Again for Anti-Gay Comments." *ESPN.com*. ESPN, 19 Feb. 2007. Web. 12 Feb. 2014. <http://sports.espn.go.com/nba/news/story?id=2770738>.
60. "Tim Hardaway Becomes First To Sign Florida Gay Marriage Petition." *The HuffingtonPost.com*. Huffington Post, 7 July 2013. Web. 12 Feb. 2014. <http://www.huffingtonpost.com/2013/07/04/tim-hardaway-gay-marriage-petition_n_3544558.html>.
61. Benoit, 76–77.
62. Madden, Bill. "Dropping Lawsuits Means Alex Rodriguez Will Be Gone for Good." *NYDailyNews.com*. New York Daily News, 7 Feb. 2014. Web. 12 Feb. 2014. <http://www.nydailynews.com/sports/baseball/yankees/madden-a-rod-finally-article-1.1606611>.
63. "A-Rod Admits, Regrets Use of PEDs." *ESPN.com*. ESPN, 10 Feb. 2009. Web. 12 Feb. 2014. <http://sports.espn.go.com/mlb/news/story?id=3894847>.
64. Matthews, Wallace. "A-Rod to Miss All of 2014 Season." *ESPNNewYork.com*. ESPN, 12 Jan. 2014. Web. 12 Feb. 2014. <http://espn.go.com/new-york/mlb/story/_/id/10278277/alex-rodriguez-suspension-reduced-162-games>.
65. "Alex Rodriguez: A Continual Stir." *NYTimes.com*. New York Times, 11 Jan. 2014. Web. 12 Feb. 2014. <http://www.nytimes.com/interactive/sports/baseball/2013alexrodrigueztimeline.html>.
66. Shaughnessy, Dan. "Alex Rodriguez in State of Denial." *BostonGlobe.com*. Boston Globe Media Partners, 17 Aug. 2013. Web. 12 Feb. 2014. <http://www.bostonglobe.com/sports/2013/08/16/dan-shaughnessy-alex-rodriguez-state-denial/ho7SuKcUPh8JuAuZY7KMjJ/story.html>.
67. Madden, Bill, Michael O'Keeffe, and Teri Thompson. "Yankees Officials Dismiss Alex Rodriguez's Suggestion That Team Is Conspiring Against Him."*NYDailyNews.com*. New York Daily News, 3 Aug. 2013. Web. 12 Feb. 2014. <http://www.nydailynews.com/sports/i-team/yanks-dismiss-a-rod-conspiracy-theory-article-1.1416746>.
68. West, Ed. "Lance Armstrong's doping confession – why does no one say sorry properly any more? – Telegraph Blogs." Ed West. 18 Jan. 2013. Telegraph Media Group. 24 Apr. 2014. <http://blogs.telegraph.co.uk/news/edwest/100198746/lance-armstrongs-doping-confession-why-does-no-one-say-sorry-properly-any-more/>.
69. Holpuch, Amanda. "Lance Armstrong says sorry during emotional meeting with Livestrong staff." The Guardian. 15 Jan. 2013. Guardian News and Media. 24 Apr. 2014. <http://www.theguardian.com/sport/2013/jan/14/lance-armstrong-livestrong-sorry-emotional-meeting>.
70. Dwyre, Bill. "Ohio State's Jim Tressel Reinvigorates Use of the Word 'Smarmy.'" *LATimes.com*. Los Angeles Times, 11 Mar. 2011. Web. 12 Feb. 2014. <http://articles.latimes.com/2011/mar/11/sports/la-sp-dwyre-jim-tressel-20110312>.

71. Gordon Gee, E. "Opposing View: A 'Tough' Friend to Athletics." *USA Today*. Gannett, 31 May 2011. Web. 12 Feb. 2014. <http://www.usatoday.com/news/opinion/editorials/2011-05-31-Ohio-State-president-defends-himself-as-tough_n.htm>.

72. Watson, Graham. "Ohio State President E. Gordon Gee: 'Can't Trust Those Damn Catholics'." *Yahoo! Sports*. Yahoo!, 30 May 2013. Web. 12 Feb. 2014. <http://www.nytimes.com/interactive/sports/baseball/2013alexrodrigueztimeline.html>.

73. "Quotes By Yogi Berra—Yogi-isms." *Yogiberra.com*. LTD Enterprises Inc, n.d. Web. 2 Oct. 2013. <http://www.yogiberra.com/yogi-isms.html>.

CHAPTER 8

1. Dorfman, Sid. "It's Time for the NFL to Go on a Diet." *NJ.com*. Star-Ledger, 28 May 2013. Web. 10 Feb. 2014. <http://www.nj.com/sports/ledger/dorfman/index.ssf/2013/05/its_time_for_the_nfl_to_go_on.html>.

2. Clark, Kevin. "Game Changer: NFL Scrambles to Fill Seats." *WSJ.com*. Wall Street Journal, 2 July 2012. Web. 10 Feb. 2014. <http://online.wsj.com/article/SB10001424052702303561504577495083707417526.html>. "NFL Attendance—2012." *ESPN.com*. ESPN, n.d. Web. 25 Sept. 2013. <http://espn.go.com/nfl/attendance/_/year/2012>.

3. Rovell, Darren. "Patriots Latest to Install Wi-Fi in Stadium." *ESPN.com*. ESPN, 10 Sept. 2010. Web. 10 Feb. 2014. <http://espn.go.com/blog/playbook/dollars/post/_/id/1561/patriots-latest-to-install-wi-fi-in-stadium>.

4. Barnhart, Tony. "Attendance Lags Put SEC on Offense, Looking to Enhance Fan Experience." *CBSSports.com*. CBS Interactive, 27 May 2013. Web. 11 Feb. 2014. <http://www.cbssports.com/collegefootball/story/22311553/attendance-lags-put-sec-on-offense-looking-to-enhance-fan-experience>.

5. Cohen, Ben. "Declining Student Attendance Hits Georgia." *WSJ.com*. Wall Street Journal, 26 Sept. 2013. Web. 27 Sept. 2013. <http://online.wsj.com/article/SB10001424052702304795804579097223907738780.html>.

6. "Not a Fantasy: Teams to Show Stats." *ESPN.com*. ESPN, 8 Sept. 2011. Web. 10 Feb. 2014. <http://espn.go.com/nfl/story/_/id/6943058/nfl-stadiums-directed-show-real-time-fantasy-football-statistics-stadiums>.

7. Cohen, "Declining Student Attendance."

8. Clark, "Game Changer: NFL Scrambles."

9. Cohen, "Declining Student Attendance."

10. Wakefield, K. L., and H. J. Sloan. The Effects of Team Loyalty and Selected Stadium Factors on Spectator Attendance. *Journal of Sport Management* 9.2 (1995): 153–72. Print.

11. Curry, Steve. "Wembley Is a Tower of Strength at Last." *Mail Online*. Daily Mail, 16 June 2011. Web. 10 Feb. 2014. <http://www.dailymail.co.uk/sport/football/article-2004487/Wembley-Stadium-tower-strength-last.html>.

12. Marazzi, Rich. "Yale Bowl: Celebrating the 100th Anniversary of Breaking Ground on the Historic Building." *New Haven Register*. New Haven Register, 22 June 2013. Web. 25 Sept. 2013. <http://www.nhregister.com/general-news/20130622/yale-bowl-celebrating-the-100th-anniversary-of-breaking-ground-on-the-historic-building>.

13. Byrnes, Mark. "The End of the Domed Stadium." *The Atlantic Cities*. The Atlantic Monthly Group, 25 May 2012. Web. 10 Feb. 2014. <http://www.theatlanticcities.com/arts-and-lifestyle/2012/05/end-domed-stadium/2101/#slide5>.

14. "Oriole Park at Camden Yards History." *Baltimore Orioles*. MLB.com, n.d. Web. 10 Feb. 2014. <http://baltimore.orioles.mlb.com/bal/ballpark/information/index.jsp?content=history>.

15. Fenno, Nathan. "Document: NCAA schools spent more than $5 billion on facilities." 27 Feb. 2014. Los Angeles Times. 24 Apr. 2014. <http://articles.latimes.com/2014/feb/27/sports/la-sp-sn-ncaa-facilities-5-billion-dollars-20140227>.

16. Ibid.

17. Warner, Pete. "Alfond Arena Renovations Progressing on Schedule." *BangorDailyNews.com*. Bangor Daily News, 5 Aug. 2011. Web. 10 Feb. 2014. <http://bangordailynews.com/2011/08/05/sports/alfond-arena-renovations-progressing-on-schedule/>.

18. Ellin, Abby. "$60 Million High School Football Stadium." *ABC News*. ABC News Network, 25 Aug. 2012. Web. 10 Feb. 2014. <http://abcnews.go.com/blogs/business/2012/08/60-million-high-school-football-stadium/>.

19. "New Athletics Facility." *EpiscopalHighSchool.org*. N.p., n.d. Web. 10 Feb. 2014. <http://www
.episcopalhighschool.org/archive/promise/strive/athletics_complex/index.aspx>.

20. Ross, Catherine. "Allen Unveils $60 Million Eagle Stadium." *NBCDFW.com*. NBC, 17 Aug.
2012. Web. 10 Feb. 2014. <http://www.nbcdfw.com/news/local/Allen-Unveils-New-Eagle-
Stadium-164932936.html>.

21. Jaynes, Dwight. "The true cost of new Nike U. football building estimated at $138 million."
07 Aug. 2013. CSN Northwest. 24 Apr. 2014. <http://www.csnnw.com/blog/dwight/
true-cost-new-nike-u-football-building-estimated-138-million>.

22. Gribble, Andrew. "Alabama Board of Trustees Approves New 34,000 Square-Foot Athletic
Training Facility." *AL.com*. Alabama Media Group, 1 Aug. 2012. Web. 10 Feb. 2014. <http://
www.al.com/sports/index.ssf/2012/08/alabama_board_of_trustees_appr_1.html>. "K-State to
Dedicate Basketball Training Facility Friday." *KStateSports.com*. CBS Interactive, 2 Oct. 2012.
Web. 10 Feb. 2014. <http://www.kstatesports.com/sports/m-baskbl/spec-rel/100212aab.html>.

23. Yuscavage, Chris. "Oregon Ducks Tour New Football Facility (Video)." *HuffingtonPost
.com*. Huffington Post, 10 Aug. 2013. Web. 10 Feb. 2014. <http://www.huffingtonpost.com/
2013/08/10/oregon-ducks-facility-tour_n_3734962.html>. "A Look Inside the $68M Oregon
Ducks Football Center." *Portland Business Journal*. Bizjournals.com, 1 Aug. 2013. Web.
10 Feb. 2014. <http://www.bizjournals.com/portland/blog/real-estate-daily/2013/08/
a-look-inside-the-68m-oregon-ducks.html?s=image_gallery>.

24. Bishop, Greg. "Oregon Embraces 'University of Nike' Image." *NYTimes.com*. New York
Times, 2 Aug. 2013. Web. 10 Feb. 2014. <http://www.nytimes.com/2013/08/03/sports/
ncaafootball/oregon-football-complex-is-glittering-monument-to-ducks-ambitions
.html?pagewanted=all&_r=0&gwh=AA230B45BF87AEBD138091A149C67B6B>.

25. Garcia, Craig. "The Hatfield-Dowlin Complex in Perspective." *DailyEmerald*. Emerald
Media Group, 12 Aug. 2013. Web. 10 Feb. 2014. <http://dailyemerald.com/2013/08/12/
the-hatfield-dowlin-complex-in-perspective/>.

26. United States Tennis Association. *Major Upgrades to USTA Billie Jean King National Tennis
Center Will Enhance Fan Experience at 2012 US Open*. USTA, 20 Aug. 2012. Web. 10 Feb.
2014. <http://assets.usta.com/assets/643/15/Whats_New_at_the_2012_US_Open.pdf>.

27. "Year in Review: 1924 National League." *Baseball-Almanac.com*. Baseball Almanac, n.d.
Web. 10 Feb. 2014. <http://www.baseball-almanac.com/yearly/yr1924n.shtml>.

28. Covil, Eric C. "Radio and Its Impact on the Sports World." *American Sportscasters
Online*. American Sportscasters Association, n.d. Web. 10 Feb. 2014. <http://www
.americansportscastersonline.com/radiohistory.html>.

29. Murphy, Brian. "Sen. John McCain, Fans Battle NFL over Blackout Rule." *Denverpost
.com*. Denver Post, 6 July 2013. Web. 10 Feb. 2014. <http://www.denverpost.com/politics/
ci_23610220/sen-john-mccain-fans-battle-nfl-over-blackout>.

30. Fleisher, Arthur A., III., Brian L. Goff, and Robert D. Tollison. *The National Collegiate
Athletic Association: A Study in Cartel Behavior*. Chicago: U of Chicago P, 1992. 52–60. Print.

31. Habib, Hal. "Some Feel NFL's TV Blackout Policy, Which Could Affect Dolphins Fans This
Week, Is Archaic; Others Defend It." *Palm Beach Post*. Cox Media Group, 10 Oct. 2012. Web.
10 Feb. 2014. <http://www.palmbeachpost.com/news/sports/football/some-feel-nfls-tv-
blackout-policy-which-could-affe/nSZTJ/>.

32. Schweitzer, George. "The Birth of Instant Replay." *CNET.com*. CBS Interactive, 7 Dec. 2011.
Web. 10 Feb. 2014. <http://reviews.cnet.com/8301-19727_7-57337961-10170017/the-birth-of-
instant-replay/>.

33. Binnings, Thomas L., and Paul A. Rochette. *Market and Economic Impacts of Relocating
Sky Sox Stadium to Downtown Colorado Springs*. City of Colorado Springs, June 2013. Web.
10 Feb. 2014. <http://www.springsgov.com/units/communications/Econ%20Impact%20
Dwntwn%20Stad%206-27-13.pdf>.

34. "Dragons Sell-Out Streak Reaches 1,000" *Dayton Dragons*. Minor League Baseball, 10 May
2014. Web. 08 May 2015. <http://www.milb.com/news/article.jsp?ymd=20140510&content_
id=75062440&fext=.jsp&vkey=news_t459&sid=t459>.

35. Vecsey, George. "For One Minor League Baseball Team, Never an Empty Seat." *NYTimes
.com*. New York Times, 2 July 2011. Web. 10 Feb. 2014. <http://www.nytimes.com/2011/07/03/
sports/baseball/for-one-minor-league-baseball-team-never-an-empty-seat.html?_r=0>.

36. Fisher, Eric. "The Streak." *Sports Business Journal*. Mandalay.com, 2009. Web. 10 Feb. 2014.
<http://www.mandalay.com/pdf/The%20Streak.pdf>.

37. "Fifth Third Field / Dayton Dragons." *BallparkDigest.com*. Ballpark Digest, 29 Nov. 2008. Web. 10 Feb. 2014. <http://ballparkdigest.com/200811291029/minor-league-baseball/visits/fifth-third-field-dayton-dragons>.

38. Vecsey, "For One Minor League."

39. "Heater and Gem." *DaytonaDragons.com*. Minor League Baseball, n.d. Web. 10 Feb. 2014. <http://www.milb.com/content/page.jsp?ymd=20090325&content_id=40997980&sid=t459&vkey=team2>.

40. Nichols, Tom. "Dragons Concessions Stand Program for Non-Profits." *DaytonaDragons.com*. Minor League Baseball, 12 Mar. 2013. Web. 10 Feb. 2014. <http://www.milb.com/news/article.jsp?ymd=20120312>.

41. Fisher, "The Streak."

42. Cuban, Mark. "The Fan Experience at Sporting Events—We Don't Need No Stinking Smartphones!" *Blog Maverick*. N.p., 24 Dec. 2011. Web. 10 Feb. 2014. <http://blogmaverick.com/2011/12/24/the-fan-experience-at-sporting-events-we-dont-need-no-stinking-smartphones/>.

43. Katzowitz, Josh. "Not All NFL Stadiums Will Get Wi-Fi in 2012." *CBSSports.com*. CBS Interactive, 16 July 2012. Web. 10 Feb. 2014. <http://www.cbssports.com/nfl/blog/eye-on-football/19598102/not-all-nfl-stadiums-will-get-wi-fi-in-2012>.

44. Rovell, "Patriots Latest."

45. Schultz, Beth. "Context on Ice: Penguins Fans Get Mobile Extras." *Computerworld.com*. Computerworld, 2 July 2009. Web. 10 Feb. 2014. <http://www.computerworld.com/s/article/9134588/Context_on_ice_Penguins_fans_get_mobile_extras>.

46. "Deutsche Telekom Installs State-of-the-Art 802.11n Wi-Fi System in One of Germany's Largest Stadiums." *Ruckuswireless.com*. Ruckus Wireless, 11 Jan. 2010. Web. 10 Feb. 2014. <http://www.ruckuswireless.com/press/releases/20100111-hsh-nordbank-arena>.

47. Wiedeman, Reeves. "Sporting Kansas City Makes the Stadium More Like Your Couch." *Bloomberg.com*. Bloomberg, 18 July 2013. Web. 10 Feb. 2014. <http://www.businessweek.com/articles/2013-07-18/sporting-kansas-city-makes-the-stadium-more-like-your-couch>.

48. Tweney, Dylan. "New, High-Tech Stadium for the San Francisco 49ers Will Be 'Software-Driven.'" *VentureBeat.com*. VentureBeat, 30 May 2013. Web. 10 Feb. 2014. <http://venturebeat.com/2013/05/30/new-high-tech-stadium-for-the-49ers-will-be-software-driven/>.

49. Barra, Allen. "'Dempsey and Firpo': The Greatest American Sports Painting." *TheAtlantic.com*. Atlantic Monthly, 24 Apr. 2012. Web. 10 Feb. 2014. <http://www.theatlantic.com/entertainment/archive/2012/04/dempsey-and-firpo-the-greatest-american-sports-painting/256256/>.

50. "History of Yankee Stadium Football." *Pinstripe Bowl*. Yankees/cp, n.d. Web. 10 Feb. 2014. <http://web.pinstripebowl.com/history/index>.

51. Bishop, Greg. "Season Tips Off in Location Unlike Any Other." *NYTimes.com*. New York Times, 11 Nov. 2011. Web. 10 Feb. 2014. <http://www.nytimes.com/2011/11/12/sports/ncaabasketball/unc-and-michigan-state-tip-off-on-an-aircraft-carrier.html>.

52. Ibid.

53. "Carrier Classic Highest-Rated ESPN November Game." *Boston.com*. Boston Globe, 14 Nov. 2011. Web. 10 Feb. 2014. <http://www.boston.com/sports/colleges/mens_basketball/articles/2011/11/14/carrier_classic_highest_rated_espn_november_game/>.

54. Katz, Andy. "A Win-Win Situation for Huskies, Spartans." *ESPN.com*. ESPN, 12 Nov. 2011. Web. 10 Feb. 2014. <http://espn.go.com/mens-college-basketball/blog/_/name/katz_andy/id/8623349/game-ramstein-air-base-was-huge-success-connecticut-huskies-michigan-state-spartans-military-personnel-college-basketball>.

55. "TIA Survey Highlights: Tailgating Industry Takes a Long Look in the Mirror." *Tiassn.org*. Tailgating Industry Association, 7 July 2012. Web. 10 Feb. 2014. <http://tiassn.org/html/news.html>. Munro, Aria. "With 50 Million Tailgaters in the U.S., Tailgating Digest Is Launching Digital and Print Magazines to Reach This Growing Market." *ENewsChannels*. Neotrope News Network, 5 Mar. 2012. Web. 10 Feb. 2014. <http://enewschannels.com/2012/03/05/enc14419_005838.php>.

56. "Football Tailgating Trivia 2007–2008: Tailgating Enters the High-Tech Age." *Hightechtailgaiting.com*. KVH, n.d. Web. 10 Feb. 2014. <http://www.hightechtailgating.com/Portals/0/Uploads/Documents/Tailgating%20Trivia.pdf>.

57. Hamilton, William L. "At Ole Miss, the Tailgaters Never Lose." *NYTimes.com*. New York Times, 29 Sept. 2006. Web. 10 Feb. 2014. <http://travel.nytimes.com/2006/09/29/travel/escapes/29grove.html>.

58. Ibid.

59. "Tailgate 48." *Btn.com*. Big Ten Network, n.d. Web. 10 Feb. 2014. <http://btn.com/shows/tailgate-48/>.

60. Drenten, Jenna, C. Peters, T. Leigh, and C. Hollenbeck. "Not Just a Party in the Parking Lot: An Exploratory Investigation of the Motives Underlying the Ritual Commitment of Football Tailgaters." *Sport Marketing Quarterly* 18.2 (2009): 92–106. Print.

61. Meryhew, Richard. "Minneapolis, Vikings on Board for Pregame 'Railgating.'" *StarTribune Minneapolis*. StarTribune, 19 Sept. 2012. Web. 10 Feb. 2014. <http://www.startribune.com/local/minneapolis/170270226.html>.

62. "Turnkey Tailgating Comes to Autzen Stadium This Fall." *Goducks.com*. University of Oregon, 13 Aug. 2012. Web. 10 Feb. 2014. <http://www.goducks.com/ViewArticle.dbml?DB_OEM_ID=500&ATCLID=205585664>.

63. Heinz, Frank. "Rangers Change Tailgating Rules for 2013." *NBCDFW.com*. NBC, 28 May 2013. Web. 10 Feb. 2014. <http://www.nbcdfw.com/blogs/red-fever/Rangers-Change-Tailgating-Rules-for-2013-200493961.html>.

64. Hall, Matthew T. "Tailgating Gets Boot in Stadium Plan." *Utsandiego.com*. San Diego Union-Tribune, 6 Feb. 2010. Web. 10 Feb. 2014. <http://www.signonsandiego.com/news/2010/feb/06/tailgating-gets-boot-stadium-plan/>.

65. "Gus Miller's Store in Oakland, Pittsburgh, 1950s." *Pittsburgh History Journal*. N.p., n.d. Web. 10 Feb. 2014. <http://thepittsburghhistoryjournal.com/post/558166743/gus-millers-store-in-oakland-pittsburgh>.

66. Lancaster, Donald G. "Forbes Field Praised as a Gem When It Opened." *Sabr.org*. Society for American Baseball Research, n.d. Web. 10 Feb. 2014. <http://research.sabr.org/journals/forbes-field-praised-as-a-gem-when-it-opened>.

67. Kemp, Roger L. *Community Renewal through Municipal Investment: A Handbook for Citizens and Public Officials*. Jefferson, NC: McFarland & Company, Inc., 2003. 198–202. Print.

68. Ibid.

69. Borchers, Callum. "Businessman Offers to Outbid Red Sox for Yawkey Way License." *BostonGlobe.com*. Boston Globe Media Partners, 14 June 2003. Web. 26 Sept. 2013. <http://www.bostonglobe.com/business/2013/06/13/lawyer-offers-outbid-red-sox-for-yawkey-way-concession-license/sBEFE2CoRzo1suCqj2UYfK/story.html>.

70. "2013–14 Official Blackhawks Bars." *Chicago Blackhawks*. NHL.com Network, n.d. Web. 10 Feb. 2014. <http://blackhawks.nhl.com/club/page.htm?id=57901>.

71. Rovell, Darren. "Blackhawks Rewarded for Taking Risks." *ESPN.com*. ESPN, 7 Mar. 2013. Web. 10 Feb. 2014. <http://espn.go.com/blog/playbook/dollars/post/_/id/3086/blackhawks-rewarded-for-taking-risks>.

72. "Running USA Annual Marathon Report | Running USA." 23 Mar. 2014. Running USA. 24 Apr. 2014. <http://www.runningusa.org/marathon-report-2014?returnTo=annual-reports>.

73. "Running USA Annual Half-Marathon Report | Running USA." 23 Mar. 2014. Running USA. 24 Apr. 2014. <http://www.runningusa.org/marathon-report-2014?returnTo=annual-reports>. <http://www.runningusa.org/index.cfm?fuseaction=news.details>.

74. "Race Day in Columbus—a Recap." *Tweetmytime.com*. N.p., 21 Oct. 2009. Web. 10 Feb. 2014. <http://tweetmytime.com/blog/race-day-in-columbus>.

75. "About Nike+ Challenges." *Nikeplus.com*. Nike+, n.d. Web. 10 Feb. 2014. <https://support-en-us.nikeplus.com/app/answers/detail/a_id/32082/p/3169,3195>.

76. "1962 Major League Baseball Attendance & Miscellaneous." *Baseball-Reference.com*. Sports Reference, n.d. Web. 10 Feb. 2014. <http://www.baseball-reference.com/leagues/MLB/1962-misc.shtml>.

77. "MLB Attendance Report—2013." *ESPN.com*. ESPN, n.d. Web. 2 Oct. 2013. <http://espn.go.com/mlb/attendance>.

78. Kronheim, David P. "Minor League Baseball 2011 Attendance Analysis." *Numbertamer.com*. N.p., 2012. Web. 10 Feb. 2014. <http://numbertamer.com/files/2011_Minor_League_Analysis.pdf>.

79. Newman, Mark. "MLB.TV Price Drops as Action Heats up." *MLB.com*. MLB, 31 May 2013. Web. 16 Aug. 2013. <http://mlb.mlb.com/news/article.jsp?ymd=20130531&content_id=49177566&vkey=news_mlb&c_id=mlb>.
80. Salter, Chuck. "MLB Advanced Media's Bob Bowman Is Playing Digital Hardball. And He's Winning." *Fast Company*. Fast Company, Inc., 19 Mar. 2012. Web. 10 Feb. 2014. <http://www.fastcompany.com/1822802/mlb-advanced-medias-bob-bowman-playing-digital-hardball-and-hes-winning>.
81. *Changing the Game—Outlook for the Global Sports Market to 2015*. PwC, Dec. 2011. Web. 27 Sept. 2013. <http://www.pwc.com/en_GX/gx/hospitality-leisure/pdf/changing-the-game-outlook-for-the-global-sports-market-to-2015.pdf>.
82. Chiappetta, Mike. "UFC and FOX Officially Announce Details of Landmark 7-Year Broadcast Deal." *Mmafighting.com*. SB Nation, 18 Aug. 2011. Web. 10 Feb. 2014. <http://www.mmafighting.com/2011/08/18/ufc-and-fox-officially-announce-details-of-landmark-7-year-broad>.
83. Miller, Matthew. "Ultimate Cash Machine." *Forbes.com*. Forbes, 17 Apr. 2008. Web. 10 Feb. 2014. <http://www.forbes.com/forbes/2008/0505/080.html>.
84. Bearak, Barry. "Ultimate Fighting Dips a Toe into the Mainstream." *NYTimes.com*. New York Times, 11 Nov. 2011. Web. 10 Feb. 2014. <http://www.nytimes.com/2011/11/12/sports/ultimate-fighting-championship-comes-of-age-financially.html?pagewanted=all&gwh=9F25BA02FF359596F2A4148F4A37A735>.

CHAPTER 9

1. Bishop, Greg. "A Company That Runs Prisons Will Have Its Name on a Stadium." *NYTimes.com*. New York Times, 19 Feb. 2013. Web. 2 Oct. 2013. <http://www.nytimes.com/2013/02/20/sports/ncaafootball/a-company-that-runs-prisons-will-have-its-name-on-a-stadium.html?pagewanted=all>.
2. O'Matz, Megan. "Immigrants with No Criminal History Get Lengthy Stays at Little-Known Jail." *Sun Sentinel*. Sun Sentinel, 5 Jan. 2013. Web. 2 Oct. 2013. <http://articles.sun-sentinel.com/2013-01-05/news/fl-private-immigration-jail-20130105_1_illegal-immigrants-deutch-human-rights-abuses>.
3. Troop, Don. "Florida Atlantic U. Students Stage Sit-In to Protest 'Owlcatraz' Stadium Deal." *Bottom Line*. Chronicle of Higher Education, 25 Feb. 2013. Web. 2 Oct. 2013. <http://chronicle.com/blogs/bottomline/florida-atlantic-u-students-stage-sit-in-to-protest-owlcatraz-stadium-deal/>.
4. Sherman, Rodger. "Video: Stephen Colbert Takes on FAU's Prison-Sponsored Stadium." *SBNation.com*. SBNation, 22 Feb. 2013. Web. 2 Oct. 2013. <http://www.sbnation.com/college-football/2013/2/22/4017374/stephen-colbert-fau-football-stadium-geo-group>.
5. Bishop, "A Company That Runs Prisons."
6. Myerberg, Paul. "Prison Operator Withdraws Naming Rights Offer for FAU Stadium." *USA Today*. Gannett, 2 Apr. 2013. Web. 2 Oct. 2013. <http://www.usatoday.com/story/gameon/2013/04/02/florida-atlantic-fau-geo-group-stadium-withdraws-offer/2045581/>.
7. "FAU—President Announces Resignation." Florida Atlantic University, n.d. Web. 2 Oct. 2013. <http://www.fau.edu/explore/homepage-stories/2013_05re.php>.
8. Connor, Tracy. "Giants, Jets End Stadium Naming Negotiations with Allianz over Past Nazi Ties." *NYDailyNews.com*. New York Daily News, 13 Sept. 2008. Web. 26 Jan. 2014. <http://www.nydailynews.com/sports/football/giants-jets-stadium-naming-negotiations-allianz-nazi-ties-article-1.325107>.
9. "Allianz's Past Ties with Nazis Led to Widespread Criticism; Teams Still Negotiating." *ESPN.com*. ESPN, 12 Sept. 2008. Web. 26 Jan. 2014. <http://sports.espn.go.com/nfl/news/story?id=3584453>.
10. Kercheval, Nancy, and Eben Novy-Williams. "MetLife Sets 25-Year Naming Rights Deal for Jets-Giants New Jersey Stadium." *Bloomberg.com*. Bloomberg, 23 Aug. 2011. Web. 26 Jan. 2014. <http://www.bloomberg.com/news/2011-08-23/metlife-sets-25-year-naming-rights-deal-for-jets-giants-new-jersey-stadium.html>.
11. *The Set-Up*. Dir. Robert Wise. RKO Radio Pictures, Inc., 1949. Film.
12. "1954: Bannister Breaks Four-Minute Mile." *BBC News*. BBC, 5 June 1954. Web. 26 Jan. 2014. <http://news.bbc.co.uk/onthisday/hi/dates/stories/may/6/newsid_2511000/2511575.stm>.
13. "TV Ratings: 'SportsCenter' Still Tops 'Fox Sports Live' (Also: PGA/CBS, Usain Bolt)." *Sports Media Watch*. Sports Media Watch, 3 Sept. 2011. Web. 22 Feb. 2014. <http://www

.sportsmediawatch.com/2013/08/sportscenter-still-tops-fox-sports-live-also-pga-on-cbs-usain-bolt/>.

14. Paulsen. "TV Ratings for Nationally Televised Sporting Events (January 28–February 3)." *Sports Media Watch*. Sports Media Watch, 29 Feb. 2012. Web. 6 Sept. 2013. <http://www .sportsmediawatch.com/2012/02/tv-ratings-for-nationally-televised-sporting-events-january-28-february-3/>.

15. Futterman, Matthew. "Tiger Woods Is No. 1 Again, but Golf Hardly Missed Him." *WSJ.com*. Wall Street Journal, 10 Apr. 2013. Web. 26 Jan. 2014. <http://online.wsj.com/article/SB100014 24127887323646604578402891124694264.html>.

16. Watson, Phil. "Ben Johnson Disqualification in 1988 an Olympic-Sized Shocker." *Yahoo! Sports*. Yahoo!, 9 Aug. 2012. Web. 27 Jan. 2014. <http://sports.yahoo.com/news/ben-johnson-disqualification-1988-olympic-sized-shocker-194500522--oly.html>.

17. "Track CEO Blames industry." *ESPN.com*. ESPN, 22 Jan. 2009. Web. 27 Jan. 2014. <http:// sports.espn.go.com/oly/trackandfield/news/story?id=3852967>.

18. "Manchester United Survey Reveals They Have Doubled Their Global Fan Base to 659 Million over Five Years." *The Telegraph*. Telegraph Media Group, 29 May 2012. Web. 11 Feb. 2014. <http://www.telegraph.co.uk/sport/football/teams/manchester-united/ 9298384/Manchester-United-survey-reveals-they-have-doubled-their-global-fan-base-to-659-million-over-five-years.html>.

19. American Medical Society for Sports Medicine. "Effectiveness of Early Sport Specialization Limited in Most Sports, Sport Diversification May Be Better Approach at Young Ages." *ScienceDaily*, 23 Apr. 2013. Web. 5 Sept. 2013. <http://www.sciencedaily.com/releases/ 2013/04/130423172601.htm>.

20. Anderson, Lars. "NASCAR Chase Scandal Costs Michael Waltrip Racing Big Time."*SI.com*. Sports Illustrated, 16 Oct. 2013. Web. 17 Jan. 2014. <http://sportsillustrated.cnn.com/racing/ news/20131016/nascar-michael-waltrip-racing-cheating-fallout/>.

21. McNamee, M. J., and S. J. Paree. *The Ethics of Sports: A Reader*. London: Routledge, 2010. 166. Print.

22. Perry, Dayn. "Just Because: Gaylord Perry, Roberto Clemente and the Hint of a Spitter." *CBSSports.com*. CBS Interactive, 23 May 2013. Web. 27 Jan. 2014. <http://www.cbssports .com/mlb/eye-on-baseball/22290070/just-because-gaylord-perry-roberto-clemente-and-the-hint-of-a-spitter>.

23. Ibid.

24. Gavett, Gretchen. "HBR Blog Network / The Shortlist." *The Shortlist*. Harvard Business Review, 30 Aug. 2013. Web. 5 Sept. 2013. <http://blogs.hbr.org/shortlist/2013/08/has-maximizing-shareholder-val.html>.

25. Hsieh, Tony. *Delivering Happiness: A Path to Profits, Passion, and Purpose*. New York: Business Plus, 2010. Print.

26. "Leading Across Sectors." *HBR Ideacast*. Harvard Business Review, 12 Sept. 2013. Web. 27 Sept. 2013. <http://blogs.hbr.org/2013/09/leading-across-sectors/>.

27. deHaan, Ed. "How to Rebuild Trust After a Scandal." Stanford Graduate School of Business, 14 Jan. 2014. Web. 17 Jan. 2014. <http://www.gsb.stanford.edu/news/headlines/ ed-dehaan-how-rebuild-trust-after-scandal?utm_source=twitter>.

28. McCabe, Theresa. "The Best and Worst Baseball Promotions." The Street, 29 Mar. 2010. Web. 17 Jan. 2014. <http://www.thestreet.com/story/10713002/1/the-best-and-worst-baseball-promotions.html>.

29. Staples, Andy. "Ed O'Bannon v. the NCAA: A Complete Case Primer." *SI.com*. Sports Illustrated, 2 Apr. 2013. Web. 17 Sept. 2013. <http://sportsillustrated.cnn.com/college-football/news/20130402/ed-obannon-ncaa-case-primer/>.

30. "Players to Receive $40 million." *ESPN.com*. ESPN, 27 Sept. 2013. Web. 27 Sept. 2013. <http://espn.go.com/college-football/story/_/id/9731696/ea-sports-clc-settle-lawsuits-40-million-source>.

31. "Athletic Scholarships." *National Letter of Intent*. NCAA, n.d. Web. 27 Sept. 2013. <http:// www.ncaa.org/wps/wcm/connect/nli/nli/document library/athletic scholarship>.

32. Staples, "Ed O'Bannon v. the NCAA."

33. Solomon, Jon. "Jay Bilas Shuts Down Player Memorabilia Sales on NCAA Web Site." *Al.com*. Alabama Media Group, 8 Aug. 2013. Web. 17 Sept. 2013. <http://www.al.com/sports/index .ssf/2013/08/jay_bilas_shuts_down_player_me.html>.

34. Rovell, Darren, and Justine Gubar. "Sources: Two More Manziel Signings." *ESPN.com.* ESPN, 13 Aug. 2013. Web. 17 Sept. 2013. <http://espn.go.com/espn/otl/story/_/id/9562044/texas-aggies-qb-johnny-manziel-signed-two-more-sessions-sources>.

35. "Half-Game Penalty for Johnny Manziel." *ESPN.com.* ESPN, 29 Aug. 2013. Web. 17 Sept. 2013. <http://espn.go.com/college-football/story/_/id/9609389/johnny-manziel-texas-aggies-suspended-1st-half-season-opener-rice-owls>.

36. Berri, David. "One More Reason to Pay College Athletes." *TIME.com.* Time Magazine, 17 Aug. 2013. Web. 27 Jan. 2014. <http://ideas.time.com/2013/08/17/one-more-reason-to-pay-college-athletes/>.

37. Peach, Jim. "College Athletics, Universities, and the NCAA." *Social Science Journal* 44 (2007): 11–22. Web. 27 Jan. 2014. <http://www.suu.edu/faculty/berri/PeachNCAA2007.pdf>.

38. Berri, "One More Reason."

39. Sports, Steve Berkowitz. "NCAA Increases Value of Scholarships in Historic Vote." *USA Today.* Gannett, 17 Jan. 2015. Web. 07 May 2015.

40. Staples, Andy. "Delany: Big Ten Could De-Emphasize Athletics If O'Bannon Plaintiffs Win." *SI.com.* Sports Illustrated, 18 Mar. 2013. Web. 2 Oct. 2013. <http://sportsillustrated.cnn.com/college-football/news/20130318/big-ten-jim-delany-ncaa-obannon/>.

41. Solomon, Jon. "Desmond Howard on Manziel: Where Was Public Support for Terrelle Pryor and A. J. Green vs. NCAA?" *AL.com.* Alabama Media Group, 16 Aug. 2013. Web. 27 Jan. 2014. <http://www.al.com/sports/index.ssf/2013/08/desmond_howard_on_johnny_manzi.html>.

42. Parker, Willie. "Amateur Sports in America: The Effect of the Olympic and Amateur Sports Act." *Yahoo! Contributor Network.* Yahoo!, 6 Apr. 2007. Web. 27 Jan. 2014. <http://voices.yahoo.com/amateur-sports-america-effect-olympic-275063.html>.

43. Dauster, Rob. "The Latest in the Ed O'Bannon Case, and Why the NCAA's Headed for Change." *CollegeBasketballTalk.* NBC Sports, 8 May 2013. Web. 27 Jan. 2014. <http://collegebasketballtalk.nbcsports.com/2013/05/08/the-latest-in-the-ed-obannon-case-and-why-the-ncaas-headed-for-change/>.

44. Cohen, Ben. "The Case for Paying College Athletes." *WSJ.com.* Wall Street Journal, 16 Sept. 2011. Web. 27 Jan. 2014. <http://online.wsj.com/article/SB10001424053111904060604576572752351110850.html?mod=WSJ_hps_editorsPicks_1>.

45. "Pick Me Out a Winner, Bobby." *Season Ticket Game Plans.* Minor League Baseball, n.d. Web. 5 Sept. 2013. <http://www.milb.com/content/page.jsp?sid=t459&ymd=20111115&content_id=25976680&vkey=tickets>.

46. Rovell, Darren. "New NBA Site to Sell Fans' Tickets, too." *ESPN.com.* ESPN, 20 Aug. 2012. Web. 6 Sept. 2013. <http://espn.go.com/los-angeles/nba/story/_/id/8284251/nba-ticketmaster-launch-one-stop-shop-website>.

47. Ibid.

48. "The Open Source Initiative." *Open Source Initiative.* N.p., n.d. Web. 22 Jan. 2014. <http://www.opensource.org/>.

49. "Welcome to the Android Open Source Project!" *Android Developers.* N.p., n.d. Web. 22 Jan. 2014. <http://source.android.com/>.

50. Kingsley-Hughes, Adrian. "How Much Money Does Google Make from Mobile?" *ZDNet.* N.p., 16 Oct. 2011. Web. 22 Jan. 2014. <http://www.zdnet.com/blog/hardware/how-much-money-does-google-make-from-mobile/15539>.

51. Bradley, Tony. "Android Dominates Market Share, But Apple Makes All The Money." *Forbes.com.* Forbes, 15 Nov. 2013. Web. 22 Jan. 2014. <http://www.forbes.com/sites/tonybradley/2013/11/15/android-dominates-market-share-but-apple-makes-all-the-money/>.

52. Maisel, Ivan. "Urban Planning: Existing Alongside NFL." *ESPN.com.* ESPN, 18 June 2011. Web. 30 Sept. 2013. <http://sports.espn.go.com/ncf/columns/story?id=6676377>.

53. "National Lacrosse Participation Nears 750,000." Press Release & News. USLacrosse, 10 Apr. 2014. Web. 05 May 2015. < http://www.uslacrosse.org/multimedia-center/press-releases-news/postid/583/national-lacrosse-participation-nears-750000.aspx>

54. Craft, Kevin. "Will Lacrosse Ever Go Mainstream?" *The Atlantic.* 13 Apr. 2012. Atlantic Media Company. 24 Apr. 2014. <http://www.theatlantic.com/entertainment/archive/2012/04/will-lacrosse-ever-go-mainstream/255690/>

55. Forman, Matt. "30 in 30: How Will New Rules Impact the Game?" Division I Men. 24 Sept. 2012. US Lacrosse, Inc. 24 Apr. 2014. <http://www.laxmagazine.com/college_men/DI/2012-13/news/092412_30_in_30_how_will_new_rules_impact_the_game>.

56. Roan, Dan. "Olympics 2020: Wrestling Reinstated to Games." *BBC News.* BBC, 8 Sept. 2013. Web. 9 Sept. 2013. <http://www.bbc.co.uk/sport/0/olympics/24009517>.

57. Whiteside, Kelly. "Wrestling had cash, charisma backing it in Olympic bid." *USA Today Sports*, Gannett, 8 Sept. 2013. Web. 9 Sept. 2013. <http://www.usatoday.com/story/sports/olympics/2013/09/08/why-wrestling-won-spot-olympics-2020/2783711/>.
58. Kerr, Peter. "Now It Can Be Told: Those Pro Wrestlers Are Just Having Fun." *NYTimes.com*. New York Times, 10 Feb. 1989. Web. 17 Sept. 2013. <http://www.nytimes.com/1989/02/10/nyregion/now-it-can-be-told-those-pro-wrestlers-are-just-having-fun.html>.
59. Belzer, Jason. "Elimination of Guarantee Games Increases Likelihood of NCAA Breakup." *Forbes.com*. Forbes, 19 Feb. 2013. Web. 27 Jan. 2014. <http://www.forbes.com/sites/jasonbelzer/2013/02/19/elimination-of-guarantee-games-increases-likelihood-of-ncaa-breakup/?utm_source=twitterfeed>.
60. McMurphy, Brett. "Seven FCS Teams Cash in Via Upsets." *ESPN.com*. ESPN, 1 Sept. 2013. Web. 9 Sept. 2013. <http://espn.go.com/college-football/story/_/id/9624936/seven-fcs-teams-pull-23m-upsets>.
61. "2013 NCAA Division I-A Football Schedule - Week 1." *ESPN.com*. ESPN, n.d. Web. 11 Feb. 2014. <http://espn.go.com/college-football/schedule/_/seasontype/2>.
62. Kurtenbach, Dieter. "FAU Trades Mismatches for Millions." *Sun Sentinel*. Sun Sentinel, 14 Sept. 2012. Web. 9 Sept. 2013. <http://articles.sun-sentinel.com/2012-09-14/sports/fl-fau-georgia-alabama-money-games-0915-20120914_1_fau-coach-carl-pelini-owls-athletics-program>.
63. Cohen, "Declining Student Attendance."
64. Solomon, Jon. "Smaller Alabama Football Schools Worry About Potential Impact of Big Ten Ending FCS Games." *Al.com*. Alabama Media Group, 21 Feb. 2013. Web. 28 Sept. 2013. <http://www.al.com/sports/index.ssf/2013/02/samford_and_jacksonville_state.html>.
65. Russo, Ralph D. "FCS Teams to Lose Pay Day Games, Revenue." *Augusta Chronicle*. Augusta Chronicle, 26 July 2013. Web. 27 Jan. 2014. <http://chronicle.augusta.com/sports/2013-07-26/fcs-teams-lose-pay-day-games-revenue>.
66. Tannenwald, Jonathan. "Ivy League Strikes Major National Television Deal with NBC Sports Network." *Philly.com*. Interstate General Media, 7 May 2012. Web. 27 Jan. 2014. <http://www.philly.com/philly/sports/colleges/Ivy-League-strikes-major-national-television-deal-with-NBC-Sports-Network.html>.
67. Rachac, Greg. "Big Sky, Root Sports TV Deal Official." *Billings Gazette*. Billings Gazette, 17 Jan. 2012. Web. 27 Jan. 2014. <http://billingsgazette.com/sports/college/big-sky-conference/montana-state-university/big-sky-root-sports-tv-deal-official/article_38a72dd8-b437-5922-89cd-d93d3c9ff442.html>.
68. Ecker, Danny. "How Mountain West Football Could Help the Sox Win a Title." *Crain's Chicago Business*. Crain Communications, Inc., 26 Aug. 2013. Web. 5 Sept. 2013. <http://www.chicagobusiness.com/article/20130826/BLOGS04/130829880/how-mountain-west-football-could-help-the-sox-win-a-title>.
69. Cuban, Marc. "Help the Mavs Design Our Next Uniform!" *Blog Maverick*. N.p., 13 May 2013. Web. 18 Sept. 2013. <http://blogmaverick.com/2013/05/13/help-the-mavs-design-our-next-uniform/>.
70. Surowiecki, James. *The Wisdom of Crowds: Why the Many Are Smarter than the Few and How Collective Wisdom Shapes Business, Economies, Societies, and Nations.* New York: Doubleday, 2004. Print.
71. Silver, Nate. *The Signal and the Noise: Why So Many Predictions Fail—but Some Don't.* New York: Penguin, 2012. Print.
72. Armstrong, Jim. "Aggressive Index 2011." *Football Outsiders*. Football Outsiders, 27 Jan. 2012. Web. 18 Sept. 2013. <http://www.footballoutsiders.com/stat-analysis/2012/aggressiveness-index-2011>.
73. Monkovic, Toni. "On Fourth Down, Coaches Aren't Going for It." *The Fifth Down*. New York Times, 29 Jan. 2012. Web. 18 Sept. 2013. <http://fifthdown.blogs.nytimes.com/2012/01/29/on-fourth-down-coaches-arent-going-for-it/?_r=0>.
74. Silver, *The Signal and the Noise*.
75. Bee, Colleen C., and Mark E. Havitz. "Exploring the Relationship Between Involvement, Fan Attraction, Psychological Commitment and Behavioural Loyalty in a Sports Spectator Context." *International Journal of Sports Marketing & Sponsorship* 11.2 (2010): 140–57. Print.
76. Brydum, Sunnivie. "Putin Signs Russian Ban on 'Homosexual Propaganda'." *Advocate.com*. Here Media, 1 July 2013. Web. 27 Jan. 2014. <http://www.advocate.com/news/world-news/2013/07/01/putin-signs-russian-ban-homosexual-propaganda>.

77. Longman, Jeré. "On Olympics: Outrage Over an Antigay Law Does Not Spread to Olympic Officials." *NYTimes.com*. New York Times, 6 Aug. 2013. Web. 6 Sept. 2013. <http://www.nytimes.com/2013/08/07/sports/games-officials-tiptoeing-around-russias-antigay-law.html?_r=1&>.

78. Ibid.

79. "NHL, NHLPA Announce Partnership with You Can Play." *NHL.com*. NHL, 11 Apr. 2013. Web. 6 Sept. 2013. <http://www.nhl.com/ice/news.htm?id=665247>.

80. "America's LGBT 2012 Buying Power Projected at $790 Billion." Witeck Communications, 27 Mar. 2012. Web. 6 Sept. 2013. <http://www.witeck.com/pressreleases/americas-lgbt-2012-buying-power-projected-at-790-billion/>.

81. Lopez, Tyler. "For One Lucky NFL Franchise, Thousands of New Gay Fans (and a Better Defense)." *Slate*. The Slate Group, 10 Feb. 2014. Web. 11 Feb. 2014. <http://www.slate.com/blogs/outward/2014/02/10/football_player_mike_sam_gay_which_lucky_nfl_franchise_will_sign_him.html>.

82. Connolly, Kate. "Gay Games in Cologne Set to Welcome 10,000 Competitors." *The Guardian*. Guardian News and Media Limited, 30 July 2010. Web. 11 Feb. 2014. <http://www.theguardian.com/world/2010/jul/30/gay-games-cologne>.

83. Snider, Mike. "Gay Sports Fans Are More Likely to Attend Games Live." *For The Win*. USA Today, 26 June 2013. Web. 18 Sept. 2013. <http://ftw.usatoday.com/2013/06/gay-sports-fans-are-more-likely-to-attend-games-live>.

84. Ibid.

85. Anderson, Mae. "Chevy Olympic Ads Feature Gay Couples." *The Big Story*. Associated Press, 7 Feb. 2014. Web. 11 Feb. 2014. <http://bigstory.ap.org/article/chevy-olympic-ads-feature-gay-couple>.

86. "Be True Pride Pack." *Nikeinc.com*. NIKE, Inc., 15 June 2012. Web. 27 Jan. 2014. <http://nikeinc.com/news/be-true-pride-pack>.

87. Heitner, Darren. "How Does Jason Collins' Coming Out Statement Affect His Off-Court Opportunities?" *Forbes.com*. Forbes, 29 Apr. 2013. Web. 27 Jan. 2014. <http://www.forbes.com/sites/darrenheitner/2013/04/29/how-does-jason-collins-coming-out-statement-affect-his-off-court-opportunities/>.

88. Zeigler, Cyd. "Jason Collins Jersey Sales Spike for Washington Wizards." *Outsports.com*. SB Nation, 30 Apr. 2013. Web. 27 Jan. 2014. <http://www.outsports.com/2013/4/30/4287418/jason-collins-jersey-sales-washington-wizards-gay>.

89. "Collins' No. 98 Brooklyn Nets jersey selling well." NBA.com. 26 Feb. 2014. Associated Press. 25 Apr. 2014. <http://www.nba.com/2014/news/02/26/collins-jersey-sales.ap/>.

90. Snyder, Whitney. "Gareth Thomas: 'I'm Gay'—Welsh Rugby Player Comes Out." *HuffingtonPost.com*. Huffington Post, 20 Dec. 2009. Web. 27 Jan. 2014. <http://www.huffingtonpost.com/2009/12/20/gareth-thomas-im-gay-wels_n_398611.html>.

91. "Gareth Thomas Speaker Profile." NOPACTalent, n.d. Web. 9 Sept. 2013. <http://www.nopactalent.com/celebrity/gareth-thomas-speaker-appearance-booking-agent.php>.

92. Hart, Simon. "Tom Daley Reveals He Is in a Relationship with a Man in Frank YouTube Video from Olympic Diver." *The Telegraph*. Telegraph Media Group, 2 Dec. 2013. Web. 22 Jan. 2014. <http://www.telegraph.co.uk/sport/olympics/diving/10487809/Tom-Daley-reveals-he-is-in-a-relationship-with-a-man-in-frank-YouTube-video-from-Olympic-diver.html>.

93. Drehs, Wayne. "A Coming-Out Party for Professional Sports." *Page2*. ESPN, n.d. Web. 6 Sept. 2013. <http://espn.go.com/page2/s/drehs/010524.html>.

EPILOGUE

1. Haudricourt, Tom. "Ryan Braun Comes Out Swinging, Explains Innocence." *JSOnline*. Milwaukee Wisconsin Journal Sentinel, 24 Feb. 2012. Web. 28 Sept. 2013. <http://www.jsonline.com/sports/brewers/Braun_live22412-140317723.html>.

2. Kevin Zimmerman. "Lions' Ndamukong Suh Voted NFL's Least Liked Player by Fans." *SBNation.com*. Vox Media Inc., 25 Oct. 2012. Web. 9 Jan. 2014. <http://seattle.sbnation.com/seattle-seahawks/2012/10/25/3554964/seahawks-lions-suh-least-liked>.

3. Gantt, Darin. "New Lions Captain Suh Calls Players-Only Meeting." *ProFootballTalk*. NBC Sports, 6 Sept. 2013. Web. 28 Sept. 2013. <http://profootballtalk.nbcsports.com/2013/09/06/new-lions-captain-suh-calls-players-only-meeting/>.

Index

transportation-imagery model, 45
trap questions, 176–77
Tressel, Jim, 173–74
Tripathi, Manish, 102
Trudeau, Garry, 56
Trudell, Mike, 90–91
Truex, Martin, Jr., 208
Tunney, Gene, 192
Tustin Pee Wee Red Cobras, 149
TVtag, 76
TweetDeck, 86
Tweet my Time, 199
Twitter, 12, 78–79, 84–85, 87
   controversies, 154–56
   Earnhardt and, 86
   NBA and, 80–81
   Nike and, 80–81
   Swisher and, 152
   Trudell and, 91

UDiligence, 158
Uecker, Bob, 62
UEFA. *See* Union of European Football Associations
UFC. *See* Ultimate Fighting Championship
The Ultimate Fighter (television series), 200–201
Ultimate Fighting Championship (UFC), 60, 143–44, 200–201
uncertainty, of details, 150
Under Armour, 116
underdog, 46–47, 59
uniforms, 222–23
Unione Sportiva Triestina, 96–97
unionization, 213–14
Union of European Football Associations (UEFA), 4–5, 114
United States Tennis Association (USTA), 186
University of Alabama, 134, 180
University of California, Berkeley, 140
University of California, Riverside, 141
University of Chicago, 53
University of Connecticut, 5, 118–19
University of Georgia, 180
University of Hartford, 118–19
University of Iowa, 32–33, 220
University of Michigan, 123, 183
University of Minnesota, 139
University of Mississippi, 158, 194
University of Mount Union, 60
University of North Carolina, 149
University of Northern Iowa, 220
University of Oregon, 88, 184–85, 195
University of South Florida, 217
University of Tennessee, 159–60
University of Texas, 158
University of Texas at Tyler, 141–42
University of Utah, 127
University of Washington, 129
University of Wisconsin, 220
Uphoria, 191
USA Today, 149
US Open, 186
USTA. *See* United States Tennis Association

value-generating framework, 104*f*
Verbeck, Sibley, 72
Verizon, 93–94
Verizon Center, 196–97
Veronica Mars Movie Project, 138
Vick, Michael, 170
The Victory Lab: The Secret Science of Winning Campaigns (Issenberg), 51

Vietnam War, 56
Viggle, 73, 76
Vila, Joe, 147
Vine, 87
Virginia Tech, 32
virtual experiences, 186–88, 200–201
Visible Measures, 47–48
Vogel, Meghan, 61

Wacha, Michael, 27
Wakefield, Kirk, 9, 181
Wallace, Gerald, 18–19
Wall Street Journal, 55, 140
Walt Disney Company, 28
Wambach, Abby, 25
Warner, Glenn "Pop," 30
Washington Capitals, 50, 93
The Washington Post, 100–101
Washington Redskins, 100–102
Washington Wizards, 156
Weidman, Chris, 60
Weingartner, Tom, 53
White, Dana, 200–201
Whittington, Richard, 13
Whyte, Charles, 4
Wieden+Kennedy, 42–44
Williams, Deron, 18–19
Williams, Roy, 61
Williams, Ted, 152
willingness-to-pay, 104
win-loss record, 2–3
winners
   perennial, 3–5
   periodic, 3, 6–7
winning
   attendance and, 4
   as commodity, 7–8
   fallacy, 3–4
   as success factor, 8
Wirtz, Rocky, 197–98
Wise, Mike, 100–101
WNBA. *See* Women's National Basketball Association
Women's National Basketball Association (WNBA), 10, 110–11
Woodley, LaMarr, 129
Woods, Tiger, 160
World Track and Field Championships, 207
World Wrestling Entertainment (WWE), 219
W Partners, 35
wrestling, 219
Wrigley Field, 6, 161–62
WWE. *See* World Wrestling Entertainment

Xbox One, 83–84

Yale Bowl, 182
Yale University, 55–56
Yang, Y. E., 59
Yankee Stadium, 192
Yao Ming, 47
Yormark, Brett, 17
You Can Play Project, 225
Youth America's Cup Regatta, 138–39
YouTube, 12, 84, 87

Zappos, 210–11
Zeebox, 73, 76
Zierden, Ben, 114
Zimbalist, Andrew, 123
Zoley, George, 203